INTERNATIONAL DESIGN ORGANIZATIONS

INTERNATIONAL DESIGN ORGANIZATIONS

Histories, Legacies, Values

Edited by
Jeremy Aynsley,
Alison J. Clarke and
Tania Messell

BLOOMSBURY VISUAL ARTS
LONDON • NEW YORK • OXFORD • NEW DELHI • SYDNEY

BLOOMSBURY VISUAL ARTS
Bloomsbury Publishing Plc
50 Bedford Square, London, WC1B 3DP, UK
1359 Broadway, New York, NY 10018, USA
29 Earlsfort Terrace, Dublin 2, Ireland

BLOOMSBURY, BLOOMSBURY VISUAL ARTS and the Diana logo are
trademarks of Bloomsbury Publishing Plc

First published in Great Britain 2022
Paperback edition published in 2026

© Editorial content and introduction, Jeremy Aynsley, Alison J. Clarke and
Tania Messell, 2026
© Individual chapters, their authors, 2026

Jeremy Aynsley, Alison J. Clarke and Tania Messell have asserted their right under the Copyright,
Designs and Patents Act, 1988, to be identified as Editors of this work.

Cover design: Louise Dugdale
Cover image © troyka / iStock

All rights reserved. No part of this publication may be: i) reproduced or transmitted in any form, electronic or mechanical, including photocopying, recording or by means of any information storage or retrieval system without prior permission in writing from the publishers; or ii) used or reproduced in any way for the training, development or operation of artificial intelligence (AI) technologies, including generative AI technologies. The rights holders expressly reserve this publication from the text and data mining exception as per Article 4(3) of the Digital Single Market Directive (EU) 2019/790.

Bloomsbury Publishing Plc does not have any control over, or responsibility for, any third-party websites referred to or in this book. All internet addresses given in this book were correct at the time of going to press. The author and publisher regret any inconvenience caused if addresses have changed or sites have ceased to exist, but can accept no responsibility for any such changes.

Every effort has been made to trace copyright holders of images and to obtain their permission for the use of copyright material. The publisher apologizes for any errors or omissions in copyright acknowledgement and would be grateful if notified of any corrections that should be incorporated in future reprints or editions of this book.

A catalogue record for this book is available from the British Library.

Library of Congress Cataloging-in-Publication Data
Names: International Design Organizations: Histories, Values, Legacies
(Conference) (2017 : University of Brighton), author. | Messell, Tania, editor. |
Clarke, Alison J., editor. | Aynsley, Jeremy, editor.
Title: International design organizations : histories, legacies, values /
edited by Jeremy Aynsley, Alison J. Clarke amd Tania Messell.
Description: London ; New York : Bloomsbury Visual Arts, 2022. | Includes
bibliographical references.
Identifiers: LCCN 2021040303 (print) | LCCN 2021040304 (ebook) |
ISBN 9781350112513 (hardback) | ISBN 9781350112520 (epub) |
ISBN 9781350112537 (pdf) | ISBN 9781350112544
Subjects: LCSH: Design–Societies, etc.–Congresses.
Classification: LCC NK21 .I58 2017 (print) | LCC NK21 (ebook) |
DDC 745.406–dc23
LC record available at https://lccn.loc.gov/2021040303
LC ebook record available at https://lccn.loc.gov/2021040304

ISBN:		
	HB:	978-1-3501-1251-3
	PB:	978-1-5266-9712-7
	ePDF:	978-1-3501-1253-7
	eBook:	978-1-3501-1252-0

Typeset by Integra Software Services Pvt. Ltd.
Printed and bound in Great Britain

For product safety related questions contact productsafety@bloomsbury.com

To find out more about our authors and books visit www.bloomsbury.com
and sign up for our newsletters.

CONTENTS

List of Figures vii
List of Tables xiii
List of Contributors xiv
Preface xv

Introduction 1
Jeremy Aynsley, Alison J. Clarke and Tania Messell

PART ONE PROFESSIONS – RULES – INSTITUTIONS – PERSONALITIES 17

1   Professional graphic design and Cold War politics: National and transnational design organizations 19
    Dora Souza Dias

2   One step before organizations: Networks, actors and trajectories in Argentine design (1938–1962) 39
    Verónica Devalle

3   International design organizations and émigré identity: Peter Muller-Munk and American representation in ICSID, 1950–1967 63
    Tania Messell

4   International design organizations as global design advocates: Romance, reality and relevance? 83
    Jonathan M. Woodham

PART TWO NATIONAL – INTERNATIONAL – TRANSNATIONAL 107

5   Becoming the International Design Conference in Aspen 109
    Robert Gordon-Fogelson

6 ALADI, a Latin American voice of design 131
Juan Buitrago

7 Internationalizing Japanese graphic design: From the pre-war period to today 157
Yasuko Suga

8 Shaping national and international design policies: The transnational trajectory of the Belgian policymaker Josine des Cressonnières (1926–1985) 179
Katarina Serulus

PART THREE DESIGN DEFINITIONS – EPISTEMOLOGIES – DIFFERENCES 203

9 Negotiating graphic design between national and international design organizations: The case of the Associazione per il Design Industriale in Milan 205
Chiara Barbieri

10 *Tööstuskunsti komitee*: A case study of an invisible design organization in Soviet Estonia 223
Triin Jerlei

11 Design for development, ICSID and UNIDO: The anthropological turn in 1970s design 247
Alison J. Clarke

12 No good (design) would come of it: The International Design Conference in Aspen, 1977–2004 267
Penelope Dean

13 XIN, A message with strategic vision – an analysis of the meaning of the 2009 Icograda Beijing Congress 291
Yun Wang

Select Bibliography 311
Index 314

FIGURES

1.1 Map projection showing only the associations with representatives at the Icograda Inaugural Meeting. Map by the author 33
2.1 Grupo Austral. Silla BKF prototipo, c. 1937. Courtesy of Fundación IDA, Investigación en Diseño Argentino Fondo Bonet Antonio 43
2.2 Boletín CEA, 1949. Courtesy of Fundación IDA, Investigación en Diseño Argentino Fondo Maldonado Tomás 48
2.3 Silla W, 1944. Courtesy of Fundación IDA, Investigación en Diseño Argentino Fondo Jannello César 50
2.4 Feria de América calco, 1953–1954. Courtesy of Fundación IDA, Investigación en Diseño Argentino Fondo Jannello César 51
2.5 *nueva visión* journal, issue 1 (5.1) and issue 2/3 (5.2). Courtesy of Fundación IDA, Investigación en Diseño Argentino Fondo Maldonado Tomás 53–54
2.6 Editorial NV Max Bill, 1955. Courtesy of Fundación IDA, Investigación en Diseño Argentino Fondo Maldonado Tomás 56
3.1 Tea service designed by Peter Muller-Munk in The Metropolitan Museum of Art, 'American Industrial Art', 11th Exhibition (11 February to 2 September 1929). Courtesy of BPK/ The Metropolitan Museum of Art 67
3.2 Ilona and Peter Muller-Munk upon their return from travels in Europe, *Pittsbugh Press* (12 October 1936). Courtesy of the Pittsburgh Post-Gazette 71
3.3 Sigvard Bernadotte and Peter Muller-Munk at the Special Exhibition of Industrial Design held at the Moderna Tekniske Museet during ICSID's General Congress in Stockholm, 1959. Ulf Hård af Segerstad, 'The Congress for Industrial Design will Open the Eyes of the Sceptics', Svenska Dagbladet (1959): 11. Courtesy of the Svenska Dagbladet / Keystone/TT 77
4.1 Geographical distribution of ICSID/WDO Executive Board of Directors membership 95
4.2 Geographical distribution of icograda/ico-D Board of Directors 95

4.3	ICSID/WDO Executive Board of Directors Membership	96
4.4	icograda/ico-D Executive Board of Directors Membership	96
5.1a	Herbert Bayer, logo designed for the Aspen Institute for Humanistic Studies and later used for the Aspen design conference, c. 1950. Aspen Historical Society, Bayer Collection. © 2020 Artists Rights Society (ARS), New York/VG Bild-Kunst, Bonn	110
5.1b	Unknown designer, International Design Conference in Aspen (IDCA) pamphlet, n.d. International Design Conference in Aspen records, 1949–2006, Getty Research Institute, Los Angeles (2007.M.7). © J. Paul Getty Trust	110
5.2	Leo Lionni, personal letterhead for the 'International Design Conference,' 1953. Buckminster Fuller Papers, M1090, Series 2, Box 79, Folder 6. Courtesy of the Department of Special Collections, Stanford University Libraries. © Leo Lionni. Used with permission of the Lionni family	116
5.3	Robert Hunter Middleton, temporary letterhead for the 'ASPEN International Design Conference,' 1954. International Design Conference in Aspen records, 1949–2006, Getty Research Institute, Los Angeles (2007.M.7). © J. Paul Getty Trust	122
5.4	Unknown designer, International Design Conference in Aspen (IDCA) letterhead, 1955. Will Burtin Papers, Cary Graphic Design Archives, Rochester Institute of Technology	124
5.5	Unknown designer, International Design Conference in Aspen (IDCA) letterhead, 1956. Will Burtin Papers, Cary Graphic Design Archives, Rochester Institute of Technology	124
5.6	Unknown designer, International Design Conference in Aspen (IDCA) stationery, 1964. International Design Conference in Aspen records, 1949–2006, Getty Research Institute, Los Angeles (2007.M.7). © J. Paul Getty Trust	127
6.1	Black and White version of the ALADI logo, c. 1980. Designed by Jesús Gámez. Digital reproduction by the author. Personal collection of the author	142
6.2	Presentation of the proposal for ALADI at the 11th Congress of ISCID, Mexico City, October 1979. From left to right: Rómulo Polo (Colombia), Basílio Uribe (Argentina), Gui Bonsiepe (Germany-Argentina), Roberto Napoli (Argentina) and Mario Mariño (Argentina). Taken from the book 'Crónicas del Diseño Industrial en la Argentina' [Chronicle of Industrial Design in Argentina] by Ricardo Blanco (2005). Fundación IDA, Investigación en Diseño Argentino. Fondo: Blanco, Ricardo	143
6.3	Statement by the Colombian designers. Document drafted and signed in Bogotá in June 1979. Taken from the journal *La Carreta*	

del Diseño no. 3 (Gutiérrez et al., 1980, p. 19). Personal collection of Rómulo Polo, Bogotá, Colombia 146

6.4 Proposal for the formation of ALADI. Bombay, January 1979. *La Carreta del Diseño*, no. 3 (Abramovitz, Polo, & Uribe, 1980, p. 18). Personal collection of Rómulo Polo, Bogotá, Colombia 147

6.5 The first page of the 'Document of intent' Conceived in Mexico in November 1978 and drafted by Rómulo Polo. Personal collection of Luiz Blank, Rio de Janeiro, Brazil 150

7.1 Satomi's poster (Gebrauchsgraphik, vol. 11, 1938). Author's collection 160

7.2a Poster announcing the 3rd Exhibition of JAAC (Modern Publicity, vol. 24, 1954–1955). Author's collection 163

7.2b Posters sent from JAAC to Graphis (Graphis, 1953). Author's collection 164

7.3 WoDeCo exhibition sites (Dezain no. 9, 1960). Author's collection 165

7.4 Judging scenes at JAAC (Dezain no.13, 1960). Author's collection 168

7.5 A notice made by All-Campus Struggle League for Crushing JAAC (Dezain no. 126, 1969). Author's collection 171

7.6 Scenes from 1st NAAC Exhibition (IDEA, no. 146, 1978). Author's collection 174

7.7a ICOGRADA-JAGDA Pan-Pacific Design Congress '89 Tokyo, pamphlet cover. Courtesy of University of Brighton Design Archives 176

7.7b ICOGRADA 'Visualogue', pamphlet cover. Courtesy of University of Brighton Design Archives 177

8.1 Josine des Cressonnières at the 8th ICSID Congress in Kyoto, 1973. ICSID Archive, University of Brighton Design Archives 180

8.2 Josine des Cressonnières, Secretary of the Signe d'Or. Private archive Geraldine des Cressonnières 183

8.3 The first Signe d'Or jury in 1957. From left to right: M. Stoffel, Robert Giron, Alberto Rosselli, Jaap Penraat, Josine des Cressonnières, Peter Muller-Munk and Louis Desamory. Private archive Geraldine des Cressonnières 184

8.4 Josine des Cressonnières at the Second ICSID Seminar on The Teaching of Industrial Design in Ulm, together with Arthur Pulos (US), Roger Tallon (France), André De Poerck (Belgium), Misha Black (UK), Zvonimir Radic (Yugoslavia), Tomàs Maldonado (West Germany), Shinji Koioke (Japan), Nathan Shapira (US), Basilio Urbine (Argentina), Gino Valle (Italy), Manuel Villazón Vázquez (Mexico) and Alexandre Wollner (Brazil), 1965. © HfG-Archiv/Museum Ulm 189

8.5 Josine des Cressonnières and Prince Albert at the opening of the Design Centre, 1964. Private archive Geraldine des Cressonnières 194

8.6 Kenji Ekuan at the Brussels Design Centre exhibition 'Design for the State'. In front a model of a pilot boat made by a temporary association of the shipbuilding yards 'Langerbrugge' and 'Fulton Marine'. Belgium, Brussels, State Archives, BE- A0545/Fic 2000, Archive Design Centre, 263 201

9.1 One page from *Poliedro* no. 5 (January–April 1968). In the picture (from left to right), the Aiap president Franco Mosca visits the exhibition 'Today's Italian Publicity and Graphic Design' with the Italian ambassador to the UK Gastone Guidotti and the chairman of the D&AD Edward Booth-Clibborn. Courtesy of Aiap CDPG, Centro di Documentazione sul Progetto Grafico, Milan 219

10.1 Ingi Vaher, head of the Council of Industrial Art and the Industrial Art Committee. Photo by: Oskar Juhani, April 1969. Estonian National Archives, EFA.252.0.71275 231

10.2 Ingi Vaher (third from right) with colleagues at the evaluation of Olympic souvenirs. Photo by: Arnold Moskalik, April 1977. Copyright: Estonian Public Broadcasting, Estonian National Archives 232

10.3 Fragment from the archives, a short article from Russian newspapers Izvestija, announcing the establishment of the committee. The reason for the graphic design still remains unclear – certain pages of minutes are decorated in a haphazard manner. Estonian National Archives, ERA.R-1906.1.478 234

10.4 Ingi Vaher. Vases produced by Tarbeklaas in early 1960s. Copyright: Estonian Museum of Applied Arts and Design 236

11.1 Ahmedabad Congress, 1979. © University of Applied Arts Vienna, Victor J. Papanek Foundation. Reproduced with permission from University of Applied Arts Vienna 256

11.2 Cobold, 'India's Design Dilemma', *DESIGN*, vol. 336, 1979, figs 1–5. Reproduced with permission from the Royal College of Art Archive 262

11.3 The Tin Can Radio: Designed by Victor Papanek and George Seeger at North Carolina State College for 'developing countries' using recycled and locally sourced materials. Courtesy: UNESCO. © University of Applied Arts Vienna, Victor J. Papanek Foundation. Reproduced with permission from University of Applied Arts Vienna 263

11.4 Decorated Tin Can Radio: Designed by Victor Papanek and George Seeger at North Carolina State College for 'developing countries' using recycled and locally sourced materials. Courtesy: UNESCO.

© University of Applied Arts Vienna, Victor J. Papanek Foundation. Reproduced with permission from University of Applied Arts Vienna 264

12.1 Certificate of Incorporation for the International Design Conference in Aspen, as provided by the 'General Not For Profit Corporation Act' in the State of Illinois, 22 October 1954. IDCA_0001_0014_032–1, International Design Conference in Aspen papers, Special Collections and University Archives, University of Illinois at Chicago 269

12.2 Publicity poster, 27th International Design Conference in Aspen, 'Shop Talk,' 1977. IDCA_0002_0023_010, International Design Conference in Aspen papers, Special Collections and University Archives, University of Illinois at Chicago 272

12.3 Frame from proof sheet, Daniel Boorstin at lecture podium at the 32nd International Design Conference in Aspen, 'The Prepared Professional,' 1982. International Design Conference in Aspen Record, 1949–2006. Getty Research Institute, Los Angeles (2007.M.7) 274

12.4 Program booklet cover, 28th International Design Conference in Aspen, 'Making Connections,' 1978. Design by John Massey. Box 16, Folder 750, International Design Conference in Aspen papers, Special Collections and University Archives, University of Illinois at Chicago 277

12.5 Frame from proof sheet, participants in costume at the 28th International Design Conference in Aspen, 'Making Connections,' 1978. Photograph by James O. Milmoe. International Design Conference in Aspen Record, 1949–2006. Getty Research Institute, Los Angeles (2007.M.7) 279

12.6 Tent interior at the 45th International Design Conference in Aspen, 'New Business of Design,' 1995. International Design Conference in Aspen Record, 1949–2006. Getty Research Institute, Los Angeles (2007.M.7) 282

12.7 Half empty tent interior at the 51st International Design Conference in Aspen, 'The More Things Change,' 2001. Photograph by Burnham W. Arndt. International Design Conference in Aspen Record, 1949–2006. Getty Research Institute, Los Angeles (2007.M.7) 288

12.8 Organizational restructuring diagram for the International Design Conference in Aspen, 2001. International Design Conference in Aspen Record, 1949–2006. Getty Research Institute, Los Angeles (2007.M.7) 289

13.1 and 13.2 China National Centre for the Performing Arts; The banner of 2009 Icograda Beijing Congress inside the China National Centre

13.3   He Jun, 2009 Icograda Beijing Congress poster, 2009 (© Wang Min) 294

13.4   Brainstorm for the meaning of XIN, the theme of the 2009 Icograda Beijing Congress at CAFA Design School, 2007 (© Zheng Tao) 296

13.5   Lu Jingren, Zhu Xi Bangshu Thousand-Character essay (《朱熹榜书千字文》), 1999. Counterclockwise (© Lu Jingren) 301

13.6   The main entrance of the National Museum of China where Design as Productive Force, the sub-theme exhibition of the 2009 Icograda Beijing Congress was organized, 27 October 2009 (© Wang Min) 305

(…continued from previous: for the Performing Arts, 26 October 2009 (© Arnold Schwartzman (photo on the top) / © Wang Min (photo on the bottom)) 293)

TABLES

6.1 ALADI Executive Board, 1980–1997. Sources: Meeting minutes (ALADI, 1980; 1984; 1995); (Lobato et al., 1982); (Espín et al., 1989); (Rivera et al., 1991); (Barragán et al., 1993) 132

6.2 Founding members of ALADI. The spelling corresponds to the original writing. Source: Opening minutes of ALADI (1980) 137

6.3 Signatories for the proposal to form ALADI, Mexico City, 1979. Sources: Journal 'La Carreta del Diseño' (Polo, Gámez, Lozano, 1980, pp. 20–2); Journal 'Módulo' (Pamio, 1980, pp. 30–2) 144

6.4 Schedule at Valle de Bravo from 22 to 29 November. Sources: CODIGRAM report on Interdesign '78 (Martínez & Gallardo, 1978) and Working Programme, given to participants by the organizers (CODIGRAM et al., 1978) 148

7.1 The rise in applicants to the JAAC exhibition. Table by Yasuko Suga 166

CONTRIBUTORS

Jeremy Aynsley is Professor of History of Design at the University of Brighton, UK.

Chiara Barbieri is Researcher in Design History at Ecal/University of Art and Design Lausanne (HES–SO), Switzerland.

Juan Buitrago is Associate Professor in History and Theory of Design at the Universidad del Valle (University of the Valley), Cali, Colombia.

Alison J. Clarke is Professor of Design History and Theory at the University of Applied Arts Vienna, Austria.

Penelope Dean is Associate Professor, School of Architecture, University of Illinois at Chicago, USA.

Verónica Devalle is Professor at the School of Architecture, Design and Urbanism. Universidad de Buenos Aires (University of Buenos Aires), Argentina.

Dora Souza Dias is Lecturer in Design at Brunel University, London, UK.

Robert Gordon-Fogelson is PhD candidate in the Department of Art History, University of Southern California, USA.

Tr'in Jerlei is Lecturer in History of Interiors, Estonian Academy of Arts, Tallinn, Estonia.

Tania Messell is Researcher in Design History at the University of Applied Sciences and Arts Northwestern Switzerland (FHNW), Basel, Switzerland.

Katarina Serulus is Research Fellow at KU Leuven Department of Architecture and Project Manager at Flanders Architecture Institute, Belgium.

Yasuko Suga is Professor of British Culture and History at Tsuda University, Tokyo, Japan.

Yun Wang is a librarian at the China Design Museum, Hangzhou, Republic of China.

Jonathan M. Woodham is Emeritus Professor of Design History at the University of Brighton where he is an associate of the Centre for Design History.

PREFACE

The book *International Design Organizations: Histories, Values, Legacies* has its roots in the conference of the same name that was held in Brighton, UK, in 2017. The conference marked a collaboration between the Papanek Foundation at the University of Applied Arts Vienna and the Centre for Design History at the University of Brighton, and we are grateful for the sustained support of these institutions. This location was in part informed by the location of the Design Archives held at the University of Brighton where two archives central to these histories, those of ICSID and Icograda, are held.

To our knowledge, the conference marked the first coming together of a group of international scholars interested to approach the histories of international design organizations from a global perspective. The editors would like to thank the contributors to the volume for their sustained interest and collaboration in the project.

INTRODUCTION

Jeremy Aynsley, Alison J. Clarke and Tania Messell

International Design Organizations: Histories, Legacies, Values presents the first scholarly selection of essays to offer contemporary perspectives drawn from new research into a range of design organizations across the globe. Mostly established in the second half of the twentieth century, in their relatively short lives, international design organizations formed an important platform for raising awareness of design issues. Their primary purpose was advocacy, and this involved setting standards of design practice and education, as well as the promotion of the status of design as a profession. As the chapters in this volume reveal, the organizations combined the pursuit of varied economic, professional and national interests and informed diverse ways of how to be or become 'international'. Embedded in asymmetrical power relations that reflected the wider geopolitical world of which they were an active part, these organizations and their programme of events, congresses and conferences were sites of dynamic exchange that could lead towards an agreed consensus, or equally to local and vocal resistance to the organizations' expressed prevailing values and structures. Significantly, in partnership with governmental, corporate and cultural agencies, many design organizations went on to build initiatives through their membership which sought to address pressing social issues and concerns, including world poverty, sustainable development and gender inequalities.

Design historians have consistently recognized the influence of design organizations for the ways that design is shaped.[1] Initially, emphasis was focused on those considered to be the largest or most overarching in their ambition, among them are the International Council of Societies of Industrial Design (ICSID) formed in 1957 and International Council of Graphic Design Associations (Icograda) formed in 1963. The International Design Conference held in Aspen, Colorado, from 1951 until 2004, also garnered early historical

---

[1] Penny Sparke, *Consultant Design: The History and Practice of the Designer in Industry* (London: Pembridge Press, 1983); Jonathan M. Woodham, *The Industrial Designer and the Public* (London: Pembridge Press, 1983).

and critical attention.[2] However, as many chapters in this volume reveal, other design organizations, often with a national focus, were forming at the same time but their histories were only told later. Belatedly, attention turned towards extending the range and number of national design organizations to receive considered historical acknowledgement.[3] These more recent studies highlighted how such national bodies were embedded in transnational flows of individuals, ideas and objects, and the nature of multidirectional networks in which they operated. Through this, these studies prepared the ground to develop a more nuanced understanding of how national organizations participated in, shaped or contested the assumptions of those founding international design organizations. It is from this base that *International Design Organizations: Histories, Legacies, Values* grew.

The approaches taken by contributors to the collection reflect recent wider developments in historical perspectives. Since the late 1980s, design historians have argued that the study of design institutions and their structures, among them design schools, museums, official bodies and organizations, can reveal how 'different ideas about design are made explicit and struggled over',[4] and that their study can help to disclose how the design profession has become aware of its inner-workings and self-image.[5] Further, the late 2000s witnessed a 'mediatization turn' in the field,[6] emphasizing the need for extended research into design's structures.[7] The 'global turn' in design history, informed by wider critiques of Eurocentrism across the arts and humanities, stressed the necessity to recognize other histories and the networked, heterogeneous character of design activities. These approaches furthermore stressed that design exchanges were often historically embedded in geographies shaped by 'asymmetrical power and exchange' and local processes of

---

[2] Reyner Banham, ed., *The Aspen Papers: Twenty Years of Design Theory from the International Design Conference in Aspen* (London: Pall Mall Press, 1974).
[3] Helena Čapková, 'Transnational Networkers – Iwao and Michiko Yamawaki and the Formation of Japanese Modernist Design', *Journal of Design History* 7, no. 4 (2014); Samer Akkach, 'Professional Identity and Social Responsibility', in *Design in the Borderlands*, ed. Eleni Kalantidou and Tony Fry (Abingdon / New York: Routledge, 2014); Artemis Yagou, 'Unwanted Innovation: The Athens Design Centre (1961–1963)', *Journal of Design History* 18, no. 3 (2005); Katarina Serulus, '"Well-Designed Relations": Cold War Design Exchanges between Brussels and Moscow in the Early 1970s', *Design and Culture* 9, no. 2 (2017).
[4] John Walker, *Design History and the History of Design* (London: Pluto Press, 1989), 67. Cited in Katarina Serulus, 'Design & Politics: The Public Promotion of Industrial Design in Postwar Belgium (1950–1986)', Doctoral Thesis, University of Antwerp, 2016, 15.
[5] Guy Julier, 'Re-Drawing the Geography of European Design: The Case of Transitional Countries', *Contextual Design – Design in Context*, 2nd European Academy of Design Conference, Stockholm, April 1997.
[6] Serulus, 'Design & Politics', 15. See also: Grace Lees-Maffei, 'The Production-Consumption – Mediation Paradigm', ibid., 22, no. 4 (2009); Kjetil Fallan, *Design History. Understanding Theory and Method* (Oxford/New York: Berg, 2010), cited in Serulus, 'Design & Politics'.
[7] Kjetil Fallan, 'Our Common Future: Joining Forces for Histories of Sustainable Design', *TECNOSCIENZA Italian Journal of Science & Technology Studies* 5, no. 2 (2015): 17–18. Cited in Serulus, 'Design & Politics'.

negotiation, translation and rejection.[8] To understand how design organizations operated, the tracing of people, epistemologies and objects across and beyond national borders therefore drew on the precepts of transnational histories. Through this, previously accepted analytical categories of the local, the national, the international and the global as they had been applied to design cultures were questioned.[9] In part, the contribution of design historians is to suggest that the study of international design organizations can unveil some of the many ways in which design cultures have been entangled and developed in an expanded geography. In 2005, for example, Jonathan M. Woodham predicted such an endeavour would lead to new insights into 'design practice, promotion, context and consumption in many more corners of the globe than have been explored by design historians to date'.[10] Ten years later, Daniel Huppatz extended this point of view, highlighting how the study of multidirectional exchanges between professional organizations and international design organizations was a powerful means to 'globalize history and historicize globalization'.[11]

This edited collection is distinctive in bringing together essays which shed light on the histories, legacies and values of international design organizations as they have extended across and between Latin America, Asia, Europe and the United States since their formation. Taking this wide geography is an important first step in showing that their composition was diverse and multiple, not homogenous or singular. They provide important sources of evidence of the formation and institutionalization of design standards. Some histories focus on individuals responsible for this shaping, others on the social interactions or rituals involved in their operation, and others on the materiality through which design organizations could function. Together, they shed light on the diverse and interconnected issues that working towards internationalism can raise and the negotiation of national

---

[8] Glenn Adamson, Sarah Teasley and Giorgio Riello, eds., *Global Design History* (London/New York: Routledge, 2011).

[9] Karen Fiss, 'Design in a Global Context: Envisioning Postcolonial and Transnational Possibilities', *Design Issues* 25, no. 3 (2009): 3–10, 2; Yuko Kikuchi and Yunah Lee, 'Transnational Modern Design Histories in East Asia: An Introduction', *Journal of Design History* 27, no. 4 (2014); Joana Ozorio de Almeida Meroz and Katarina Serulus, 'A Theoretical Straddle: Locating Design Cultures Between National Structures and Transnational Networks', in *Design Culture: Objects and Approaches*, ed. Guy Julier et al. (London: Bloomsbury, 2019).

[10] Jonathan M. Woodham, 'Local, National and Global: Redrawing the Design Historical Map', Special Issue: The Global Future of Design History, *Journal of Design History* 18, no. 3 (2005).

[11] Daniel Huppatz, 'Globalizing Design History and Global Design History', *Journal of Design History* 28, no. 2 (2015): 182. See also: Alison J. Clarke, 'Design for Development, ICSID and UNIDO: The Anthropological Turn in 1970s Design', *Journal of Design History* 29, no. 1 (2015); Dora Souza Dias, 'International Design Organizations and the Study of Transnational Interactions: The Case of Icogradalatinoamérica80', *Journal of Design History* 32, no. 2 (May 2019); Tania Messell, 'Globalization and Design Institutionalization: ICSID's XIth Congress and the Formation of ALADI, 1979', *Journal of Design History* 32, no. 1 (2019); Juan-Camilo Buitrago-Trujillo, 'The Siege of the Outsiders ALADI: The First Latin American Design Association and its Discourse of Resistance', *Journal of Design History* 34, no. 1 (2021).

interests within this process. In line with the views of historian Patricia Clavin, this edited volume therefore advances the study of cross-border networks as they were enacted through international design organizations to offer 'an unrivalled lens through which to see the world afresh'.[12]

From *inter*-national to transnational networks

The establishment of the first large international design organizations took place in the years following the Second World War. At that time, heightened efforts to institutionalize the design profession were seen by those involved as a response to the expansion of trade networks and interlinked economic systems. These were profoundly shaped by competing US and Soviet hegemonies and global Cold War politics that divided a substantial part of the world between 1947 and 1991. Although the first steps towards international legislative, commercial and industrial co-operation and forms of internationalism in Europe and North America can be traced to the mid-nineteenth century, the period after 1945 witnessed a moment in which the world's interconnectedness reached new heights. During this period, international organizations, located predominantly in the West, were in large part established in reaction to the experience of devastating nationalism that had resulted in two world wars, in an alleged attempt to forge progress towards shaping better societies. Moreover, in addition to the growing entry of African, Asian and Latin American countries in international organizations, world states not formally aligned with major post-war power blocs also promoted co-operation and a united front against colonization, such as through the Non-Aligned Movement (NAM). This surge towards increased connectedness between nation and federal states was facilitated by the development of technical innovations such as satellite technology that contributed to a new understanding of the world map.

In the immediate post-war years, design as a profession still held a tenuous and ill-defined status in many countries and it continued to struggle to receive recognition from governments, industry and commerce. In response to this, there was a move among some designers to join forces to 'campaign collectively for a greater recognition of their value to business, commerce, and society', which resulted in the gradual multiplication of professional design organizations.[13] Alongside the promotion of the profession, these associations aimed to provide practitioners with fora in which they could exchange ideas, receive their awards and establish

---

[12] Patricia Clavin, 'Roundtable: "Governing the World" by Mark Mazower', *History Workshop Journal Online*, 8 October 2013. http://www.historyworkshop.org.uk/roundtable-governing-the-world-by-mark-mazower/. Cited in Jessica Reinisch, 'Introduction: Agents of Internationalism', *Contemporary European History* 25, no. 2 (2016): 202.

[13] Jonathan M. Woodham, *Twentieth-Century Design* (Oxford/New York: Oxford University Press, 1997), 175.

international connections.¹⁴ While some designers at the peak of their careers had been able to travel and operate internationally prior to these developments,¹⁵ improved communication technologies and more readily available air travel facilitated much wider-spread design connections and exchanges.¹⁶ Operating in varying degrees by virtue of governmental and industrial funding, such networks brought together actors from promotional, professional and educational design circles whose design understanding and disciplinary divisions often differed. Similarly to many international non-governmental organizations, such platforms were established as a result of 'cultural internationalism', a phenomenon which the historian Akira Iriye defined as the assumption that cultural and social questions knew no boundaries and that international networks would help to promote common interests.¹⁷ Such organizations however rapidly became the site of professional, but also diplomatic and economic manoeuvring.

As historians have argued, the study of international institutions and networks is crucial for uncovering the connections and cross-fertilizations that have so often been neglected within the framework of national case studies. Historian Sandrine Kott writes,

> International organisations and associations are particularly fertile areas of study in this regard: they represent spaces in which one can reveal the existence of networks of relationships and systems of circulation […] and explore the connections between the local, the national, and the global and, indeed, the process of internationalisation itself.¹⁸

Similar to international governmental organizations, international design organizations were composed of government representatives, professional members, headquarters and secretarial staff, as well as a wider constellation of regional branches and members. Brought together under one roof, individuals who operated at the intersection of national, transnational and local networks pursued overlapping and diverse interests that revealed the intermeshed character of such networks. In order to shed light on the circulations and connections that shaped local, regional and international design cultures, it is useful to examine micro-histories and the social phenomena that extend beyond nation-states as

---

¹⁴ Penny Sparke, *An Introduction to Design and Culture*, 3rd ed. (Abingdon: Routledge, 2013), 152; Wendy Siuyi Wong, 'Detachment and Unification: A Chinese Graphic Design History in Greater China since 1979', *Design Issues* 17, no. 4 (Autumn 2001).
¹⁵ Adamson, Teasley and Riello, *Global Design History*.
¹⁶ Huppatz, 'Globalizing Design History and Global Design History'.
¹⁷ Akira Iriye, *Global Community: The Role of International Organisations in the Making of the Contemporary World* (Oakland: University of California Press, 2002), 25.
¹⁸ Sandrine Kott, 'Towards a Social History of International Organisations: The ILO and the Internationalisation of Western Social Expertise (1919–1949)', in *Internationalism, Imperialism and the Formation of the Contemporary World*, ed. Miguel Bandeira Jerónimo and José Pedro Monteiro (Cham: Palgrave Macmillan, 2017), 33–4.

'containers of society'.[19] This is not to say that the national as a unit of analysis should altogether be put aside, as international and national aims are intimately connected. As historian Pierre-Yves Saunier writes, modern nation-states have sought 'to control, rebut or eradicate flows, ties and formations across borders', yet they have also led 'projects to nurture and orient' transnational phenomena 'if only to increase or protect what was defined as "national"'.[20] Indeed, international governmental organizations often understood themselves as summations of nations, which were celebrated as stepping stones towards building international society,[21] and such dynamics extended to cross-border professional networks. While studies have highlighted the shifting and heterogeneous bond between expert organizations and the state in transnational networks,[22] their establishment and running were often triggered by the logics of 'strategic internationalisation'.[23] In this way, international design organizations at times became sites of soft power,[24] through their advancement of so-called 'national' design doctrines, the promotion of national industries and goods, and processes which were at times embedded in the pursuit of ideological political aims, such as the Cold War containment strategies or the strengthening of newly decolonized states.

In line with this scholarship, international design organizations can furthermore be examined in their own right as 'sites of internationalisation'.[25] Shaped by cross-border encounters, orchestrated gatherings, headquarters and secretariats, designed artefacts and exhibitions, and often clear-cut hierarchies, much can be unveiled about the formation, transfers and local translations of design cultures. As Woodham suggested in the context of ICSID, since 2017 the World Design Organization (WDO):

> the globally dispersed ICSID General Assemblies, Seminars, Interdesign workshops, numerous Working Groups and the emergent World Design Capitals merit further detailed examination as important ingredients in an understanding of the complexities of design practices, protocols and policies in a global context.[26]

---

[19] Ulrich Beck, *What Is Globalization?* (New York: Wiley, 2000), 63.
[20] Pierre-Yves Saunier, *Transnational History* (Basingstoke: Palgrave, 2013), 8. Cited in Daniel Laqua, 'Internationalism and Nationalism in the League of Nations' Work for Intellectual Cooperation', in *Internationalism, Imperialism and the Formation of the Contemporary World*, ed. Miguel Bandeira Jerónimo and José Pedro Monteiro (Cham: Palgrave Macmillan, 2017), 60.
[21] Glenda Sluga, *Internationalism in the Age of Nationalism* (Philadelphia: University of Pennsylvania Press, 2013).
[22] Martin H. Geyer and Johannes Paulmann, *The Mechanics of Internationalism: Culture, Society, and Politics from the 1840s to the First World War* (Oxford: Oxford University Press, 2001); Patricia Clavin, 'Defining Transnationalism', *Contemporary European History* 14, no. 4 (2005); Reinisch, 'Introduction'.
[23] Geyer and Paulmann, *The Mechanics of Internationalism*.
[24] On the concept of 'soft power', see Joseph Nye, *Power in the Global Information Age: From Realism to Globalization* (London/New York: Routledge, 2004), 5.
[25] Kott, 'Towards a Social History of International Organisations', 34.
[26] Jonathan M. Woodham, 'Design, Histories, Empires and Peripheries', in *Design Frontiers – Territories, Concepts, Technologies*, ed. Farias Priscila et al., 8th Conference of the International Committee of Design History and Design Studies (São Paulo: Blucher, 2012), 456.

Despite their stated aims, design organizations regularly failed to represent their constituents, to consolidate cross-border norms, or to harness wider design discourses. Similar to other international networks,[27] international design organizations often held a weak legal status. Their restricted budgets led them to struggle in carrying out even daily tasks, let alone ambitious large-scale initiatives. For some of their members, international organizations also regularly failed to address diverse local professional interests and needs,[28] leading to dissatisfaction from those with divergent design understandings, professional priorities or ideological positionings. From a contemporary perspective, it is clear that such weaknesses did not always detract from the symbolic weight that their cross-border networks acquired, nor their impact in enabling transnational connections that helped shape professional and promotional design practices in local and regional contexts. Yet such a perspective aligns this design historical position with the approaches of disciplines such as anthropology and ethnographic studies, which have sought to challenge 'the monolithic representations of international institutions', as it has been 'produced by their mandates and by the outside perspectives that focus only on the content of their documents and public statements'.[29]

Cross-border professionalization: Power and knowledge production

While historical studies of international expert networks have revealed that they were established to bring order to unregulated domains, diverging national agendas, inherent rivalries and the meeting of diverse professional cultures nevertheless often affected their aims and functioning.[30] For interpreting complex entities such as those that occur across the design profession, the sociologist Ellen Kuhlmann recommends 'context-sensitive approaches that take into account the intersecting dynamics of different sets of governance in global, local and transnational perspective and the various ways professions are nested in these contexts'.[31] As the chapters in this volume show, international design organizations held within them a diversity of professional, national and international interests

---

[27] Sandrine Kott, 'Towards a Transnational History of International Organisations: Methodology/Epistemology', Paper given at the UNESCO Conference, King's College, Cambridge, 2009; Mary Fulbrook, German History seminar, Faculty of Modern History, Oxford, 2004.
[28] Marcos Braga, *ABDI e APDINS-RJ*, 2nd ed. (São Paolo: Editora Edgar Blücher, 2016), 134.
[29] Ronald Niezen and Maria Sapignoli, eds., 'Introduction', in *Palaces of Hope: The Anthropology of Global Organizations* (Cambridge: Cambridge University Press, 2017), 2–3.
[30] Daniel Laqua, ed., *Internationalism Reconfigured: Transnational Ideas and Movements between the World Wars* (London: I.B. Tauris, 2011); Bruno Strasser, *La Fabrique d'une Nouvelle Science: La Biologie Moléculaire à l'Âge Atomique (1945–1964)* (Florence: Olschki, 2006).
[31] Ellen Kuhlmann, 'Sociology of Professions: Towards International Context-Sensitive Approaches', *South African Review of Sociology* 44, no. 2 (2013).

that require such sensitive attention to contexts. The coming together of members and representatives of the various design interests in such organizations could influence their internal operations or their definitions of design but could not escape the inherent asymmetrical power relations and frictions. For as historian Patricia Clavin has written, power is intrinsic to transnational processes, both the power to 'dominate peoples, and the will to resist'.[32]

International governmental and non-governmental organizations have been defined as Western constructs, whose Eurocentric structures, regulations and working languages resulted in inequalities throughout history.[33] Furthermore, such networks were inevitably shaped by overlapping and shifting issues of gender, race and class of their time.[34] According to historian Jessica Reinisch, histories of power relations must take account of the political and cultural contexts within which international networks are embedded,[35] such as the exclusionary dynamics in professional projects that undermine claims to universalizing knowledge of design. Feminist scholars have also noted how connections can be traced between the disembodiment of knowledge and the processes of creating and legitimizing hierarchies, which has assisted ambitious white middle-class men in their social ascension, so prevalent in the formative years of these design organizations.[36] In considering Western design circles, design historians Gerry Beegan and Paul Atkinson write that professionalization intentionally or unintentionally excludes individuals and groups on 'the basis of money, class, ethnicity and gender', through the setting up of narrow criteria. Symptomatic of this process, they furthermore argue that 'professionalization in Europe and the USA became a means of creating business networks and social arenas that were largely middle class, white and male, maintaining the gentlemanly hierarchies characteristic of divinity, law and medicine'.[37] As will be discussed, such élites, from their positions of power, defined objectives that resulted in excluding other social groups, knowledges and practices.[38]

---

[32] Patricia Clavin, 'Defining Transnationalism', *Contemporary European History* 14, no. 4 (2010): 626.
[33] Toshiki Mogami, 'On the Concept of International Organization: Centralization, Hegemonism, and Constitutionalism', in *Networking the International System Global Histories of International Organizations*, ed. Madeleine Herren (New York: Springer, 2014).
[34] See, for instance, Glenda Sluga, 'UNESCO and the (One) World of Julian Huxley', *Journal of World History* 21, no. 3, Cosmopolitanism in World History (2010); Michael Barnett, *Empire of Humanity: A History of Humanitarianism* (Ithaca, NY: Cornell University Press, 2011); Karen Garner, *Women and Gender in International History, Theory and Practice* (London: Bloomsbury, 2018).
[35] Reinisch, 'Introduction'.
[36] Donna Haraway, 'Situated Knowledges: The Science Question in Feminism and the Privilege of Partial Perspective', *Feminist Studies* 14, no. 3 (1988); Magali Sarfatti Larson, *The Rise of Professionalism: A Sociological Analysis* (Oakland, CA: University of California Press, 1977).
[37] Gerry Beegan and Paul Atkinson, 'Professionalism, Amateurism and the Boundaries of Design', *Journal of Design History* 21, no. 4 (2008): 305. See also: Armstrong, Leah, 'Steering a Course Between Professionalism and Commercialism: The Society of Industrial Artists and the Code of Conduct for the Professional Designer, 1945–1975', *Journal of Design History* 29, no. 2 (2016).
[38] Keith Macdonald, *The Sociology of the Professions* (London: SAGE Publications, 1999).

International design organizations were often the product of restricted networks of professionals, whose design visions and value systems excluded younger practitioners and expansive design definitions. As design historian Alice Twemlow has shown, this was the case at the 1970 International Design Conference in Aspen, when vocal protests led by students, activists and some of the guest speakers against the values, modes and manners of the design establishment demanded the introduction of revised agendas for future meetings, with topics that addressed 'the major socio-political issues of the moment such as sexual politics and third world hunger', and a format which 'accommodated disruption [and] self-critique'.[39] As several chapters in this volume reveal, post-war international design organizations were also predominantly male-dominated environments, in which women had to continuously negotiate their position and battle to gain executive roles. Moreover, unequal relations and processes of exclusion were evident in international design organizations with their shifting geographies of power. The designer and researcher Danah Abdulla has argued that this process has remained engrained among Western-based organizations such as ICSID (World Design Organisation), which still tend to reduce the concept of global design to narratives of the 'West and the rest'.[40] As could be expected, Western-led international design organizations favoured dominant narratives of modernization and development which by implication asserted hegemonic Anglo-European ways of thinking and designing. In the case of ICSID and Icograda, for example, imbalances were reflected in the composition of their Executive Boards, the locations of their headquarters and the fee structures for membership. The latter excluded organizations from weaker economies, unable to cover their fees.[41] The organizations' membership criteria were so defined as to undervalue diverse understandings of design, stances which prevented individuals and groups from joining who were deemed not fit to practise. In her analysis of exchanges and initiatives conducted between Icograda and Latin American graphic design circles, design historian Dora Souza Dias has thus shown how, 'placed in a position of disadvantage (as part of the periphery) [...] individuals had (and still have) to negotiate their position in the international context, affecting the direction of cultural flows'.[42]

However, the dominant Western perception of internationalism risks overshadowing alternative possibilities that existed. History shows how groups that were geographically or politically distanced from the decision-making centres of

---

[39] Alice Twemlow, 'I Can't Talk to You if You Say That: An Ideological Collision at the International Design Conference at Aspen, 1970', *Design and Culture* 1, no. 1 (2009).
[40] Danah Abdulla, Contribution to the Plenary Discussion, 'International Design Organisations: Histories, Legacies, Values', University of Brighton, Brighton, 9–10 November 2017.
[41] Souza Dias, 'International Design Organizations and the Study of Transnational Interactions', 202; Tania Messell, 'Constructing a "United Nations of Industrial Design": ICSID and the Professionalization of Design on the World Stage, 1957–1980', Doctoral Thesis, University of Brighton, 2018.
[42] Souza Dias, 'International Design Organizations and the Study of Transnational Interactions', 195.

international organizations used their situations to stake claims and assert the right to economic development, nation building and the crafting of cultural identities.[43] Indeed, as historians Miguel Bandeira Jerónimo and José Pedro Monteiro note, 'there was never a single internationalism, but several internationalisms that have intersected and competed with each other', a diversity that needs to 'gain a proper place in studies of the contemporary world'.[44] Therefore, the meeting of diverse professional design cultures in other settings can be seen as allowing for multidirectional exchanges and the expression of alternative visions for design. This was the case for designers representing Asian nations in the context of Western-based international design organizations, as famously happened in the case of the Ahmedabad Declaration in 1979 that grew from the ICSID-UNIDO (United Nations Industrial Development Organization) conference held at the National Institute of Design in that city.[45] The recognition of other voices also contributed to the polycentric regionalization of the organization's membership, a process which resulted in exchanges on common issues and interests at a regional level. Subsequent initiatives brought forth processes of local translation of established 'global' design agendas, where these have been re-combined in line with local aims and realities, as urban geographer Laura Nkula-Wenz writes in the context of ICSID/WDO's 'World Design Capital' programme in Cape Town.[46]

By way of conclusion, the edited collection approaches international organizations as spaces of intersections, exchanges and professional formation, shaped by competing visions and agendas, and dynamics that both excluded and also at times was negotiated and hybridized.

In this sense, it contributes to scholarship on how design became a much discussed and debated profession, industry and potential force for global change. By challenging a one-way diffusionist approach to explore a wide set of issues, *International Design Organisations: Histories, Values, Legacies* contributes to deepening our understanding of international design networks, the formation of design practices and epistemologies. This is at a time when moves to internationalize design have been condemned for homogenizing design cultures and calls to decolonize design practices and epistemologies are being increasingly being heard. While its focus is on international design organizations, a further

---

[43] Sunil Amrit, closing remarks, Transnational History of International Organizations: Methodology/Epistemology Conference, King's College, Cambridge, 6–7 April 2009. Cited in Glenda Sluga, 'Editorial: The Transnational History of International Institutions', *Journal of Global History* 6, no. 2 (2011); Sluga, *Internationalism in the Age of Nationalism*.

[44] Miguel Bandeira Jerónimo and José Pedro Monteiro, *Internationalism, Imperialism and the Formation of the Contemporary World* (Cham: Palgrave Macmillan, 2017).

[45] In the case of ICSID, the Council's development initiatives and the Ahmedabad Declaration in 1979 were instigated by actors in so-called 'developing countries'. Balaram Singanapalli, 'Design in India: The Importance of the Ahmedabad Declaration', *Design Issues* 25, no. 4 (2009): 55. On this initiative, see also: Clarke, 'Design for Development, ICSID and UNIDO'.

[46] Laura Nkula-Wenz, 'Worlding Cape Town by Design: Encounters with Creative Cityness', *Environment and Planning A: Economy and Space* 51, no. 3 (2018).

hope is that the assembled new knowledge will also contribute to the wider understanding of how international networks operate beyond design.

Structure

A significant proportion of the historical period covered in this book was marked by the political circumstances of the Cold War that divided the world between 1947 and 1991. During this time, in the West a model of consumer capitalism was consolidated to compete with the alternative model of the command economy of nations and states within the Soviet Bloc. The period was also a time of change in the manufacturing base on a global scale that formed the context in which design operated. While the West moved towards technological, service and digital economies characteristic of post-industrial societies from the last decades of the twentieth century, the impact of globalization and the changing map of major centres of industrial manufacture led to the intensification of cultural exchange across the world.[47] International design organizations were inevitably implicated in these changes that also entered among the subjects that were addressed at their meetings, conferences and congresses.

Historians of international design organizations navigate this complex terrain. It is important to draw attention to the varied terminology that appears in the period at a macro-level, to characterize this global landscape. Sources on international design organizations reveal a general concern with what is described variously as the division between the 'First', 'Second' and 'Third Worlds'. Also, terms such as the 'developed' and 'developing world' frequently occur, as do 'Centre/Periphery' and more recently, the 'Global North' and 'Global South'.[48] Together, these terms point towards shifting geopolitical imaginations, as Arturo Escobar writes, the 'social production of space implicit in these [...] is bound with the production of differences, subjectivities, and social orders'.[49] Authors in this book employ the terms with great care, concerned to distinguish how they are found and were used in the primary sources of documents, the organizations' own minutes and records of meetings, their conferences and congresses or subsequent commentary by the press and specialist journals or through oral testimony. In their subsequent interpretation and analysis, they take care to assess such terms critically for the value judgements and assumptions that informed them.

---

[47] Saskia Sassen, *A Sociology of Globalization* (New York: Norton, 2007).
[48] On the origins and value systems inherent in such terminologies, see Duanfang Lu, ed., 'Introduction: Architecture, Modernity and Identity in the Third World', in *Third World Modernism: Architecture, Development and Identity* (Abingdon/New York: Routledge, 2010) and Marcin Wojciech Solarz, *The Language of Global Development: A Misleading Geography* (Abingdon/New York: Routledge, 2014).
[49] Arturo Escobar, *Encountering Development: The Making and Unmaking of the Third World* (Princeton, NJ: Princeton University Press, 2011), 9.

In addition to terminology of the world's divisions, the literature on design's professionalization highlights its gendered nature. As suggested above, the histories of the first period of design organizations are largely one in which men are the protagonists. Here, two chapters, by Katarina Serulus and Triin Jerlei, show the pivotal but all too infrequent role of women as leading actors in their design organizations. The question remains whether it is possibly still too soon to know whether women are hidden from history and if future research may answer this, placing their contributions more centrally to correct this imbalance.

Finally, as readers of this volume will become aware, the focus of the chapters is mainly on organizations that represented and promoted the genres of industrial and graphic design, along with their frequent interaction. To some extent, this choice reflects the current state of research on international design organizations, which to our knowledge has not yet awarded as much attention to the histories of international fashion and interior design networks.[50] In contrast, the professionalization and international organization of architecture that constituted an important prior model for the fields of design and at many points overlapped with international design organizations[51] have received historical attention.[52]

Professions – rules – institutions – personalities

The opening section of the book presents the diverse dynamics at play with complex design organizations, tracing how they were formed, structured and functioned, and in particular highlighting that they were sites of contested values. In the first chapter Dora Souza Dias looks at distinct design organizations operating in the post-war period, focusing more intently on those dedicated to graphic design practice. Taking a post-colonial perspective, the chapter critically assesses the manners in which professionalization has often favoured a Eurocentric understanding of design during the Cold War period, which both excluded and contributed to shaping transnational design connections. As she moreover argues, the formation of international non-governmental design organizations was grounded in the belief of the universalism of Western design values, which have very much remained

---

[50] See, for instance, the International Federation of Interior Architects/Designers (IFI) formed in 1963 with parallel aims to those of ICSID and Icograda, www.ifiworld.org, and The International Apparel Federation (IAF) founded in 1972, www.iafnet.com.

[51] Mark Mazower, *Governing the World: The History of an Idea* (London: Allen Lane, 2012), 106.

[52] Christiane Crasemann Collins and Mark Swenarton. 'CIAM, Teige and the Housing Problem in the 1920s', *Habitat International* 11, no. 3 (1987); Eric Paul Mumford, *The CIAM Discourse on Urbanism, 1928–1960* (Cambridge, MA: MIT Press, 2002); International Union of Architects, *L'UIA, 1948–1998* (Paris: Epure, 1998); Marcela Hanáčková, 'CIAM and the Cold War Post-war Discussions on Modernism and Socialist Realism', Doctoral Thesis, ETH Zurich, 2012; Aymone Nicolas, *L'Apogée des Concours Internationaux d'Architecture: L'Action de l'UIA 1948–1975* (Paris: Editions A&J Picard, 2007).

today through the excluding frameworks of professionalization. In this way, the chapter signals sites of contestation that are discussed in further detail by individual cases in the chapters that follow. In the second chapter, Veronica Devalle sheds light on the emergence of design as a modern discipline in mid-twentieth-century Argentina. The chapter reconstructs the relations between architects, designers and intellectuals, their editorial initiatives, and the public and private institutions in which they were active. This set of networks linked artistic, promotional and architectural practices with institutions in the region that prepared the ground for professional design organizations to be created from the 1960s onwards. This culminated in Buenos Aires in the first institution of public policy on design, the Centre for Research on Industrial Design (CIDI). In the third chapter Tania Messell contributes to post-war histories of international design organizations by examining the central contribution of émigré designers to such cross-border networks, in this case, of ICSID. The chapter follows the path of designer Peter Muller-Munk from Vienna to the United States, whose migration presents a case of translation and mediation by crossing the fault-line between design cultures, in an organization shaped by the Cold War and professional imperatives. When interests in international alliances materialized in the early formative years of these organizations, the contribution of émigré practitioners was a crucial factor. In the final chapter of Part One, Jonathan M. Woodham considers how in their mature stages, International Council of Societies of Industrial Design (ICSID) and the International Council of Graphic Design Organizations (Icograda) moved beyond the international development of the design profession and design standards in their quest to become recognized authoritative non-governmental global advocates for design. Tracing ICSID's reincarnation as the World Design Organization (WDO) and Icograda as the International Council of Design (Ico-D), the chapter asks to what extent such global design organizations became effective promoters of their own globally oriented agendas.

National – international – transnational

The chapters in the second section address the ways that individuals, groups and organizations defined themselves and set goals for design. Together, they reveal how it is not always possible to draw straightforward distinctions on the basis of their national, international and transnational operation, but rather, they underline the interlinked and interdependent character of these concepts. Part Two opens with first of two chapters on IDCA, in which Robert Gordon-Fogelson focuses on the reorganization of the conference during the mid-1950s and the repercussions on its mission to promote comprehensive, integrated approaches to design. By revealing archival details of the conference's identity, he suggests that these changes reflected the image of internationalization developed by the IDCA organizers and supported their vision of design as a fundamentally integrative force at a time of political instability facing the world. The sixth chapter by Juan Buitrago considers the professionalization of design in Latin America from the 1960s onwards, to show how the process was entangled with matters of regional identity and conflicts on the adoption of foreign influences, namely those from Europe and the United States. As a defence of 'lo latinoamericano', as well as its design, the Latin American Design Association (ALADI) was founded in Colombia in 1980 by delegations from nine countries. Central in this, one of ALADI founders, Oscar Pamio, claimed that this was a strategy to protect the 'Imagined Community' and its people from not being allowed to create their own reality. In the seventh chapter, Yasuko Suga examines the post-war formations and activities of two major graphic design professional groups, the Japan Advertising Artists' Club (JAAC, 1951–1970) and the Japan Graphic Design Association (JAGDA, 1978–), to show how they balanced or failed to balance their international experiences, such as the coming of WoDeCo (World Design Conference) in Tokyo in 1960 and the formation of Icograda with domestic social issues. In turn, the chapter sheds light on understanding some of the tensions facing contemporary graphic design in Japan. In the eighth chapter, Katarina Serulus highlights how, when studying the institutionalization of industrial design in Western Europe, strong personal and professional networks that reached far beyond borders are often overlooked. Its focus is on the Belgian policymaker Josine des Cressonnières, who, as director of the Brussels Design Centre (1962–1985) and Secretary General of ICSID from 1961 until 1977, among other roles, operated as a pivotal figure and one of the rare women in this male-dominated context. Following an individual as she moved between national, international and transnational networks shaped by political and economic interests in the wider Cold War context, the chapter offers key insights into the formation of design policies at the crossroad of national and transnational design cultures.

Design definitions – epistemologies – differences

Building on the framework established by the chapters in the first two sections, this final group of chapters offers detailed considerations of the circumstances in which definitions of design changed, evolved and/or were challenged in a number of different organizational settings across the world. In the first chapter of this section, Chiara Barbieri shows how, in 1962, a group of graphic designers who were members of the Italian Association for Industrial Design (ADI) launched a graphic design division that turned to international design organizations, offering Italian graphic designers a crucial opportunity to be part of an international community. This enabled new thinking in visual communication and fostered professionalization on both a local and global scale. Such contact within transnational circuits asserted their distinctive professional identity as equal partners with industrial designers. The tenth chapter by Triin Jerlei focuses on the Industrial Art Committee, an institution that existed in Soviet Estonia from 1967 to 1989, and shows how the IAC functioned very differently from its Western counterparts. Through this case study of the political processes underlying the negotiation of the 'Western' and 'Socialist' in industrial design within a local peripheral context of the Soviet Union, the chapter explores the inner workings of the so-called peripheral design organizations and the methodological challenges faced when researching organizations regarded as having played a minor role internationally. Led by Ingi Vaher from the onset, a study of the organization furthermore sheds a much-needed light on the contribution of women to international design networks. Alison J. Clarke, in the eleventh chapter, examines the crucial dispersion of anthropology within design and its culmination in the 'Ahmedabad Declaration' in 1979. Launched at an ICSID/UNIDO congress under the title 'Design and Development', this formalized the emergence of a specific genre of 'development design' based on quasi-anthropological paradigms. The author considers how the informal 'alternative design' movement was incorporated into industrial design's role in 1970s entente Cold War politics. In the second chapter to consider ICDA, Penelope Dean turns to events in the conference's final years. It chronicles the changing discursive landscape of design from the rise of neoliberalism, a digital revolution and impending economic crises. It shows that any consensus on what actually constitutes design disintegrated, revealing the IDCA as neither an organization of the design establishment nor the outsider, but both of them at once. In the final chapter in this collection, Yun Wang explores the changes in Chinese graphic design since 1980s, following China's implementation of the Reform and Opening-up policy of 1978. This political change prompted international design organizations, including AGI (Alliance Graphique Internationale) and Icograda, to hold their conferences in Beijing in 2004 and 2009, respectively. These exerted a profound influence on many aspects of Chinese graphic design, at a stage the graphic design profession was confronting the real problems and challenges involved in applying the knowledge gained abroad to a local context. The chapter thereby reflects some of the central contributions of the edited collection by highlighting how international design organizations have constituted spaces formed and transformed by the meeting of diverse constituencies embedded in transnational political, economic and professional contexts, thereby contributing to expose cultures of internationalism and mechanics of cultural exchanges.

PART ONE

PROFESSIONS – RULES – INSTITUTIONS – PERSONALITIES

1 PROFESSIONAL GRAPHIC DESIGN AND COLD WAR POLITICS: NATIONAL AND TRANSNATIONAL DESIGN ORGANIZATIONS

Dora Souza Dias

The entwined histories of modernism, modernization, industrialization and the professional practice of design offer a significant challenge for the study of design history. Historically, the role of the designer as a full-time professional occupation has appeared in societies where increasingly complex production systems have resulted in the fragmentation of work, further emphasized by the introduction of mechanical devices into production systems.[1] For instance, the development of paper and printing systems enabled the development of new ways of reproducing and distributing texts and images, from manuscripts produced one by one, to the mass printing of texts and books by a number of skilled workers dedicated to specialized tasks in graphic reproduction.[2] Similarly specialization occurred in the pottery and textiles industries in Europe during the nineteenth century, where a division of labour was established to increase production, differentiating the act of designing from that of making.[3]

However, one needs to consider the possible underlying conundrum within the very own concept of design. Considering design – as suggested by design historians Grace Lees-Maffei and Kjetil Fallan – as an activity that 'extends to everything that is planned and/or made […] not limited to high or official culture'[4] offers an opportunity for design to be seen as an activity independent of modernization, modernity or industry. Instead, if one considers the professional practice of design or its connection to mass production, the story takes a different

---

[1] Peter Dormer, *Design since 1945* (London: Thames & Hudson, 1993).
[2] Philip B. Meggs and Alston W. Purvis, eds., *Meggs' History of Graphic Design*, 5th ed. (Hoboken: John Wiley & Sons, [1998] 2012).
[3] Dormer, *Design since 1945*.
[4] Grace Lees-Maffei and Kjetil Fallan, 'Introduction: National Design Histories in an Age of Globalization', in *Designing Worlds: National Design Histories in an Age of Globalization*, ed. Grace Lees-Maffei and Kjetil Fallan (Oxford: Berghahn Books, 2016), 3.

turn. It could be said that the tensions between design practice and modern design practice lie between two extremes; on the one hand, that of design as a human-led process that is independent of mechanization, and, on the other, that of design as a profession that is primarily related to mass production and, therefore, seen by some as inevitably linked to industrialization.

Yet it is important to consider that the development of design into a field of professional practice was not determined by specialization itself. According to sociologists Andrew Abbott[5] and Pierre Bourdieu,[6] professional boundaries depend on a number of social conventions that separate fields of practice from each other in order to regulate entry and limit competition. The separation of fields of practice not only delineates what is considered to be legitimate practice but also, more importantly, defines which practitioners are allowed to perform certain occupations.

An important part of the process of professionalization is the establishment of forms of control that help regulate the professions and professionals, such as 'schools that train practitioners, the examinations that test them, the licenses that identify them, and the ethics codes they are presumed to obey'.[7] In the case of design, as in many other professions, the history of such institutions has favoured Eurocentric perspectives, not only due to the fact that the history of professional boundaries and professional organizations are somewhat rooted in European traditions, but also because design, or at least its modern form, was generally understood as a specialized practice associated with industrial production and, therefore, intrinsically connected to the industrial revolution that took place in Europe. In the past decades, these ideas have been under scrutiny for they restrict the comprehension of design to industrial development, compromising equitable comparisons and inevitably promoting Eurocentric ideas around design practice.[8]

Issues of professionalism

Professionalism is related to the creation of institutions and boundaries considered as professional practice, and the professional organizations were and are established to be the gatekeepers of such boundaries. Yet professional design organizations have not yet been approached from the perspective that these were

---

[5] Andrew Abbott, *The System of Professions: An Essay on the Division of Expert Labor* (Chicago: The University of Chicago Press, 1988).

[6] Pierre Bourdieu, 'Political Representation: Elements for a Theory of the Political Field' [1981], in *Language and Symbolic Power*, ed. John B. Thompson, trans. Gino Raymond and Matthew Adamson (Cambridge: Polity Press, 1991), 171–202.

[7] Abbott, *The System of Professions*, 79.

[8] Daniel J. Huppatz, 'Globalizing Design History and Global Design History', *Journal of Design History* 28, no. 2 (2015): 182–202.

initially developed within European social contexts and frameworks of knowledge. Professional organizations as we know them today were not necessarily common in other regions of the world – certainly not previously to colonization – such as the Americas, Africa and Oceania. As stressed by sociologist Aníbal Quijano, in nations that have been colonized, native forms of social organization and local knowledge have been suppressed and substituted by the colonizer's social structures, eliminating knowledge about their stories and forms of social organization predating colonization.[9]

Even though design has been portrayed, particularly in its modern version, as if it could not have originated anywhere else but in Western Europe, this does not mean that there was no design practice elsewhere. Particularly, if one disconnects its practice from industry and formal organizations. The issue at stake is that the act of designing outside of Western Europe and, later, the United States might not have been organized in the same way or not use the same vocabulary and methodologies, but that does not mean that it did not take place. It is only a matter of how design is defined. Alternative design practices have been overlooked or misunderstood in the past when analysed in comparison to the way design practice was established and developed in Europe and in the United States.[10]

One could say that the idea of professionalism fits within the definition coined by historian Dipesh Chakrabarty in his book *Provincializing Europe*. As put by him, certain categories and concepts – whose genealogies 'go deep into the intellectual and even theological traditions of Europe'[11] – are so entangled with the idea of modernity that it becomes impossible to address modernity without them, in such a way that European thought becomes 'both indispensable and inadequate' when addressing 'the various life practices that constitute the political and the historical'.[12]

Historical knowledge has reflected the structural reality of organizations related to the design profession, which inevitably consider the first organizations dedicated to the promotion and development of design practice, to have been established in Western Europe. From the second half of the twentieth century onwards, designers located in other regions shaped their vocabularies and methodologies in an attempt to integrate themselves into the international scene of professional

---

[9] Aníbal Quijano, 'Colonialidad del poder, cultura e conocimiento en América Latina', *Dispositio/n* 24, no. 51 ([1997] 1999): 137–48.

[10] H. Alpay Er, 'Development Patterns of Industrial Design in the Third World: A Conceptual Model for Newly Industrialized Countries', *Journal of Design History* 10, no. 3 (1997): 293–307; Anna Calvera, 'Local, Regional, National, Global and Feedback: Several Issues to Be Faced with Constructing Regional Narratives', *Journal of Design History* 18, no. 4 (2005): 371–83; Dora Souza Dias, 'International Design Organizations and the Study of Transnational Interactions: The Case of Icogradalatinoamérica80', *Journal of Design History* 32, no. 2 (2019): 188–206.

[11] Dipesh Chakrabarty, *Provincializing Europe: Postcolonial Thought and Historical Difference* (Princeton: Princeton University Press, 2000), 4.

[12] Ibid., 6.

design, by structuring local practice and organizing professionals in similar ways to those seen in Europe. This process gave rise to the flawed idea that all design practice – only considered as valid in its modern form – was born in and exported by Europe to the rest of the world.

Even though design can be considered 'a fundamental human activity'[13] that takes place regardless of institutions and forms of controls, the way in which design was shaped into a profession delimited its access and its definitions.[14] Understanding the formation of professional design organizations offers an opportunity to locate the symbolic systems and conventions established by them. It also allows for a critique of the ways in which particular perspectives of design became perceived to be of universal significance and value, ideas that became particularly relevant in the formation of international non-governmental design organizations after the end of the Second World War. Looking at distinct design organizations operating in the post-war period, this chapter focuses more intently on those associations dedicated to graphic design practice and on the formation of international non-governmental design organizations whose establishment was based on the belief of the universalism of Western design values.

From promotional to professional organizations

One of the earliest design organizations on record is the Swedish *Svenska Slöjdföreningen* that was established in 1845 to safeguard the quality of Swedish craft.[15] This organization was responsible for one of the first design periodicals, launched in 1904 as *Svenska Slöjdföreningen Tidskift* and renamed in 1932 as *Form*.[16] In the early twentieth century, other organizations and groups concerned with the quality of industrial production were slowly established in other European countries. In 1907, the *Deutscher Werkbund* was established in Germany, bringing industrial workers, craftsmen and artists together with the aim of refining industrialized production and improving the quality of the products available nationally. The organization of exhibitions by the *Deutscher Werkbund* became the main means of promotion of its achievements and relevance, serving as stimuli for the foundation of other nations to establish organizations dedicated

---

[13] Christine M. E. Guth, 'Design Before Design in Japan', in *The Routledge Companion to Design Studies*, ed. Penny Sparke and Fiona Fisher (London: Routledge, 2016), 508–17.
[14] For an interesting paper on debates about graphic design regulation in the 1990s, see Jacques Lange, 'Tested and Detested Designers: Conflicting opinions on title protection and industry regulation', in *Image & Text: Journal for Design* no. 8 (1998).
[15] Katarina Öhlin, 'Svenska Slöjdföreningen (1845–1976)', *Riksarkivet* (22 March 2010). https://sok.riksarkivet.se/ [accessed 23 December 2019].
[16] Jonathan M. Woodham, 'Form', in *A Dictionary of Modern Design*, ed. Jonathan M. Woodham (Oxford: Oxford University Press, 2004), 152.

to similar goals in the 1910s.¹⁷ In 1912, the Austrian *Österreichischer Werkbund* and US American *National Alliance of Art and Industry* were founded, while the Swiss, Czech and Hungarian Werkbunds were created in 1913 and the *Design and Industries Association* was established in Britain, in 1915.¹⁸

These early promotional organizations, however, usually included both industrialists and practitioners, while also not distinguishing between specializations within the realm of design practice. Organizations entirely dedicated to exclusively gathering professional practitioners – which defined the symbolic systems and regulations for design practice and professional designers – were established later, entangling the history of design as a professional practice with the history of European design. In the world of European design, the creation of professional organizations was not only a way to set standards and internal codes, it also 'became a means of creating business networks and social arenas'.¹⁹

Graphic design organizations

It was between 1900s and 1930s that organizations dedicated to graphic arts and design started taking shape: the *American Institute of Graphic Arts* was established in the United States in 1914, the German *Bund Deutscher Gebrauchsgraphiker* was created in 1919, the Austrian *Bund Österreichischer Gebrauchsgraphiker* and the US American *Society of Typographic Arts* were both created in 1927.²⁰ The number of associations for practitioners of graphic arts increased with the establishment of a number of other associations in the 1930s such as the French *Syndicat National des Graphistes Publicitaires*, the Finnish *Taidepiirtäjäin Liitto GRAFIA Tecknarförbund*, the *Association of Commercial Artists* in Israel and the Swedish *Svenska Affischtecknare*.²¹

The increasing interest in graphic arts and advertising in the early twentieth century also created an opportunity for the development of specialized periodicals. In the United States, the emphasis on advertisements led to the creation of the *Art Directors Club* and the development of a dedicated publication – the *Advertising*

---

[17] Winfried Nerdinger, ed., *Deutscher Werkbund: 100 Anos de Arquitetura e Design na Alemanha*, trans. Virginia Blanc de Sousa (São Paulo: CCSP and VG Bild-Kunst, Boon, 2007).
[18] Jonathan M. Woodham, 'Timelines', in *A Dictionary of Modern Design*, ed. Jonathan M. Woodham (Oxford: Oxford University Press, 2004), 490–506.
[19] Gerry Beegan and Paul Atkinson, 'Professionalism, Amateurism and the Boundaries of Design', *Journal of Design History* 21, no. 4 (2008): 305–13.
[20] AIGA, 'How AIGA Is Organized', *AIGA* (n.d.). http://www.aiga.org/ [accessed 23 August 2017].
E. Hölscher, 'Germany', in *Who's Who in Graphic Art: An Illustrated Book of References to the World's Leading Graphic Designers, Illustrators, Typographers and Cartoonists* (Zürich: Amstutz & Herdeg Graphis Press, 1962), 180.
[21] Icograda, *Societies Participating at the I Icograda General Assembly* (1964). University of Brighton Design Archives, Icograda Archive, ICO/6/1/4; Grafia, 'About Grafia', *Grafia* (n.d.). www.grafia.fi/in-english/about-grafia/ [accessed 11 April 2017]; H. E. Kjellberg, ed., *Svenska Dagbladets Årsbok* (Stockholm: Åhlén & Holms Boktryckeri, 1937).

Arts – first published in 1921. In Britain, the magazine *Commercial Art* 'devoted to all aspects of graphic design and display was launched at a time when "commercial artists" were striving hard to be recognized as design professionals'.[22] In 1924, the German association *Bund Deutscher Gebrauchsgraphiker* published the first issues of its magazine known as *Gebrauchsgraphik* or *International Advertising Art*. These were soon followed by other publications, such as the Swiss *Typographische Monatsblätter* (1932–), the Italian magazine *Campo Grafico* (1933–1939) and the US American *Print* (1940–).[23]

Yet, before graphic design was widely recognized as a professional practice in its own right, a number of other professionals undertook the task of designing graphic solutions to resolve communicational needs. Between 1920s and 1960s, the vocabulary and symbolic systems of the graphic design profession were being developed and defined, which meant that throughout this time there was no specific term used to indicate the professional who later became widely known as the 'graphic designer'. The term 'graphic designer' dates back to the early 1920s when coined by William Addison Dwiggins to define his own professional practice.[24] During the first half of the twentieth century, terms such as 'graphic artist', 'graphic designer', 'commercial artist' and 'advertising artist' transitioned between numerous languages, and their meanings usually varied depending on which country one was in. In Europe, commercial artists were known to employ their talents to fulfil commercial needs, while in the United States, art directors led the way towards recognition.[25] In many Latin American countries, graphic artists worked on advertisements and packaging while architects became known for their involvement in the design of corporate identity and information systems.[26]

Before the Second World War there was already a sense of recognition, but it was after its end that the numbers of professional graphic design associations had the

---

[22] Jonathan M. Woodham, 'Commercial Art', in *A Dictionary of Modern Design*, ed. Jonathan M. Woodham (Oxford: Oxford University Press, 2004), 90.

[23] Jeremy Aynsley, 'The Cultural Representation of Graphic Design in East and West Germany, 1949 to 1970', in *The Routledge Companion to Design Studies*, ed. Penny Sparke and Fiona Fisher (London: Routledge, 2016), 242–65; Campo Grafico, 'Welcome', *Campo Grafico* (n.d.). www.campografico.org/ [accessed 11 July 2019]; PRINT, 'About Us', *PRINT* (n.d.). www.printmag.com/about-us/ [accessed 11 July 2019].

[24] Philip B. Meggs, *A History of Graphic Design*, 3rd ed. (New York: John Wiley & Sons, [1983] 1998); Paul Shaw, 'Tradition and Innovation: The Design Work of William Addison Dwiggins', *Design Issues* 1, no. 2 (1984): 26.

[25] Ellen Lupton and J. Abbott Miller, *Design Writing Research: Writing on Graphic Design*, 2nd ed. (London: Phaidon, [1996] 1999).

[26] Chico Homem de Melo and Elaine Ramos, eds., *Linha do Tempo do Design Gráfico* (São Paulo: Cosac & Naify, 2011); Pedro Álvarez Caselli, *História del Diseño Gráfico en Chile* (Santiago: Pontificia Universidad Católica de Chile, Escuela de Diseño, 2004); Luz del Carmen A Vilchis Esquivel, *História del Diseño Gráfico en México, 1910–2010* (México, DF: INBA-Conacultura, 2010); Giovani Tronconi, ed., *Diseño Gráfico en Mexico: 100 años, 1900–2000* (México, DF: Artes de México, 2010); Rafael Cardoso, *O Design Brasileiro antes do Design: aspectos da história gráfica, 1870–1960* (São Paulo: Cosac & Naify, 2015); Silvia Fernández and Gui Bonsiepe, eds., *Historia del diseño en América Latina y Caribe: Industrialización y Comunicación Visual para la Autonomía* (São Paulo: Blücher, 2008).

most significant increase. In many countries, design became part of governmental strategies for modernization and development, not only in the democratic but also in the socialist world.

Design associations in the Cold War period

After the end of the Second World War, an undeclared state of war between the Soviet Union and the United States dominated the global scene. At the core of the conflict known as the 'Cold War' was a competition between these 'superpowers' for allies who would embrace either of their opposing ideologies, dividing the world between socialist nations, democratic nations and those that refused to embrace either.[27]

These underlying ideologies defined the ways in which social and cultural life was organized on each side, being a 'clash of ideas and cultures as much as a military and strategic conflict'.[28] Inevitably, designers, as other professionals, had to adapt to the political frameworks within their contexts, be it Western and capitalist ideals based on individual liberty, liberalism and market values; or socialist or communist values of collectivism and state planning or any other forms of national or federal government. Yet, differently from other professionals, designers needed to be aware of the aesthetics and values associated with the ideologies promoted by their governments.

Between 1945 and the early 1960s, even though professional associations and unions were still more significantly concentrated in Western Europe and the United States, design organizations appeared around the globe, following the overall trends of the Cold War. On the side of the US allies, these organizations appeared in the shape of professional associations and design councils, whilst in socialist and communist states the professional practice of design mostly occurred within governmental structures, within governmental divisions, cultural institutions or research centres, while unions seem to be the only form of design organization to appear in both.

The political polarization created challenges for the exchange of knowledge between designers and associations based in countries of opposing perspectives, as technological development was a central part of the dispute. Yet there were also efforts to foster transnational connections with the intention to overcome

---

[27] Odd Arne Westad, *The Global War: Third World Interventions and the Making of Our Times* (New York: Cambridge University Press, 2005); Shu Guang Zhang, 'The Sino-Soviet Alliance and the Cold War in Asia', in *The Cambridge History of the Cold War, Volume I: Origins*, ed. Melvyn P. Leffler and Odd Arne Westad (Cambridge: Cambridge University Press, 2010), 353–75.

[28] Odd Arne Westad, 'The Cold War and the International History of the Twentieth Century', in *The Cambridge History of the Cold War, Volume I: Origins*, ed. Melvyn P. Leffler and Odd Arne Westad (Cambridge: Cambridge University Press, 2010), 1–19.

the restrictions created by national governments and promote cosmopolitan ideals of international understanding, further motivated by the foundation of the United Nations. As is going to be seen later in this chapter, international design organizations founded in the post-war period attempted to create a forum for exchange across political division, with the aim to allow for the encounter between designers and representatives of design associations of different ideologies. But before looking into the formation of international organizations dedicated to graphic design, it is important to briefly understand the distinctions between the national design organizations being established in the post-war period.

In China, the birth of the People's Republic of China in 1949 and its alliance with the Soviet Union in 1950 defined the practice of graphic arts under tight state control. Before 1949, a number of civil associations existed within Chinese society, but the new government reorganized existing associations and established new ones, such as the *China Federation of Literacy and Art Circles*.[29] Propaganda policies were defined by the Chinese Communist Party and implemented through hierarchical networks and mass union organizations. Posters took central stage as the main means to promote the governmental ideologies given the high illiteracy rate of the population, being produced by either governmental propaganda units or independent groups allied with the government. The production of posters by peasants and workers with no professional training was encouraged, yet being usually aided by trained experts who were not given due credit.[30]

In Cuba, the domestic frameworks within which social, political and cultural changes took place were shaped – to a very large extent – by Soviet Union's interventionist strategies. In the 1950s, graphic design in Cuba was dominated by advertising agencies, magazines following US and European styles and Cuban brands for export products such as cigars, sugar and rum. However, after the Cuban revolution in 1959, the government suppressed advertising spaces on radio and television and in the press, creating a number of cultural institutions owned by the state, such as the *Instituto Cubano del Arte y la Industria Cinematográfica*, known as ICAIC for short.[31] The nationalization of the cinema circuits in 1961 made the ICAIC the only institution in Cuba allowed to produce national films and to import foreign ones; while also being responsible for the production of film posters having an in-house graphic design team.[32] In 1961, a union was established – the

---

[29] Chen Guangjin, 'Organizational Structure', in *Social Structure of Contemporary China*, ed. Xueyi Lu (Singapore: World Scientific Publishing, [2011] 2012), 337–96.
[30] Lincoln Cushing, 'Revolutionary Chinese Posters and Their Impact Abroad', in *Chinese Posters: Art from the Great Proletarian Cultural Revolution*, ed. Lincoln Cushing and Ann Tompkins (San Francisco: Chronicle Books, 2007), 7–23.
[31] Jorge Bermúdez, 'Eduardo Muñoz Bachs: una sonrisa en la pared', *La Jiribilla: Revista de Cultura Cubana* 6, no. 338 (2007). www.lajiribilla.co.cu/ [accessed 16 May 2018].
[32] Bermúdez, 'Eduardo Muñoz Bachs'.

Unión de Escritores y Artistas de Cuba – including writers, artists and also graphic designers that became renowned for their posters.[33]

In the USSR, as put by writer and critic Igor Lvov in the early 1960s, 'graphic design in the Western sense has made comparatively little headway in the USSR'. It was only in 1962 that an organization dedicated to design matters was established within the Soviet Union.[34] As other organizations in Western Europe and the United States, the *Vserossiyskiy Nauchno-Issledovatel'skiy Institut Tekhnicheskoy Estetiki* (VNIITE – All-Union Scientific Research Institute for Technical Aesthetic) was created for the improvement of the quality of industrial production and some consumer goods through research and development of design practice and theory. The name of the organization reflected the avoidance of words associated with the 'West' such as design, where 'industrial design' became known as 'artistic engineering' and industrial design theory as 'technological aesthetics'. Despite attempts of the Soviet government to prevent transnational contact, VNIITE was unusually open to international connections and exchange of knowledge.[35]

In Czechoslovakia, after the political coup in 1948, significant interventions began to occur adapting current social structures and organizations to the Soviet model. This included the introduction of a system to supervise and control artists, grouping them according to their disciplines and the liquidation of existing associations. All remaining associations became part of a federal union, the *Svaz Ceskoslovenskych Vytvarnych Umelcu*, which dictated the rules of operation within each association and united members on a federal level. In the early 1950s, the existing associations went through a process of 'cleansing' that decreased significantly the number of its members, who were selected accordingly to their position within the socialist establishment.[36] All changes were subject to revision by the government and to political requirements.[37] In countries aligned with the rules of the Soviet State, any practice related to cultural expression was followed by close governmental watch and regulated in a way that those professionals endorsed as members of unions and associations were aligned with the federal policies.

However, in socialist but non-aligned countries, the situation was significantly different. In Yugoslavia, the *Savez Likovnih Umjetnika Primenjenih Umetnosti*

---

[33] Héctor Villaverde, *Testimonios del Diseño Gráfico Cubano: 1959–1974* (La Habana, Cuba: Ediciones La Memoria, Centro Cultural Pablo de la Torriente Brau, 2009).

[34] Triin Jerlei, Industrial Designers within the Soviet Estonian Design Ideology of the Late Socialist Period, 1965–1988, Doctoral Thesis, Brighton: University of Brighton, 2005.

[35] Dmity Azrikan, 'VNIITE, Dinosaur of Totalitarianism or Plato's Academy of Design?' *Design Issues* 15, no. 3 (1999): 45–77.

[36] For more on Czech graphic artists, see the section on Czechoslovakia on *Who's Who in Graphic Art: An Illustrated Book of References to the World's Leading Graphic Designers, Illustrators, typographers and cartoonists* (Zürich: Amstutz & Herdeg Graphis Press, 1962), 98–118.

[37] Alena Binarová, *Svaz Výtvarných Umělců v Českých Zemích V Letech 1956–1972: Oficiální Výtvarná Tvorba v Proměnách Komunistického Režimu*, Doctoral Thesis, Olomouc: Univerzita Palackého v Olomouci, 2016; Oskar Brůža, 'Poúnorové a Normalizační Svazy', *UVUCR* (2010). http://www.uvucr.cz/archiv/ [accessed 12 July 2019].

Jugoslavije was the federal union in operation in the early 1960s, while there were also associations operating within the constituent republics, such as the Slovenian *Drustvo Likovnih Umetnikov Uporabne Umetnosti Slovenije*, the *Udruženje Likovnih Umjetnika Primijenjene Umjetnosti Hrvatske* established in Croatia in 1950,[38] and the Serbian *Udruzenje Likovnih Umetnika Primenjenih Umetnosti i Dizajnera Srbije* founded in 1953.[39] As part of the non-aligned movement, Yugoslavia was home for a number of events during the Cold War period that allowed designers from every side of the war to meet.[40] As in many other non-aligned countries, Yugoslav graphic design threaded the tensions between traditional and modern approaches where the 'strict separation and often mutual demeaning between applied arts and design unfortunately greatly reduced the possibilities of both areas'.[41]

At the same time, in Western Europe, the combination of capitalist crises and previous two world wars led to the collapse of European colonial empires and growing disbelief in totalitarianism. In many nations, design became part of the efforts of reconstructions and economic stability. An increasing number of associations appeared in the region, such as the *Associazione Italiana Artisti Pubblicitari*, created in Italy in 1954, and the *Agrupació de Directors d'Art, Dissenyadors Gràfics i Il·lustradors*, established in Barcelona, Spain, in 1961.[42] Publications specialized in design also increased, such as in the United States, *Design Quarterly* published for the first time in 1946[43] (–1996), the British *Design* in 1949 (–1999) and the German magazines *Ulm* in 1958 (–1967) and *Form* in 1957 (–present).

The number of publications dedicated to graphic arts and graphic design also grew considerably, and some publications – particularly from Western Europe and the United States – travelled internationally, such as the Swiss *Neue Graphik* or *New Graphic Design* (1958–1965), *Graphis* (1944–1964, 1966–present) and US American *Communication Arts* (1959–present). These titles became reference for designers world-wide and its issues were collected in many libraries of educational institutions dedicated to design, helping to build a connected transnational design scene that was not restrained by national borders or, even, political alliances.

---

[38] ULUPUH, 'O nama', *ULUPUH* (n.d.). http://www.ulupuh.hr/hr/onama.asp [accessed 12 July 2019].
[39] ULUPUDS, 'Istorijat', *ULUPUDS* (2010). http://www.ulupuds.org.rs/Istorijat.htm [accessed 12 July 2019].
[40] Cvetka Požar, 'Continuity and Change: The Biennial of (Industrial) Design over the First Twenty Years', *Journal of the Museum of Applied Art*, no. 11 (2015): 18–26. https://mpu.rs/zbornik/lat/svi_zbornici.php?zbornik=11 [accessed 8 September 2021].
[41] Dejan Kršić, 'Graphic Design and Visual Communications 1950–1975', in *Socialism and Modernity. Art, Culture, Politics 1950–1974*, ed. Ljiljana Kolešnik (Zagreb: Muzej Suvremene Umjetnosti, 2012), 211.
[42] Jonathan M. Woodham, 'Japan Advertising Artists Club', in *A Dictionary of Modern Design*, ed. J. M. Woodham (Oxford: Oxford University Press, 2004), 407–9; ADG F AD, 'About ADG-Fad', *ADG FAD* (n.d.). www.adg-fad.org/ca/about-adg-fad [accessed 12 July 2019].
[43] Between 1946 and 1953, the magazine was known as Everyday Art Quarterly having its name changed to Design Quarterly in 1954.

In countries that were under US American interventionism, conforming to the Western and capitalist rules was part of the game. In the second half of the twentieth century, modernization and development seemed to be the only option for 'Third World'[44] designers to escape the stigmas of 'underdevelopment', by modernizing themselves and incorporating the First World's structure for design practice and professional organizations. The so-called 'Third World' was seen as the collective of underdeveloped nations deemed to have non-existent or inferior technology and industry that did not fit into either the capitalist or the communist alliances. Yet it was no mere coincidence that the disputed 'Third World' was mainly composed of nations that had been colonies impoverished by colonialism.[45]

In Latin American countries, the injection of US capital in the post-war period spurred industrialization, but also suffocated these nations under the clauses of the financial agreements and dictatorial regimes. In Africa and the Caribbean, the disintegration of the imperial order allowed for newly decolonized nations to focus their efforts on reconstruction through the development of national governments as well as cultural and social life, nations disputed by the Cold War 'superpowers'. As in Japan, many governments framed 'their own political agendas in conscious response to the models of development presented by the two main contenders of the Cold War',[46] and local elites either kept connections with former colonies or established completely independent nations, depending on what served better their own ends.

The struggle for development, however, proved an uphill battle for many 'Third World' countries, primarily – it could be argued – because they were forced to compete within an international system that was geared towards the interests of their 'allies'. Across the 'Third World', in nations allied with the 'Western' ideals, many professional associations were founded, aiming at the organization and further development of the design profession within their nations. These professionals were frequently caught in debates about the development of a national design and the conflicts and contradictions on their engagements with design from the US and Western Europe. Most design associations established in these nations during this period were dedicated to the whole of design practice as, for example, the *Society of Industrial Artists and Designers of South Africa* created in 1953[47] and the Brazilian *Associação Brasileira de Desenho Industrial* founded in 1963.[48] In India, the magazine *Design* – very similar to the British *Design* – had its first number published in 1957, preceding the foundation of the Indian *National Institute of Industrial Design* set up in 1961. In Latin America, during the 1950s

---

[44] Even though the 'three worlds' theory is problematic, its concepts are used in this chapter to contextualize the way transnational power relations took place during the Cold War.
[45] Gearóid Ó Tuathail, 'Introduction: Thinking Critically About Geopolitics', in *The Geopolitics Reader*, ed. Gearóid Ó Tuathail, Simon Dalby and Paul Routledge (London: Routledge, 2003 [1998]), 6.
[46] Westad, *The Global War*.
[47] Lange, 'Tested and Detested Designers'.
[48] Marcos da Costa Braga, *ABDI e APDINS-RJ*, 2nd ed. (São Paulo: Blücher, [2011] 2016).

and 19560s, a number of higher education design courses appeared all over[49] as did the publications dedicated to design, such as the Argentinian *Nueva Visión* (1951–1957) and *Summa* (1963–1993), Mexican *Artes de México* (1953–), and Brazilian *Produto e Linguagem*.[50]

In Africa by the end of the Second World War, most territories were still colonies. Since early interactions, African indigenous art and design practices had been exoticized and debased by the European gaze. In the twentieth century, Western artists and intellectuals assumed African cultural production to be 'the antithesis of modernity' and a reflexive tool for the modern condition without ever considering their original use and meaning.[51] With the end of the Second World War, liberation movements sprung across the continent resulting in a significant change in the way local practices were seen. By the mid-1960s, most of the territories in the continent had become independent nations, yet the conflict between traditional, modern and vernacular African art and design persisted.[52] In the Nigerian and Kenyan postcolonial contexts, for example, modern design was approached carefully, mostly because it was seen as a foreign practice, distant from indigenous ones and, therefore, not seen with good eyes by the newly established nation-states.[53]

Yet higher education institutions that included design – as understood within the Western European and US American framework – in their curriculum slowly appeared all over the continent. For instance, in 1969, a Department of Industrial Design was established at the University of East Africa in Nairobi, Kenya,[54] while other active higher education courses in the early 1970s in Khartoum, Sudan, and in the 1980s in Port Harcourt, Nigeria.[55] Attempts to establish graphic design organizations which followed the European structure also took place, such as the *Society of Industrial Artists and Designers of South Africa* mentioned previously and the *Nigerian Association of Graphic Designers* that was active in the 1980s.

---

[49] Silvia Fernández, 'The Origins of Design Education in Latin America: From the HfG in Ulm to Globalization', *Design Issues* 22, no. 1 (2006): 3–19.

[50] Verônica Devalle, 'Hacia la síntesis de las artes. El proyecto cultural y artístico de la revista Nueva Visión', *Anclajes* 13, no. 13 (2009): 61–70; JSTOR, 'Artes de Mexico', in *JSTOR* (n.d.). www.jstor.org/journal/artesmexico [accessed 12 July 2019]; Dora Souza Dias and Marcos da Costa Braga, 'A revista Produto e Linguagem e a arte gráfica de Fernando Lemos', *Agitprop* 5, no. 52 (2013): n.p.

[51] Carole Sweeney, *From Fetish to Subject: Race, Modernism, and Primitivism: 1919–1935* (Westport: Praeger, 2004), 13.

[52] Prita Meier, 'Authenticity and Its Modernist Discontents: The Colonial Encounter and African and Middle Eastern Art History', *Arab Studies Journal* 18, no. 1 (2010): 12–45; Dipti Bhagat, 'Designs on/in Africa', in *Designing Worlds: National Design Histories in an Age of Globalization*, ed. Kjetil Fallan and Grace Lees-Maffei (New York: Berghahn Books, 2016), 23–41.

[53] Icograda and UNESCO, Regional Seminar: Design for Development, programme (1987). University of Brighton Design Archives, Icograda Archive, ICO/10/18/4; and Haig David-West, ed., 'Port Harcourt Protocol', Dialogue on Graphic Design Problems in Africa, ed. Haig David-West (Unknown: NAGD, 1983), 121. University of Brighton Design Archives, Icograda Archive, ICO/10/18/2.

[54] Walter Plata, 'Visual Communication in East Africa', *Icographic*, no. 4 (1972): 6–7.

[55] Icograda and UNESCO, *Regional Seminar*.

In Japan, the Americanization of popular culture that was intensified after the war and US American lifestyle became a fashionable symbol of 'modern life'.[56] Design associations emerged reflecting the same structures and terminology as those from the 'West'. According to specialist in Japanese design Christine Guth the 'ideology of rupture intended to promulgate an image of Japan as a country that had undergone a radical transformation'.[57] In the 1950s, the first association related to graphic design was founded – the *Japan Advertising Artists Club* – and two specialized magazines had their first numbers published: *Idea* or *International Advertising Art* (1953–) and the グラフィックデザイン or *Graphic Design* (1959–1986).[58]

International design organizations

Even though the end of the Second World War resulted in somewhat divided world, the establishment of transnational organizations changed the political landscape by facilitating transnational connections and exchanges. The foundation of the United Nations in 1945 prompted a global political turn that transformed the nature of the relationships between nation-states and peoples, in many ways surpassing the limitations imposed by national and federal governments. This new context favoured connections among actors across the globe with common problems and interests, stimulating the creation of a number of international non-governmental organizations.[59]

The first international organizations related to the design profession appeared in the early 1950s. The *Alliance Graphique Internationale* (AGI), for example, was formulated by five Western European graphic artists, who conceived the alliance as a way to formalize their friendships into an official professional network. The Alliance was established in 1952 and originally gathered 65 members from 10 countries with the aim to 'share common interests and friendships across national and cultural borders'.[60] In 1957, another international design organization was established, the *International Council of Societies of Industrial Design* (ICSID). Differently from the AGI, ICSID was a council dedicated to gathering Industrial

---

[56] Sayuri Guthrie-Shimizu, 'Japan, the United States, and the Cold War, 1945–1960', in *The Cambridge History of the Cold War, Volume I: Origins*, ed. Melvyn P. Leffler and Odd Arne Westad (Cambridge: Cambridge University Press, 2010), 248.
[57] Guth, 'Design Before Design in Japan', 509.
[58] Sarah Teasley, 'IDEA: International Graphic Arts, Japan (1953–)', in *The Bloomsbury Encyclopedia of Design, Volume 2*, ed. Clive Edwards (London: Bloomsbury Academic, 2016), 175–6; Tadasu Fujii (藤井 匡), '展覧会報告：勝見勝 桑澤洋子 佐藤忠良－東京造形大学 教育の源流 (Exhibition Report: Masaru Katzumie, Yōko Kuwazawa and Churyo Sato)', *Tokyo Zokei University Research Report* (東京造形大学研究報) no. 19 (2018): 100–18; Woodham, '*Japan Advertising Artists Club*', 407–9.
[59] John Boli and George M. Thomas, 'Introduction', in *Constructing World Culture: International Nongovernmental Organizations since 1875*, ed. John Boli and George M. Thomas (Stanford: Stanford University Press, 1999), 1–10.
[60] AGI, 'How It All Began', *AGI* (n.d.). preview.a-g-i.org/about/ [accessed 21 November 2016].

Design associations rather than a congregation of individual designers. ICSID was registered in France and its first meeting held in the headquarters of the British *Society of Industrial Artists* (SIA) in London, being attended by representatives and proxies from societies from Denmark, Italy, Norway, Sweden, the Netherlands, India, Japan and the United States.[61] ICSID was established with the aim to promote the interests of industrial designers and its success stimulated graphic designers within the SIA to push for the creation of a parallel body that, instead, would be dedicated to graphic design associations.[62]

The International Council of Graphic Design Associations, known as Icograda for short, was founded in 1963 during a meeting convened in London by the SIA and became an important network in the international scene of graphic design practice.

International Council of Graphic Design Associations

Icograda was established to be an international forum for national graphic design associations aiming to improve the standards of professional practice and the status of the graphic designer within their nations. The Council aimed to unify codes of conduct and professional practice internationally, exchange information on the training of graphic designers on an international level, organize international assemblies and congresses, distribute information about member societies and, 'to include […] organizations of graphic designers and supporting organizations in all countries of the world and thus contribute to *international understanding*' as well as 'to function as a *non-political* organisation'.[63] However, even though the Council was meant to be an international affair, Icograda was, initially, more regional than global.

From the 41 associations invited, only delegates and observers from 24 associations were able to attend the inaugural meeting (see Figure 1.1), amounting to a total of 17 countries represented from which only two were situated outside of Europe, namely the Australian Commercial and Industrial Artists Association and the Association of Commercial Artists in Israel. The majority of European representatives inevitably meant that the decisions regarding the Council's

---

[61] Tania Messell, Constructions a 'United Nations of Industrial Design': ICSID and the Professionalisation of Design on the World Stage, 1950–1980, Doctoral Thesis, Brighton: University of Brighton, 2018.

[62] F. H. K. Henrion, 'Speech', in Icograda, *Minutes Inaugural Meeting*, 1963. University of Brighton Design Archives, Icograda Archive, ICO/1/1/1.

[63] Icograda, *Icograda Constitution: As Agreed at the Inaugural Meeting Held in London from April 26th to April 28th 1963 and Amended by the Executive Board at a Meeting Held in Amsterdam on July 19th/20th 1963 and Stockholm on January 23rd 1964* (1964). University of Brighton Design Archives, Icograda Archive, ICO/1/2/1.

FIGURE 1.1 Map projection showing only the associations with representatives at the Icograda Inaugural Meeting. Map by the author

formation privileged a Western European perspective.[64] Associations in Socialist and Communist countries such as Czechoslovakia, East Germany and Yugoslavia were also invited, but were unable to send representatives.

In the first years, a number of documents were drafted in order to eliminate what was seen as wasteful duplication of effort by a number of associations and unify codes of practice. According to Icograda's First President Willy de Majo, it seemed incredible that a number of graphic design organizations in Europe were all engaged in drawing up similar documents, such as codes of practice and constitution.

This explains the focus of the Executive Board in preparing a number of model-documents in the interim between the inaugural meeting and the first General Assembly, namely *The International Code of Ethics and Conduct for Graphic Designers*, the *Conditions of Contract and Engagement for Graphic Designers*, and the *Regulations Governing Conduct of International Competitions*.[65]

Within Icograda, the fact that activities were restricted to a small area of the world was not perceived as an issue, at least until the Council was informed that UNESCO's only reason to withhold Icograda's recognition was its lack of geographical spread.[66]

However, there was a failure to understand within the Council that design practice was not necessarily shaped in the same way in different parts of the globe. The Council insisted on gathering associations that fulfilled a set of restrictions,

---

[64] Dora Souza Dias, *Icograda: The International Council of Graphic Design Associations, 1963–2013: Transnational Interactions and Professional Networks in Graphic Design*, Doctoral Thesis, Brighton: University of Brighton, 2019.

[65] Icograda, *Report on the 1st ICOGRADA General Assembly and International Congress* (1964). University of Brighton Design Archives, Icograda Archive, ICO/6/1/2.

[66] Knut Iran, Icograda President 1966–1968. Icograda, *Minutes III General Assembly* (1968), 9. University of Brighton Design Archives, Icograda Archive, ICO/6/3/7.

which proved impossible to satisfy. Icograda President Knut Iran affirmed that even though representatives from the Council had travelled throughout Asia, Africa and South America during the 1960s, 'it had unfortunately become apparent that in many countries, a designers' association which fulfilled the membership conditions of ICOGRADA did not exist'.[67]

As a way to circumvent what was seen as a setback, a new category of membership was created. The Corresponding Member was an individual appointed honorarily who would be responsible for acting as a liaison between Icograda and designers and design educators in their own countries, but who had no right to vote in the Council's matters.

There was no consideration whether Icograda's 'membership conditions', or even Icograda's attitude towards design practice in other continents might be the reason preventing the expansion of Icograda's reach. As an association of associations, the membership of Icograda was predicated on the existence of professional associations formed mainly by commercial artists and graphic designers, and based on the assumption that in countries where there was graphic design practice, practitioners would always be organized in associations similar to Western European ones.

However, the awareness created by UNESCO's repeated rejection directed the Council in a new direction, understanding that an international organization was not simply inter-nations, but had to be more globally representative. In the 1970s, the Council entered a new phase in which it became an organization not only interested in expanding its reach but actively working towards it. During the early 1970s, Icograda gathered members from all sides of the Cold War, including the Czech Svaz Ceskoslovenskych Vytvarnych Umelcu, Verband Bildender Kuenstler Deutschlands from East Germany, Savez Likovnih Umetnika Primenjenih Umetnosti from Yugoslav and three associations from the United States, namely the American Institute of Graphic Arts, the Society of Typographic Arts and the Art Directors Club.

In 1975, for the first time, an Icograda event was held outside of Europe.[68] The conference *Education for Graphic Design, Graphic Design for Education*, *Edugraphic* for short, was held in Edmonton, Canada, and became an important milestone in the Council's activities, opening Icograda to expand not only its geographical reach but also its knowledge about graphic design practice in other regions of the world. With the shift in the Council's approach to its geographical reach in the mid-1970s, Icograda's Membership grew considerably in numbers as well as in spread. For instance, between 1964 and 1977, the Council's membership grew from 23 members representing 17 countries to 27 member associations

---

[67] Knut Iran, Icograda President 1966–1968. Icograda, *Minutes III General Assembly* (1968), 9.
[68] Edugraphic, 'Edugraphic Conference', Press Release (1975). University of Brighton Design Archives, Icograda Archive, ICO/6/6/4.

representing 20 countries,[69] while between 1977 and 1983, the membership almost doubled. By 1983, the Council gathered 51 member associations representing 30 countries, with at least one association in every continent.[70]

One of the ways in which Icograda reached to designers outside of Europe was the organization of regional meetings. Icograda Regional Meetings were events sponsored by Icograda but financed and organized by its hosts. The regional meetings held in Latin America, Africa and Asia were organized by individuals connected to these regions, who had the opportunity to be also connected with Icograda. The organizers of the regional meetings, as members of the Council, believed in the value of design but also in the value of Icograda as a professional network.

From Icograda's point of view, the main intention of these meetings was to foster the creation of associations that could become Icograda members and a way to engage with graphic designers in other regions of the world. These meetings were not, however, considered as an opportunity for the exchange of knowledge about professional practice between Icograda and designers practising in these regions. The Council's main goals with such meetings was to 'spread over the globe as widely as possible'.[71] Yet, inevitably, this resulted in the Council's awareness that there was design practice outside of Europe and Anglo America, and that it should be acknowledged. As a result of the regional meetings, throughout the 1980s the policies, governance schemes and, more importantly, the Council's discourse were quickly adapted to this newly found perspective of the state of design practice in other areas of the globe.

However, even though there was a shift in the discourse, professional associations were still expected to be aligned with the Council's parameters, even if the professional practice was not originally understood or organized by them in the same way. This meant that they had, at times, to adapt to meet Icograda's parameters. For example, in Nigeria, the structure of the Nigerian Association of Communication Designers was reassessed in the early 1980s 'to delimit its scope to address itself to the specificity of graphic design' and further align its programmes and definitions with those of Icograda, being renamed as the Nigerian Association of Graphic Designers.[72] In Latin America, new associations dedicated exclusively

---

[69] Icograda, *Minutes VII General Assembly* (1977). University of Brighton Design Archives, Icograda Archive, ICO/6/7/3.

[70] Icograda, *Minutes X General Assembly* (1983). University of Brighton Design Archives, Icograda Archive, ICO/6/11/3.

[71] Icograda Executive Board (1977–1979), *Minutes of Board Meeting Number 6* (1979), 5. University of Brighton Design Archives, Icograda Archive, ICO/2/2/7. Two years after the event, in 1982, a similar event occurred in Nigeria, with the aim of promoting a dialogue about the situation of graphic design in Africa. However, these were Regional events. It wasn't until the late 1980s that the International Congresses started taking place in countries that were not part of Europe or North America.

[72] NAGD, NAGD University of Brighton Design Archives, Icograda Archive, ICO/10/18/2.

to gathering graphic design practitioners were founded after the 1980s, allowing for the possibility to become members of the Council.

By the late 1980s, Icograda counted 54 member associations between professional and promotional memberships. In a book prepared to celebrate its 25th Anniversary, the diversity of accounts shows how in the late 1980s the Council had embraced the diversity of graphic design practice, including accounts from graphic designers from India, China, Argentina, Mexico, the Soviet Union, the Middle East, the United States and so on. Beyond the geographical spread, the diversity in participation resulted in a shift in the Council's discourse, in terms of how to address practice in different areas of the world. The book prepared to celebrate Icograda's 25th Anniversary *Graphic Design, World Views* evidenced such shift. As stated by then former President of Icograda Jorge Frascara, the book created 'space for a wide range of voices' facing 'the complexity of graphic design head-on, without attempting to present a simple picture'.[73] Frascara's statement about the book was an echo of Icograda's newly espoused disposition.

During the 1980s, the Council embraced in its move towards diversity with the organization of regional meetings in areas of the world not previously approached by the Council and election of increasingly diverse Executive Boards. From 1980 – when the first regional meeting was held – to the end of the decade, the events that drove the growth in the remit of Icograda also altered the Council's perception of itself, its discourse and the practice of graphic design. There was a significant change in the Council's approach to the practice of graphic design in different regions of the world, as well as an abandonment of absolute values and standards of graphic design practice.

Beyond the Cold War

The increased opportunities for travel and communications combined with the end of conflicts of the Cold War period in the early 1990s allowed the Council to enter a new phase of more ambitious goals in terms of its global remit. The ease of global communications and the transnational movements gave people unprecedented opportunities to connect with others 'wherever on earth they might be'.[74] However, the intensification of processes of globalization also led to global anxieties about the uncertainty of the future. On the one hand, these changes enabled the development of the belief in worldwide cooperation, while on the other, they stimulated a fear that globalization could mean the end of diversity through global cultural homogenization.

---

[73] Jorge Frascara, 'Preface: A Celebration of Graphic Design', in *Graphic Design, World Views: A Celebration of Icograda's 25th Anniversary*, ed. Jorge Frascara (Tokyo: Kodansha, 1990), 92.
[74] Jan Aart Scholte, *Globalization: A Critical Introduction*, 2nd ed. (Hampshire/New York: Palgrave Macmillan, [2000] 2005), 241.

From the mid-1990s onwards, the fear of 'globalization' was replaced within Icograda by an effort towards change. The terms 'globe', 'global' and 'world' became frequent, as members of the Executive Board and representatives of member associations constantly referred to the 'global situation' and 'world changes'. From the early concerns with the inevitability of globalization, the Executive Board members went on to treat the world as a globalized entity and, rather than speculating over what a globalized world would look like, or what the role of the profession was, focused on defining 'the future of Icograda'.

For Icograda, embracing globalization meant becoming 'a global community',[75] benefiting from the opportunities of globalization and allegedly addressing its potential issues. Within Icograda, there was a growing sense of duty towards collective solidarity that surpassed regional, national or local identities. For instance, Icograda President Guy A. Schockaert advocated that Icograda members needed 'to learn to say "us" instead of "them"' and 'to communicate and work together, far beyond all divisions'.[76] His statement evidences a self-conscious awareness of postcolonial debates, and an attempt to erase social difference within the Council by eliminating otherness, through the symbolic suggestion of eliminating the use of the pronoun 'them' in favour of the pronoun 'us'.

Conclusion: The limitations of professionalism

This chapter has shown that professionalism in design practice has acted as a restricting and Eurocentric framework within which transnational design connections were being established during the Cold War. The limitations imposed were even more relevant in the context of international design organizations such as Icograda, where the delimitations of professional practice and its definitions deterred the Council from an earlier more comprehensive networks with professionals in diverse regions of the world. The broadening of Icograda's scope resulted in a shift of discourse towards diversity and inclusion and an expansion of its remit and influence farther than ever before. Within graphic design, professionalism does not necessarily act as a restriction to practice given that it can be understood to embrace practice by non-professional designers, but so is the nature of professions as professional associations certainly exclude all but those designers officially recognized as professionals. As such, Icograda and its regulations reflect the normalization of graphic design practice within the realm of Western European practice, perpetuating models and standards which were, to some extent, extended as a transnational normalization of the profession during the Cold War period by the Council.

---

[75] Icograda, *A Global Community*, folder (April 2001). Personal Archive of Ruth Klotzel.
[76] Guy-A. Schockaert, 'The Winds of Change: Guidelines for a Presidency', XVII Icograda General Assembly (1997), item 7.1. University of Brighton Design Archives, Icograda Archive, ICO/6/18/7.

2 ONE STEP BEFORE ORGANIZATIONS: NETWORKS, ACTORS AND TRAJECTORIES IN ARGENTINE DESIGN (1938–1962)

Verónica Devalle

Introduction

In Argentina, like other countries in Latin America, the professionalization and institutionalization of design, regardless of area, was an outgrowth of its prior constitution as an artistic-cultural practice. In other words, in Latin America, unlike in much of Europe,[1] design was not initially the product of a process of industrial transformation. Nor was it conditioned by the production of a new material culture in nascent mass societies.[2] On the contrary, design was one of the many consequences of the processes of cultural modernization for which the Latin American avant-gardes – including avant-garde architecture – were so fruitful.[3]

This tight bond between the avant-garde and design proved short-lived, however. During the post-war period, Argentina developed an industrialization policy based on import substitution and the domestic market – an economic framework in effect from the mid-1950s until the mid-1970s – the period during which design began to be envisioned as a component of production. This was when the organizations and institutions that gathered the players in the realm of design were formed, in particular the *Centro de Investigación en Diseño Industrial* [Industrial Design Research Center] (CIDI) (1962–1988) and the *Asociación de Diseñadores Industriales* [Association of Industrial Designers] (ADIA) (1962–1975). Be that as it may, those organizations and institutions were conceptually tied to that earlier moment and, hence, informed by the language of the region's

---

[1] Ana Calvera, 'Cuestiones de fondo: la hipótesis de los tres orígenes del diseño', in *Diseño e historia. Tiempo, lugar y discurso*, ed. Campi Isabel (México: Designio, 2010).
[2] Victor Margolin, *The Politics of the Artificial: Essays on Design and Design Studies* (Chicago: Chicago University Press, 2002).
[3] Carlos Méndez Mosquera, 'Retrospectiva del diseño gráfico', *Contextos*, no. 1 (1997): 46–51.

abstract-constructive avant-gardes and, in architecture, by the international style.[4] This chapter focuses on the 20 years prior to the creation, in 1958, of the first university design programme, housed at the Design and Decoration Department of the Universidad Nacional de Cuyo's School of Visual Arts (Mendoza province) and, in 1962, of the CIDI, the first and most important entity insofar as a public design organization with ties to universities and companies.[5]

This period sheds light on how a group of actors, with their specific trajectories and the networks and exchanges they formed, produced an initial design identity. I do not, here, venture an explanation that focuses on the actors' individual intentions as agents of change, that is, as individuals outside their inter-social ties. Nor do I rest my analysis of the shape that design – and the organizations and institutions that legitimized and consolidated it – assumed on structural considerations (whether economic, political or social in nature). I believe that an inter-social analysis shows how initiatives worked together as an international network to usher in a set of social developments. Before embarking on a discussion of specific events, I will describe the context.

The context

The Southern Cone of Latin America was, in the early twentieth century, home to truly remarkable modern art and cultural movements. The 1920s, 1930s, and 1940s witnessed the emergence of Creationism, an avant-garde literary movement, in Chile and of Pau Brasil and Verde Amarelo, avant-garde art movements, in Brazil, in addition to the *Antropofagia* journal and the group around it. Meanwhile, in Argentina the Boedo and Florida groups were laying the basis for what would prove an enduring literary tradition; in Uruguay, the *Asociación Arte Constructivo* [Constructive Art Association] brought to the south the robust body of work the artist Joaquín Torres García had produced while in Europe.[6, 7] Modern literary movements influenced by Surrealism were the first to develop in the region; they were soon followed by music and the visual arts, where emerging movements updated and questioned the European tradition, attempting to reformulate it for the local scene without diminishing its staunch modern and avant-garde bent.[8]

The Latin American avant-garde cannot then be read linearly as a blunt rendering of European influences. Latin American creators looked at the European tradition from a critical distance; many of them played an active role

---

[4] María Amalia García, *El arte abstracto. Intercambios culturales entre Argentina y Brasil* (Buenos Aires: Siglo XXI, 2011).
[5] Ricardo Blanco, *Crónicas del diseño industrial en Argentina* (Buenos Aires: Ediciones FADU, 2005).
[6] García, *El arte abstracto*.
[7] Nelly Perazzo, *El arte concreto en la Argentina* (Buenos Aires: Ediciones Gaglianone, 1983).
[8] Alejandro Crispiani, *Objetos para transformar el mundo. Trayectorias del arte concreto-invención, Argentina-Chile, 1940–1970* (Buenos Aires: Editorial Prometeo, 2011).

in the European scene in the 1910s and 1920s. For this reason, the relationship between the European and the Latin American avant-gardes must be envisioned as an *exchange*, as a series of networks sustained by trips, friendships, patronages, prolonged visits and periods of exile, as well as shared projects. If, until the mid-1930s, Europe's influence on the region was largely exercised through local creators travelling there, with the outbreak of the Second World War an already abundant flow of European immigrants to the region grew; a great deal of the continent's cultural life migrated to the United States and Latin America.

Ships carrying emigrants and exiles from the First World War, the Russian Revolution and the Spanish Civil War headed to Rio de Janeiro, Montevideo, Buenos Aires and Santiago.[9] The passengers on these transatlantic voyages included intellectuals, journalists, visual artists, musicians, writers, architects, engineers and poets who then joined the local avant-garde movements.[10] They had little trouble fitting in. After all, there was a solid groundwork of existing friendships and comradery. Chilean poet Vicente Huidobro was friends with Juan Gris, Pablo Picasso and Jean Cocteau. Uruguayan painter Torres Garcia had worked with Theo van Doesburg, Piet Mondrian, Hans Arp and Sophie Taeuber Arp. Tarsila do Amaral had close ties to Cubism thanks to a prolonged stay in Europe during which she held frequent gatherings in her Paris *atelier*. Swiss poet Blaise Cendrars, fascinated with Brazil pursuant to a visit there in 1924, became an advocate of Brazilian culture in Europe (indeed, it is likely that Le Corbusier first came into contact with the Brazilian group of artists and poets in Paris through him).[11] Argentine writer Victoria Ocampo visited Ortega y Gasset, Tagore, Albert Camus, Virginia Woolf, Paul Valéry and others, on a regular basis.

The Austral network

But what was the relationship between the Austral network and the design organizations in Argentina like? In particular, how did that network relate to the CIDI – the first of those organizations – and to the ADIA, also created in 1962? In the 1960s, design was institutionalized through organizations that bolstered its practice and communicated the concepts and procedures crucial to the profession in the country. The practitioners behind those new organizations had either participated personally in the Austral network or been trained in its principles through work on publications like *Tecné* (1942–1944) and *Ciclo* magazines (1948–1949) or, later, *nueva visión* magazine (1951–1957). Those magazines played a central role in the circulation of a modern framework of ideas and of design

---

[9] Gino Germani, *Estructura social de la Argentina* (Buenos Aires: Raigal, 1955).
[10] Beatriz Sarlo, *Una modernidad periférica. Buenos Aires 1920–1930* (Buenos Aires: Nueva Visión, 1988).
[11] Jorge Francisco Liernur and Pablo Pschepiurca, *La red Austral: obras y proyectos de Le Corbusier y sus discípulos en la Argentina, 1924–1965* (Buenos Aires: Universidad Nacional de Quilmes, 2008).

understood as a new practice to make the human environment. The extension of the network is evident in the trajectories of its members, who in their studios and university classes in disciplines like architecture and art would train the generation that founded the first university design programme in the country.[12] Architect Amancio Williams and Le Corbusier were regular correspondents from the time they met in 1946. Williams's students included architect and designer César Jannello. Indeed, early Argentine industrial designers considered Williams a point of reference thanks to his way of understanding interior residential space.[13] It was in this context that, in 1929, Le Corbusier arrived in Buenos Aires. He not only became fast friends with art patron and cultural advocate Ocampo, but also gave a series of lectures where he presented the preliminary ideas of a Master Plan for the city.[14]

As historian Federico Deambrosis points out:

> The relative stagnation of much of Europe in the second half of the 1930s may well be why Le Corbusier saw in Argentina an opportunity to express himself professionally. He developed a plan for Buenos Aires on his own, that is, without having been commissioned to do so by the local authorities. Though Le Corbusier was determined to materialize his ideas for a city in any way possible, he did seek to win the commission for his project.[15]

That did not come to pass, though. All that is left of that frustrated plan is an assortment of letters to and from the Swiss master and his disciples in Argentina who, meanwhile, began making use of modern architecture typologies.

Young architects around Argentina began designing modern projects for cities like Mendoza, La Plata, Tucumán and Rosario. While most were never constructed, they were envisaged according to the precepts of the *Congrès internationaux d'architecture moderne* [International Congresses of Modern Architecture] (CIAM).[16] The first avant-garde architecture group Austral was founded in 1938 by Jorge Ferrari Hardoy and Juan Kurchan. They had recently returned from Europe,

---

[12] Initially, only in industrial design.
[13] Blanco, *Crónicas del diseño industrial;* Luis Müller, 'Amancio Williams. La invención como proyecto' (Ph.D. dissertation, Facultad de Arquitectura, Planeamiento y Diseño, Universidad Nacional de Rosario. Rosario, 2019).
[14] Buenos Aires, Rio de Janeiro and Bogotá were the three Latin American cities where Le Corbusier drew up a Master Plan.
[15] Federico Deambrosis, *Nuevas visiones* (Buenos Aires: Ediciones Infinito, 2011), 45.
[16] *Congrès internationaux d'architecture moderne* (CIAM) are considered the main laboratory of the ideas at play in the International Style. They were essential to the development of functionalism as a core architecture ideology. With the expansion of major metropolises at the dawn of the twentieth century, urbanism and city planning emerged as disciplines to tackle new and urgent problems. Functionalism attempted to organize the urban space on the basis of the principal human activities, that is, work, leisure, housing and transportation. Those ideas were endorsed, but also debated, at the different meetings of CIAM held from 1928 to 1959. Le Corbusier was a cornerstone of the CIAM's vision.

FIGURE 2.1 Grupo Austral. Silla BKF prototipo, c. 1937. Courtesy of Fundación IDA, Investigación en Diseño Argentino Fondo Bonet Antonio

where they worked at Le Corbusier's *atelier* and met Catalan architect Antoni Bonet. The group was short-lived (in 1941 it was disbanded), and its members scattered; most of its initiatives never made it beyond the preliminary phase. Notwithstanding, Austral did produce a number of acclaimed works, among them the BKF (Bonet, Kurchan, Ferrari Hardoy) chair (see Figure 2.1).[17, 18]

Like all avant-garde groups, Austral issued a manifesto in June 1939. In it, it called for the re-foundation of modern architecture in Argentina which, the group believed, had lost sight of its founders' spirit and become an empty reflection of what was known as the 'international style'.[19, 20]

Later, between 1942 and 1944, the architects and artists close to Austral published three issues of *Tecné* journal, a publication that tied the most forward-looking architecture projects in Argentina to the international networks that sustained them. Victor Bourgeois, Edgard Kaufmann, Alfred Roth, Richard Neutra and Le Corbusier were among the foreign contributors to *Tecné*. The journal upheld Austral's tenets: to build on the basis of the country's lived reality, to focus on local

---

[17] In addition to Ferrari Hardoy, Kurchan and Bonet, members of the group included Horacio Caminos, Eduardo Catalano, Carlos Coire, Samuel Sánchez de Bustamante, Alberto Le Pera, Humberto Vera Barrios, Jorge Vivanco, Simón Ungar and Hilario Zalba.
[18] The chair gets its name (BKF) from the last names of its creators: Bonet, Kurchan, Ferrari Hardoy.
[19] Liernur and Pschepiurca, *La red Austral*.
[20] From the beginning, Austral attempted to gain membership, especially among architecture students. To that end, it issued a manifesto, published as an insert in *Nuestra Arquitectura* magazine, the most important architecture publication in Argentina in the 1930s, 1940s and 1950s.

conditions and use local materials, to increase architecture and urbanism's social commitment, to champion a free assimilation of works by master architects, to build relationships with industry and to strengthen ties between architecture and urbanism. As stated in the editorial:

> *Tecné* is not about simply taking pleasure in pondering ideas or in gazing at works of art. It is a tool and a goad to production [...][21]
>
> The greatest defect of local constructions, which are naturally influenced by Europe, is the lack of continuity and connection with their surroundings (soil, weather, people) [...] It is time to come clean and begin building here, with our feet on the ground.[22]

The never-built Master Plan for the city of Buenos Aires was the springboard of what architecture historians Francisco Liernur and Pablo Pschepiurca call the 'Austral network' – a metaphor that captures two important phenomena. First, the extension of the network of relationships formed through the creation of Austral, a network that had considerable consequences for how architecture, urbanism and, later, design were envisioned in Argentina. Second, to use a chemistry metaphor, how the introduction of one element – in this case, Le Corbusier – altered the very substance of the original elements.[23] The ideas, projects and productions of a group of young Argentine architects were palpably modified by this exchange; Le Corbusier's ideas about urbanism also seemed to have undergone major alterations after he came to the Americas. As recent works produced in Latin America on Le Corbusier's brief stay in the region show, he was receptive to the specificities of a context with which he was – furthermore – in constant contact. That does not mean, however, that he was immune to prejudices, and his vision of the population was informed by a hackneyed notion of folk culture.[24] Le Corbusier's correspondence with friends and colleagues in Latin America evidences major discoveries on his part regarding the scale, complexity, density and magnitude of cities like Rio de Janeiro, Buenos Aires and São Paulo. He found what Beatriz Sarlo has described as a peripheral modernity marked by cultural hybridization.[25, 26]

During the 1940s, the group of architects who had first become involved in modern architecture through Austral, along with contributors to *Tecné*, came into

---

[21] Editorial, *Revista Tecné*, no. 1 (1942).
[22] Editorial, *Revista Tecné*, no. 3 (1944).
[23] Liernur and Pschepiurca, *La red Austral*.
[24] Carlos Martins, 'Una Lectura Crítica de Precisiones', in *Le Corbusier: Precisiones sobre un estado presente de la arquitectura y del urbanismo* (São Paulo: Cosac&Naify, 2004), 276 and Carlos Eduardo Dias Comas, *Le Corbusier y Sudamérica: viajes y proyectos* (Santiago de Chile: Editorial ARQ, 1991).
[25] Sarlo, *Una modernidad periférica*; Liernur and Pschepiurca, *La red Austral*.
[26] It is striking that Le Corbusier drew a parallel between Buenos Aires and New York, both of which had, by the 1920s and 1930s, adopted the imaginary of modernity to which the construction of skyscrapers was central (that was not the case in most other cities in the Americas or Europe).

contact with the Argentine artists in the *Movimiento Arte Concreto* [Concrete Art Movement], which was founded around that time. In that convergence lay the conceptual and ideological foundations of modern design in Argentina.[27] We shall next discuss the characteristics of that avant-garde movement both internationally and in Argentina.

Tomás Maldonado's pre-Ulm period (1942–1954)

The International Concrete Movement is usually considered to have been begun in 1930, when Dutch artist Van Doesburg published a six-point manifesto in the sole issue of the magazine *Art Concret*. In it, he lay the theoretical basis for a new art, a logical, rational and geometric art.[28] One year later, in 1931, the *Abstraction-Création* group was founded in Paris in keeping with the tenets of that manifesto. Its aim was to foment different strains of abstraction. In 1937, Max Bill, who had studied at the Bauhaus, and Leo Leuppi founded the Allianz group in Switzerland in order to promote Swiss modern art and build alliances between different tendencies. Allianz ultimately turned into the group of Concrete artists in Zurich and the main point of reference for Argentine Concrete artists.[29]

Arte Concreto [Concrete Art], the group founded in Argentina in 1944 by Tomás Maldonado, Lidy Prati, Alfredo Hlito and Edgar Bayley, adhered to Concretism because, in the view of its members, it took the Cubist revolution to another level.[30] Their concerns with painting – the questions they asked of it – were bound to space, geometry, light, colour and sound. That led them – as it had led the Russian Constructive avant-gardes – to concerns akin to those of modern architecture and the world of utilitarian objects. Visual artist and theorist Maldonado's home, located at Uriburu Street in Buenos Aires, was, by 1948, a sort of laboratory of ideas and a gathering place where artists and architects would meet to discuss the relationship between aesthetics and function, between art and the transformation of society.[31] As Carlos Méndez Mosquera recalled:

> Tomás's house was a sort of power station where architecture students at the Universidad de Buenos Aires [University of Buenos Aires] would get together. It

---

[27] Verónica Devalle, *La travesía de la forma. Emergencia y consolidación del diseño gráfico (1948–1984)* (Buenos Aires: Paidós, 2009); Crispiani, *Objetos para transformar el mundo*.

[28] Bear in mind that the term 'Concrete' refers here to a strain of abstraction that eschews any reference to a model rooted in nature to propose instead an objective system of composition based on geometric forms.

[29] María Amalia García, 'Arte Concreto entre Argentina, Brasil y Suiza. Max Bill y sus conexiones latinoamericanas'. *Crítica Cultural*, no. 4 (2009): 21.

[30] Known later, after an internal division, as *Arte Concreto Invención* [Concrete Invention Art].

[31] Méndez Mosquera, *Retrospectiva*.

was there that we first came into contact with – and later discussed and debated – terms like 'visual arts, space, industrial design', not only with Maldonado, but with the whole group of Argentine Concrete artists.[32]

At the same time, the *Instituto de Arquitectura y Urbanismo* [Institute of Architecture and Urbanism] was opened at the Universidad Nacional de Tucumán [National University of Tucumán], a university located in a city in northern Argentina. Even by contemporary standards, the institute's programme is one of the most experimental in the history of architecture and urbanism education in Argentina. The idea was to change the parameters for urban construction, to make them coherent with the industrialization taking place in mid-size cities in Argentina. For the first time, modern architecture and urbanism – their theory and practice – were taught at an Argentine public university. In this context, in 1947 Jorge Vivanco – Director of the *Instituto de Arquitectura y Urbanismo* – brought in as visiting professors Italian architects Ernesto Nathan Rogers, Cino Calcaprina, Luigi Piccinato and Enrico Tedeschi alongside the civil engineer Guido Oberti. He had met them at the sixth *Congrès international d'architecture moderne* (CIAM) that had taken place in Bridgwater, Somerset, in the UK. The faculty in Tucumán also included Argentine architects from the Austral group.

Concrete artists and modern architects came together in a number of projects, most of them led by Maldonado. The 1948 art exhibition *Nuevas Realidades* [New Realities], for instance, featured projects by the Italians working in Tucumán – it was novel to include architecture and urbanism in an art show. The exhibition ended with a lecture by Rogers called *Ubicación del arte concreto* [The Place of Concrete Art] that called for joining constructivist visual arts and modern architecture (International Style). By 1947, Maldonado was in touch with Swiss Concrete artist Bill. As Maldonado stated:

> My idea was to travel around Europe and meet as many Concrete artists as possible. That was why I wrote to Max Bill, who lived in Switzerland. We set a date to meet. Then I received another letter from Bill saying that on that very day he would be visited by two young Germans who wanted to talk to him – that was the only day they could meet. He asked me if we could change the date of our meeting. I couldn't because I had planned to be in Switzerland for only a few days. So we agreed I would also go to the meeting with the Germans – and that is just what happened. Since I did not speak German yet, they kindly held the meeting in French. Those two young Germans were Inge Scholl and Otl Aicher, who had come to propose to Bill taking part in the creation of a school that would continue the Bauhaus's work […] As you can see, life-changing

---

[32] Ibid., 50–1.

events are sometimes by chance. Who would have said I would take part in that meeting?[33]

In 1947 and 1948, Maldonado travelled to continental Europe to experience in person the modern art tradition which, until then, he had only seen in journals and catalogues or in the works and accounts of European artists in exile in Argentina.[34] He visited Paris where he met artist and architect Georges Vantongerloo; Zurich where he met Bill and other Swiss concrete artists; and Italy where he met artists Max Huber, Bruno Munari, Gillo Dorfles and Gianni Dova.

When Maldonado returned from Europe, he shared what he had experienced there with the Concrete artists and architecture students who would gather in his house. He brought the lead moulds for Spartan (Futura) typeface, which were later used for several catalogues of the *Arte Concreto* [Concrete Art] group.[35] The group grew as the Italians architects who taught at the Universidad de Tucumán joined. Its theoretical points of reference expanded to encompass not only Marxism and Concrete art, but also the Bauhaus and concrete abstraction from France, Switzerland and Italy. To look, once again, to Méndez Mosquera's recollection:

> The typeface created at the Bauhaus by Moholy-Nagy and Herbert Bayer and then perfected by Max Bill arrived in Argentina. We came into contact Moholy-Nagy´s magazine *Telehor* – where the famous letter to Kalivoda was published, a piece that opened up whole new spheres in the language of vision; Jan Tschichold's book *Die Neue Typographie*; Max Bill's article *Ubertypographie*; the Bauhaus-Bucher; Morancé editions on architecture; Georges Vantongerloo's ideas; the catalogues to Concrete art exhibitions in Switzerland and Italy; the Stijl movement; Mondrian; Constructivism; Russian Suprematism; and Apollinaire's poetry.[36]

After returning to Argentina in June 1948, Maldonado began corresponding almost daily with Bill. In the letters, they worked on a number of joint projects, among them a Bill exhibition in Argentina and Brazil (the show would never make it to Argentina due to lack of government support and bureaucratic obstacles, but it was held at the Museu de Arte de São Paul in March 1951).[37]

By 1949, Concretism was a well-established movement 'Billism',[38] like the teachings of the Bauhaus school, was slowly gaining ground with figures such as László Moholy-Nagy and Hannes Meyer. Maldonado's exchange with young

---

[33] Maldonado, Interview. Verónica Devalle interviewer, in the framework of the television programme 'Diseñadores argentinos' [Argentine Designers] directed to be aired in Argentina, 2014.
[34] García, *El arte abstracto*.
[35] Maldonado also brought back with him Huber's posters like *sinerella* and *arte astratta e concreta*.
[36] Méndez Mosquera. Interview. Devalle interviewer. Buenos Aires, Argentina, 1998.
[37] García, *El arte abstracto*.
[38] Crispiani, *Objetos para transformar el mundo*, 253.

Boletín 2 del
Centro Estudiantes de Arquitectura
Perú 294
Octubre-Noviembre de 1949 Buenos Aires

Comité de Redacción:
Juan Manuel Borthagaray
Gerardo Clusellas
Carlos Mendez Mosquera
Pino Sivori

1

Lo que nos impulsa hoy a publicar este boletín es el deseo de difundir, en la medida de nuestras posibilidades, los principios artísticos y técnicos que mejor enseñen a comprender el fenómeno de la arquitectura moderna; queremos así concretar, de una vez por todas, un órgano capaz de reflejar las más renovadoras inquietudes del estudiantado.

En nuestra época se presentan nuevos problemas que requieren nuevas soluciones. Los adelantos técnicos han modificado la fisonomía de nuestro tiempo, pero los intereses creados y la falta de visión han obstaculizado su desarrollo progresista, desaprovechando tanto los materiales manufacturables como las preciosas energías humanas. Contra esto, nuestro boletín ha de esforzarse por difundir todo lo que contribuya, directa o indirectamente, a encontrar una solución estable de los problemas a que acabamos de referirnos. Tales son nuestros propósitos.

El arquitecto van der Rohe   Edoardo Pérsico

Ludwig Mies van der Rohe, nacido en Aachen en 1886, puede ser considerado como el paladín de los arquitectos modernos.

Quien mire atentamente toda su obra percibe al instante que la inspiración de este artista se ha manifestado en los temas máximos del nuevo arte de construir: desde la búsqueda de una "línea" original hasta la afirmación de un nuevo concepto de "espacio".

En el "Baukunst der neuesten Zeit", de Gustav Adolf Plots, frente a las "realizaciones" de todos los demás arquitectos europeos, Mies van der Rohe está representado únicamente por una serie de proyectos y bocetos; este hecho puede servir para entender mejor el espíritu de intransigencia y el deseo de perfección absoluta en Mies van der Rohe, el arquitecto más representativo de esa amplia corriente innovadora que es la arquitectura moderna.

Los temas que ha preferido Mies van der Rohe, son, en el fondo, los mismos de Le Corbusier o Gropius, pero la importancia de Mies está en el estilo con el cual ha pensado nuevas soluciones y en la posibilidad de desarrollo "universal" de sus conceptos.

Le Corbusier, por ejemplo, es el inventor de alguna nueva "línea" en arquitectura. Pero ¿quién llevó más lejos que Mies van der Rohe la capacidad de dibujar los "Metallmöbel"? El concepto de "espacio" compromete toda la obra de Gropius, pero nadie pudo, ni siquiera los más audaces suprematistas rusos, expresar leyes espaciales tan nuevas y exactas como las que están contenidas en algunos proyectos, y en el pabellón alemán de la Exposición de Barcelona 1929, de este arquitecto.

La casa Tugendhat confirma la ley expresada en el pabellón de 1929, y establece con autoridad que el deber de un constructor moderno es de superar los simples problemas del oficio, para desembocar en una forma lírica, capaz de dar

Fachada de la casa Tugendhat de Mies van der Rohe

a los hombres de nuestra época otras interpretaciones originales de la belleza.

Mies van der Rohe proyectó la casa Tugendhat con la máxima libertad respecto a los problemas

FIGURE 2.2 Boletín CEA, 1949. Courtesy of Fundación IDA, Investigación en Diseño Argentino Fondo Maldonado Tomás

architects was increasingly intense, and he was becoming a widely recognized thinker in university circles. In 1949, the second issue of the *Boletín del Centro de Estudiantes de Arquitectura* [Architecture Students' Centre Bulletin] was published and, for it, Maldonado wrote the first article on industrial design ever published in Argentina (see Figure 2.2).

In it, he defined design as follows:

> Design unquestionably represents, for the time being, the most immediate, the most social, way of expressing what has been called the new vision, which comprises – to define it briefly – all the activities, artistic or not, that tend to undermine the morphological repertoire of today's visual world.[…] design today is the only possibility to actually solve one of the most dramatic and acute problems of these times: the divorce between art and life, between artists and all other human beings.
>
> […]Rather than proposing that artists limit themselves to being skilful copyists of styles and forms from other times, the new vision proposes that artists expand their horizons to reach new creative spheres, to reach the thriving social universe of mass-produced everyday objects, which constitute, in the end, the human being's most immediate reality.[39]

'Design' was a new concept and its introduction in the academy part of a new vision that attested to, among other things, the influence of Moholy-Nagy's experiments with perception (Moholy-Nagy, [1929] 1963). That, along with the concept of 'form' as understood by Bill, began to shape a cluster of interests: the social objectives of design, the universalization of forms set forth by Concrete Art, the rationalization of the production process and hope grounded in technological development.

'Design', 'new vision', 'visual culture' and 'typography' were among the terms that, starting in 1951, began to appear in a number of initiatives: the *nueva visión* journal (1951–1957), the Nueva Visión publishing house and the Vision course launched at a number of architecture schools in Argentina. Those notions were also central to shaping design as a new area of academic instruction. At the forefront of all of those initiatives was the figure of Jannello.[40]

César Jannello: A key figure to the design network in Argentina and internationally

In 1947, after intense study of modern architecture at the Universidad de Buenos Aires and of constructive art under the influence of the avant-garde, Jannello and his wife, architect Colette Boccara, moved to the city of Mendoza, at the foot of the Andes. In Buenos Aires in 1944, he had designed the W chair inspired by the aforementioned BKF chair (see Figure 2.3).

In Buenos Aires, he had a large circle of friends, among them were Williams and Maldonado. Like Maldonado, Jannello was interested in architecture and art

---

[39] Tomás Maldonado, 'El diseño y la vida social', *Boletín CEA*, no. 2 (1949): 7–8.
[40] Devalle, *La travesía de la forma*.

FIGURE 2.3 Silla W, 1944. Courtesy of Fundación IDA, Investigación en Diseño Argentino Fondo Jannello César

theory and in experimentation and multidisciplinary projects. In Mendoza, he designed and built apartment buildings. He worked with architect Tedeschi from 1949 to 1956. He spent 1953 and 1954 designing the *Feria de América* [Americas Fair], a public initiative envisioned to showcase the industrial potential of the continent; he commissioned his friend Maldonado to come up with the fair's visual identity (see Figure 2.4).

During his years in Mendoza (1947–1958), Jannello corresponded with his friends and colleagues on a regular basis, telling them about his projects and discussing his vision of architecture and design. In addition to references to the political events taking place in the country at the time, his epistolary exchanges with Maldonado and architect Gerardo Clusellas included invitations to Mendoza and Buenos Aires – as the case may be – to give lectures, as well as opinions of art exhibitions, recommendations for the architecture curriculum, comments on books and accounts of the sale of the *nueva visión* journal and Jannello's W chair. While his tie to both Maldonado and Clusellas was multifaceted, it was based on comradery and intellectual exchange.

FIGURE 2.4 Feria de América calco, 1953–1954. Courtesy of Fundación IDA, Investigación en Diseño Argentino Fondo Jannello César

Jannello, like Williams and Maldonado, formed part of a tight international network as well. He corresponded with Joseph Albers and with the circle of professors who had emigrated from Germany to the United States.[41] Unlike Williams and Maldonado, though, Jannello kept a low profile and published a great deal of theoretical work, as well as teaching, within the Argentine borders. His interest in architecture grew out of his interest in Constructive art; his approach to design was always interdisciplinary, and his theoretical research was coupled with the need to root the discipline in the regional context. That meant casting off an orthodox stance on architecture and art and heeding local cultural factors as a constituent part of design. In 1956 and 1957, he put together the first degree programme in design in Argentina. It was launched in 1958 at the *Universidad Nacional de Cuyo* [Cuyo National University] in Mendoza. That same year, having decided that his work in Mendoza was done, he returned to Buenos Aires, where modern design and its discourse were, by now, well established – thanks, in no small measure, to the *nueva visión* journal.

In 1956, now back in Buenos Aires, he taught the Vision course given at the architecture schools of the *Universidad Nacional de La Plata* [National University of La Plata] and the *Universidad de Buenos Aires* [National University of Buenos Aires]. The course was part of a process of reworking the curriculum and pedagogical models. Key to those changes was the 'vertical studio class', an idea and method brought over from the architecture school at the *Universidad de la República* [University of the Republic] in Uruguay in 1952.[42] According to Méndez Mosquera,

---

[41] Crispiani, *Objetos para transformar el mundo*; Devalle, *La travesía de la forma*; García, *El arte abstracto.*; Müller, 'Amancio Williams. La invención como proyecto'.

[42] The 'vertical studio' is an architecture teaching modality whereby a number of professors can teach different aspects of the same subject in parallel. The 'Vision' course, for example, could be taught by Jannello and by Breyer at the same time to allow for different approaches to architecture's problems to interact. Students were able to choose in which studio and, hence, with which professor, to take the course.

The course's name, Vision, was clearly influenced by the Bauhaus as expressed in Moholy-Nagy's art. It replaced the course entitled 'art', which was linked to L'École des Beaux Arts in Paris. The name meant envisioning architecture as part of the still-incipient concept of design, ushering in a focus on questions like representation and analysis of forms – disciplines and topics currently addressed in courses with names like morphology, expressive media, and heuristics.[43]

The research orientation of the course meant that, in teaching it, Jannello was able to develop a theory of design based on rational systems. Jannello and architect Gastón Breyer were two key points of reference in the development of a colour theory and in understanding the problem of form; they were also pivotal to the 'morphology programmes' at architecture schools, natural heir to the Vision course first taught in 1956.

From its beginnings, the morphology programme was experimental. At Jannello's initiative, it included, for instance, a semiotic reading of space. In the 1960s, Jannello corresponded with Roland Barthes, Umberto Eco and the young and then-lesser known Julia Kristeva. His interest in semiotics and discourse theories was responsible, in part, for the launching of the semiology course at the Universidad de Buenos Aires, Facultad de Arquitectura [National University of Buenos Aires, Arquitecture] in the early 1970s.[44]

This was the culmination of a process where form, as theoretical problem, ceased to be interrogated in the terms of Bill's mathematics or of the Ulm school's scientificity to be addressed instead in terms of French semiology – that is, in relation to its meaning. And this had serious repercussions when it came to founding departments in graphic design, industrial design, and image and sound design (also known as media), all of which were engaged as communication. Design departments, starting with the first one, founded in 1958, were almost always housed in schools of architecture and urbanism at educational institutions like the Universidad del Litoral [University of Litoral], the Universidad de Buenos Aires [University of Buenos Aires], the Universidad de Mar del Plata [University of Mar del Plata], the Universidad de Córdoba [University of Córdoba] and others. Hence, teaching morphology in design programmes furthered an academic tradition tied to the old Vision course – indeed, it was from that course that it drew its sustenance. It did that while expanding on the question of meaning, a concern not only for architecture and work with space, but also – and from then on – for all disciplines connected to vision and objects. That transfer was not problematic when it came to putting together design programmes' curricula: thanks to the legacy of the Vision course, form as problem – that is, form as outgrowth of an experimental conception of space – was understood as going beyond architecture.

---

[43] Méndez Mosquera, Retrospectiva, 49.
[44] The author's unpublished research in the Jannello archives housed at Fundación IDA.

Though Jannello was central to this entire process and he regularly exchanged ideas with his colleagues in the United States and Europe, he was not considered an international intellectual as his friend and interlocutor Maldonado was – or an international architect as another of his friends, Williams, was. He was more concerned with research and teaching in Argentina and with the production of a rational theory of design.

Publication projects

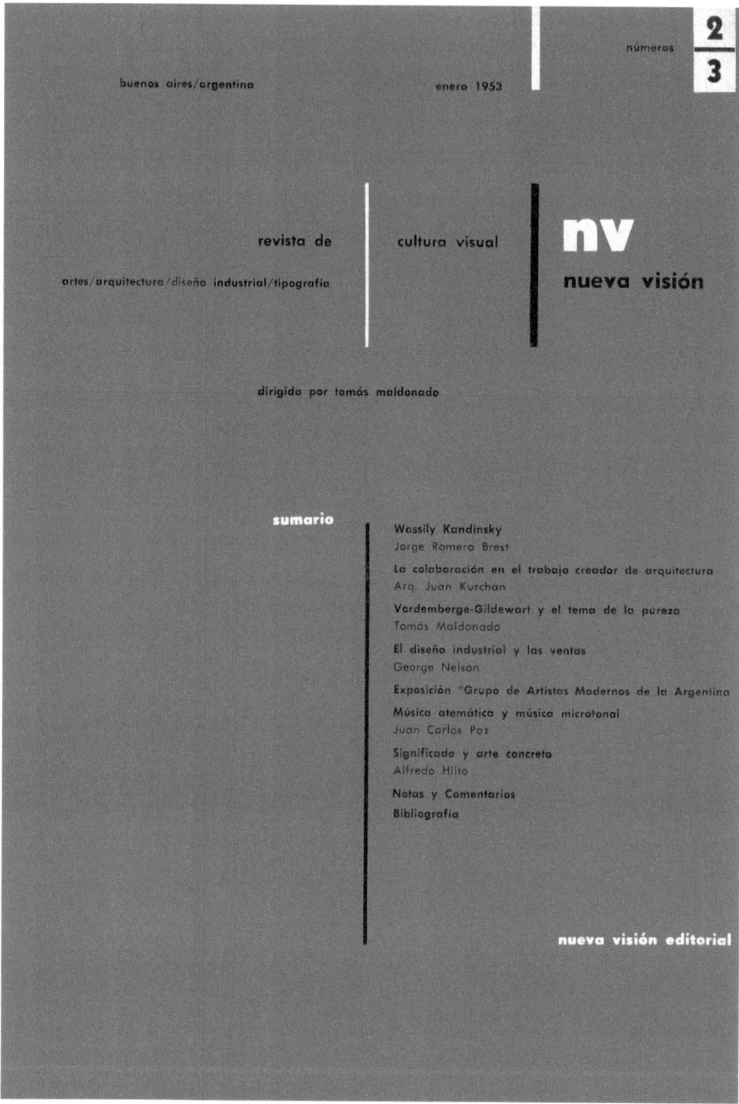

FIGURE 2.5 *nueva visión* journal, issue 1 (5.1) and issue 2/3 (5.2). Courtesy of Fundación IDA, Investigación en Diseño Argentino Fondo Maldonado Tomás

As mentioned above, the magazines *Ciclo* and *nueva visión* were media for criticism of modern architecture and art and, hence, they furthered the development of the concepts that were shaping design in Argentina. *nueva visión*, specifically, and its later incarnation, *Summa* (1963–1993), was the conceptual engine that provided the country's first university design programmes with contents.[45]

---

[45] It was in 1963 that the Universidad Nacional de La Plata launched the second university design programme in Argentina, one in industrial design and the other in visual communication.

nueva visión journal was founded in 1951 by Hlito, Méndez Mosquera and Maldonado, the latter was also the publication's director almost until it folded. Published until 1957, its nine issues dealt with the concept of 'visual culture' understood to encompass expressions of modern art, (industrial) design and modern architecture. It published the work carried out at schools like the Bauhaus and the Chicago Institute of Design; constructions by architects like Frank Lloyd Wright, Alvar Aalto, Pier Luigi Nervi, Bruno Zevi and Walter Gropius; works by artists like Mondrian, Bill, Wassily Kandinsky, and Moholy-Nagy, as well as by local pioneers in modern architecture (Bonet, Ferrari Hardoy, Kurchan, Williams, Jannello), and Concrete art (Maldonado, Hlito, Bayley and Prati).[46]

The title of the journal left no doubt about its roots. The term *nueva visión* is a direct reference to Moholy-Nagy's seminal text *The New Vision* and to the classic *Vision in Motion*. The journal looked, then, to the German and Swiss tradition, which did not preclude references to Constructive modern art or modern architecture.

The Hochschule für Gestaltung (HfG) figures centrally in a number of issues of the journal. The school and its educational project were essential to Maldonado's development (he ultimately moved to Ulm to teach there in 1954). In issue 4 (1953), Bill mentioned plans to found the HfG in Ulm and recalled, in vague terms, earlier failures to establish a Bauhaus-like school.

> With varying degrees of success, many efforts have been made to open institutions analogous to the Bauhaus or to transform existing schools to reflect its model. None of those projects, though, has gone as far as the Hochschule für Gestaltung, created in Ulm by Inge Aicher-Scholl in memory of her two siblings killed by the Nazis [...] The school's statement of purpose opens as follows: 'The school is the continuation of the Bauhaus (Weimar-Dessau-Berlin). Its curriculum includes topics more important today than they were twenty or thirty years ago [...]'
>
> The school strives to guide the enterprising spirit characteristic of youth, to cultivate its sense of responsibility in our common life, to lead it to solve social problems, and to put into practice this technical era's lifestyles.[47]

It should come as no surprise that Bill chose an organ like *nueva visión* to announce the opening of the HfG and to describe its educational project. He was an active advisor and contributor to the journal to the point of having suggested – if not outright imposed – the change in its cover design starting in the double issue put out in 1953 (2/3) (see Figure 2.5). *nueva visión* reproduced a number of Bill's works and published Spanish translations of his texts. Perhaps more than any other publication, *nueva visión* journal – its first issues, that is – evidenced

---

[46] Devalle, *La travesía de la forma*.
[47] Max Bill, 'Educación y creación', *Revista nueva visión*, no. 4 (1953): 8.

FIGURE 2.6 Editorial NV Max Bill, 1955. Courtesy of Fundación IDA, Investigación en Diseño Argentino Fondo Maldonado Tomás

the friendship and shared artistic and intellectual interests connecting Bill and Maldonado (starting in 1956, a distance would set in between the two men and they would eventually clash).

The seventh issue of the journal, published in 1955, discussed the first stage of the HfG and presented the book *Max Bill* (see Figure 2.6), with texts by Maldonado.[48] In it, Bolivian Concrete poet Eugen Gomringer – Bill's secretary at the HfG from 1954 to 1957 – wrote:

> There have been repeated attempts to found institutions like the Bauhaus after its closing in 1933. They have all failed because they took into account only some components of the Bauhaus idea – and those parts alone could not join

---

[48] Significantly, *Max Bill* was the first book put out by Nueva Visión.

art and life. Max Bill, who was named dean of the HfG in 1951 and who also directed its architecture department, speaks of the difference between the Bauhaus and the school he directs in these terms:

The professors at the Bauhaus – that generation – were divided between artists and technicians. My generation produced a type of designer for whom art is a vital need, but who sees its vitality as tied to collaboration to solve society's daily problems.[49]

nueva visión gradually moved away from modern art criticism to form part of a broader project, namely forging the conceptual tools necessary for a scientific and technical understanding of design. It was the first publication in Spanish – and, along with the HfG's journal, one of the only publications in any language – to participate in that effort. The fact that its affinity with the HfG's project was as absolute as its support for Maldonado should come as no surprise.

Together, its nine issues shed light on how the synthesis of the arts that had so rallied Concrete artists turned into focus on design, and how design in turn veered away from a formal aesthetic framework to take root in a technical-social universe, hence the journal's growing attention to modern architecture and urbanism.

The journal was published until 1957, when the ninth and final issue came out. Through issue eight, Maldonado directed it from Ulm. The growing conflict between him and Bill and the broader schism at the HfG made it impossible for Maldonado to direct the final issue, which Jorge Grisetti, who had gradually been taking over, edited.[50, 51] Three years before, in 1954, Grisetti had created the *nueva visión* publishing house which, through its collections of books on design, architecture and modern art, continued the journal´s project.

In 1954, *nueva visión* publishing house launched one of the most important collections of conceptual writing on the fields of architecture, art and modern design in Spanish. It included texts by Maldonado, photographer and painter Moholy-Nagy, art critic Giulio Argan, architect Marina Waisman, architecture critic Rayner Banham, architect Wladimiro Acosta, and writer and philosopher Benedetto Croce. *nueva visión*'s books, thanks to its sound distribution network, gradually formed part of the collections of university libraries, of schools of architecture and design, as well as the collections of critics, collectors and gallerists

---

[49] Eugen Gomringer, 'La Escuela Superior de Diseño de Ulm', *Revista nueva visión*, no. 7 (1955): 7–10.
[50] Paul Betts, *The Authority of Everyday Objects. A Cultural History of West German Industrial Design* (California: University of California Press, 2007), 139–77; Gui Bonsiepe, 'The Invisible Facets of the HfG Ulm', *Design Issues*, no. 11 (1995): 11–20; Rene Spitz, *The View behind the Foreground: The Political History of the Ulm School of Design (1953–1968)* (London: Edition Axel Menges, 2002).
[51] The differences between Bill, on the one hand, and Otl Aicher and Maldonado, on the other, that would eventually lead them to part ways set in 1956. The main point of contention was the profile most befitting the HfG. Aicher and Maldonado believed that the school should be less oriented to art – the profile Bill advocated – and more oriented to the industrial needs of the post-war world. These differences led Bill to resign from the HfG in 1957.

all over the Spanish-speaking world. They helped spread ideas about design that, as we have seen, began to take shape decades before.[52]

The first design organizations in Argentina

The 1960s witnessed the first design organizations in the country, first in the capital city, Buenos Aires, and then in the rest of Argentina. Since this chapter focuses on the earlier networks that led to those organizations, I will discuss, and only briefly, the first two organizations, the CIDI and the ADIA.

The CIDI was created in Buenos Aires in September 1962 in the framework of the *Instituto Nacional de Tecnología Industrial* [National Institute of Industrial Technology] (INTI). It was a public entity aimed at supporting industrial design and graphic design in Argentina through, among other things, technical assistance from the industrial sector (Rey, 2009). To that end, it attempted to connect universities and private companies. The CIDI upheld as canon the notion of Good Design, even creating a prize with that term in its name (*Premio al Buen Diseño*).

The first president of the CIDI was Basilio Uribe, an engineer and the head of the largest plastics company in Argentina at the time (the company advertised in *nueva visión*). Uribe invited *nueva visión*'s staff writers and professors of the Vision course at the Universidad Nacional del Litoral and the Universidad de Buenos Aires to participate in the CIDI. Uribe organized lectures by international figures in industrial and graphic design to coordinate university instruction with the needs of the private sector. The Ulm school was a major presence at the CIDI in its early years, which meant – among other things – that Gui Bonsiepe, Herbert Ohl and Maldonado all gave seminars there. Maldonado was always close to the group of friends and colleagues with whom he had worked at *nueva visión*. In 1964, in the framework of the invitation from the CIDI, Maldonado and Bonsiepe helped develop a school of design envisioned as a point of reference in design instruction in Latin America. According to those who took part in the project, the vision of design underlying the never-opened school was a bit elitist.[53]

The CIDI also invited Finnish designer Ilmari Tapiovaara and English designer Misha Black to give lectures. In 1964, it applied for admission to the International Council of Societies of Industrial Design (ICSID). When it was accepted in 1965, Argentina became the first country in the region recognized by the ICSID as a producer of design. The CIDI later applied for membership to the International Council of Graphic Design Associations (ICOGRADA).

The CIDI's activities and accomplishments included the *Primera Exposición Internacional de Diseño Industrial* [First International Exhibition of Industrial Design] held in 1963 and curated by Clusellas. According to designer Ricardo

---

[52] Devalle, *La travesía de la forma*.
[53] Blanco, *Crónicas del diseño industrial*, 136.

Blanco, '[t]hat exhibition was, arguably, the moment when industrial design erupted in Argentina. It aptly reflected what was happening around the world'.[54, 55]

The purpose of the *Asociación de Diseñadores Industriales* [Association of Industrial Designers] (ADIA), founded in December 1962, was to gather all the professionals in the broad realm of design.[56] Less active than the CIDI, the ADIA mostly selected products to participate in the CIDI's Good Design prize and in the *Primera Exposición Internacional de Diseño Industrial* [First International Exhibition of Industrial Design]. It also helped put together juries for competitions and shows. In 1965, it was also admitted to the ICSID. A number of the ADIA's own members called it 'insular', and it eventually petered out.

The CIDI's focus differed from the ADIA's. The CIDI had an international bent; it was committed to instructing industries in design and designers in production processes. The ADIA, meanwhile, was more concerned with honing design standards; its members were industrial designers. The two organizations shared, however, a conception of design rooted in the tenets of Good Design, undoubtedly due to the influence in Argentina of the network tying Swiss and Italian Concrete artists and their Argentine counterparts in the 1940s and the one that later, through Maldonado, linked Argentine and German designers.

Later – after the period covered here – a series of regional organizations were formed. Most of them did not prosper for a number of reasons, such as the drop in employment opportunities for designers due to de-industrialization policies in the country starting in the mid-1970s, the lack of government support and the infighting between members.

Conclusions

This chapter discussed the two decades before the first design organizations were founded in Argentina, a period when the networks that shaped design as discipline and practice in Argentina were being assembled. I emphasized national and international exchanges between groups of avant-garde artists and architects from Argentina and Brazil, Switzerland, France, Germany and other countries in an attempt to show how the initiatives at the origin of design were largely the fruit of those connections. Though the Austral network was the first one I addressed, no less important is the network that later formed around the concept of 'new vision'. Indeed, a magazine, a publishing house and a university course of that name were fundamental to feeding educational contents and modalities in early design courses in Argentina.

---

[54] Ibid.
[55] Blanco is considered an essential point of reference in industrial design in Argentina. He was a disciple of Acosta, Breyer and Jannello. In addition to his extensive professional work, Blanco designed the curriculum for most of the industrial design university programmes in Argentina in the 1980s.
[56] Blanco, *Crónicas del diseño industrial*.

I have thus provided a framework for trajectories that, were it not for the concept of the 'network', would be considered individual efforts.[57] Nothing could be further from the case. The profile of a figure of the stature of Maldonado, a man who played a major role in design organizations – he was even the President of the ICSID from 1967 to 1969 – changes if his artistic, theoretical and ideological alignments in Argentina before working in Ulm, along with the multiple connections that characterized his youth, are taken into account.

Design organizations can be seen as either a point of departure for a series of initiatives or – as this chapter affirms – as their end result. They bear traces of earlier conceptions of design, professional identities and interlinked genealogies that have, on occasion, been silenced through the institutionalization and formalization of design education. I hope that this chapter has captured the embers of the networks that made design in Argentina so remarkable.

References

Betts, Paul. *The Authority of Everyday Objects. A Cultural History of West German Industrial Design*. California: University of California Press, 2007.

Bill, Max. 'Educación y creación'. *Revista nueva visión*, no. 4 (1953): 8.

Blanco, Ricardo. *Crónicas del diseño industrial en Argentina*. Buenos Aires: Ediciones FADU, 2005.

Bonsiepe, Gui. 'The Invisible Facets of the HfG Ulm'. *Design Issues*, no. 11 (1995): 11–20.

Calvera, Ana. 'Cuestiones de fondo: la hipótesis de los tres orígenes del diseño'. In Isabel, C. (ed.)., *Diseño e historia. Tiempo, lugar y discurso*. México: Designio, 2010.

Crispiani, Alejandro. *Objetos para transformar el mundo. Trayectorias del arte concreto-invención, Argentina-Chile, 1940–1970*. Buenos Aires: Editorial Prometeo, 2011.

Deambrosis, Federico. *Nuevas visiones*. Buenos Aires: Ediciones Infinito, 2011.

Devalle, Verónica. *La travesía de la forma. Emergencia y consolidación del diseño gráfico (1948–1984)*. Buenos Aires: Paidós, 2009.

Dias, Comas and Eduardo, Carlos. *Le Corbusier y Sudamérica: viajes y proyectos*. Santiago de Chile: Editorial ARQ, 1991.

Editorial. *Revista Tecné*, no. 1 (1942).

Editorial. *Revista Tecné*, no. 3 (1944).

Fundación IDA. *Investigación en Diseño Argentino*. Fondo Bonet, Antonio. Fondo Maldonado, Tomás y Fondo Jannello, César.

Fundación IDA. *Investigación en Diseño Argentino*. Jannello Archive, box 7.

García, María Amalia. 'Arte Concreto entre Argentina, Brasil y Suiza. Max Bill y sus conexiones latinoamericanas'. *Crítica Cultural*, no. 4 (2009): 209–17.

García, María Amalia. *El arte abstracto. Intercambios culturales entre Argentina y Brasil*. Buenos Aires: Siglo XXI, 2011.

Germani, Gino. *Estructura social de la Argentina*. Buenos Aires: Raigal, 1955.

Gomringer, Eugen. 'La Escuela Superior de Diseño de Ulm'. *Revista nueva visión*, no. 7 (1955): 10.

---

[57] Bruno Latour, *Reassembling the Social: An Introduction to Actor-Network-Theory* (Oxford: Oxford University Press, 2005).

Latour, Bruno. *Reassembling the Social: An Introduction to Actor-Network-Theory*. Oxford: Oxford University Press, 2005.

Liernur, Jorge Francisco and Pschepiurca, Pablo. *La red Austral: obras y proyectos de Le Corbusier y sus discípulos en la Argentina, 1924–1965*. Buenos Aires: Universidad Nacional de Quilmes, 2008.

Maldonado, Tomás. 'El diseño y la vida social'. *Boletín CEA*, no. 2 (1949): 7–8.

Maldonado, Tomás. Interview. Verónica Devalle interviewer, in the framework of the television programme 'Diseñadores argentinos' [Argentine Designers] directed to be aired in Argentina, 2014.

Margolin, Victor. *The Politics of the Artificial: Essays on Design and Design Studies*. Chicago: Chicago University Press, 2002.

Martins, Carlos. 'Una Lectura Crítica de Precisiones'. In *Le Corbusier: Precisiones sobre un estado presente de la arquitectura y del urbanismo*. São Paulo: Cosac&Naify, 2004.

Méndez Mosquera, Carlos. 'Retrospectiva del diseño gráfico'. *Contextos*, no. 1 (1997): 46–51.

Méndez Mosquera, Carlos. Interview. Verónica Devalle interviewer. Buenos Aires, Argentina, 1998.

Moholy-Nagy, Laszlo. *La nueva visión*. Buenos Aires: Ediciones Infinito, 1963.

Müller, Luis. 'Amancio Williams. La invención como proyecto' (Ph.D. dissertation, Facultad de Arquitectura, Planeamiento y Diseño, Universidad Nacional de Rosario. Rosario, 2019).

Neiburg, Federico and Plotkin, Mariano. *Intelectuales y expertos. La construcción del conocimiento social en Argentina*. Buenos Aires: Paidos, 2004.

Perazzo, Nelly. *El arte concreto en la Argentina*. Buenos Aires: Ediciones Gaglianone, 1983.

Rey, José. *Historia del CIDI. Un impulso de diseño en la industria argentina*. Buenos Aires: Red Amigos CMD, 2009.

Sarlo, Beatriz. *Una modernidad periférica. Buenos Aires 1920–1930*. Buenos Aires: Nueva Visión, 1988.

Spitz, Rene. *The View behind the Foreground: The Political History of the Ulm School of Design (1953–1968)*. London: Edition Axel Menges, 2002.

3 INTERNATIONAL DESIGN ORGANIZATIONS AND ÉMIGRÉ IDENTITY: PETER MULLER-MUNK AND AMERICAN REPRESENTATION IN ICSID, 1950–1967

Tania Messell

After the Second World War an international change occurred in the design profession, which witnessed an increase in the number of international conferences and awards, and designers' growing realization of the need to collectively position design as a fully fledged profession.[1] Moreover, the growth of international trade, led to intensified debates on the contribution of design to the positioning of nations, which alongside the necessity to give visibility to the profession, resulted in the proliferation of national bodies for design promotion and of professional design organizations. Arising from such circumstances, international design organizations developed, which fuelled by what can be seen as 'strategic internationalization' aimed to strengthen the position of design locally and nationally while answering business imperatives, alongside the sharing of design knowledge and skills.[2] This chapter contributes to post-war histories of international design organizations by examining the central contribution of émigré designers to such cross-border networks. The twentieth century had witnessed important migration flows from and within Europe, and when interests in international alliances materialized in such organizations, which were predominantly established in Western contexts in the post-war period, the latter often witnessed the contribution of émigré practitioners.[3]

---

[1] Jonathan M. Woodham, *Twentieth-Century Design* (Oxford/New York: Oxford University Press, 1997); Penny Sparke, *An Introduction to Design and Culture*, 3rd ed. (Abingdon: Routledge, 2013), 152.
[2] On cross-border professional organizations and 'strategic internationalisation' see Martin H. Geyer and Johannes Paulmann, eds., *The Mechanics of Internationalism: Culture, Society, and Politics from the 1840s to the First World War* (Oxford: Oxford University Press, 2001).
[3] On the International Design Conferences in Aspen (IDCA): Alison J. Clarke and Elana Shapira, 'Introduction – Emigrés Cultures and New Design Directions', in *Émigré Cultures in Design and Architecture*, ed. Alison J. Clarke and Elana Shapira (London/New York: Bloomsbury, 2017), 10. On Icograda: Jonathan M. Woodham, 'De Majo, William', in *A Dictionary of Modern Design*, ed. Jonathan M. Woodham, 2nd ed. (Oxford: Oxford University Press, 2016), 206. On F. H. K. Henrion's involvement with the Alliance Graphique Internationale and Icograda, see Jonathan M. Woodham, 'Henrion, F. H. K.', in *A Dictionary of Modern Design*, ed. Jonathan M. Woodham, 2nd ed. (Oxford: Oxford University Press, 2016), 328.

This was particularly the case in the International Council of Societies of Industrial Design (ICSID), which was founded in 1957 by designers representing professional organizations in Europe and the United States to raise the professional status of designers, and to establish international standards for the profession and design education. Symptomatic of this, ICSID's founders included the Russian-born British architect and designer Misha Black, the German-born American designer Peter Muller-Munk, and the Hungarian-born French architect Pierre Vago, who would all hold important positions within the Council subsequently.[4] Promoting the pacifist qualities of cross-border exchanges alongside the economic and professional benefits of international cooperation and shared design standards, all three practitioners acted as central cultural brokers during ICSID's establishment and development. Their discourse was grounded in the belief of 'cultural internationalism', which, having foregrounded the establishment of many international non-governmental organization after the Second World War, advanced that cultural and social questions knew no boundaries and that international cooperation could help to promote common interests.[5] ICSID's establishment however rapidly witnessed attempts at overseeing the organization's aims and functioning by its founders, strategies which were fuelled by political, economic and professional imperatives, and which from the very onset shaped the organization on a Western-centric model.

Championing the leading role of American designers in the global development of the profession and the necessity to establish an organization advancing raised professionalization and business interests, Muller-Munk's contribution to ICSID particularly influenced the organization's inner-workings during its early years. Born in Berlin in 1904 and having left Germany seeking the economic boom in America in 1926, Muller-Munk had rapidly built a reputation for himself in the United States, where he pursued a successful career as a silversmith in New York, and from 1935 onwards as a designer and design educator in Pittsburgh. Interested in contributing to design professionalization too, Muller-Munk became closely involved in the Society of Industrial Designers (SID) subsequently, an organization which was established by fifteen industrial designers in 1944, and which was renamed as the American Society of Industrial Designers (ASID) in 1955. Muller-Munk acted as SID's president between 1954 and 1955 and as the Chairman of its Foreign Affairs Committee subsequently.[6] Muller-Munk represented SID within ICSID, through which he became one of the driving forces behind the Council, as one of its founding members, president and past-president between 1953 and 1967.

---

[4] Muller-Munk, who was to become ICSID's first President, Black, became ICSID's first Vice-President, and Vago was to become ICSID's first Secretary General and third President. Ibid.
[5] Akira Iriye, *Global Community: The Role of International Organisations in the Making of the Contemporary World* (Oakland, CA: University of California Press, 2002), 25.
[6] Rachel Delphia, 'PMMA: Product Design', in *Silver to Steel: The Modern Designs of Peter Muller-Munk*, ed. Rachel Delphia and Jewel Stern (London: Prestel, 2015), 106.

Throughout this period, the designer strove to shape ICSID as an organization steeped in design specialization, while pursuing political and personal objectives. In particular, Muller-Munk capitalized on the duality of his European origins and embeddedness in American professional spheres to pursue his aims. Muller-Munk's émigré status and belief in cultural internationalism led him to become a central advocate of the benefits of cross-border professional exchanges within American design organization, resulting in the latter to be represented in ICSID. On the other hand, Muller-Munk regularly instrumentalized his involvement in American design circles to promote American design standards within ICSID's membership, efforts which contributed to the dominance of an Anglo-American model during the organization's early years. The designer's actions were thereby fuelled by overlapping professional interests, political pursuits and personal experience, which shaped his influence within ICSID's transnational network.

Recent scholarship has highlighted the fluid and contingent nature of émigré identity.[7] Informed by the realization that a significant proportion of migrants move across borders and between diverse social and cultural systems, transnational perspectives have challenged the singular narrative of the 'uprooted' migrant, instead suggesting that such individuals 'move freely back and forth across international borders, and between different cultures and social systems'.[8] Histories of individuals whose profiles circumvent settled categories of national, social or cultural identities have revealed how they often 'acquire their individual frames of action and identification through the characteristic of challenging established categories and criss-crossing between several identities'.[9] This overstepping of categories can result in incompatibilities and frictions,[10] but also spur economic and social change in local communities.[11] As design historians Alison J. Clarke and Elana Shapira have noted, 'it was through hybridity that [émigré designers] asserted their authority' in professionalization, promotion and education, in the form of 'new design vocabularies based on constructed hybrid cultures'.[12] As

---

[7] Akhil Gupta and James Ferguson, 'Culture, Power, Place: Ethnography at the End of an Era', in *Culture, Power, Place: Explorations in Critical Anthropology*, ed. Akhil Gupta and James Ferguson (Durham: Duke University Press, 1997); Yen Fen-Tseng, 'From "Us" to "Them": Diasporic Linkages and Identity Politics', in *Global Studies in Culture and Power* 9, no. 3 (2002). Sue Breakell and Lesley Whitworth, 'Archives, Collections and Curatorship: Émigré Designers in the University of Brighton Design Archives', *Journal of Design History* 28, no. 1 (2013).

[8] Caroline B. Brettell, 'Theorizing Migration in Anthropology: The Social Construction of Networks Identities, Communities, and Globalscapes', in *Migration Theory: Talking across Disciplines*, ed. Caroline B. Brettell and James F. Hollifield, 3rd ed. (London/New York: Routledge, 2015), 157.

[9] Cornelia Knaab, 'Civil Society Diplomacy? W. T. Stead, World Peace, and Transgressive Journalism', in *Lives beyond Borders: A Social History 1880–1950*, Special Issue, ed. Madeleine Herren and Isabella Löhr 23, no. 6 (2013): 25–6.

[10] Madeleine Herren, 'Between Territoriality, Performance, and Transcultural Entanglement (1920–1939): A Typology of Transboundary Lives', in *Lives Beyond Borders: A Social History 1880–1950*, Special Issue, ed. Madeleine Herren and Isabella Löhr 23, no. 6 (2013): 105.

[11] Brettell, 'Theorizing Migration in Anthropology', 157.

[12] Clarke and Shapira, 'Introduction – Emigrés Cultures and New Design Directions', 4.

this chapter argues, Muller-Munk's personal connections to Europe and North America, allied with his involvement in cross-border commercial networks and American Cold War operations, paved the way for the designer to become a central agent of internationalism within ICSID. Design historians have examined Muller-Munk's personal and professional trajectories in an expanded geography, and special attention has been awarded to the designer's role in the Cold War technical aid programmes, in particular at the intersection of American and Turkish contexts.[13] Building on this scholarship and drawing from the ICSID Archives and the Industrial Designers Society of America (IDSA) Records, the chapter untangles the overlapping set of imperatives and experiences that fuelled Muller-Munk's action at the intersection of national design organizations and ICSID, and by extension some of the processes that shaped the organization within wider political, economic and cultural contexts. It thereby offers a dual contribution to reconfigured histories of émigré designers and to histories of international design organizations.

Establishing ICSID

Similar to others among ICSID's founders, narratives of mobility and international awareness pervaded Muller-Munk's upbringing and early adulthood. Born into a culturally enlightened family with Jewish roots of the professional bourgeoisie, his mother's side in particular had favoured education, culture and travelling.[14] He was trained as a silversmith in Berlin in the early 1920s, and later enrolled at the city's Friedrich-Wilhelms-Universität, where he studied topics ranging from philosophy and politics to art history.[15] The economic and political uncertainty of the early years of the Weimar Republic led to a lack of clientele for luxury silverware, which resulted in Muller-Munk's departure for America in 1926, in search of financial security and artistic freedom.[16] There, the designer obtained the American citizenship, and after three years being employed at Tiffany's as a metalworker, he established his own silver studio. During this period, much of Muller-Munk's pieces were influenced by Bauhaus functionalism, and German and Scandinavian metalwork, while he

---

[13] See, for instance, Jewel Stern, *Modernism in American Silver: 20th-Century Design*, ed. Kevin W. Tucker and Charles L. Venable (New Haven and London: Yale University Press, 2005); Rachel Delphia and Jewel Stern, eds., *Silver to Steel: The Modern Designs of Peter Muller-Munk* (London: Prestel, 2015); Alpay Er et al., 'U.S. Involvement in the Development of Design in the Periphery: The Case History of Industrial Design Education in Turkey, 1950s–1970s', *Design Issues* 19, no. 2 (Spring 2003); Bahar Emgin, 'Traces of Peter Muller-Munk Associates in the History of Industrial Design in Turkey', *A/I/S Design Storia e Ricerche* (2017).

[14] Jewel Stern, 'Berlin: Family', in *Silver to Steel*, 17–19.

[15] Stern, 'Berlin: Family', 20–1.

[16] Jewel Stern, 'New York: Silver to Industrial Design', in *Silver to Steel*, 24.

FIGURE 3.1 Tea service designed by Peter Muller-Munk in the Metropolitan Museum of Art, 'American Industrial Art', 11th Exhibition (11 February to 2 September 1929). Courtesy of BPK/The Metropolitan Museum of Art

would compare silverwork to architecture and sculpting, as opposed to what he considered temporary novelties (see Figure 3.1).[17]

In a context of economic depression, Muller-Munk however became increasingly interested in design for mass production and received a growing number of industrial design commissions, before being invited to teach the first university course in industrial design at the Carnegie Institute of Technology, in Pittsburgh. Alongside his years teaching, Muller-Munk pursued his own practice, which flourished, leading him to form Peter Muller-Munk Associates (PMMA) in 1944, a design consultancy that by the mid-1960s would specialize in product, transportation and exhibition design, and which employed nearly fifty employees at its height. As written above, Muller-Munk moreover played a central role in SID, through which he continuously strove to expand the organization's international reach, and thereby disseminate American models of design practice and manufacturing. In particular, Muller-Munk became increasingly involved in

---

[17] Stern, 'New York', 24.

international initiatives abroad during this period, where his path often intersected with that of ICSID's other founders. In 1951, he attended the Milan Triennale, where talks were already held to establish an international design body among the participants, including Misha Black.[18] Two years later the American designer attended an international design congress in Paris as a delegate of SID, and from 1957 acted as a jury member for the design award Signe d'Or scheme, held by design organizations in the Benelux countries and operating with international juries, and which included some of ICSID's board members.[19] Alongside his involvement in the professional design community, Muller-Munk also participated to the Cold War efforts. The designer served as advisor on the International Cooperation Administration (ICA) programme,[20] and from 1955 PMMA was appointed to help the so-called developing countries raise the quality of their domestic products as part of the United States' wider attempt to win support in the Cold War race.[21] Muller-Munk was also actively spreading the gospel of raised productivity in the Organisation of European Economic Co-operation (OEEC) seventeen member states, where from 1960 he would conduct seminars and workshops on the relationship between management, engineering, marketing and industrial design.[22] Thus both professionally and politically, Muller-Munk looked inward and outward, a stance that was facilitated by his diplomatic know-how, prestigious address book and multilingual skills.

The idea of ICSID had originated in France, where the first official presentation of such a global design body took place at the Congrès International d'Esthétique Industrielle (International Congress of Industrial Aesthetics), organized by the President of the Institut d'Esthétique Industrielle, the design promoter Jacques Viénot, in 1953. Viénot organized the congress following his attendance to an international industrial design congress held in London in 1951, and organized by the CoID as part of the Festival of Britain, where more than 300 participants from thirteen different countries had been present. Amazed by the scale of the festival and by the international design congress, Viénot set out to host a similar gathering in Paris. The event featured sixty-nine speakers from thirteen countries and witnessed Viénot's attempt to promote the creation of an international 'liaison committee' for design. While the majority of participants at this event deemed the establishment of such an organization to be premature, Muller-Munk quickly sided with Viénot, as he also believed that the international growth of design activities

---

[18] Misha Black, 'International', 1957, DCA/12/165, Design Council Archive of the University of Brighton Design Archives.
[19] Javier Gimeno-Martínez, 'The Signe d'Or Award Scheme from 1956 to 1960: The Economic Reasons for "Good Design"', *Konsthistorisk Tidskrift/Journal of Art History* 79, no. 3 (2010): 130.
[20] Arthur Pulos, *The American Design Adventure, 1940–1975* (Cambridge, MA: MIT Press, 1988), 242.
[21] Er et al., 'U.S. Involvement in the Development of Design in the Periphery', 20–3.
[22] By then, several of these member states housed ICSID's member societies. Pulos, *The American Design Adventure*, 242.

made 'urgent the formation of an organisation for liaison and coordination'.[23] Two years later, SID formally agreed to continue to discuss the foundation of an international committee of coordination with the British Society of Industrial Artists (SIA) and the Institut d'Esthétique Industrielle.[24] The 'International Liaison Committee of Esthétique Industrielle' was subsequently created during a constitutive meeting in Paris, in 1956.[25] By then, societies that were primarily located in industrialized countries had been invited to join the venture,[26] with representatives from the United States, Britain, France, West Germany, Belgium, Italy and India attending the constitutive meeting; members from Swedish, Dutch, Swiss, Canadian, Japanese, Danish and Finnish societies, although they had been invited, were not able to attend or failed to answer the invitation.[27] Muller-Munk rapidly dominated ICSID's first gatherings. During the 1956 meeting, the designer was appointed as President of the Provisional Committee, while Misha Black was appointed as Vice-President, Pierre Vago as Secretary-General and the Belgian designer Robert Delevoy as Treasurer.[28] A year later, the American designer was voted as ICSID's President during ICSID's first formal meeting in London, on 29 June 1957.[29] Overseeing ICSID's operations, Muller-Munk rapidly set out to pursue political and economic interests within the organization, as its founder and long-standing board member.

Exporting American professional standards

Defender of the philosophy of *esthétique industrielle* (industrial aesthetics), Viénot had founded his design vision on progressive humanism, an ideology which was grounded in the notion of 'useful beauty'. Through this approach, Viénot believed that the overall enhancement of 'industrial aesthetics' would help society to modernize while achieving aesthetic harmony, a contribution which would benefit humankind morally, spiritually and socially.[30] After having institutionalized this discipline through the establishment of the Institut d'Esthétique Industrielle

---

[23] Peter Muller-Munk report, 1955, IDSA Archives, Box 68.
[24] Peter Muller-Munk to Pierre Vago, 20 June 1955, IDSA Archives, Box 68.
[25] Peter Muller-Munk report, 1955, IDSA Archives, Box 68.
[26] Jacques Viénot, 'Fondation du Comité de Liaison Internationale d'Esthétique Industrielle', *Esthétique Industrielle*, no. 22 (1956): 33.
[27] Minutes of Meeting held on 13 April 1956, Paris, p. 2, AAD/3/1980/44, MBA.
[28] Pierre Vago, 'Paris-Londres-Stockholm-Venise', *Esthétique Industrielle*, no. 42–43 (1959): 7.
[29] Minutes of first meeting of International Council of Societies of Industrial Designers, 1957, p. 11, The Archive of Art and Design, Misha Black holdings, AAD 3-1980, 44.
[30] Catherine Millet, 'Roger Tallon Designer', in *Roger Tallon, Itineraires d'un Designer Industriel* (Paris: Editions du Centre Pompidou, 1993), 29; Jocelyne Le Bœuf, 'Jacques Viénot and the "Esthétique Industrielle" in France, 1920–1960', *Design Issues* 22, no. 1 (2006): 50.

(Institute of Industrial Aesthetics, IEI) in 1950,[31] Viénot envisioned an organization that would assist in disseminating industrial aesthetics beyond French borders. Such an organization also needed to coordinate professional as well as social, artistic and philosophical matters. Viénot was nevertheless quickly put aside, and a coalition was formed between Muller-Munk, Black and Vago, who together favoured a focus on professional standards and business interests.[32] Muller-Munk believed in the necessity to create an organization that would develop the quality of design practice internationally, ultimately securing trade and economic benefits. During this period, the design profession still had a tenuous status in most industrialized countries and struggled to receive recognition from governments, industry and commerce, leading to raised attempts at establishing a professional model by the early 1950s.[33] In contrast, by the 1950s, industrial design in the United States had already made significant progress towards its public and legal recognition, partly through its professional organizations, the IDI (Industrial Designers Institute) and SID.[34] Moreover, within the wider containment and economic strategies of the US abroad, a marketing-led approach to the profession became increasingly exported to the so-called developed and developing nations.[35] This process took place when new technologies, which were mainly exported by the United States, 'dramatically influenced the way in which industry organised its manufacturing almost on a worldwide basis'.[36] In this context, Muller-Munk ceaselessly promoted the necessity to develop the maturity of the design profession internationally, an endeavour he acknowledged as essential to 'help to establish the designer for industry as a key technician in the modern world'.[37] Regarding American design expertise as the most advanced, the designer on multiple occasions presented it as the ultimate stage of development for the design profession,[38] a discourse which fuelled his attempts to export American design standards through SID. During his presidency of the American organization, the designer orchestrated the presentation of SID's products abroad, such as through travelling photographic exhibitions, which were sent to France, Austria, England, India and Australia (see Figure 3.2).[39]

---

[31] 'Inauguration de l'Institut d'Esthétique Industrielle', *Esthétique Industrielle*, no. 1 (1951): 16.
[32] Tania Messell, 'Constructing a "United Nations of Industrial Design": ICSID and the Professionalization of Design on the World Stage, 1957–1980', Doctoral Thesis, University of Brighton, 2018, 62.
[33] Jocelyne Le Boeuf, *Jacques Viénot (1893–1959): Pionnier de l'Esthétique Industrielle en France* (Rennes: Presses Universitaires de Rennes, 2006), 114.
[34] Er et al., 'U.S. Involvement in the Development of Design in the Periphery', 20.
[35] Sparke, *An Introduction to Design and Culture*, 186; Er et al., 'U.S. Involvement in the Development of Design in the Periphery', 22.
[36] Ibid., 137.
[37] Peter Muller-Munk, 'Report on Meeting of International Council of Societies of Industrial Designers', *ASID* Newsletter supplement XII, no. 7 (1957), Misha Black Archive, The Archive of Art and Design, AAD 3-1980, 43.
[38] Peter Muller-Munk, 'L'Esthétique Industrielle aux Etats-Unis', *Esthétique Industrielle* (1953): 73.
[39] Ibid., 108.

Muller-Munk also often received designers and industrialists from abroad and oversaw tours of foreign designers throughout the country during this period, which points at his active attempts at disseminating American manufacturing and design methods.[40] As an extension to these initiatives, Muller-Munk also shaped the image of SID abroad to differentiate itself from foreign organizations. It was indeed under Muller-Munk's initiative that the name of the organization was changed from the 'Society of Industrial Designers' to the 'American Society of Industrial Designers' (ASID) in 1955, a process which underlined Muller-Munk's

FIGURE 3.2 Ilona and Peter Muller-Munk upon their return from travels in Europe, *Pittsburgh Press* (12 October 1936). Courtesy of the Pittsburgh Post-Gazette

---

[40] Delphia, 'PMMA', 106.

dual pursuit of international exchanges and American interests. As seen next, the designer pursued these efforts once again within ICSID.

Muller-Munk would use several strategies to promote American design expertise during the Council's early years. These involved the coordination of American products or photographic displays in the international exhibitions held by the international council in the 1950s and 1960s and shaping ICSID's innerworking and outlook on design professionalization by promoting American ways of designing during ICSID's General Assemblies and Congresses. Between June 1957 and June 1958 ICSID's Executive Board conducted a survey, the findings of which were reported upon by Muller-Munk. The survey examined the geographical spread of the profession and the characteristics of design organizations located in twenty countries throughout Latin America, Asia and Africa. Applying ICSID's design definition, which reduced the industrial designer's practice to industrial and craft processes defined by commercial nature, Muller-Munk considered only nine out of thirty-three bodies surveyed as qualifying as societies of professional industrial designers, societies that were based in the United States, Canada, Denmark, France, Holland, Japan, Norway, Sweden and Britain.[41] The designer moreover regarded the ASID as 'The [underlined in original] recognised society of professional industrial designers in the world'.[42] Having established these differentiations, Muller-Munk set out to increase the design expertise of ICSID's membership, in particularly in Europe, where he saw the newly established Common Market has affording ample opportunities to strengthen commerce between countries through the pursuit of good design.[43] Hence as ICSID's president told delegates in Stockholm, 'in this dawn of industrial design […] actual professional competence is the first demand raised by ICSID towards its members'.[44]

To achieve the latter, Muller-Munk regularly admonished the profession to develop its own standards of practice and to harness the growing complexity of management and manufacturing. To begin with, Muller-Munk advocated the need for ICSID's members to cut their bonds with peripheral professions. For the designer, a focus on professional interests was necessary within ICSID to 'unify the creative people connected with industry', as by including architects, graphic designers and stage designers, industrial design risked losing its distinctiveness.[45] Moreover, as part of PMMA, Muller-Munk had promulgated the necessity for the designer to operate as a coordinator among other experts, who would oversee the

---

[41] Peter Muller-Munk, 'Report Number One', December 1958, pp. 2–4. Misha Black Archive, The Archive of Art and Design, AAD 3-1980, 51.

[42] Peter Muller-Munk, 'Report on International Coordinating Committee of Industrial Design Societies', IDSA Archives, Box 68.

[43] 'Industriella Formgivningen Bevarar Nationalkaraktären', *Dagens Nyheter* (17 September 1959): 6.

[44] R. S., 'The Glamorous Designer Yields to the Professional Industrial Designer', *Stockholms-Tidningen*, no. 52 (17 September 1959): 2–3.

[45] Letter from Peter Muller-Munk to André Hermant (Formes Nouvelles), 3 September 1957, ICSID Archive, University of Brighton Design Archives, ICD/09/11/1.

development of a product from initial market research to manufacturing methods and final rendering.[46] This design vision, grounded in a rhetoric of long-range planning and problem-solving, similarly permeated the designer's discourse in ICSID. During his presidency, Muller-Munk promoted the notion of industrial design expertise as inextricably linked with the idea of planning and efficient modernity, through which he aimed to communicate America's leading position in modern management and technology, and by implication, design. For the designer, the logic of design reflected the growing rationality of planning sciences, at a time when there was a growing admiration for the American model for productivity and management in Europe.[47] In contrast with his early years as a silversmith, Muller-Munk rejected the understanding of the designer as a secluded artist, which he saw as prevailing in Europe. Indeed, while he acknowledged 'the flash of discovery, the lonely agony of artistic creation' of design practice, the philosophy through which design was created did not represent the determining factors of practice.[48] As shared in his valedictory address during ICSID's first General Assembly in Stockholm, in 1959, Muller-Munk rather regarded ICSID as a manifestation of a larger movement towards political and economic international collaboration, in which 'economic isolationism and sovereignty are dead-unworkable-suicidal, and [where] only the team can survive and prosper in a world of the fair-play of teamwork'.[49] In his view, a shift was needed from the European belief in the notion that the designer is 'the hero, the genius, the boss, […] the only agent of creation, of authority, and of progress' to the team action and group responsibility, which he regarded as 'one of the most revolutionary developments of our age'.[50]

Muller-Munk's attempts to transform ICSID into an essentially professional design organization succeeded. Proposing to change ICSID's name from the 'International Council of Societies of Industrial Design' to the 'International Council of Societies of Industrial Designers', this action received the majority of votes during ICSID's first formal meeting in 1957.[51] Such a change implied that the Council represented practitioners mainly, as opposed to promotional members, thereby putting the accent on the organization's overarching professional character. As part of this strategy, Muller-Munk also divided the organization into professional and non-professional organizations and worked towards awarding the control of the organization to the former during his presidency. As was voted during ICSID's first formal meeting in June 1957, under Muller-Munk's instigation, the organization was to host two categories of membership: 'Full

---

[46] Delphia, 'PMMA', 84–7.
[47] Bruno Strasser, *La Fabrique d'une Nouvelle Science: La Biologie Moléculaire à l'Age Atomique, 1945–1964* (Florence: Olschki, 2006), 364.
[48] Polly Miller, 'ICSID: Stockholm Convention', *Industrial Design* 6, no. 10 (October 1959): 73.
[49] Ibid., 73.
[50] Ibid.
[51] Messell, 'Constructing a "United Nations of Industrial Design"', 77.

Members' and 'Associate Members'. While Full Members represented societies that included more than half industrial designers, Associate Members represented the remaining of societies, including councils of industrial design. Muller-Munk, backed up by ICSID's British members, removed Associate Members' voting rights on professional issues, a decision which for the American designer constituted 'a measure of maturity in this field'. This was so since reserving professional affairs to recognized practitioners would contribute to the profession's recognition nationally and abroad and would help to dissociate the profession from allied disciplines,[52] thereby drastically reducing the agency of members representing diverse professional models. Alongside shaping ICSID on a specific professional standard, this decision also helped preserving the control of the organization by American societies: the United States was indeed the only country that was represented by two Full Members, the IDI and the ASID. Their voices could therefore not be dismissed within the international forum. Tirelessly advocating the use of the terminology 'industrial design' among ICSID's members, Muller-Munk also led the latter to be voted as the official term during ICSID's first General Assembly, held in Stockholm in 1959. This decision was met with discontent by several of ICSID's members, who had favoured the preservation of local terms. However, as the term 'industrial design' was voted, it sealed the dominance of the English language and a particular design heritage within ICSID, while the terminology was officially adopted in many nations subsequently. In particular, this decision for Muller-Munk reflected 'the significant influence of the United States on European design'.[53] Thus championing the leadership of American design within ICSID, Muller-Munk's actions radically transformed the outlook and membership policies of the organization during its early years. As seen next, these efforts were also sparked by overlapping Cold War and cross-border commercial interests.

Furthering political and economic agendas

Muller-Munk was closely involved in contributing to American Cold War containment strategies in the 1950s. The decade witnessed the involvement of American designers in the Cold War efforts, through which the practitioners gained access to new spheres of influence. As Alpay Er, Fatma Korkut and Özlem Er write, this situation resulted from two developments: On the one hand, the US government set out to increase its participation to overseas international trade

---

[52] Peter Muller-Munk to André Hermant, 3 September 1957, ICSID Archive, University of Brighton Design Archives, ICD/09/11/1.

[53] Peter Muller-Munk, 'Situation of Industrial Design in the European Market', extract from *Product Engineering* (1959) in *Esthétique Industrielle*, no. 44 (1959): 36.

fairs in response to the Soviet Union's extensive representation at such gatherings. On the other, the International Cooperation Administration (ICA), the State Department agency responsible for all US foreign assistance programmes, had launched its technical assistance programme aimed at pro-Western or neutral so-called 'developing countries' to build a positive image of the American way of life overseas and to prevent the spread of Soviet influence in non-communist nations.[54] In this context, the ICA programme strengthened the view of the designer as 'a generalist rather than a specialist' and by employing a large number of American designers for the ICA's undertakings,[55] 'cast the American designer in the role of "economic diplomat".'[56] Under this guise, design was to enhance the competitiveness of national production through assistance with design and marketing, thereby increasing commerce and stabilizing political elements 'in favour of American democracy'.[57] Muller-Munk was closely involved in the trade fair exhibitions abroad, and in the ICA's design assistance programme in the so-called developing countries, which he saw as essential in the wider Cold War context. As he shared with the American House Foreign Affairs Committee in 1957, the year ICSID was established: the 'weaker [...] needy nations [have] only two places to look for [technical help] – to the Soviets and to us'.[58]

Muller-Munk became involved with the design of American exhibitions in trade fairs abroad following the Office of International Trade Fairs (OITF)'s turn towards designers to contribute to such important political and commercial undertakings. Here, as the American magazine *Industrial Design* reported, designers were charged with being 'propagandists', by both presenting America and formulating the nation's approach to other nations through ingenious exhibit designs.[59] At the time when Muller-Munk presided over the ASID, the design organization cooperated with the OITF to locate practitioners who could oversee such assignments. As a result of this, PMMA was charged with the exhibit designs of several fairs, which could show between fifty to two thousand American products, and which taking place in Turkey, Syria, Yugoslavia and Italy and other nations, 'often confronted communist displays head-on'.[60] On the other hand, Muller-Munk became also closely involved with the ICA. Interestingly, the latter appeared to be aware of the ICSID initiative, most likely through Muller-Munk. In 1955, James M. Silberman of the ICA had invited SID, which was then presided over by Muller-Munk, to form a subsidiary corporation charged with coordinating knowledge transfers between American and foreign practitioners and managers.

---

[54] Er et al., 'U.S. Involvement in the Development of Design in the Periphery', 21.
[55] Ibid., 33.
[56] Ibid., 24.
[57] Pulos, *The American Design Adventure*, 224.
[58] Rachel Delphia and Catherine Walworth, 'New Frontiers', in *Silver to Steel: The Modern Designs of Peter Muller-Munk*, ed. Rachel Delphia and Jewel Stern (London: Prestel, 2015), 125.
[59] Jane Fiske Mitarachi, 'Design as a Political Force', *Industrial Design* 4, no. 2 (February 1957): 39.
[60] Delphia and Walworth, 'New Frontiers', 125.

This body was to be named the 'International Council for Industrial Design' (ICID), and would handle tours for foreign industrial designers, managers and other interested individuals from Europe and 'under-developed areas [sic]' to study industrial design and manual industry in the United States, and vice versa.[61] The initiative was dismissed as 'overambitious' by some members of SID,[62] however following this event Muller-Munk became involved in assisting with a study tour of European executives of industrial firms in the United States in 1957, and possibly on other occasions thereafter, as written above.[63]

Moreover, Muller-Munk became an advisor on the ICA's industrial technical cooperation programmes, within which PMMA was contracted to assist Turkey and Israel to increase the competitiveness of their products in 1955.[64] In Turkey PMMA was employed to enhancing traditional craft products such as woodwork, ceramics and copperware to cater for the tastes of foreign markets, and to develop the cross-border distribution and promotion of such goods.[65] These assignments were pursued through the Turkish Handicraft Development Office (THDO), established by the Turkish Handicraft Development Board, and which was led by a member of PMMA and a Turkish industrial engineering graduate from Cornell University. In Israel Muller-Munk focused in enhancing domestic and exportable goods, while offering industrial design training. It resulted in the establishment of the Israel Product Design Office (IPDO) in Haifa, an industrial design office funded by the American and Israeli governments. There, design assignments were carried out by Israeli and American designers, while seminars on design practice were regularly held. While these appointments resulted in financial returns for PMMA, they were also used to enhance the image of the firm. Indeed the THDO and the IPDO were often promoted as extensions of PMMA, through shared letterheads graphics and the inclusion of Israeli and Turkish products in the firm's promotional documents, as Rachel Delphia and Catherine Walworth have noted.[66] Thus beyond political objectives, Muller-Munk also benefitted from the financial benefits of such Cold War assignments, an approach he also embraced within ICSID.

Arthur Pulos has suggested that the German-born American designer became involved with the design assistance programme of the ICA due to his role as a founding member of ICSID.[67] Conversely, Muller-Munk's pursuit of American Cold War interests extended to the international design organization, which

---

[61] SID Executive Secretary to Peter Muller-Munk, 22 July 1955, IDSA Archives, Box 67.
[62] Ibid.
[63] Pulos, *The American Design Adventure*, 234.
[64] Er et al., 'U.S. Involvement in the Development of Design in the Periphery'.
[65] Bahar Emgin, 'Traces of Peter Muller-Munk Associates in the History of Industrial Design in Turkey', *A/I/S Design Storia e Ricerche* (2017), p. 10. http://www.aisdesign.org/aisd/en/traces-of-peter-muller-munk-associates-industrial-design-turkey [accessed 12 April 2019].
[66] Delphia and Walworth, 'New Frontiers', 124.
[67] Pulos, *The American Design Adventure*, 236.

the designer regarded as an effective forum to instrumentalize during its early years. Firstly, Muller-Munk capitalized on ICSID's internationalist aims to shape its membership. The designer invited the Indian Institute of Art in Industry and the Japan Industrial Designers' Association to join the organization in 1956,[68] these countries at the time saw ICA interventions on local design practices.[69] The designer also pressed for the exclusion of Soviet involvement during ICSID's early years. As he wrote to Pierre Vago in 1955, while ICSID was not be affected by racial questions, 'political considerations, however, would have to be considered in their proper perspective, as we have already agreed on the exclusion of government-controlled societies'.[70] Indeed, 'the Americans are very sensitive about the whole

FIGURE 3.3 Sigvard Bernadotte and Peter Muller-Munk at the Special Exhibition of Industrial Design held at the Moderna Tekniske Museet during ICSID's General Congress in Stockholm, 1959. Ulf Hård af Segerstad, 'The Congress for Industrial Design Will Open the Eyes of the Sceptics', Svenska Dagbladet (1959): 11. Courtesy of the Svenska Dagbladet/Keystone/TT

---

[68] Misha Black, 'International Committee for Industrial Design', Misha Black Archive, The Archive of Art and Design, 1956, AAD 3-1980, 44.
[69] Pulos, *The American Design Adventure*, 241.
[70] Peter Muller-Munk to Pierre Vago, 29 August 1955, IDSA Archives, Box 68.

question of representation from "Iron Curtain" countries on [sic] ICSID', while it was 'difficult to find an organization of Russian designers who represent industrial designers in our sense of the word', as Misha Black noted in 1959.[71] This decision affected ICSID, as it was not before the mid-1960s that contact was initiated between ICSID and societies in the Soviet Union.

Moreover, Muller-Munk's stress on professional development of ICSID's membership aimed at contributing to Cold War efforts by assisting countries in preserving their political independence by securing a stable and promising economy (see Figure 3.3).[72] Alongside professional competence, Muller-Munk and ICSID's American Council Members, SID and the IDI, also advocated the need for the organization's membership to favour trade interests. In 1955 they proposed the creation of an international exhibition calendar, an international directory of professionals and the creation of documents aimed at facilitating international collaborations.[73] As Arthur Pulos writes, while between 1957 and 1958 more than 1,600 American corporations had established new quarters in Europe, by 1963, 'sixteen American design firms had offices abroad and thirty were serving foreign clients from the United States'.[74] In total, American designers had contracts with manufacturers in twenty-two European and Latin American countries and in Japan.[75] The creation of an international organization facilitating international business alliances was therefore essential for Muller-Munk. The organization thus witnessed Muller-Munk's attempts to pursue political, economic and professional interests, which would ultimately serve American imperatives. However, as seen next, while Muller-Munk tirelessly defended the interests of American design profession and Cold War efforts, his involvement in ICSID was also shaped by a personal belief in the benefits of cross-border exchanges, while Muller-Munk was very much alone in contributing to ICSID's norm production and activities on the American side, which further constrained his actions. The designer thus continuously straddled the border between national and international professional spheres, a strategic albeit tenuous position, which would ultimately affect American representation in ICSID.

International aspirations and cultural brokering

While Muller-Munk pursued political and professional agendas, the designer also acted as a cultural broker, a go-between, whose transnational life and values also

---

[71] Quoted in Messell, 'Constructing a "United Nations of Industrial Design"', 96.
[72] Pulos, *The American Design Adventure*, 224.
[73] Jacques Viénot, 'Productivité de l'Esthétique Industrielle: Conférence prononcée à Liège le 9/12/54', *Esthétique Industrielle*, no. 15 (1953): 33.
[74] Pulos, *The American Design Adventure*, 235.
[75] Ibid.

shaped his actions in ICSID and the American design community. To begin with, Muller-Munk was acutely aware of the necessity to avoid the homogenization of cultural aspects of design practices. Muller-Munk's appreciation of European designs, which had shaped his early metal work as seen earlier, later on extended to the region's mass-produced products. As the designer admitted in 1959, in some instances 'on finds a higher level of aesthetic understanding and knowledge [in Europe] than in the US'.[76] As part of his design consultancy abroad, the designer moreover believed that industrial designers needed to preserve national heritage alongside the opening of 'worth-while vista into the future',[77] and that growing standardization should not eradicate national product specificities, but on the contrary clarify the national characteristics of products in an increasingly competitive marketplace.[78] While this discourse was harnessed by other nations in the same period,[79] Muller-Munk's appreciation of foreign ways of doing transcended business interests, at times countering American perspectives. When members of the IDI critiqued the theoretical debates that had taken place during ICSID's General Assembly and Congress in Paris in 1963, Muller-Munk indeed deemed the discussions of high interest, and noted that 'when Paris gets to be like New York, it will no longer be Paris'.[80]

Moreover, Muller-Munk had anglicized and hyphenated his name following his arrival to the United States from Müller Munk to Mueller-Munk, and later to Muller-Munk,[81] which denoted a desire to assimilate with American spelling and customs. Muller-Munk's awareness of dual identity nevertheless remained, as the designer acknowledged in a report submitted to the ASID in 1959, that he was of 'pragmatic American-European or European-American nature'.[82] Thus while Muller-Munk's actions within ICSID often prioritized American design ways, his origins remained part of his public persona and professional and personal outlooks. Beyond valuing European ways of doing and recognizing his composite identity, Muller-Munk also became an advocate of the pacifying qualities of international cooperation. He had entered adolescence in the midst of the First World War, during which he lost his uncle, Ernst Munk, on the Russian front.[83] Later on, when conditions worsened in Nazi Germany, Muller-Munk's family was forced to flee the country, with drastic consequences. Among Muller-Munk's close family,

---

[76] Peter Muller-Munk, 'Situation de l'Esthétique Industrielle dans l'Europe du Marché Commun', *Esthétique Industrielle* 9, no. 44 (1959): 36.
[77] ASID, 'Industrial Designers Hold International Meeting in Venice, Italy', IDSA Archives, Box 67.
[78] Muller-Munk, 'Situation de l'Esthétique Industrielle dans l'Europe du Marché Commun', quoted in Katarina Serulus, *Design and Politics: The Public Promotion of Industrial Design in Postwar Belgium (1950–1986)* (Leuven: Leuven University Press, 2018), 121.
[79] Serulus, *Design and Politics,* 121.
[80] Peter Muller-Munk to Ramah Larisch, 19 August 1963, IDSA Archives, Box 67.
[81] Delphia and Stern, *Silver to Steel.*
[82] Peter Muller-Munk, 'Report on the International Council of Industrial Designers', 1959, IDSA Archives, Box 68.
[83] Stern, 'Berlin: Family', 20.

his mother and aunt fled to the United States, and his father and second wife, Franz and Susanne Müller, sought refuge in France. While Müller died of natural cause there, Susanne Müller's escape was short-lived as she perished at Auschwitz, ultimately.[84] These events could have led the designer to consider cross-border exchanges as the answer to conflicts, a belief he continuously advocated during his involvement with ICSID. As Muller-Munk shared with the members of SID in 1953, regarding the international coordination committee,

> I am deeply convinced that individually and collectively we have only two choices. We can erect walls and barriers behind which to live in seclusion in imaginary protection of our safety. We can even prosper for a while yet behind an intellectual and creative Maginot line; but I do not believe that our peace, our safety, and our prosperity will last very long in such isolation. It is my conviction that we must go out and meet each other, that we must expose ourselves to new ideas.[85]

Beyond the 'enlightened self-interest' that would result from such expansion,[86] Muller-Munk displayed a belief in the peace-inducing role of international cooperation, which, as he wrote in correspondence, had always been an issue 'close to [him]'.[87] This conviction reflected a wider belief in the pacifying qualities of international organizations in the immediate post-war period.[88] For Muller-Munk, this belief nevertheless did not contradict with the open pursuit of American professional and political interests.

Muller-Munk was also a key driver of American involvement in ICSID. As Misha Black shared with the delegates of ICSID's General Assembly in Stockholm, without the 'tireless enthusiasm' of Muller-Munk, 'ICSID could not have survived'.[89] The designer's commitment to contribute to ICSID, and to act as spokesperson for American industrial designers was however very much a 'one-man affair', as Muller-Munk noted in 1963.[90] ICSID was not very popular in the United States by the late 1950s. Muller-Munk struggled for IDI and the ASID to present a unified front within ICSID,[91] as inter-institutional conflicts prevailed between both organizations, due to diverging understandings of design definitions and other matters.[92] Moreover, both societies were wary of the alleged

---

[84] Rachel Delphia, 'Professor Muller-Munk, Industrial Designer', in *Silver to Steel: The Modern Designs of Peter Muller-Munk*, ed. Rachel Delphia and Jewel Stern (London: Prestel, 2015), 65.
[85] Peter Muller-Munk, 'Report on International Coordinating Committee of Industrial Design Societies', IDSA Archives, Box 68.
[86] Ibid.
[87] Peter Muller-Munk to Misha Black, 3 May 1955, IDSA Archives, Box 68.
[88] Iriye, *Global Community*.
[89] Miller, 'ICSID: Stockholm Convention', 71.
[90] Peter Muller-Munk to Ramah Larisch, 19 August 1963, IDSA Archives, Box 67.
[91] Peter Muller-Munk to Georges Beck, 17 July 1959, IDSA Archives, Box 68.
[92] Delphia and Stern, *Silver to Steel*, 106.

lacking expertise of ICSID's wider membership, whose members were attributed the same number of votes as the American societies.[93] This worry reflected a wider insecurity regarding the international spread of industrial design practice and institutionalization, which prevailed in the subsequent decades. As Pulos noted in 1988, while designers in other countries and on an international level were moving towards a common centre, 'Americans [were still] repairing the fences that kept them apart'.[94] Muller-Munk, in contrast, had embraced this phenomenon since the very beginning.

Incidentally, practical and personal considerations also affected Muller-Munk's involvement in ICSID, which was regularly restricted by overlapping engagements and a lack of financial means. As he reported to the ASID in 1959, 'this can no longer be delegated to a single interested individual. Speaking for myself, I have had it – believe me!'[95] Muller-Munk's triple commitment to the ASID, ICSID and his design studio made it an everyday struggle, and the designer at times longed to reduce his functions. As he wrote in 1959, following the General Assembly in Stockholm:

> As it is, I would be ready for a fine case of schizophrenia – acting one minute as President of ICSID and then the next one as Chairman of the ASID Foreign Relations Committee, were it not for the fact that every once in a while I still get pretty much involved with the practice of industrial design. I look forward to next year when I will be able to enjoy being nothing else but a local character.[96]

In particular, Muller-Munk struggled to fulfil his duty within ICSID due to the distance and slow communication, much of which his design studio, PMMA, covered.[97] As he communicated to ICSID's General Secretary Josine Des Cressonnières in 1964, 'even though jet travel has done a lot of distance, distance is still here and so are money and time'.[98] The designer moreover regularly complained that ICSID expected funds to come from the United States, expectations which Muller-Munk regularly had to temper. Thus, while Muller-Munk ruthlessly pursued Cold War agendas and the spread of American professional design models, his involvement in ICSID was also shaped by overlapping beliefs and

---

[93] Letter from John Blake to Josine des Cressonnières, 16 November 1961, ICSID Archive, University of Brighton Design Archives, ICD/10/25/3.
[94] Pulos, *The American Design Adventure*, 255.
[95] Peter Muller-Munk, 'Report on the International Council of Industrial Designers', 1959, IDSA Archives, Box 68.
[96] Peter Muller-Munk to Donald L. McFarland, President of ASID, 16 March 1959, IDSA Archives, Box 68.
[97] Peter Muller-Munk to Sally G. Swing, Executive Secretary of ASID, 16 March 1957, IDSA Archives, Box 68.
[98] Letter from Peter Muller-Munk to Josine des Cressonnières, 16 November 1964, ICSID Archive, University of Brighton Design Archives, ICD/06/10/6.

imperatives alongside material restrictions, which highlights the complexity of the émigré condition within such an environment.

Conclusion: Peter Muller-Munk and American legacy on ICSID

The chapter traced Muller-Munk's multiple trajectories between American design circles and ICSID's transnational network and activities, within the wider Cold War context. In particular, it outlined how it was through the designer's multifaceted identity and allegiances that American representation was secured within the organization, whose inner-working and design outlooks became predominantly shaped on Western and in particular Anglo-Saxon design visions and practices. Muller-Munk achieved this by shaping ICSID's membership criteria, ICSID's official design terminology, and the organization's name, which answered American political and economic interests, as well as professional imperatives. While the dominance of American and British practices prevailed in the decades that followed, ICSID expanded its professional aims to embrace wider issues, such as design promotion and the social contribution of the profession from the 1960s onwards. This expansion took place alongside the rapid entry of societies from the so-called developing and socialist economies, which also affected the organization's activities and outlooks.[99] Alongside these shifts, and following Muller-Munk's death in 1967, American involvement in ICSID became more sporadic,[100] and it was not until the 1980s that the United States gained its place again in the organization, with Arthur Pulos's Presidency between 1979 and 1981, and the first ICSID Congress and General Assembly held in the United States, and planned by the IDSA, 'Worldesign', in Washington in 1985.[101] Within a renewed interest in Muller-Munk's life and career,[102] the designer's central role in international professional initiatives is therefore important to understand, both as an example of émigré actors within transnational design networks and of international diplomacy informed by the émigré condition.

---

[99] Messell, 'Constructing a "United Nations of Industrial Design"'.

[100] In 1970, IDSA's President, Eugene Smith, complained that the organization was not involved in any of ICSID's activities, for instance. Eugene Smith to Richard Latham, 12 May 1970, IDSA Archives, Box 67.

[101] ICSID, 'Worldesign 95', *ICSID News* (October 1984), ICSID Archive, University of Brighton Design Archives, ICD/09/1/5.

[102] The first monographic museum exhibition of Muller-Munk's life and work was held at the Carnegie Museum of Art in 2015–2016, 'Silver to Steel: The Modern Designs of Peter Muller-Munk'. An exhibition catalogue accompanied the exhibition: Delphia and Stern, *Silver to Steel*.

4 INTERNATIONAL DESIGN ORGANIZATIONS AS GLOBAL DESIGN ADVOCATES: ROMANCE, REALITY AND RELEVANCE?

Jonathan M. Woodham

Introduction

The origins of many design organizations in the industrialized world in the years following the end of the Second World War lay in their collective desire to advance the notion of the designer as a valued member of society alongside architects, engineers, scientists, lawyers, medics and other groups with recognized professional standards. Despite a number of notable – largely national – precedents, this aspiration assumed a more international edge in the post-1945 decades when bodies such as the International Council of Societies of Industrial Design (ICSID), the International Council of Graphic Design Organizations (Icograda) and the International Federation of Interiors Architects/Designers (IFI) were launched in 1957, 1963 and 1963, respectively. Over succeeding decades the international membership of all three organizations underwent considerable growth, their executive ambitions moving beyond the transnational development of the design profession, and design standards in their quest to become recognized as authoritative non-governmental global advocates for design itself. In the twenty-first century such aspirations re-emerged formally with ICSID's re-designation as the World Design Organization (WDO)™ in 2015 and Icograda's recasting as the International Council of Design (Ico-D) in 2013. However, the extent to which such global design organizations have genuinely become effective promoters of 'a better environment and society' through design or, in effect, brand agencies acting on behalf of their own globally oriented agendas is open to question even if the latter are the embodiment of a romantic attachment to an idea that has been ever present in their outlook for almost sixty years. There has been an increasing number of doctorates and articles addressing particular aspects of these professional design organizations[1] as well as bringing new knowledge to the fore through archival and other forms of primary research. However, the activities of these leading design bodies have not always been systematically appraised in terms of the explicit ways in which they have actually changed subsequent behaviours or strategies in the wider world. For example, the activities of Giu Bonsiepe, ICSID Vice-President 1973–1975, and a prominent figure in ICSID discussions about design in so-called developing countries,[2] were later reappraised from different perspectives. Sulfikar Amir considered that

> [o]ver two decades after Papanek and Bonsiepe first conveyed their ideas of design for Third World societies [sic], the social and economic condition of these societies has not changed much if one compares them today with thirty years ago … The idea of design for the third world advocated by either Papanek or Bonsiepe did not really work because they lacked political dimensions in their implementation.[3]

Similarly, Singanapalli Balaram, organizer of the first joint meeting of the UNIDO and ICSID at the National Institute of Design (NID) in Ahmedabad that resulted in the widely referenced 'Ahmedabad Declaration' (1979), wrote thirty years later that

> [t]he 1979 Declaration should have been a watershed event for design in India, inspired as it was by the Indian experience. Yet in India the 'Declaration' remained largely as a statement of intent and less a thing of achievement … this perception remained until India in the 1990s gave up its over-protective economic and industrial policies.[4]

---

[1] These include T. Messell (2018) 'Globalization and Design Institutionalisation: ICSID's XIth Congress and the Formation of ALADI, 1979', *Journal of Design History* 13, no. 1 (February 2019): 88–104; T. Messell 'Contested Development: ICSID's Design Aid and Environmental Policy in the 1970s', in *The Culture of Nature in the History of Design(ed)*, ed. K. Fallan (London: Routledge, 2019), 131–46; D. Souza-Diaz, 'International Design Organizations and the Study of Transnational Interactions: the Case of Icogradalatinoamérica80', *Journal of Design History* 32, no. 2 (May 2018): 188–206; and A. J. Clarke, 'Design for Development ICSID and UNIDO: The Anthropological Turn in 1970s Design', *Journal of Design History* 29, no. 1 (2016): 43–55; also 'Design, Development and its Legacies: A Perspective on 1970s Design Culture and its Anthropological Intents', in *Flow of Forms/Forms of Flow: Design Histories between Africa and Europe*, ed. K. Pinther and A. Weigand (Bielefeld: transcript Verlag, 2018), 110–23.
[2] Such as Giu Bonsiepe. (1975) 'Development through Design', UNIDO, a Working Paper prepared for UNIDO at the request of ICSID. University of Brighton Design Archives: ICSID at DES/ICD/6/4/1/5.
[3] S. Amir, 'Rethinking Design Policy in the Third World', *Design Issues* 20, no. 4 (2004): 69. 'Third World' was a term adopted in the post Second World War era but with the increasing lack of specificity of the term 'Second World', generally identified with the Communist Soviet Bloc, following the end of the Cold War became less useful.
[4] S. Balaram, 'Design in India: The Importance of the Ahmedabad Declaration', *Design Issues* 25, no. 4 (Autumn 2009): 54–79. Balaram was an advisory board member of *Design Issues* and a winner of the UNIDO-ICSID award for Design Development. See also Darlie Koshy, *Indian Design Edge: Strategies for Success in the Creative Economy* (New Delhi: Lotus Collection, 2008), 24. Koshy was Director of NID (2000–2008) and drafted the Indian National Design Policy (2007).

And design writer Victor Margolin, commenting on the *Worldesign 85* ICSID Congress in Washington D.C. in a 1985 *Design Issues* editorial, felt that 'little has been achieved in shifting the paradigm of design from a client-oriented perspective to one that defines its own purposes and finds ways to achieve them'.[5]

Unlike the majority of nationally based and publicly funded design bodies around the world which have to answer to their paymasters through annual reports and other documentation produced, at least in part, to secure continued funding from the public purse, independent design organizations in general do not face such intense scrutiny in terms of their continuity. It is comparatively straightforward to find supportive documentation about the ways in which bodies, such as ICSID and Icograda, were founded, along with their aims and activities, as their most obvious traces mainly take the form of narratives of success. Understanding and analysing failure is an important but often underplayed facet of the design world, its leaders, internal and external discussions, politics, publications, funding and influence. Although the availability of a design organization's archives considerably enhances this dimension of research, the extent to which content has been assembled, shaped, edited and preserved is dependent on the professionalism and diligence of its board members and, most particularly, administrative officers or often powerful Secretary Generals whose interests in telling or concealing a particular story may encourage selectivity, report writing or even omission. This chapter seeks to consider ways in which international design organizations have sought to position themselves as global design advocates from the 1960s to the present.

ICSID: Early years

ICSID was originally formed as the International Council of Societies of Industrial Designers in 1956 at the instigation of the French Institut d'Esthétique Industrielle, itself established in 1951 by Jacques Viénot (leading figure in the promotion of industrial design in France), the American Society of Industrial Designers (formerly the Society of Industrial Designers) and the British Society of Industrial Artists (SIA, established in 1930). Although ICSID's HQ was provisionally located at 17 Quai Voltaire, Paris 7ème, the organization's first formal meeting was held in London on 27 June 1957 where representatives from nine countries proposed a provisional constitution that was formally adopted at ICSID's First General Assembly in Stockholm, Sweden, in September 1959. At this stage it was agreed that the Council's working languages would be English and French, raising some interesting contrasts between the two. For example, the capitalized 'Industrial Designer' equivalent in French was 'styliste industrielle', an instance perhaps of what presaged the Council's serial preoccupation with definitions and redefinitions of the term 'industrial design' on and off over the next six decades, whether as

---

[5] Victor Margolin, 'Editorial', *Design Issues* 2, no. 1 (1985): 3.

ICSID, as a member of the International Design Alliance (IDA), or its current nomenclature as World Design Organisation (WDO). It is maybe worth noting that the sister organization IFI's official language was German until 1972 when its outlook and engagement had become far more international in its membership and outlook and it took up English as its official language of communication and business.

Key among ICSID's early aims and functions, like so many other national and international design organizations that proliferated throughout the industrialized world in the post-1945 decades, was its mission to improve standards in industrial design, to raise the professional standing of industrial designers, and to develop national and international exchange of, and networks for, teaching and learning practices in higher education. The Council also expressed keenness to exchange ideas and information across the spectrum of the creative visual arts, architecture and design, as well as engineering and technology, and to disseminate information on major national and international exhibitions in order to prevent unnecessary duplication.

From the early days there were ongoing concerns about the shape, nature, purpose and modus operandi of ICSID with Misha Black,[6] a founder member and the organization's second President (1959–1961), already proposing amendments to the original constitution in a document tabled for the General Assembly of 1961, held in Venice. Among them was the decision to change the name of the organization to the International Council for Societies of Industrial Design (rather than Industrial Designers). Reflecting the views of the Executive Board in a draft letter to all Presidents of ICSID's Constituent Societies, Black also suggested that 'the main concern is that the existing Constitution is based on the assumption that each country should have the same number of votes irrespective of the number of constituent societies in each country and the size or status of these societies'.[7] He was concerned that when 'societies from the emergent industrialized countries in Africa and elsewhere become affiliated to ICSID as we hope they will' the Council would need to reconsider voting rights in order to address current 'anomalies' and 'less satisfactory' situations, presumably centred around notions of 'leadership' or 'control'.

ICSID experienced considerable growth, increasing representation from nine countries at its 1957 inauguration to sixteen full member and eleven associate member societies from nineteen countries by the time of its third Congress in Paris in 1963. Though unevenly spread, the Council's geographical coverage

---

[6] Misha Black (1910–1977) was a leading figure of the British design establishment. In addition to a variety of important public and private posts in industrial design consultancy, education and promotion he was also President of the Society of Industrial Artists (1954–1956), Master of the Faculty of Royal Designers for Industry (1955–1957).

[7] ICSID Archive File 01-1-2 *Constitution* 1961. Unless otherwise stated all ICSID Archive files are held in the Design Archives at the University of Brighton.

included Europe, North America, Europe (including countries from the Eastern bloc), Asia, Africa and Oceania-Australasia. Nonetheless, it can be inferred that in its earlier decades the ICSID leadership saw industrial design as a field where expertise was firmly vested in the countries of the (Western) industrialized world, although this view was increasingly contested in the 1970s and 1980s.

ICSID in the changing world of the late 1960s and 1970s

Precisely what Misha Black had in mind in terms of ICSID Constitutional membership voting rights in Paris in 1963, the year in which ICSID was granted special status with UNESCO (United Nations Educational, Scientific and Cultural Organization), remains somewhat opaque. However, at a number of later ICSID Congresses, especially from the late 1960s onwards, the interventionist ideology of ICSID and UNIDO (United Nations Industrial Development Organization), in respect of the wider role and significance of industrial design, came under fire from many delegates representing the 'developing countries' – the professional design societies of which were increasingly represented in the ICSID membership.[8] As a result, the position of the ICSID Executive Board became both ambivalent and uncomfortable in the shaping of the Council's international aims, as will be discussed further below. Nonetheless, the core of ICSID's executive ambitions remained focussed on the professional standing and high-level competence of industrial designers seeking to align themselves with international organizations, government departments and societies of industrial design around the globe, as well as with disciplines germane to a successful implementation of industrial design policy as they saw it. But this miscellany of wide-ranging aspirations was also held in check by critical voices and realities outside the design world.

The 1969 ICSID London Congress

In his opening address at the 1969 Sixth ICSID Congress held in London on the theme of 'Design, Society and the Future', Lord Blackett, a distinguished scientist and policy advisor to the British Labour Party, drew attention to the so-called developing countries when commenting that most delegates were concerned with the ills of the affluent world, only a fifth of the world's population: 'The problems of the rest – the other four fifths – are vastly greater. Their problems are not so much

---

[8] See A. J. Clarke, op.cit. and footnotes 2, 3, 4, a short overview in Jonathan M. Woodham, 'Design, Histories, Empires and Peripheries', in *Design Frontiers: Territories, Concepts, Technologies*, ed. P. L. Farias et al. (São Paolo: Blucher, 2012), 454–7; and Gabriel Patrocínio and José Mauro Nunes, *Design & Development: Leveraging Social and Economic Growth through Design Policies* (São Paolo: Blucher, 2019). English edition. Originally published in Portuguese in 2016.

pollution and congestion but the elementary needs of [what Blackett saw as] a civilised life.'[9] What he may not have realized was that at the immediately preceding ICSID General Assembly[10] the membership had approved the establishment of a Special Commission to explore and advise on the best means utilizing design in so-called developing countries.

As a Nobel Prize-winning scientist Blackett also sought to moderate what he clearly felt were the overly unrealistic ambitions of the design world to lay claim to areas of knowledge and expertise that were beyond their capacities. He expressed the view that 'the words "Design" and "Designer" should not be overworked' and that designers should

> carefully avoid giving an impression that they intend to invade verbally large areas of industrial and national management, economics, sociology, operational research and in fact, planning in general.[11]

However, the question remains, even today, about the extent to which designers – many of whom have achieved international recognition and celebrity status in relation to the prominent bodies that they have worked for and advised or iconic objects that they have designed – are strategically expert in those areas highlighted by Lord Blackett.

Student voices and the ICSID Sixth General Assembly (1969)

In 1967 ICSID's Education Commission had unsuccessfully proposed to set up a commission for students and yet there was a clear ongoing unwillingness of the ICSID Board to allow a platform for student participation at the London ICSID Congress of 1969 despite the fact that the ICSID 1969 General Assembly held immediately before the Congress had found a way to recognize future student involvement. However, the appointment of a student working party to consider the 'extent and nature' of the ways in which students might 'collaborate with ICSID at world level'[12] was in reality only a minor concession as students attending the Congress were allocated little opportunity to hold any meaningful debates or even ask questions of the speakers. Nonetheless, student opinion was far more radically expressed than had been anticipated, as seen in a statement released at the 1969

---

[9] 'ICSID comes to town', News Section, *Design* magazine, October 1969, 16.
[10] General Assemblies immediately precede the ICSID Congresses and are restricted to ICSID members only, providing an opportunity for electing the Executive Board, amend the Constitution, and bring the membership up to date on the work carried out by the Board over the previous two years.
[11] Ibid.
[12] 'Assembly votes for Reid and emergent nations', News Section, *Design* magazine, October 1969, 16.

ICSID Congress itself. In this the students were highly critical of their elders, feeling that the 'real problems' relating to the Congress theme 'Design, Society and the Future' had been 'systematically eluded', particularly in relation to the word 'Design' that was felt to lack definition, 'especially [with] no new definition corresponding to the needs of the future'.[13] Students also felt that although Congress had been critical of many of the real problems facing society it was unrealistic in its view that 'the designer, as an environment "Gestalter", has capacity but also the power of creating a better world for the future'. The students' uncompromising conclusion was that

> [s]ince the true causes of the evil we are in are essentially political and have a name i.e. exploitation of man by man, and on a more acute level, exploitations of underdeveloped countries [sic] by rich countries, this is the level where the discussions should have taken place.[14]

This disassociation of student activists and young professionals from the orthodoxies of mainstream industrial design was in some ways analogous to the situation at the 1970 International Design Conference at Aspen (IDCA) where the theme was 'Environment by Design'. Dissenters, like their student predecessors at the 1969 London ICSID Congress, were also opposed to the lack of political engagement and the non-participatory format of the Aspen conference.[15]

But it was not just in terms of ICSID's design ideology that a somewhat negative overview of its 1969 London Congress was framed. The News Section of *Design* magazine, published monthly by the state-funded Council of Industrial Design in the UK, provided a thumbnail sketch of the somewhat elitist social atmosphere given off in London. In addition to an evening reception for delegates in the presence of Princess Margaret (sister of Queen Elizabeth II) at Lancaster House, London, hosted by President of the Board of Trade Anthony Crossland, and dinner and a champagne reception at the Royal College of Art, it was reported that

> off stage, delegates and their wives enjoyed a seemingly endless round of cocktail parties, coffee breaks and exhibitions – finally whooping it up at the Designers Ball in the doomed [sic] setting of the Clapham Transport Museum.[16]

---

[13] 'ICSID Parthian Shot' in the News Section, *Design* magazine, November, 1969, 23. Tania Messell, in her PhD thesis *Constructing 'A United Nations of Industrial Design': ICSID and the Professionalisation of Design, 1957–1980*, University of Brighton, discusses other aspects of ICSID specific student friction with the organization's Executive in section ix of Chapter 3: 'Negotiating "Design, Society and the Future": ICSID's London Congress', 141–4.

[14] Ibid. The use of terms such as 'developed world', 'underdeveloped world' and 'developing world' were widespread during the earlier historical timeframe covered in this chapter.

[15] See, for example, Alice Twemlow, 'A Look Back at Aspen 1970', *Design Observer*, 28 August 2008. https://designobserver.com/feature/a-look-back-at-aspen-1970/7277/ [accessed 5 December 2019].

[16] 'ICSID comes to town', loc.cit.

The latter event was in fact the Annual Designers Ball given by the Society of Industrial Artists and Designers (SIAD). The roots of the SIAD were grounded in the Society of Industrial Artists (SIA, founded in 1930) that, like many other artistic societies at the time, can be seen to have existed as much as a gentlemen's club as a tightly organized pressure group campaigning for the improved status of professional designers.[17] The ways in which this restricted the opportunities for women in the design and architectural worlds of that era have been explored in a number of publications.[18] Before the Second World War, there was no rigorous process for admitting members, the majority being drawn from the ranks of what was known as 'commercial art' with a number showing their talents in the design of the menus that accompanied the lunches and dinners of their many restaurant-based meetings.[19] There is considerable room for further research into the ways in which education, club, society and organizational membership, class and gender have influenced the ways in which design organizations and design policymakers interlink, think and legislate.[20] This might usefully be extended to ICSID's and Icograda's Executive Boards and influential members.

The Seventh ICSID Conference in Ibiza, Spain

'Design in a Changing Society' was the theme chosen for the Seventh ICSID Congress of 1971 held in Cala de Sant Miquel on the Spanish holiday island of Ibiza. Organized by the Spanish industrial design society ADI-FAD (Agrupacíon de Diseño Industrial-Fomento de las Artes Decorativas, established in 1960 and a member of ICSID since 1961), it was seen by many critics, delegates and visitors to have been a reaction against the previous heavily structured, stage-managed and organized ICSID Congresses to date. The 1969 London Congress had typified such a controlled approach: the London-centric Society of Industrial Artists and Designers (SIAD, established in 1930) and the UK's Council of Industrial Design (COID, established in London in 1944), funded by the British state's Board

---

[17] Armstrong, Leah, 'A New Image for a New Profession: Self-image and Representation in the Professionalization of Design in Britain, 1945–1960', *Journal of Consumer Culture* 19, no. 1 (2017): 377–401.
[18] See, for example, the collection of essays in J. Seddon and S. Worden, *Women Designing: Redefining Design in Britain between the Wars* (Brighton: University of Brighton, 1994).
[19] This is well observed in Armstrong, Leah, 'Steering a Course Between Professionalism and Commercialism: The Society of Industrial Artists and the Code of Conduct for the Professional Designer 1945–1975', *Journal of Design History* 29, no. 2 (May 2016): 161–79.
[20] See, for example, J. M. Woodham, 'Managing British Design Reform I: Fresh Perspectives on the Early Years of the Council of Industrial Design', *Journal of Design History* 9, no. 1 (1996): 55–65; see also J. M. Woodham, 'British Modernism between the Wars: An Historical "Léger de main"?' in *Tradizione e Modernismo: Design 1918/1940 – Atti del convegno*, ed. A. Pansera (Milano: L'Arca, 1988), 7–10.

of Trade, were influential in its structured organization. This unspoken British projection of itself as an international design leader was a microcosm of one facet of a particular profile of the design establishment[21] that many younger designers were keen to dissipate.

The Ibiza Congress provided a decidedly more relaxed environment than its immediately preceding General Assembly in Barcelona on mainland Spain, a country in the final years of Franco's authoritarian regime, marking a wider, more politically, socially and environmentally charged climate for design discourse in the 1970s. Research carried out over four decades later for the MACBA (Museum of Contemporary Art of Barcelona) multimedia exhibition commemorating the Ibiza ICSID Congress positioned the event as a turning point for Catalan design. Entitled *La utopía es possible* the MACBA exhibition included magazines, correspondence, film and sound and ran from June 2012 to January 2013. It saw the republication of a number of contemporary *Domus* magazine articles[22] and viewed the original event as 'an experiment in socialization, an example of how communal work, vitality, intellectual reflection and leisure can be used to promote dialogue between different practices'.[23] Ibiza had opened up to international tourism in the 1960s and the Spanish organizers of 1971 event sought to promote a far more informal atmosphere than had pervaded previous ICSID Congresses. Organized as an 'open' congress the official conference hub and accommodation was housed in the recently opened package holiday Hotel Cartago where there were a number of 'Speaking Rooms' where themes chosen by the delegates could be discussed. The strikingly colourful, inflatable and impermanent 'Instant City' was an architectural experiment in new forms of communal living and provided students and delegates with alternative, flexible accommodation on the beach, in marked contrast to the fixed, static, ziggurat-like concrete forms of the official Congress hotel built into the side of the valley above. Led by Spanish architecture students Carlos Ferrater and Fernando Bendito, working with pneumatic architectural expert Professor José Miguel de Prada Poole[24] from the Calculus Centre of the University of Madrid (CCUM), students were heavily involved in Instant City's construction on the Ibiza site, one that had been widely associated as an enclave for artists and intellectuals since the 1930s. Bendito and Ferrater oversaw the creation of a fluid set of spaces

---

[21] In the 1960s, John Reid was President of the SIAD and of ICSID, FHK Henrion President of the SIAD and of Icograda, and Lord Paul Reilly the Director of the UK Council of Industrial Design (later Design Council) and Treasurer of ICSID. At this time Edgar Kauffman Jr and Eliot Noyes were also members of the ICSID Executive Board.

[22] Including 'Ibiza: the 1971 ICSID Congress', *Domus* 509, originally published April 1972, reflecting a number of different national perspectives, and republished 18 November 2012. https://www.domusweb.it/en/from-the-archive/2012/11/18/ibiza-the-1971-icsid-congress [accessed June 2019].

[23] Ethel Baraona Pohl, 'Utopia Is Possible', *Domus*, 15 October 2012, a review of the MACBA exhibition. https://www.domusweb.it/en/art/2012/10/15/utopia-is-possible.html [accessed 29 June 2016].

[24] Prada Poole, José Miguel de. (1972). 'La ciudad instantánea, la ciudad cambiante', *Arquitectura*, no. 157.

in which students and professionals could gather, engage, discuss, communicate, work, perform and socialize. Seen from an historical distance, Ibiza's Instant City might be seen to represent an ICSID-driven aspiration to project itself as a more liberal and progressive organization. However, the differences between the ways in which the Congress ethos was characterized by ICSID's Secretary General, Josine de Cressonnières[25] in her accounts of the event and the momentum on the ground, are rather different. With an invitational manifesto written by urbanist, economist and writer Luis Racionero, Instant City featured in many underground magazines of the time as well as more mainstream publications such as *Architectural Design*[26] which, in its December 1971 issue, devoted several pages to it alongside propositions by Peter Cook, a prominent figure in the UK collective Archigram whose own concept of Instant City had emerged in 1968–1969, and the Florence-based Superstudio.

Kyoto's ICSID Congress 1973: 'Soul and Material Things'

ICSID's next Congress was held in Kyoto. Hosted by the Japanese Industrial Designers' Association, an ICSID member from the organization's earliest days, and chaired by Kenji Ekuan, President of the Japan Industrial Design Association, the chosen theme was 'Soul and Material Things'. The event attracted almost 1,800 Japanese delegates outnumbering the 448 from 37 countries. It was a landmark event, bringing together for the first time the Western and Asian design worlds and also marked a 'post-European' sense of global inclusivity as it attracted speakers from Africa, Brazil, Mexico and Taiwan.[27] The topics discussed in Kyoto generally inclined towards the philosophical and spiritual rather than economics and science, marked by a keynote on 'The Soul and Material Things' by Japanese social anthropologist Tadao Umezawa.[28] This talk appeared to confuse many non-Japanese delegates while Jean Baudrillard's special lecture on 'Design between Political Economy and Symbolic Exchange' unsettled many Japanese attendees. Other key addresses included Sen Sushitsu, head of the Urasenke Japanese tea school, on 'The spirit of tea in everyday life' and Frederic Vester, a German

---

[25] K. Serulus, *Design& Politics: The Public Promotion of Industrial Design in Postwar Belgium (1950-1986)* (Leuven: University of Leuven, 2018), 187.
[26] Toal O'Muiré, 'Instant City, Ibiza', *Architectural Design*, 12 December 1971, 762–7.
[27] Toshino Iguchi, 'Reconsideration of the World Design Conference 1960 in Tokyo and the World Industrial Design Conference 1973 in Kyoto: Transformation of Design Theory' (2013). http://design-cu.jp/iasdr2013/papers/1183-1b.pdf [accessed March 2016].
[28] ICSID (1975). Hito no kokoro to mono no sekai = Soul and material things: ICSID '73, Tokyo: Hozansha.

expert on biochemistry and ecology, on 'The environment in an age of crisis'. The sociocultural differences between the Japanese and non-Japanese delegates inhibited discussion, something that a number of delegates and commentators regretted, particularly since opportunities to reflect at length on contemporary social, political, economic and environmental concerns that had begun in the 1960s were not to the forefront of the professional design agenda despite the fact that Western society's growing concerns about the impact of ecological damage had been put on notice for more than a decade. Several speakers at the Kyoto Congress expressed concern that attitudes to design for the 'developing' world were paternalistic, that resources were finite and that the countries of the industrialized world were unable to handle technological growth. This equivocal position of designers at the 1973 Congress was reflected in an Editorial in *Design* magazine that stated that

> contrasted with all this was the conspicuous consumption apparent at the conference: the over abundance of specially produced attache [sic] cases full of reams of bumph, the 2000 specially painted bicycles provided for the use of participants (which lay idle outside the conference hall because the conference programme was so heavy), free gifts of whisky and disposable razors for all.[29]

As already indicated, professional design organizations such as ICSID were finding it difficult to locate themselves in the fast-changing world of the 1960s and 1970s. There was an increasing credibility gap between what was increasingly seen as the need for designers to respond meaningfully to society's growing concerns about the social, environmental and ecological consequences of relentless technological 'progress' and their meaningful capacity to do so.

It should be mentioned briefly that the path for other prominent international professional design organizations, such as Icograda, ICSID's sister organization representing visual communication design across the globe, was also beset with difficulties – especially financial – in a period of rapid social, economic, cultural, technological and environmental change. At the Council's 1974 General Assembly in Krefeld, Germany, Kurt Weidermann, the outgoing President, felt it necessary to report that he was 'convinced that icograda [was] in need of reform from top to bottom in order to exist'.[30] *Design* magazine also reported that the gap between the design world and specialist external expertise in related fields was significant at the 1974 Congress since

---

[29] 'ICSID in Japan', *Design*, 300, December 1973, 26.
[30] Editorial Comment, 'icogrumble', *Design*, 312, December 1974, 30.

what worried many of the 200 designers who attended was that a number of distinguished non-designers from the fields of communication and education had been invited, and they can hardly be impressed by what they saw.[31]

ICSID: From the 1970s and the 1980s into the new millennium

Increased emphasis on the potential importance of a central future role for design in a world threatened by the social and environmental consequences of continuing to stoke the fires of global consumption was taken further at the 1976 ICSID Conference on 'Design for Need: the Social Contribution of Design', the papers of which were published in book form.[32] Held at the Royal College of Art (RCA), London, in April 1976, the conference raised many pressing social and environmental issues, although the extent to which it generated real change is rarely articulated. This may be accounted for straightforwardly, as Madge indicated in a seminal historiographic article in 1993: '"Design for Need" simply went out of fashion in the 1980s'.[33] The history of design over the past 50 years has been heavily populated by design manifestos, reports and conference papers that highlight contemporary concerns rather than realistic agendas for action or result in demonstrable impact, in common with the generation of national design policies over a longer duration.[34]

Such a global trajectory continued through the following decades as ICSID facilitated the establishment of a number of Regional Working Groups in the 1970s and 1980s including the Asian, Mediterranean, Latin-European, Eastern European and Nordic Groups. Particularly visible over these years in the ICSID Archives are papers and correspondence relating to the Associación Latino de Diseño Industrial (ALADI, founded in Bogotá in November 1980) as well as those of the Asian Regional Group that first met in Tokyo in May 1979 and was formed of members of leading public and private design organizations from Australia, Taiwan, Hong Kong, Japan, South Korea and the Philippines. Nonetheless, as ICSID's Executive Board membership profile suggests (see Figure 4.1), through its very heavy domination by European and North American interests, the design priorities of emerging economies elsewhere in the world were somewhat overshadowed by more mainstream activities.

---

[31] Ibid.
[32] Julian Bicknell and Liz McQuiston, eds., *DESIGN FOR NEED: The Social Contribution of Design* (ICSID: Pergamon Press, 1977).
[33] Pauline Madge, 'Design, Ecology, Technology: A Historical Review', *Journal of Design History* 6, no. 3 (1993): 156.
[34] Jonathan M. Woodham, 'Formulating National Design Policies in the United States: Recycling the Emperor's New Clothes', *Design Issues* 26, no. 2 (2010): 27–46.

The changing executive board profiles of ICSID and Icograda: Geography and gender

Figures 4.1 and 4.2 are revealing in terms of the evolution of the composition of the ICSID and Icograda Boards in their transition to becoming the World Design Organization (WDO) and International Council of Design (icoD). Both

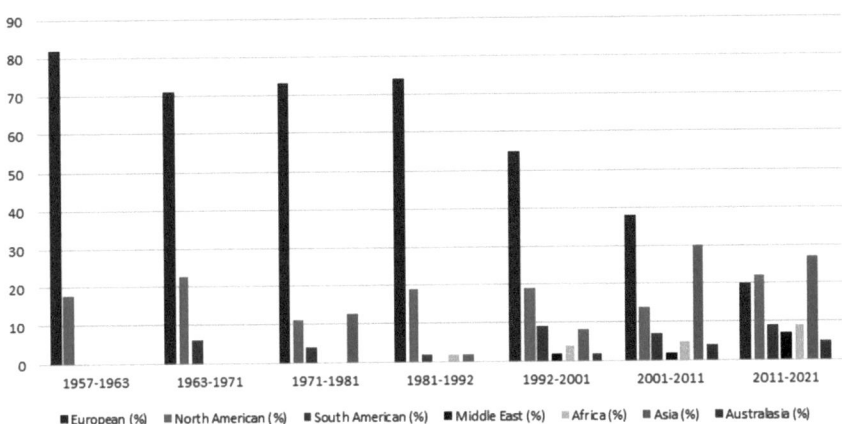

FIGURE 4.1 Geographical distribution of ICSID/WDO Executive Board of Directors Membership

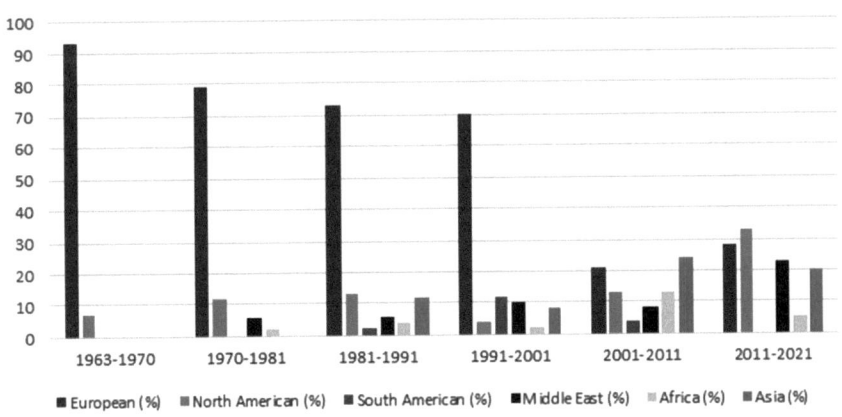

FIGURE 4.2 Geographical distribution of Icograda/ico-D Board of Directors

show a very strong European and North American domination from foundation to the millennium, with a rather more marked geographical distribution since 2010 when their respective self-generated moves to 'world' status have been enacted.

Figures 4.3 and 4.4 show the relative conservatism of both ICSID (WDO) and Icograda (ico-D) in terms of gender balance at Executive Committee/Board of Director level, although ico-D between 2011 and 2021 shows a more inclusive outlook (39: 61 per cent compared to 18: 82 per cent).

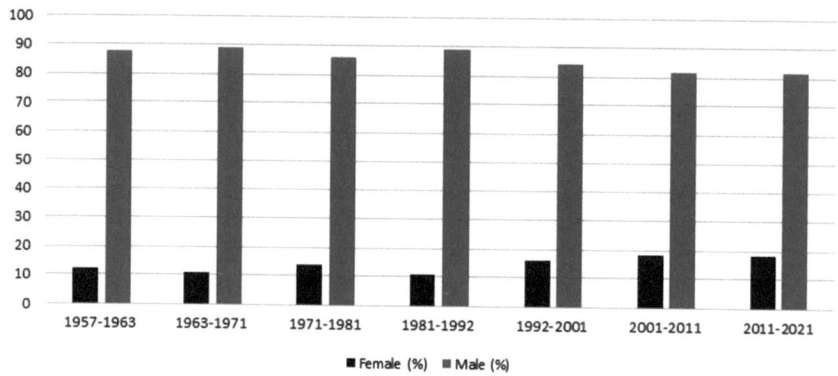

FIGURE 4.3 ICSID/WDO Executive Board of Directors Membership

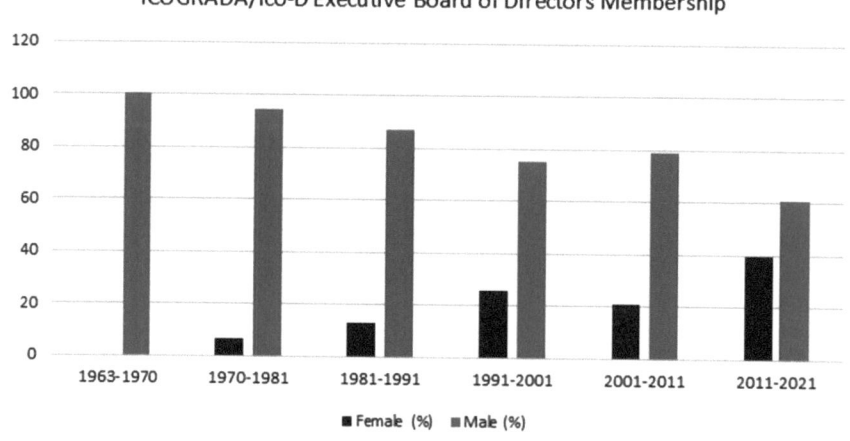

FIGURE 4.4 Icograda/ico-D Executive Board of Directors Membership

Global visions: 'World Cities of Design' and other projects

ICSID's aspirations to play an influential role in casting design as a major element in the making of a better world was part of an evolutionary process, building on the organization's consultative status with UNESCO, initiated in 1963, the United Nations Economic and Social Council (ECOSOC) in 1974, and the establishment of the ICSID-UNIDO Special Commission in 1973. Other significant collaborative initiatives included 'Design for the World' (established 1998), involving the three major international professional design organizations – ICSID, Icograda and IFI – with the assistance of the Barcelona Design Centre. 'Design for the World' supported the delivery of key design skills, knowledge and processes to those who most needed them, including victims of disasters, the disadvantaged, those in poverty and 'beyond the confines of the consumer market'. Supported by sponsorship and donations, it made possible the direct engagement of hundreds of designers in social housing projects, a refugee camp in Tanzania, and a graphic design AIDS awareness campaign. However, like so many design-led initiatives before it, Design for the World ceased to operate in 2003 due to a lack of sponsorship.

The ambition of assuming the mantle of design leadership on the world stage was also reflected in ICSID's 2003 Memorandum of Understanding with Icograda, its graphic communication professional counterpart, to establish a consolidate and more powerful federal body, the International Design Alliance (IDA). They were joined in 2008 by the third of the major professional international design organizations, the International Federation of Interior Architects/Designers (IFI).[35] And in 2011 the inaugural Annual IDA Congress was launched in Taipei, Taiwan, to replace the biennial Icograda World Design Congress as well as the joint Congresses of ICSID, Icograda and IFI that had taken place every six years since 1981. However, the International Design Alliance (IDA) was short-lived and was dissolved in 2013 with the cancellation of the projected IDA Congress in Istanbul, Turkey, due to political events. The IDA Executive had delegated the responsibility for the IDA Congresses to ICSID 'primarily because [the members] all believed that ICSID had the experience to handle this task'.[36] ICSID's unilateral withdrawal from the IDA in 2013 necessitated its dissolution, in line with the MoU on which the latter had been formed. ICSID stated that it intended to focus its 'limited'

---

[35] Confusingly, in this period of proliferation of design organizations and awards, an International Design Awards (IDA) Scheme was initiated in 2007 in the United States to mark design achievements in architecture, interior, product, graphic and fashion design.

[36] IFI Press Release of 17 September 2013: 'Reaction to Dissolvement of International Design Allowance (IDA) due to ICSID's Retirement'. http://kollectif.net/announcement-international-federation-of-interior-architectsdesigners-reaction-to-dissolvement-of-international-design-alliance-ida-due-to-icsids-retirement/ [accessed 2 January 2020].

financial resources to develop global collaborations with professional industrial design organizations. On 17 September 2013, on behalf of the IFI Executive Board, IFI President Shashi Caan sent a message to all IFI members communicating this news and, although highly diplomatic about the aims and operation of the IDA, mentioned that 'it became IFI's role to often act as a mediator' between ICSID and icograda; also that IDA, like 'all new and untested ventures ... came with inherent challenges of procedures, policy and finances'.[37]

The strategic use of the word 'world' in association with ICSID had been reinforced with the launch of the organization's annual 'World Industrial Design Day' on 29 June in 2007, ICSID's 50th anniversary. Mildly confusingly, in its own attempt to gain wider recognition as a world-relevant design organization, Icograda had launched its 'World Graphics Day' in 1995 on 27 April, morphing into 'World Communication Design Day' in 2012 – reflecting the organization's change of name to the International Council of Communication Design in the previous year – and then World Design Day in April 2015 following the organization's self-designation as the International Council of Design (ico-D). This followed the decision of the Council Members to adopt 'a visionary strategy to become a multidisciplinary design body' at the organization's 25th Anniversary General Assembly in 2013.

During these years ICSID also launched its biennial World Capitals of Design (WCD) programme with the designation of Torino, Italy, as the first of these capitals in 2008. Applications were invited against defined criteria that included information about the ways in which municipal government, industry, educational institutions and the population were able to demonstrate high levels of commitment to sustainable design-led urban policy and innovation that would result in a better quality of life. However, the very small Selection Group of five experts, including Past Presidents, considers applications and the number of cities applying for the distinction is generally modest, with a sole application for 2016. The designation of Torino as WDC was followed by Seoul, South Korea (2014); Helsinki, Finland (2012); Cape Town, South Africa (2014); Taipei, Taiwan (2016); Mexico City (2018); and Métropole europénne de Lille, France (2020).

A number of other ICSID projects featuring the word 'World' – such as the World Design Impact Prize, launched in 2012 – ultimately culminating in the decision of the organization to self-designate itself as the World Design Organisation (WDO) supported by a new Constitution to match. This was formally endorsed at the ICSID General Assembly in Gwangju in 2015. In the following year a series of World Design Talks were initiated by ICSID in the six regions of the organization (Africa, Asia, Europe, Latin America and Oceania) in the form of workshops that discussed local and regional challenges around the world that had widespread relevance and provided an agenda that promoted more sustainable consumption

---

[37] Ibid.

and production in line with the UN Sustainable Development Goals (SDGs) by 2030. These included 'Traffic Congestion' in Istanbul, Turkey (2016); 'Navigating Mobility Issues in Megacities' in Shanghai, China (2016); a return to 'Traffic Congestion' in Toluca, Mexico (2017); 'Responsible Consumption and Production in Rabat Morocco' (2017), 'Co-Living in Izmir', Turkey (2017); 'Designing the Futures of Water in Mexico' in Mexico City (2018); and 'Sustainable Cities and Communities' in Ljubljana, Slovenia (2019). Like many gatherings that are recorded in organizational histories and promotional ephemera, it is highly problematic to weigh up the *actual* impact that such events truly exerted, particularly given the rapid acceleration of numerous international design initiatives and activities on so many other national and global fronts, a number of which will be indicated below.

WDC counterparts: Creative cities, capitals of culture, global and international networks

In reality the notion of ICSID's World Capitals of Design was being enacted alongside a much wider unrelated drive across the world to highlight design as fundamental to urban enhancement. Among such projects was UNESCO's Creative Cities Network (UCCN) that was set in place in 2004 with nine creative cities from 9 countries, four years prior to the realization of ICSID's first WDC in Torino, Italy. The UCCN figure grew exponentially: by 2015 there were 180 Creative Cities from 72 countries; by 2019 a total of 246 Creative Cities with a commitment towards realizing UNESCO's 2030 Agenda for Sustainable Development (2019).[38] These globally scattered cities were designated in recognition of their commitment to embrace creativity as a strategic factor in sustainable urban development, of situating the creative and cultural industries at their centre and actively networking across the world. Forms of creativity associated with the 246 cities were distributed across seven fields: crafts and folk, art, design, film, gastronomy, literature, music and media arts. The first UNESCO Creative City of Design was Buenos Aires (2005) and by 2020 more than 30 cities in Africa, Asia, Australasia/Oceania, Europe, Eurasia, North and South America had been similarly designated. This compares with seven World Capitals of Design designated by ICSID (and its successor the WDO) between 2008 and 2020, with five of these WCDs recognized in both programmes.

Another scheme that predated ICSID's World Capitals of Design (WCD) was the European City of Culture programme established in 1985 by the French and Greek Ministers of Culture, Fritz Lang and Melina Mercouri, as a prospective

---

[38] *Voices of the City: UNESCO Creative Cities Moving towards the 2030 Agenda for Sustainable Development* (Paris: UNESCO, 2019).

network that would forge a closer bond between European nations through raising awareness of common histories and values, on the one hand, and the richness and diversity of European culture, on the other. In 1999 the designation was modified to European Capital of Culture and the aims embraced the ways in which cultural, social and economic benefits could underpin urban regeneration and raise cities' international profile, thus sharing some of the values of both the UNESCO Creative Cities of Design and later WCDs. By the time of ICSID's designation of Torino as the first World City of Design (WDC) in 2008, there had already been thirty-seven designated European Capitals of Culture in more than twenty countries.[39]

Other twenty-first-century design activities

The twenty-first-century global design calendar is heavily populated with design festivals, design weeks and activities associated with Cities of Design, as well as numerous other design and design-related conferences of many kinds that are independent of the WDO, ico-D or IFI. World's Fairs and Expos where design has been a prominent feature have been attracting many millions of visitors as well as being subject to considerable contemporary and historical analysis. Prominent among them were Paris (1900, 1925, 1937), New York (1939–1940, 1964–1965), Brussels (1935, 1958), Montréal (1967), Osaka (1970), Brisbane (1992), Seville (1992), Daejeon (1993), Aichi (2005), Shanghai (2010) and Milan (2015). A considerable array of other noteworthy design events throughout the year has also accelerated sharply in the late twentieth and early twenty-first centuries. For example, Designersblock (DB) was established in 1998 and has produced more than sixty festivals of architecture, design and illustration involving more than 3,000 creative companies with venues in more than a dozen countries. World Design Weeks, independent of the WDO, have also become a distinctive ingredient of the global design calendar. They are often held alongside major design festivals networking vehicles by connecting designers and companies on a local, regional, national and international stage, as well as integrating design educators, institutions and museums. Among the founders of the Design Week network were Dutch Design Week (established in 2005) with origins in late 1990s Eindhoven, Helsinki Design Week (also established in 2005), the largest design festival in the Nordic countries, and Design Week Mexico (established in 2009). Other early Design Week venues were established in Beijing (from 2009), Tokyo (2005–2016), Seoul (from 2002), Barcelona (established 2006) and Toronto (since 2011). Globally there are now more than fifty Design Weeks and closely related events taking place regularly across all continents.

---

[39] *European Capitals of Culture: The Road to Success from 1985 to 2010* (Luxembourg: Office for Official Publications of the European Communities 2009).

Design awards have also enjoyed a dominant profile in the world design calendar. Many were first awarded after the Second World War when design was seen to represent important added value in the fiercely competitive economic marketplace. Perhaps the most widely known in terms of cultural prestige were the Good Design Awards linked to the 'Good Design' Exhibitions (1950–1955) held at the Museum of Modern Art (MOMA), New York, curated by Edgar Kaufman Jr., Director of Industrial Design at the Museum (later a member of the ICSID Executive Board, 1969–1971). The scheme was originally held in partnership with the Merchandise Mart in Chicago and the prevailing aesthetic was attuned to European Modernism. In the twenty-first century, the GOOD DESIGN® Awards scheme is organized through the Chicago Athenaeum: Museum of Architecture and Design with designers and manufacturers from around 50 countries receiving awards annually.

In Europe, other awards came into being in the same years as the MOMA Good Design awards, including the Beauté France, the Compasso D'Oro (Italy) from 1954, the Design Innovationen award (Germany) from 1955, the Belgian Signe d'Or awards from 1956 and the UK's Council of Industrial Design's (COID) Design Centre Awards from 1957 to 1988. Josine de Cressonnières, who was also a long-standing stalwart in the organization of ICSID from 1963 to 1977 as its Secretary General, managed the Signe d'Or awards as well as the Belgian Design Centre from 1963.[40] Well connected with the politics of Belgian design and design policy, she was a major tour de force in building national and international connections such as inviting Misha Black (ICSID President from 1959 to 1961, and Board Member from 1957 to 1963) to serve on the selection committee of the Signe d'Or. There was a consciousness among many designers that, like a number of design organizations of this era, ICSID was something of a private club where personal friendships, design leadership and design jury roles overlapped, as they did across the wider Design Establishment.[41]

In Asia a similar austere aesthetic to that of 'good design' awards elsewhere also characterized the G-Mark Awards first organized through the Japanese Ministry of International Trade and Industry (MITI) from 1957. In 1998 the 'G-Mark' was reborn as the Good Design Award with very different criteria and areas of focus including sustainability and the environment. In 2019, 1,420 awards from a total entry of 4,772 were made across an extensive range of categories from 940 companies worldwide. The Korea Institute of Design Promotion (KIDP) established its GD (Good Design) Mark in 1985 and is managed by KIDP and sponsored by the Korean Ministry of Trade, Energy and Innovation. From the late twentieth century onwards, there has been a proliferation of such glittering

---

[40] Serulus, *Design & Politics*.
[41] For a discussion of Design Centres as shapers of, and shaped by, the transnational design community, see K. Serulus, '"Well-Designed Relations": Cold War Design Exchanges between Brussels and Moscow in the early 1970s', *Design and Culture: The Journal of the Design Studies Forum* 9, no. 2 (2017): 149–50.

prizes, including the Red Dot Awards that had evolved from the German Design Innovationen awards, winners of which had been incorporated into a permanent display in the Haus Industrieform in Essen, West Germany. There were major shifts in the closing years of the twentieth century when the Haus Industrieform was renamed Design Zentrum Nordrhein Westfalen, complete with a new corporate identity. Peter Zec, who was appointed to run it, became the founder and CEO of the Red Dot Award. He brought with him considerable experience of international design, including the Presidency of the Federation of German Graphic Designers and of the Association of German Industrial Designers. He also went on to serve on the ICSID Board from 1999 to 2007, including tenure as President (2005–2007). As its head, Zec oriented the Design Zentrum towards becoming a centre for hosting design congresses, trade fairs and seminars and exhibitions and was keen to promote German design leadership in Asia. The first Red Dot Award Museum had opened in Essen in 1997, followed by its counterparts in Singapore (2005) and Taipei (Taiwan, 2013). The global fashionability of design was also reflected in the opening of many other new design museums across the world, including the Design Museum in Holon, Israel (2010), designed by Ron Arad; the OCT Design Museum (2011), Shenzhen, China, designed by Studio Pei Zhu; the Museu de Disseny de Barcelona (2014) by MBM Architects; and the V&A in Dundee (2018), designed by Kengo Kuma.

By the twenty-first-century design awards had become almost *de rigeur* across the industrialized world as a means of demonstrating that a trading nation's designs could compete on aesthetic as well as technical levels, with due deference to sustainability and environmental considerations as they became constituents of the global design agenda. The China Red Star Design Award, established in 2006, was co-sponsored by the China Industrial Design Association and the Beijing Industrial Design Promotion Centre. It has remained the premier Chinese award for industrial design, covering a wide range of design fields from consumer goods and fashion to computing, medicine and science. Beginning with a modest entry of about 400 designs in its first year, there were almost 4,000 by 2009 when the award was endorsed by ICSID; by 2015 the number had risen to over 5,000. By 2019 the Red Star Award attracted more than 6,000 entries from more than 4,000 international companies and many globally recognized brands. The fact that selections were carried out by more than 40 experts from China, France, Germany, Switzerland, the UK, the United States shows the extent to which the scheme itself was emerging as a globally recognized brand of its own. Emphasizing the ever-expanding global nature of award schemes, the India Design Mark (I-Mark) was established in 2011 and managed by the government-funded Indian Design Council (established 2009). The I-Mark was formed in collaboration with the Japan Institute of Design Promotion (JDP) that had experience of design awards since 1957. Just as with many earlier design awards in Europe and the United States, the I-Mark was promoted as of significance for industry, consumers, designers and society at large, as well as representing value for money.

This vast number of Design Award schemes has generated a global meta-industry for the formation of selection committees, design juries, awards ceremonies and media coverage. They have also become powerful media-centric displays for promoting designers, manufacturers, and commercial companies, and provided opportunities for showcasing national of achievements. However, although the selection criteria have increasingly featured environmental sensitivity and sustainability as important considerations alongside the introduction of categories featuring capital goods and designs for public spaces and services, many awards ceremonies may be seen to have been a triumph of marketing over design.

From global to national design policies

In the early twenty-first century, numerous reports about national design policies were published across a wide range of countries and economies,[42] from the New Zealand Design Task Force's *Success by Design: A Report and Strategy Plan* (2003) and the American design communities' *Redesigning America's Future: 10 Design Policy Proposals for the United States of America's Economic Competitiveness & Democratic Government* (2009) to the Indian Government's approval of the India Design Policy in 2008. Less developed economies were discussed in key publications such as the *Creative Economy Report: The Challenge of Assessing the Creative Economy towards Informed Policy Making* (2008), produced by the UN Conference on Trade and Development and the UN Development Department although, tellingly, despite considerable emphasis on the Creative Economy (the first time the UN had published a comprehensive analysis on it), the amount of space devoted to design was limited to a few pages in what was a very substantial publication.

During these years, members of ICSID/WDO's Executive Board sought to become ambassadors for design in developing economies where they could meet politicians to demonstrate how design could become a tool for national economic and cultural growth.[43] Membership of the ICSID/WDO Executive Board had become significantly more globally diverse since the end of the twentieth century (Figure 4.1) and a rapidly increasing number of countries had been aligning themselves with design as a part of national policy since the 1960s. In 2008 Michael Thomson, President of BEDA (European Design Association) and ICSID Executive Board Member (2001–2005), was Chair of the 'Shaping the Global Design Agenda' Conference, the concluding official event of the 2008 ICSID Torino World Design Capital programme. The conference sought to develop the case for understanding how design could be situated as an essential ingredient

---

[42] Woodham, 'Formulating National Design Policies in the United States', 45–6.
[43] J. Woodham and M. Thomson, 'Cultural Diplomacy and Design in the Late Twentieth and Twenty-First Centuries: Rhetoric or Reality', *Design and Culture* 9, no. 2 (2017): 225–41.

of national strategies that sought to stimulate sustainable economic, social and cultural growth, something that had been happening on the ground internationally for a very long time. The invited speakers brought together a considerable range of expertise, including senior figures from the Department of Innovation Policies of the European Commission, the UK's Design Council, the Beijing Design Centre, the Italian Ministry of Economic Development, the Department of Industry and Commerce in the Design City of Nagoya, design education institutions in Italy and Finland, the Costa Rican Ministry of Culture and the Arab Engineering Bureau from Qatar. In his concluding remarks, Thomson stated that

> [t]he need to develop national design policies as soon as possible is becoming an urgent requirement felt all around the world, from Qatar to Costa Rica, from New Zealand to the Far East.[44]

Ico-D, the WDO's professional design organization's counterpart for more than fifty years, also had ambitions for influencing and shaping national design policy on the global stage. Although it had considering national design strategies at various points in its history, it established its National Design Policy Work Group (NDP WG) in 2015, a time when the ico-D leadership was considerably more geographically dispersed than in the twentieth century (Figure 4.2). WG representatives from around the world held regular meetings and a dedicated half-day forum took place at the ico-D Professional/Promotion and Education Platform Meetings at Art Center Pasadena in 2016.[45] Clearly there was considerable work yet to be done in terms of making contributions of significance as many of the conclusions of this group were quite elementary by comparison with what had been a field of detailed discussion, publication and application over many decades, particularly in the late twentieth and twenty-first centuries.[46]

Of international significance in such debates was the World Design Summit (WDS) held in Montréal, the 2017 UNESCO City of Design, held in conjunction with the General Assemblies and Congresses of several organizations ranging from ico-D's General Assembly to the International Federation of Library Associations' Congress, both held in Montréal. An important member of the WDS Steering Committee was David Grosmann, a long-standing ico-D Board of Directors member (1995–2003 and from 2013 onwards, including two terms as President). The WDS theme was 'Bring about Change by Design' and provided a platform for 30 keynote speakers, with over 500 talks from disciplines including architecture, landscape architecture, urban planning, graphic design, industrial design and

---

[44] M. Thomson, 'Discussing the Development of National Design Policies', Press Release, 12 November 2008. https://wdo.org/press-release/discussing-the-challenges-of-the-development-of-national-design-policies/ [accessed 10 November 2019].
[45] https://www.ico-d.org/platforms/pasadena-2016#programme [accessed June 2019].
[46] Woodham, 'Formulating National Design Policies in the United States', 33–46.

interior design. As well as a large design expo featuring design innovations and solutions to problems, more than 50 international organizations signed up to the resulting Montréal Design Declaration.[47] This was a call to action for governments, professional and educational bodies, civil society, designers and others to mobilize design as a major tool to help solve the growing range of social, economic, cultural and environmental global problems. Signatories included ico-D; the Bureau of European Design Associations (BEDA); the Cumulus International Association of Universities and Colleges in Art, Design and Media; the Design Research Society; and the Design for Social Innovation and Sustainability Network. In attendance were representatives from UNESCO, UNEP (United Nations Environment Programme), the OECD (Organisation for Economic Co-operation and Development) and ICLEI (Local Governments for Sustainability).

Conclusion

This consideration of globally oriented design organizations such as ICSID/WDO and, to a lesser extent, icograda/ico-D has indicated that both organizations have undergone considerable change from their early preoccupations with international design protocols and professional quality standards. They have increasingly sought to promote themselves as agencies for positioning design as an important means of enhancing social and cultural well-being across the globe. However, as has been indicated, for the most part their geographical reach has been quite restricted in terms of the representative membership of their Boards that for the most part of their histories have not demonstrated an inclusive outlook. For much of the twentieth century, the latter were weighted heavily in favour of Europe and, to a lesser extent, North America. A number of ICSID Congresses, such as those of 1969, 1971 and 1973 discussed in this chapter, have demonstrated fluctuating considerations across the global design world, although the particular ways in which major independent international design organizations might be seen internally to favour particular patterns of social and cultural networking are yet to be developed in detail. In the twenty-first century there has been considerable global design activity, much of it identified with awards, commercial activities and promotions, and civic and national policy agendas, the overwhelming majority of which have been independent of the WDO, ico-D or IFI. Over fifty years ago, Lord Blackett had cautioned his ICSID audience about assuming expertise in 'areas of industrial and national management, economics, sociology, operational research and in fact, planning in general'. While it is clear that design expertise has been built up considerably in these and other related areas, more recent aspirations of the WDO to advise on national design policies may be contrasted with their development over the past 180 years, particularly since the end of

---

[47] http://www.designdeclaration.org/declaration/ [accessed April 2019].

the Second World from when they have been accelerating with increasing pace until the present day. While there has been a widespread embrace of twentieth-century concepts such as the circular economy that has been gathering pace in the twenty-first century, there has also been a considerable recycling of design policy initiatives, particularly in the early twentieth-first century.[48] Nonetheless, both ico-D and the WDO have been involved in the promotion of design as a vehicle for improving wellbeing across the globe, including programmes such as World Capitals of Design and occasional high-profile initiatives such as World Design Summits. However, it may also be argued convincingly that such global design initiatives have been anticipated by the prolific work of other national and international agencies; also that, although personnel overlap in adjudicating and managing a number of the most prestigious design awards, the latter are largely independent of the WDO and ico-D. The Montréal Design Declaration (MDD, 2017) is clear in its agenda, as have been many design manifestos before it. These include the *Cumulus Kyoto Design Declaration* (2008),[49] supported by ICSID, BEDA, AIGA (American Institute of Graphic Arts) and EIDD (Design for All Europe), the Icograda Design Education Manifesto (2000), developed in relation to the organization's Millennium Congress in Seoul and published in seventeen languages,[50] or the minimalist *Scandinavian Design Council Manifesto on Nature, Ecology and Human Needs for the Future*.[51] Two questions remain, however: will the MDD become a meaningful blueprint from which impactful action will result? Or will it take its place alongside the many dozens of other design manifestos that have been formulated over the past 50 years, signed with great pomp and ceremony, and highlight a number of the more pressing design-related issues of its day?

---

[48] Woodham, 'Formulating National Design Policies in the United States'.
[49] Yrjö Sotamaa, 'The Kyoto Design Declaration: Building a Sustainable Future', *Design Issues* 25, no. 4 (2009): 51–3.
[50] Updated in 2010 and published and presented at the 2011 IDA Congress in Taipei.
[51] Reprinted in 1991 in *Design Issues*, vol. 8, 1, 78–9.

PART TWO

NATIONAL – INTERNATIONAL – TRANSNATIONAL

5 BECOMING THE INTERNATIONAL DESIGN CONFERENCE IN ASPEN

Robert Gordon-Fogelson

Consider two logos used to identify the same organization (Figure 5.1). Herbert Bayer created the first in 1950 for the Aspen Institute for Humanistic Studies and repurposed it in 1951 for the inaugural Aspen design conference, a meeting of designers, educators and executives that aimed to clarify design's relationship to industry and commerce. The logo depicts a classical male nude standing beside a large Aspen leaf. The figure, one arm raised in a gesture of victory, proclaims an overarching belief in human potential and perhaps, more specifically, the designer's capacity to solve human problems and fulfil human needs. The leaf, identifiable by its spade-like shape, toothed margin and pinnate venation, denotes the conference's location in Aspen, Colorado, a remote mountain town named for its trademark 'trembling aspen' trees. Together these symbols suggested that the path to human progress ran through Aspen, aided by a design conference that promised to unite the efforts of America's leading creative capitalists. The second logo appeared in the mid-1960s as part of an updated image for the conference, which had reorganized in 1954 as the International Design Conference in Aspen (IDCA). This logo's leaf, devoid of many of its distinctive traits, serves as the container for a disembodied eye, whose iris takes the form of a globe rendered in lines of latitude and longitude. This global eye spotlights the IDCA's visual focus and its attempt to bring all visible surroundings into the professional designer's orbit. But it also signals the international ambitions of the IDCA, whose sights increasingly turned outward despite being tied to Aspen, confined within the metaphorical margins of the aspen leaf.

These two logos, separated by over a decade, bookend a visual debate over the identity of the Aspen design conference and, in particular, its attempt to navigate a course between design's local, national and international functions. To construct this identity, the IDCA relied on logos, letterheads and other forms of printed matter that design critics and historians often neglect. Yet these seemingly mundane materials served a vital role by helping organizations like the IDCA communicate with their far-flung publics. Indeed, mid-century design critic Ernst Lehner urged businessmen to reconsider letterheads, trademarks and packages as three interconnected 'pillars of promotion' capable of generating goodwill among 'established or prospective customers'.[1] The IDCA promoted a similar vision of

---

[1] Ernst Lehner, *The Letterhead: History and Progress* (New York: Museum Books, 1955), unpaginated.

FIGURE 5.1A Herbert Bayer, logo designed for the Aspen Institute for Humanistic Studies and later used for the Aspen design conference, c. 1950. Aspen Historical Society, Bayer Collection. © 2020 Artists Rights Society (ARS), New York/VG Bild-Kunst, Bonn

FIGURE 5.1B Unknown designer, International Design Conference in Aspen (IDCA) pamphlet, n.d. International Design Conference in Aspen records, 1949–2006, Getty Research Institute, Los Angeles (2007.M.7). © J. Paul Getty Trust

design as a multifaceted selling tool and communication aid, using its graphic materials to articulate a complex relationship between design, business and geography. However, unlike the coordinated design programmes showcased by IDCA speakers, the conference's own graphics emerged piecemeal and retained the stylistic mannerisms of their creators. Oscillating between the particularities of the Aspen landscape and the universalizing ideal of an international discourse, these idiosyncratic designs created a conflicted institutional image. By analysing select traces of this visual identity and cross-referencing them against the IDCA's recorded history, I seek to reconstruct the organization's often opposing efforts to promote professional design as both a national and an international concern.

The IDCA's attempts to parse design's socioeconomic functions assumed particular geopolitical significance in the context of the Cold War, as the United States struggled to contain the communist threat while promoting its own economic and cultural regime abroad. Brainchild of Egbert Jacobson, the art director at Container Corporation of America, and Walter Paepcke, the company's president, the Aspen design conference originated as a meeting between American designers and businessmen who perceived design as a matter of national importance. Conference organizers, many of them profit-minded businessmen, understood their effort as 'the germinal beginning of a higher American civilization' known equally for its technical and artistic achievements.[2] They regarded design as a tool alongside other sales and marketing techniques, which could help American manufacturers prosper within an increasingly competitive global marketplace. 'It is my belief', Paepcke declared at the first conference in 1951, 'that the value of design is only recently coming to be recognized fully as a new weapon in competition'.[3] The interlocking concepts of eye value, shelf appeal and selling power underpinned this militant perception of design as a commercial weapon. This narrative has dominated scholarship on Cold War design, which focuses primarily on government organizations and on design's propagandist role in the advancement of national interests.[4]

However, the IDCA's attempts to traverse professional, ideological and geographical boundaries also situated it at the centre of a parallel yet understudied history of Cold War design concerned with the international interchange of ideas. In his own 1951 Aspen talk, American designer George Nelson contrasted the industrialist's 'military tone' with the 'moral tone' of the designer, who pursued an ideal of cooperation rather than competition.[5] Austrian-born designer Herbert

---

[2] Alexander Ebin and R. Hunter Middleton, 'Impressions from the Design Conference Held at Aspen, Colorado', 1951, Box 15, Folder 734, International Design Conference in Aspen papers, Special Collections and University Archives, University of Illinois at Chicago.
[3] Walter Paepcke, 'Design in Industry: An Industrialist Looks at Design', *Better Design* (January 1952): 65.
[4] See Greg Castillo, *Cold War on the Home Front: The Soft Power of Midcentury Design* (Minneapolis: University of Minnesota Press, 2010).
[5] Ebin and Middleton, 'Impressions'.

Bayer, consultant to Container Corporation and a former Bauhaus student and master, supported this notion of cooperative design. 'We must inspire everybody with the visual experience in which we – artists and businessmen – can cooperate', he declared in 1951. 'Our future well-being depends on the concrete interchange of all human energies.'[6] In the following years, Bayer and other like-minded conferees aimed to temper design's competitive, nationalistic associations by inviting speakers with strikingly different backgrounds to share their thoughts on design. The IDCA thus aspired to an ideal of internationalism that was human rather than nation-centred and that remained elusive due in part to a lack of coordinated government support. By analysing the IDCA's identity in relation to its activities, this chapter explores the gap between the conference's international ambitions and actual achievements.

While the IDCA continually strove to delineate and depict its geographic scope, scholars have largely ignored both the imagery and the fraught internationalism of the conference altogether, focusing instead on its functions as a repository of post-war design discourse, an organ of professionalization, and a lightning rod for radical protests.[7] However, the IDCA's efforts to express its identity are central to its legacy as an international design organization. These visual and ideological debates reveal that the process of designing an organization's image, like the process of making it international, entails a dynamic negotiation between constituent parts in the pursuit of functional wholes. I argue, in other words, that the IDCA's attempt to compose a cohesive self-image intertwined with its efforts to cultivate a forum for international exchange. Although the pieces of this international image often failed to cohere, the IDCA's visual programme nevertheless became an important site for testing the integrative possibilities of design within an internationally networked post-war modernity.

Meeting in the mountains

Though not created specifically for the design conference, Herbert Bayer's 1950 logo nevertheless encapsulated Aspen's fundamental importance to the identity of the IDCA (Figure 5.1). The human figure and the Aspen leaf effectively conveyed the conference's close relationship to the cultural programme of the Aspen Institute, on the one hand, and to the recreational opportunities offered by its

---

[6] Quoted in Edgar Kaufmann, Jr., 'Design, Designer and Industry', *Magazine of Art*, no. 44 (December 1951): 325.
[7] See Joanne Leigh George, 'The Functions of Graphic Design: Sociologies, History, and the International Design Conference in Aspen' (Ph.D. Dissertation, State University of New York at Binghamton, 2002); Alice Twemlow, 'I Can't Talk To You If You Say That: An Ideological Collision at the International Design Conference at Aspen, 1970', *Design and Culture* 1, no. 1 (2009): 25–50; Wim de Wit, ed., *Design for the Corporate World: Creativity on the Line, 1950–1975* (London: Lund Humphries, 2017).

surrounding environs, on the other. In fact, these two features of the Aspen milieu were entirely entwined in the mind of Walter Paepcke, who was responsible for rehabilitating Aspen as a recreational and cultural destination. Paepcke hoped the stunning views and outdoor activities offered by the Colorado landscape would encourage visitors, especially corporate executives and designers, to reflect on the values that guided them in everyday life. Aspen thus supported Paepcke's belief that aesthetic contemplation and physical exertion were necessary corollaries to the mental labour required for economic, intellectual and creative development. The town's grassy knolls served not simply as an attractive physical setting, but also as the metaphysical wellspring of an emergent post-war design discourse.

The heroic male nude that appeared in Bayer's logo design signified the human-centred educational program sponsored by the Aspen Institute. Inspired by his experience orchestrating the Goethe Bicentennial Convocation, a major cultural event held in Aspen in 1949, Paepcke established the Aspen Institute in 1950 to continue the advancement of humanistic ideals among corporate executives.[8] The Institute's operations centred on an executive seminar series, which pursued the reform of American business culture through liberal arts education. In its aim to cultivate well-rounded and enlightened business leaders, the Institute also supported a number of local arts initiatives, including the Aspen Music Festival and School and a national photography conference. Following Aspen's first full season of educational and cultural activity, Jacobson persuaded Paepcke to incorporate a 'Design Seminar' in Aspen's summer programme. 'I am sure you will agree that questions of design are as vital to humanism as music, literature and philosophy', he insisted.[9] Jacobson thus characterized design as a related yet distinct addition to the humanistic activities taking root in Aspen. His vision of design as a matter of managerial interest aligned particularly closely with the Institute's focus on America's business elite.[10] The commanding figure in Bayer's logo might be seen not only as a symbol of human potential, then, but also and more specifically as a *leader* in the advancement of human progress.

At the design seminar's first planning session, a committee of designers, educators and executives established a core mission for the conference: 'The consensus was all in the direction of explaining "integrated design," what it is, what it can do. The discussion at Aspen would therefore include every aspect of design in business, from the graphic arts through industrial design, furniture, interiors and architecture.'[11] This comprehensive approach to design reflected

---

[8] James Sloan Allen, *The Romance of Commerce and Culture: Capitalism, Modernism, and the Chicago-Aspen Crusade for Cultural Reform* (Chicago: University of Chicago Press, 1983), 209–67.
[9] Egbert Jacobson to Walter Paepcke, 22 August 1950, Box 103, Folder 5, Walter P. Paepcke Papers, Special Collections Research Center, University of Chicago Library [hereafter WPPP].
[10] Egbert Jacobson to Walter Paepcke, 23 October 1950, Box 103, Folder 5, WPPP.
[11] Egbert Jacobson, 'Committee on Plans for Design Conference', 19 February 1951, Box 1, Folder 2, International Design Conference in Aspen records, 1949–2006, The Getty Research Institute, Accession no. 2007.M.7 [hereafter IDCA-GRI].

the humanistic principles of the Aspen Institute, translating its ideal of the well-rounded business leader into a vision of the total designer. Indeed, designers may have recognized in Bayer's logo not only the Classical Greek nude, set in *contrapposto* with one arm raised above his head, but also the more contemporary figure of Le Corbusier's Modulor man. Developed in an effort to unite the seemingly irreconcilable European metric and US customary systems of measurement, Corbusier described Modulor as a 'range of harmonious measurements to suit the human scale, universally applicable to architecture and to mechanical things'.[12] By referencing this perennial, human-centred search for ideal proportions, Bayer's logo united the design conference and the Aspen Institute in a shared mission to discover solutions to universal human problems.

Meanwhile, the symbol of the leaf effectively evoked Aspen's lush landscape, which had a profound effect on the conference participants and the nature of their discussions. Founded as a mining town in the late nineteenth century, Aspen's prospects fell with the collapse of the silver market in the mid-1890s. Reduced to a population of fewer than one thousand residents by 1930, Aspen was revived in the 1940s through the efforts of Paepcke and his wife Elizabeth, who recognized the town's great natural charm and recreational opportunities. The invitation to the first design conference capitalized on this potential by picturing visitors swimming, fishing and horseback riding. It even encouraged conferees to combine participation in the seminar with a full family vacation. Yet the invitation also presented Aspen as more than a lavish playground or picturesque backdrop by emphasizing the intimate setting as a catalyst for informal gatherings and friendly conversation. 'It creates a community of minds', the flier stated. 'Man is a socially rational animal [who] needs the company of his fellow men and the interchange of conversation as a condition of productive thought.'[13] The conference organizers viewed Aspen, disconnected from the responsibilities and minutiae of daily life, as an ideal setting for a week of focused conversation. Many, if not all, early participants agreed. Echoing the claim that sound reasoning relied on communal exchange, design critic Alexander Ebin argued that social interaction was particularly important in the United States, where 'any constructive movement [...] must be brought into being by free collaboration and this means free and friendly interaction of diverse minds in favorable circumstances'.[14] Ebin identified Aspen as a suitably communal environment in which strangers from across the country could join together in mutual exchange.

In his analysis of the Aspen design conference as characteristically American, Ebin also participated in a normative Cold War discourse that contrasted American and Soviet modes of thought. 'A design conference held in the Ural

---

[12] Le Corbusier, *The Modulor: A Harmonious Measure to the Human Scale Universally Applicable to Architecture and Mechanics* (London: Faber & Faber, 1951).
[13] 'Design as a Function of Management, a Conference at Aspen, Colorado', 1951, Box 1, Folder 5, IDCA-GRI.
[14] Ebin and Middleton, 'Impressions'.

Mountains would be more firmly "integrated" than our conference at Aspen', he speculated. Yet he also argued that 'it would be pre-planned to Marxist philosophy and imposed upon the obedient delegates', and therefore 'would not produce a profit, as we did at Aspen, of human values and creative thoughts'.[15] Of course, Aspen's fundamentally capitalist orientation was no less 'pre-planned' or 'imposed' than that of Ebin's imagined Soviet conference. Conceived as a means of improving living conditions through the twin mechanisms of capitalism and consumerism, the conference's definition of 'design as a function of management' limited who could partake in its collectivist project. While the former Axis powers of Germany, Italy and Japan eventually became central participants, the conference remained largely unwelcoming and unappealing to communist states throughout its existence. In at least one instance, an invited speaker with communist affiliations was unable to participate after having been declined a visa.[16]

While the design conference used its connections with Aspen and the Aspen Institute to communicate ideals of communal exchange and universal human progress, these affiliations also interfered with its ability to develop a diverse audience and discourse. The Goethe Bicentennial had brought Aspen to the attention of an international intellectual community, and commercial airliners made it more accessible to visitors. Yet despite its increasing prominence and accessibility, Aspen remained physically and psychologically remote from other established centres and orthodoxies of modernist design. Even as it stimulated collective debate, Aspen's idyllic enclave, hemmed in on three sides by the Rocky Mountains, also insulated it from outside influences. Furthermore, the conference's affiliation with the Aspen Institute impeded the formation of its own unique identity and objectives. In addition to sharing a logo with the Institute, conference organizers further undermined the establishment of a self-sufficient design organization by using their individual corporate letterheads to conduct official conference business. This practice generated confusion among some correspondents. For example, Container Corporation's central involvement in Aspen – made apparent by Paepcke and Jacobson's use of company letterhead for all Aspen-related matters – troubled some prospective collaborators. In a tense exchange with American designer Russel Wright, president of the Society of Industrial Designers, Paepcke sought to correct the 'misimpressions' that his company was exploiting Aspen's cultural development for commercial gain.[17] The lack of distinct and consistently applied institutional imagery thus hindered the Aspen design conference's ability to cultivate recognition and goodwill, which likely contributed to lower attendance at the 1952 conference.[18]

---

[15] Ibid.
[16] Albert Steiner to Will Burtin, 17 May 1956, Box 102, Folder 2, Will Burtin Papers, RIT Libraries: Graphic Design Archives, Rochester Institute of Technology [hereafter WBP].
[17] Walter Paepcke to Russel Wright, 8 May 1952, Box 49, Folder 13, WPPP.
[18] 'International Design Conference at Aspen, Attendance List for 1951-'52-'53-'54', Box 1, Folder 9, IDCA-GRI.

Going global

In 1953, art director Leo Lionni used his personal stationery and his position as programme chairman of the 1953 Aspen design conference to stake a claim for an international event (Figure 5.2). The words 'International Design Conference', printed in an italicized serif typeface, loomed large on his letterhead's left-hand side, while the event's location and association with the Aspen Institute appeared much smaller, relegated to secondary importance. More than a year before its official incorporation as the International Design Conference in Aspen, Lionni thus envisioned a new beginning for the conference as a self-sustaining organization that could fill a growing need for international exchange. This particular form of internationalism centred on the participation of foreign or foreign-born speakers whose self-identities had formed across national borders. This contingent included visitors from abroad – such as Swiss designer Max Bill, Japanese designer Isamu Kenmochi and British designer Willy de Majo – as well as recent émigrés – such as Austrian-born Herbert Bayer and German-born Will Burtin. The cosmopolitanism of these designers, who regularly shuttled between countries and cultural contexts, epitomized a notion of internationalism not as a collection of nations with distinct self-interests, but rather as a basis for achieving cooperation and understanding among individuals. By promoting the conference as a semi-autonomous international event with a diverse panel of speakers, Lionni challenged its original, more limited aim to unite American commerce and culture.

As early as 1951, Lionni proposed that the topic of integrated design was of international interest, and perhaps even origin. At the planning meeting for the first conference, he volunteered to prepare an exhibition devoted to the Italian manufacturer Olivetti, called 'Integrated Design'. The planning committee agreed that Olivetti was 'perhaps the most complete example of integrated design in business' and had 'given the idea its most logical and artistic expression'.[19] As director of promotional designs for Olivetti in America, Lionni contributed both

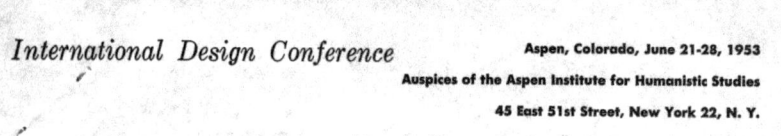

FIGURE 5.2 Leo Lionni, personal letterhead for the 'International Design Conference', 1953. Buckminster Fuller Papers, M1090, Series 2, Box 79, Folder 6. Courtesy of the Department of Special Collections, Stanford University Libraries. © Leo Lionni. Used with permission of the Lionni family

---

[19] Jacobson, 'Committee on Plans for Design Conference', 19 February 1951.

expertise and display material to the Aspen exhibition. He positioned Olivetti as a model of corporate design, but also as an example of a socially conscious and internationally active organization. In June 1951, as the 'Integrated Design' exhibition was coming together in Aspen, Lionni published an article describing Olivetti's design programme as more than a mere marketing scheme. From its headquarters in the town of Ivrea, Olivetti had become 'a symbol of progress not only in Italy but in Europe', Lionni proclaimed, 'a rallying place for young painters and graphic artists who find an air of freedom, almost of excitement, at Ivrea'.[20] Since the company's founding in 1908, Olivetti's management worked to transform the Italian village, nestled at the foot of the Alps, into an 'oasis of civilization', not unlike Paepcke's vision for Aspen. Beginning in the 1930s, Olivetti's business grew steadily until it reached far beyond the limits of the Piedmont. Through an international network of factories, showrooms and branch offices, the company spread its vision of design around the world. Not only a model for American business leaders, Olivetti also served as an example to Aspen's organizers, who sought to achieve their own balance of local and international engagement.

With its focus on Olivetti, the 'Integrated Design' show signalled a growing American preoccupation with products of Italian manufacture. The small exhibit in Aspen functioned as a testing ground for the Museum of Modern Art's (MoMA) larger exhibition, 'Olivetti: Design in Industry', which Lionni co-organized the following year. MoMA's show echoed the mission and tactics of the Aspen design conference, using Olivetti's design programme to encourage American companies to organize their own comprehensive visual identities. Olivetti products also appeared in 'Italy at Work: Her Renaissance in Design Today', an exhibition of Italian design that toured the United States between 1950 and 1951, co-sponsored by the Italian government and the United States Economic Cooperation Administration. Enthusiasm for Italian manufacturing, and the special emphasis on Olivetti as a model of excellence in corporate design, perpetuated a trope common in the history of American design by situating Europe as the fountainhead of American creative endeavour. In order to reassert the quality of US production, Aspen's organizers agreed to include examples of integrated design from American firms, such as Container Corporation, Johnson & Johnson and Martin-Senour.[21] When the first Aspen conference convened in June, work from these American corporations accompanied Lionni's main presentation of Olivetti's graphics, product design and architecture. Thus, despite the primarily national scope of the first conference, the 'Integrated Design' exhibition served as a site for negotiating America's position within an international design milieu. Yet by pitting examples of Italian and American industry against each other, the exhibition framed these international relations in competitive rather than cooperative terms.

---

[20] Leo Lionni, 'Design with a Point', *Fortune* 40, no. 6 (June 1951): 113.
[21] Egbert Jacobson, 'Committee on Plans for Design Conference', 27 March 1951, Box 1, Folder 2, IDCA-GRI.

After the Olivetti exhibition, Lionni took a leading role in broadening the geographical and cultural purview of the Aspen design conference. In 1953, he assumed chairmanship of the third conference with the belief 'that our real opportunity lay in a yearly international conference on all debatable aspects not only of design itself but of all matters that are or should be of interest to the design community'.[22] Lionni aimed to expand the scope of what he called the 'First International Design Conference' by establishing it as an annual event and opening it to foreign participants and to a wider range of topics. His vision was predicated on a broader, human-centred notion of the designer as 'an integral part of a community dedicated to a common ideology that would cover not only all formal and symbolic aspects of the visual environment but their inseparable political content as well'.[23] Rather than simply stimulate sales, Lionni believed that designers, even those working under the aegis of big business, should aim to evaluate and satisfy human needs. Guiding the conference beyond its founding concern with American industry, he pursued a more inclusive path towards the free exchange of all design-related ideas.

Lionni implemented his vision for an international conference by assembling a panel of speakers from Europe and Asia to share and debate their philosophies of design. Swiss designer Max Bill, Italian architect Enrico Peressutti, Japanese designer Isamu Kenmochi, and German émigré art historian Nikolaus Pevsner joined Hungarian-born György Kepes and Austrian-born René d'Harnoncourt as conference panelists. While in previous years speakers had shared comparable stories about corporate America's experiments with design, the 1953 group produced a more diverse discourse by recounting their experiences designing in a variety of cultural contexts. In addition to formal lectures, the speakers also conducted roundtable discussions, student forums and impromptu conversations with conferees. The programme thus reflected the relaxed attitude and composite worldview of Lionni himself, who had led a life of transience before the war, piecing together his own informal arts education around café tables in Amsterdam, Zurich and Milan.

The success of Lionni's efforts to diversify the 1953 design conference became a topic of debate among its participants. Most of the foreign speakers relished the opportunity to partake in Aspen's intellectual and recreational activities and to share their views with the predominantly American audience. Energized by his first visit to America, Bill prepared an entirely new speech, delivered in earnest yet broken English, in an attempt to better engage with his American peers on the particulars of US design. Having arrived in America by way of Brazil and Peru, he noted that differences in histories of style, traditions of craftsmanship, and modes of production engendered problems unique to Europe, South America and the

---

[22] Leo Lionni, *Between Worlds: The Autobiography of Leo Lionni* (New York: Knopf, 1997), 194.
[23] Ibid.

United States. Despite these differences, Bill also addressed what he viewed as the shared fundamentals of 'art, business, culture, and design'. He tasked all those in Aspen, 'designers and producers, artists and critics', with developing more 'honest and modest' approaches to design that might 'finally pay – perhaps not in money, but in a harmonious life'.[24] Aspen thus served as a valuable platform for Bill, allowing him to present his personal philosophy that interchange between designers, businessmen and educators could lead to a more balanced and fulfilling life.

Other conference speakers offered mixed impressions of the event and the state of design more broadly. Pevsner thanked Paepcke 'for the glorious time' in Aspen, but he also suggested improvements for future meetings.[25] Although heartened by the high attendance and the lively atmosphere, Pevsner proposed a more structured dialogue, which he hoped would lead to more concrete resolutions. His overall appraisal of the design field was similarly ambivalent. *New York Times* reporter Aline Louchheim paraphrased Pevsner in her coverage of the conference. 'There is much more going on qualitatively as well as quantitatively in architecture here [in America] than in England,' she quoted him saying.[26] Yet back in London, Pevsner was less conclusive. 'Our best [British] designs may be more refined than theirs,' he noted in a radio broadcast, 'but we have less, and certainly too few designs that pronounce frankly what century they belong to'.[27] He equivocated further that if America's obsession with novelty had produced 'modern design of the best quality', it also resulted in much 'modern vile design'. Pevsner's report thus reinforced stereotypical cultural divides, characterizing Americans not only as less literate and worldly, but also as more daring and productive, than their English colleagues. Ultimately, however, Pevsner echoed Bill's belief in the presence of common ground. Summarizing the conference themes – including the relations between manufacturing and design, artist and designer, art and science, and design and technology – he noted that 'all these topics might have been discussed in London as well'.[28] If the 'remarkably informal' Aspen conference deviated in style from European congresses, it nevertheless highlighted a shared set of concerns and the possibility of a productive international design discourse.

The 1953 conference also launched a dialogue between the United States and Japan, which positioned design as a means of overcoming cultural differences and hostilities. Isamu Kenmochi, chief of the Design Division at Tokyo's Industrial Arts Institute and design editor for the magazine *Kōgei Nyūsu* (*Industrial Art News*),

---

[24] Max Bill, 'a, b, c, d …', in *Max Bill*, ed. María Toledo (Madrid: Fundación Juan March, 2015), 292.
[25] Nikolaus Pevsner to Walter Paepcke, 7 July 1953, Box 30, Folder 10, WPPP.
[26] Aline B. Louchheim, 'U.S. Architecture Praised by Briton', *New York Times* (7 July 1953).
[27] Nikolaus Pevsner, 'At Aspen in Colorado, 1953', in *The Aspen Papers: Twenty Years of Design Theory from the International Design Conference in Aspen*, ed. Reyner Banham (New York: Praeger Publishers, 1974), 18.
[28] Ibid., 15–16.

described his experience in Aspen as 'one of the most significant parts of [his] life'.[29] After returning to Japan, he promoted the conference through a series of reports that communicated its aims and values to a Japanese audience. Impressed by the 'cross-fertilization of ideas' between American designers, businessmen and educators, Kenmochi reflected on the inferior position of design in Japan and the country's resulting economic and cultural impoverishment. 'Personally, I dream of a design conference within Japan', Kenmochi wrote, 'and eventually a day where Japan hosts an international design conference, in the spirit of a conference like this one'.[30] In addition to penning written reports, Kenmochi also spent the fall of 1953 lecturing about the conference in Japan, using 'color pictures' to help audiences feel 'as if they were at Aspen'.[31] The photographs that accompanied Kenmochi's articles are likely representative of the 'color pictures' used in his lectures. In one, a crowd of attentive conferees fills the conference tent designed by Eero Saarinen. Another shows Kenmochi himself waving a *koinobori*, a carp-shaped kite traditionally flown in Japan in celebration of Children's Day. These visual aids conveyed Aspen's atmosphere of serious intellectual activity, on the one hand, and light-hearted amusement, on the other.

Kenmochi's illustrated articles and lectures garnered positive reactions from Japanese artists, architects and designers, convincing many of them to participate in Aspen themselves. In 1955, architects Kiyoshi Seike and Koichi Ito spoke about Japan's efforts to modernize practices of building and city planning. The following year, the Japan Productivity Center sent a group of representatives to study industrial design practices in America.[32] Their itinerary included visits to major corporations, industrial design firms and the design conference in Aspen, where two of the delegates, Saburo Asaba and Sori Yanagi, gave presentations. Other 1956 conferees were impressed by the sight of 'Japanese industrial designers listening, translating, and recording every second of the sessions'.[33] Kenmochi, Yanagi and other Japanese visitors to Aspen also played central roles in organizing similar associations and events in Japan, such as the Japan Committee on International Design and the 1960 World Design Conference in Tokyo. The latter, which addressed the theme, 'Total Image for the 20th Century', modelled itself after the Aspen conference and featured talks by several Aspen organizers. By uniting designers around a common ideology of design as a 'total' process, the Japanese design community helped promote the Aspen vision of design as an opportunity for international cooperation.

---

[29] Isamu Kenmochi to Walter Paepcke, 26 December 1953, Box 103, Folder 7, WPPP.
[30] Isamu Kemmochi, 'The Aim and Character of Aspen Conference (1)', trans. Ichigo Mina Kaneko, *Kōgei Nyūsu* 21, no. 10 (November 1953): 7–10.
[31] Kenmochi to Paepcke.
[32] 'Members of Group Revealed to Study Industrial Designs', *Nippon Times* (24 June 1956): 6.
[33] Dan Aberle and Mildred Deyo, 'Design Conference Summary', Box 103, Folder 10, WPPP.

Support for an international conference was not unanimous, however. Other participants in the 1953 conference, though similarly enthusiastic about the event, questioned its success in facilitating cross-cultural exchange. Will Burtin, himself a German émigré, claimed that a deep cultural divide between America and Europe rendered the 1953 discussions ineffectual. Self-identifying as an American after fifteen years in the United States, Burtin argued that 'the issues with which our architects, designers, and artists are wrestling today [...] are on a different plane than the polished generalities of Pevsner'.[34] He contended further that 'our reality' in the United States was 'entirely different' from that of Europeans such as Pevsner and Bill. Indeed, Burtin expressed a surprisingly exceptionalist view of America, arguing that 'the historical position of our country, its intense drive towards standards of living, our super-technology, and steady dissatisfaction with existing solutions, are indicative of a deep cultural dynamicism'. He proposed that by asking 'the right visual questions' about the relationship between art and science, rather than tackling issues of humanism and internationalism, Aspen could contribute to a clearer understanding of 'the purpose of cultural activity' that 'would be refreshingly American'. Burtin's pursuit of an American design ethic, achieved through the systematic integration of art and science, earned him the position of programme chairman from 1954 to 1956.

During his tenure as chairman, Burtin permanently altered the nature of the conference by incorporating the perspectives of leading scientists and engineers, such as Albert E. Parr, Bernard S. Benson and Anatol Rapaport. His leadership also initially caused the conference to contract back within national borders. In 1954, Brazilian landscape architect Roberto Burle Marx was the lone international delegate at the speaker's podium. Burtin failed, however, to maintain a strictly American focus. Lionni's vision of an international conference had helped put Aspen on the map by drawing attendance from abroad, and the prospect of re-limiting its scope appeared to many as uncomfortably retrograde. Indeed, American polymath R. Buckminster Fuller claimed in 1953 that the conference had assumed 'true international stature', not because of the quantity of foreign participants or the magnitude of its reputation abroad, but because of 'its assimilation of controversial and live issues'.[35] Internationalism in Fuller's view thus constituted an openness to unfamiliar perspectives. It was an ongoing commitment, in other words, rather than a measurable achievement. When participants decided to incorporate the conference as a permanent organization in 1954, there was little question that it should maintain its international commitments, though what this internationalism should look like was still a matter of debate.

---

[34] Will Burtin to Walter Paepcke, 16 July 1953, Box 30, Folder 10, WPPP.
[35] R. Buckminster Fuller to Constance Steele, 7 July 1953, Box 79, Folder 3, R. Buckminster Fuller papers, M1090, Department of Special Collections, Stanford University Libraries.

Incorporating the IDCA

In the fall of 1954, Chicago designer Robert Hunter Middleton, elected as the temporary chairman in charge of incorporating a permanent Aspen design conference, introduced a personal letterhead that revealed his vision for the planned organization (Figure 5.3). Identified as a 'temporary letterhead', a work in progress like the conference itself, Middleton's two-toned design offered up a name for the organization: 'ASPEN International Design Conference'. Set in a bold, sans-serif typeface and printed in dark green, this name dominated all of Middleton's correspondence. In contrast with Lionni, whose letterhead foregrounded his international ambitions, Middleton reaffirmed the symbolic importance of 'ASPEN' by setting the word in all capitals and placing it before 'International Design Conference'. Viewed together, Middleton and Lionni's letterheads thus staged a dialogue over the public image of the conference. Would it remain physically and ideologically bound to its location in Aspen, dependent on the town's recreational and cultural offerings? Or would the conference seek out a larger milieu by promoting itself primarily as an international organization, open and accessible to participants from around the world?

This visual debate over the conference's institutional identity brings into focus a larger contest over its structure, administration and future as a centre of design discourse. During an initial planning meeting in June 1954, members of the executive committee struggled to agree on a name for the permanent organization. Suggestions included the cumbersome 'International Design Conference of the Aspen Institute of Humanistic Studies'; the distinctly European 'International Design Congress' and the more narrowly regional 'Aspen Design Conference'.[36] In a preliminary organizational plan, Middleton argued that 'the word, ASPEN, with its triple connotation of past Design conference successes, humanistic studies, and vacation promises, seems essential'.[37] While he supported the idea of opening

FIGURE 5.3 Robert Hunter Middleton, temporary letterhead for the 'ASPEN International Design Conference', 1954. International Design Conference in Aspen records, 1949–2006, Getty Research Institute, Los Angeles (2007.M.7). © J. Paul Getty Trust

---

[36] 'Aspen International Design Conference', 29 June 1954, Box 1, Folder 9, IDCA-GRI.
[37] R. Hunter Middleton, 'Suggested Plan for Permanent Organization', July 1954, Box 1, Folder 9, IDCA-GRI.

the conference to international participation, Middleton argued that Aspen had been a critical attraction for early conferees and remained imperative to the event's continued success. The organizing committee ultimately pursued a compromise between Lionni and Middleton's visions, designating their organization the 'International Design Conference in Aspen'. Typographically bookended by the words 'International' and 'Aspen', the 'Design Conference' appeared caught between its international ambitions and regional roots. While the name suggested an international scope, the membership of the first board of directors betrayed its American, and specifically Midwestern, orientation. To compensate for the board's limited reach, Middleton established a committee of regional chairmen to promote the IDCA's objectives in various geographic centres by carrying out local meetings and other activities throughout the year. At the same time, Middleton acquiesced to his colleagues' desire for 'a genuinely international character' by including provisions for extending the IDCA's network of regional chairmen worldwide.

The incorporation of the IDCA necessitated the design and printing of new stationery forms as a way to communicate its identity and mission to existing and prospective members. H. Creston Doner, chairman of the public relations committee, argued that focus should be kept on the '"International Design Conference" with "in aspen" reduced to a secondary element so it would not appear that Aspen is the headquarters'.[38] He thus voiced a concern, shared by several of his colleagues, that a conference permanently headquartered in the remote Colorado town would fail to attract the international audience promised by its new name. In 1955, the IDCA introduced a letterhead that accommodated Doner's desire for geographic flexibility (Figure 5.4). The words 'International Design Conference', set in all capitals, dominated the composition. The date appeared even larger in block numerals, a separate element that could be changed easily each year. The words 'in Aspen', which appeared smaller and to the right of the date, shunted into the letter's margin, could be altered as well if the location of the conference ever changed. Instead of adapting this letterhead, the IDCA introduced an entirely new design the very next year. In the new letterhead, 'International Design Conference', printed in black ink, appeared separate from the location and date, printed beside it in blue (Figure 5.5). The colour changed each subsequent year, and the words 'in Aspen' could be altered just as easily in case of a change in location. The executive committee thus built into its letterhead a willingness to venture beyond the limits of Aspen. The 1956 design also introduced a new logo consisting of a typographic composite of the letters 'idca'. By eliminating the Aspen leaf, so prominent in Bayer's design, and replacing it with an inscribed globe, the new IDCA logo further indicated a shift away from Middleton's focus on Aspen and towards an image of internationalism.

---

[38] H. Creston Doner, memo, 14 September 1954, Box 1, Folder 9, IDCA-GRI.

FIGURE 5.4 Unknown designer, International Design Conference in Aspen (IDCA) letterhead, 1955. Will Burtin Papers, Cary Graphic Design Archives, Rochester Institute of Technology

FIGURE 5.5 Unknown designer, International Design Conference in Aspen (IDCA) letterhead, 1956. Will Burtin Papers, Cary Graphic Design Archives, Rochester Institute of Technology

Aspen's precarious position within the IDCA's letterheads alluded to a series of planned organizational changes and administrative manoeuvres, which included attempts to promote, and even hold, the conference outside of Aspen. Doner encouraged associates in England, Italy and Mexico to publicize the design conference in the international press. Some of these contacts even proposed meetings of their own. After attending the 1955 Aspen conference, Mexican architect Manuel Pizarro invited the IDCA to convene its sixth iteration in Mexico City.[39] Postponed first to 1958 and then again to 1960, IDC Mexico ultimately foundered under logistical and political pressures. Despite having earned Pizarro's support and the consent of government authorities, the IDCA had no actual Mexican representation and thus would have operated in the country as a largely unknown foreign entity. IDCA board members further feared that in the light of Mexico's upcoming general elections, their conference, devoted to the free exchange of ideas, might be subject to some form of governmental censorship.[40]

Meanwhile, motivated by the enthusiastic reports of Kenmochi, Yanagi and other visitors to Aspen, the Japan Committee on International Design also

---

[39] Manuel Pizarro to Will Burtin, 9 September 1955, Box 102, Folder 10, WBP.
[40] Albert E. Parr, memo, 14 February 1958, Box 102, Folder 10, WBP.

pursued the possibility of holding a design conference in Japan in collaboration with the IDCA. They even selected a conference site in Hakone, a small town southwest of Tokyo with a stunning view of Mt. Fuji that resembled Aspen's scenic landscape.[41] Burtin, having reversed his earlier isolationist stance, spearheaded talks with Japan as chairman of the IDCA's international planning committee, working with his Japanese colleagues to develop a conference programme. Yet IDC Japan, alternately referred to as the East-West Design Conference and the World Conference on Design, also lost the support of the IDCA. Some members of the executive committee feared that holding the conference outside Aspen would be prohibitively expensive for most members and would result in the loss of both individual and corporate contributions. Ultimately succumbing to expediency, the executive committee 'unanimously agreed that no foreign meetings [would] be held in the near future'.[42] They did, however, take more modest administrative steps towards internationalization. In 1958, the IDCA established an International Advisory Committee consisting of members from Europe and North America, each of whom held the status and voting privileges of a board member. Beginning in the early 1960s, promotional materials listed additional contacts in Europe and Asia. By assembling and publicizing these international administrative groups, the IDCA sought to maintain open lines of communication with its constituents overseas.

Despite the diplomatic efforts of Doner, Burtin, and other board members, the IDCA's imagined international network never fully materialized. The failed attempts to hold conferences in Mexico and Japan especially called into question the organization's actual internationalism, which remained a vexed ideal well into the 1960s, disputed in board meeting minutes and memoranda. The two sides of this debate split largely along professional lines. Most of the designers supported greater internationalization, while the businessmen expressed fears that a conference held abroad might jeopardize its audience, continuity and profitability. In response to this resistance, American designer Morton Goldsholl argued that a preoccupation with cost-benefit analyses had begun to overshadow more important questions about the implications and responsibilities of an international design conference. 'Maybe the idea of design growing and flourishing in other countries makes some of our corporate members fearful of a growing competition overseas,' he speculated wryly.[43] Burtin agreed that the executive committee should approach the question of international engagement as more than a logistical consideration. He acknowledged that the conference still required sturdier financial and organizational foundations before it could become 'truly International'. But he also argued that it had already achieved 'a momentum of its own as far as the international scene and opportunities are concerned',

---

[41] Takehiko Kanakogi to Will Burtin, 18 March 1957, Box 102, Folder 8, WBP.
[42] 'Minutes of IDCA Executive Committee meeting', 26 June 1958, Box 102, Folder 11, WBP.
[43] Morton Goldsholl, memo, 24 October 1957, Box 102, Folder 8, WBP.

and demanded that the executive committee work to define its 'objectives more clearly and search for formula [sic] that will make a progressive policy possible'.[44] Burtin believed the IDCA had missed out on important opportunities in Mexico and Japan not simply because of logistical obstacles, but also because of its own internal indecision with respect to internationalization.

In a summary of the 1960 design conference, commercial illustrator Bill Tara, then-chairman of the IDCA, questioned why in its tenth year the conference still failed to achieve its full potential. 'Why is it', he wondered, 'that with our great talent our product is at best good, but not great?'[45] British designer Willy de Majo, the IDCA's primary contact in Europe and a fixture on its advisory board, identified a more specific failure of the conference: its inability to achieve true international stature. In his own post-conference memorandum, he reminded the executive committee 'that the Conference is still mainly in name only, an "International" Conference'.[46] While the IDCA had amassed upwards of five hundred members, de Majo struggled to obtain just twenty-five subscriptions overseas. The difficulty of attracting foreign members arose not only from considerations of cost and distance, he explained, but also from an underlying image problem. Having developed haphazardly over the course of a decade, the IDCA still struggled to convey the nature of its commitment to international design. When Tara asked his fellow board members to 'invent and design an ideal conference, its function and its form', he sought to render the ideal of an effective international design discourse more concrete. 'Describe it in words', he urged his colleagues, 'draw some pictures of it'.[47]

The 1964 letterhead might be understood as a picture of the 'ideal conference' designed by board members in the 1960s (Figure 5.6). A thin line marks out the space for text. At the top of this box, the organization's name appears in small sans-serif letters, while its Aspen mailing address rests at the bottom. The logo floats in empty space to the left of the text box. The nested symbols of leaf, eye and globe clearly communicate the conference's vested interests in Aspen, design, and internationalism. By subsuming the globe within the leaf, the new logo might be seen as a reflection of the IDCA's limited internationalism. But it might also be interpreted as a refusal to reckon with the question of internationalism altogether. Rather than choose between Aspen and the international scene, or between its local and global constituencies, the IDCA continued to walk a line between regional, national and international engagement. By the mid-1960s, the design world had become increasingly saturated with organizations and conferences that catered to an international audience. While the IDCA aimed to cooperate with some of these groups, it also struggled to compete for its share of attention. By

---

[44] Will Burtin to Albert Parr, 21 November 1957, Box 102, Folder 8, WBP.
[45] Bill Tara, 'Post Conference Memorandum', 15 July 1960, Box 5, Folder 7, IDCA-GRI.
[46] Willy de Majo, 'IDCA 1960/61', 25 July 1960, Box 5, Folder 7, IDCA-GRI.
[47] Tara, 'Post Conference Memorandum'.

FIGURE 5.6 Unknown designer, International Design Conference in Aspen (IDCA) stationery, 1964. International Design Conference in Aspen records, 1949–2006, Getty Research Institute, Los Angeles (2007.M.7). © J. Paul Getty Trust

maintaining its connection to Aspen, the IDCA preserved a sense of continuity while also appearing distinct from other conferences held in urban centres around the world. And while its membership was predominantly American, the IDCA's claim to internationalism and its inclusion of foreign speakers ensured it a larger and more diverse constituency than it would have enjoyed otherwise. To some extent, then, the incorporation of the IDCA as an international organization might be seen as a marketing ploy, an attempt to expand its originally limited sphere of influence.

Conclusion

In the light of the recent global turn in design history, the birth of the IDCA helps historicize the many challenges that attended the construction of an international post-war design discourse. Internal disputes over the IDCA's regional, national and international interests were more central to its formation than scholars have shown. The organization's aim to produce and participate in an international milieu competed with its roots in Aspen and its preoccupation with American industry throughout the 1950s and 1960s, resulting in a conflicted institutional identity. Indeed, just as many of its attempts at international collaboration faltered, so too did its early efforts to construct a cohesive self-image. Thus in the final analysis, it could be said that the IDCA failed to fulfil Buckminster Fuller's claim for 'true international stature' and instead remained, as Willy de Majo feared, international in name only.

Yet such an assessment minimizes the IDCA's significant role in promoting a particular vision of international cooperation as a worthy, if imperfect or perhaps even unattainable, ideal. This vision of internationalism was neither a given nor a straightforward trajectory within a design field caught amidst rising Cold War geopolitical tensions. The IDCA was certainly less internationally active than other organizations engaged in post-war cultural diplomacy, especially those that participated, directly or indirectly, in the Marshall Plan and equivalent or successor initiatives. Yet if we shift the conversation around international relations away from matters of war, diplomacy, and national interest and towards such topics as international order, cooperation and interdependence, then the IDCA's collectivist approach to design and internationalism assumes greater significance.[48] Although its visual identity lacked the cohesion exhibited by other corporate design programmes, the IDCA's graphic materials nevertheless instantiated design as an ongoing integrative process. Through continual changes to the content, composition, and style of its logo and letterhead, the IDCA tested design's capacity to reconcile competing interests and concerns.

If the image of the Aspen design conference was subject to continuous revision, so too was its position on internationalism. Indeed, the process of becoming an international design organization did not end with the IDCA's incorporation. Changes in the political climate, the availability of resources, and the views of its members led organizers to develop new ways of producing international design relations throughout the latter part of the twentieth century. For example, several

---

[48] See Akira Iriye, *Global Community: The Role of International Organizations in the Making of the Contemporary World* (Berkeley: University of California Press, 2002).

later conferences explored specifically international themes, such as 'Design and the American Image Abroad' (1963); 'Dialogues: America and Europe' (1968); 'Japan in Aspen' (1979); 'The Italian Idea' (1981); and 'Neighbors: Canada, USA & Mexico' (1984). Beginning in the mid-1960s, an international fellowship programme sponsored by IBM brought individual visitors and entire delegations from abroad to attend the Aspen conference. Further study is needed to understand if and how these and later initiatives helped diversify the programme, voice and audience of the conference. Nevertheless, they indicate that the IDCA was indeed caught in a perpetual process of becoming international. This chapter has captured only a partial, though determining, picture of the early stages of this process. By examining how organizers and participants negotiated, through both graphical and verbal means, the organization's position in an expanding field of design discourse, it invites further critical re-evaluations of the conference and its place within histories of post-war design and international exchange.

6 ALADI, A LATIN AMERICAN VOICE OF DESIGN

Juan Buitrago

Introduction

In November 1980, delegates from Argentina, Brazil, Colombia, Costa Rica, Cuba, Ecuador, Guatemala, Mexico and Puerto Rico convened in Bogotá, Colombia, and founded ALADI, Asociación Latinoamericana de Diseño (Latin American Design Association). This inaugural assembly was also attended by representatives from other countries and observers in the region. Seventy-two people signed the founding document, which was conceived and drafted during the meeting (ALADI, 1980). ALADI represented collegial work on design among fourteen Latin American countries and became a level-II consulting body of the United Nations in 1989.[1]

During the 1980s, there was true regularity neither in addressing matters nor in conceptual agreements. It can be stated, however, that there was a certain permanence in both the types of discussions held and the delegations and attendees, which more or less lent continuity to the processes. The Association entered a new phase in 1991, one that could even be seen as a break with the original discourse. The year 1993 represented an effort to return to the 'old discourse', and 1995 – lending continuity to what was conceived of in 1991 – marked a conceptual turn that kept ALADI from returning to its initial positions.

For this reason, it is possible to speak of the existence of two or three ALADIs between the late 1970s and the mid-1990s. The first originated in 1978 and was strong in the 1980s, attempting to reach 1989 when Cuba organized the fourth Congress in Havana. The second phase began in 1995, when Argentina organized the seventh Congress in Rosario. In the meantime, it is possible to locate the tension between the 1991 Congress in Mexico – which marked a different lodestar from that of the previous 13 years – and the 1993 Colombian bastion, which

---

[1] Based on the minutes of the assemblies (ALADI, 1980, 1984; Lobato et al., 1982; Espín et al., 1989; Rivera et al., 1991; Barragán et al., 1993), it is possible to infer that until 1993, there were delegations to ALADI from Argentina, Brazil, Colombia, Costa Rica, Cuba, Chile, Ecuador, Guatemala, Mexico, Nicaragua, Panama, Peru, Puerto Rico and Venezuela. From 1991 onwards, Bolivia, Paraguay, the Dominican Republic and Uruguay were members. The association continues to exist today.

sought to return to the original positions, when the sixth Congress was organized in Santa Marta.

Alternating power biannually, ALADI organized congresses and assemblies in Bogotá, Colombia (1980); Havana, Cuba (1982 and 1989); Rio de Janeiro, Brazil (1984); Mexico City (1991); Santa Marta, Colombia (1993) and Rosario, Argentina (1995). In each one of these assemblies, the Executive Committee was chosen for the two subsequent years, comprising a President, Secretary, Treasurer of the association, and two Vice Presidents, who represented sequentially the next headquarters of ALADI and the country that would organize the next two events: the first vice president for the two subsequent years and the second vice president four years later.

TABLE 6.1 ALADI Executive Board, 1980–1997

ALADI 80 – Bogotá, Colombia	
President	Rómulo Polo (Colombia)
Secretary	Luis Fernando Zapata (Colombia)
Treasurer	Jesús Gámez (Colombia)
Vice President 1	Iván Espín (Cuba)
Vice President 2	Valéria London (Brazil)
Former President	–
ALADI 82 – Havana, Cuba	
President	Iván Espín (Cuba)
Secretary	Lourdes Martí (Cuba)
Treasurer	Hugo D´Costa (Cuba)
Vice President 1	Valéria London (Brazil)
Vice President 2	Américo Tapia (Nicaragua)
Former President	Rómulo Polo (Colombia)
ALADI 84 – Rio de Janeiro, Brazil	
President	Valéria London (Brazil)
Secretary	João R. do Nascimento (Brazil)
Treasurer	Élio Grossman (Brazil)
Vice President 1	Sergio Rivera (Mexico)
Vice President 2	Enzo Grivarello (Argentina)
Former President	Iván Espín (Cuba)
Ad hoc Member	Américo Tapia (Nicaragua)
ALADI 89 – Havana, Cuba	
President	Iván Espín (Cuba)
Secretary	Manuel Miyar (Cuba)
Treasurer	Gabriel Reyes (Cuba)
Vice President 1	Sergio Rivera (Mexico)

Vice President 2	Jesús Gámez (Colombia)
Former President	Valéria London (Brazil)
ALADI 91 – Mexico City	
President	Sergio Rivera (Mexico)
Secretary	Luis Equihua (Mexico)
Treasurer	Claudio Rodríguez (Mexico)
Vice President 1	Rómulo Polo (Colombia)
Vice President 2	Enzo Grivarello (Argentina)
Former President	Iván Espín (Cuba)
Permanent Secretary	Jaime Franky (Colombia)*
ALADI 93 – Santa Marta, Colombia	
President	Jaime Franky (Colombia)
Secretary	Lourdes Martí (Cuba)
Treasurer	Jesús Gámez (Colombia)
Vice President 1	Enzo Grivarello (Argentina)
Vice President 2	Guillermo Buendía (Ecuador)
Former President	–
Permanent Secretary	Colombia*
ALADI 95 – Rosario, Argentina	
President	Paolo Bergomi (Argentina)
Secretary	Enzo Grivarello (Argentina)
Treasurer	Beatrice Segni (Argentina)
Vice President 1	Guillermo Buendía (Ecuador)
Vice President 2	Ivens Fontoura (Brazil)
Former President	Jaime Franky (Colombia)

Sources: Meeting minutes (ALADI, 1980, 1984, 1995; Lobato et al., 1982; Espín et al., 1989; Rivera et al., 1991; Barragán et al., 1993).

*The position 'Permanent Secretary' underwent a prolonged discussion in the 1980s. It is not entirely clear, but some minutes indicate this position was held by one person, another set of minutes changes the subject, and yet another set of minutes grants this position to a country. One set of minutes additionally presents the role as a temporary assignment.

The details given in Table 6.1 refer to the life of ALADI from its creation in 1980 onwards. This chapter presents the process that created what could be called 'the first ALADI', a sequence of events that is significant for how both design in Latin America and the social and cultural history of the region are understood. The founding of ALADI resembles the tail of a long comet, which has been travelling since the early decades of the nineteenth century and moves through the twentieth century energetically, attempting to survive after the asphyxia of 1982 caused by the conditions of Latin America, when neoliberalism inserted its ambition in the region. It is a process of dense genealogies and complex interrelations.

The structure of this work is regressive. To visualize some of these genealogies, arguments on which ALADI was founded in 1980 are first described. As justifications were notorious among geographically distant subjects that had not met until then, we trace 'sound boxes' from those echoing such arguments. For this purpose, presenting a far-reaching Latin Americanism proves enlightening.[2] The chapter then outlines steps taken in 1979 to materialize the association. The last section deals with the remarkable moment from which the idea of creating ALADI was born: the 1978 Interdesign workshop organized in Mexico, when several Latin Americans reacted to suspicions of cultural imperialism by the ICSID, initiating a path of enunciation for the design of the region unconsciously supported by principles of Latin Americanism of the nineteenth century, which ends with fusing design with autonomy.[3]

The First ALADI

In Bogotá, in 1980, the founders of ALADI were clearly interested in establishing the boundaries, jurisdiction and direction of design. They sought to define the profile of the Latin American designer, the matters that design should address within that territory, and the social role of its 'esotericism' as a profession.[4] While they were constructing those definitions, however, they were also reasserting the autonomy of Latin America as a technological, economic and cultural unit.

The different delegations present in Bogotá, in 1980, drafted a series of documents that were delivered to the Colombian organizers. The report of the event includes thirty typed documents and consists of the writings prepared by the delegations for the meeting, certain documents on the national discussions of the time, and some speeches that appear to have been given by experts on appropriate technologies and endogenous technologies – the latter by officials from Colombian agencies and the attaché in Bogotá of the UNDP (United Nations Development Programme). Argentina provided three of these documents, Brazil fourteen, Colombia eight (including the speeches by experts), Costa Rica one, Cuba two, Guatemala one, and Mexico four. Two things could be said about this. On the one hand, the volume of documents highlights the

---

[2] The term 'sound boxes' was taken from Serge Gruzinski (2012).
[3] The interpretations are based on the ideas that the authors themselves expressed during the processes. Expressions such as 'marginalized' or 'developed world' – among others – thus come from a long genealogy, which dialogues with different Latin American critics related to liberation and cultural autonomy. Such conceptions are mobile and are signified in the time in which they are enunciated. For that reason I try to put them in discussion with the context that produces them, regardless of whether I personally agree with them or not.
[4] Esotericism according to Eliot Freidson (1983, 2001).

active dynamics in which these countries were involved in those years. On the other, the presence in Bogotá implied a commitment to a regional effort to discuss these issues.[5]

Related to jurisdictional and discretional interests, in a first group, the Latin American authors coincided in defending design as a profession with a clear technological vocation, fundamentally committed to the satisfaction of the basic needs of the population – in general, related to a particular idea of 'the people' – and with specialized support from the State for economic performance, whether in the economy of planning – clearly expressed in the Cuban case (Fernández, 2005, 2012; Chomsky, 2015) – or in the promotion of export goods. While we will later expose some of their bifurcations, but for now, it is important to state that that conception of 'the people' included in its imagination a long list of demands in which resolving the different needs of those marginalized by the process of economic and social development was unquestionable. This representation included the so-called original inhabitants of the territory who had been plundered and exterminated after the Spanish conquest in 1492, peasants and poor people in general who had been settling in the peripheries of Latin American cities: these were the segments of the population that represented the old Latin American scourge of extreme poverty.

In contrast, the support for economic performance demonstrated an attempt to have one foot in politics – clearly an effort to make design a necessary profession in the agendas of national states.[6] As the Import Substitution Industrialization policy for the region had failed to have an impact – among others, because it did not achieve the production of capital goods, nor the expected rate of job creation, while the urbanization accelerated rapidly – several multilateral agencies had redefined its meaning. Thus, in the second half of the 1970s, it was dictated that the industrialization of Latin America would be possible once it could produce value-added products for the international market. Within this general trend, several approaches are apparent, of which two seemingly opposed cases will be described. On the one hand, is Argentina's approach to industrialization leading to an obsession among government, businesspeople and designers with creating goods for large industrial plants, primarily household appliances and some automobiles; something similar occurred in Brazil and Mexico. On the other hand was the Colombian approach that – with the advice of the United States – sought to organize and refine the products already produced by its artisans, similar to several countries around the globe – Mexico, Jamaica, Bolivia and Suriname in

---

[5] For a detailed analysis please review (Buitrago, 2017) and (Buitrago, forthcoming). Copies of the proceedings of the first ALADI congress can be found in both the Biblioteca de la Universidad Nacional in Medellín (National University of Colombia Library at Medellín) and the personal archives of Jesús Gámez in Cali.

[6] Dora Souza Dias (2018a, 2018b) states that design in Latin America is linked to expectations regarding industrial and economic development.

Latin America – fundamentally seeking to familiarize artisans with the principles of modern production and the international market.[7]

Both a satisfier of the needs of the population and supporter of economic development, to those in ALADI, design was the great enabler promising that all they dreamed of would be conquered.

Let us designate these ideas as that first block mentioned in the previous paragraph. In a sort of fusion of the two following groups of ideas, the texts presented at the ALADI conference in Bogotá defend the ways in which the technological characteristics attributed to design are the path towards the nationalist defence of the region. Through a reading of the conditions of Latin American countries, the documents use both information – certain data and reflections from multilateral agencies – and the critical rhetoric regarding economic and social development that had been circulating intensely in the region since the 1940s. Appearing with vehemence in these views are notions regarding historic patterns of inequality in Latin America, the problem of importing technology (as one of the main drivers of dependency), and the aggravating circumstance of the exercise of copy and paying royalties for products coming from the technological centres. In their rhetoric, these three aspects were seen as the sharpest teeth of an aggressive external system that would continue to harm – drain, as heterodox Communists said – the region's cultural, social and economic processes. Combined, these effects caused a lack of attention to the needs of the 'marginalized', lack of workforce absorption and underdevelopment. They also strengthened the umbilical cord that made Latin America an instrumentalized appendage in the international modernization process.

These diagnoses appearing in the documents, notably more ideological than empirical, established in the statements that social change would only be possible if a local form of design were developed, resisting the siege of intruders: '[I]n conclusion, underdeveloped countries are trapped between the option to develop their own design or be dominated colonized through foreign, colonialist design. Underdeveloped countries can either design, or others will design for them and against their interests' (Espín, 1980, p. 5).

The tone of these arguments is clearly vindicating and notably political. Beyond the ideological lean of the different subjects – several of them with opposing positions – it seemed that the majority of the authors from the different countries represented in Bogotá in 1980 shared the principle of defending the idea that Latin America is a different and sovereign territory. For this reason, it was necessary to respect its particularities as a way of achieving an image of autonomy. Along those lines, it was necessary for the exercise of design to be carried out with an understanding of the conditions that produces it, and hence, this seemed to be the beginning of a great vindication: design as a tool for ending dependency on imperialism.

---

[7] In a special chapter, the details of this issue in Colombia are addressed (Buitrago-Trujillo, 2020).

This was the key to achieving a form of autonomy that was technical (given that what one does with what one has available remains one's own knowledge), economic (working with Latin American material meant not having to pay more royalties) and finally cultural (the needs of 'our peoples' would be resolved with 'our capabilities' and 'our knowledge'), breaking the chains of dependency once and for all. Ultimately, it was the defence of an essentialist formula that inspired a group of Latin American intellectuals to create based on the circumstances in

TABLE 6.2 Founding members of ALADI. The spelling corresponds to the original writing

ALADI Founders		
Olicio C. Pelosi	Adriana Canales	Carlos Daniel Soto
Franca Rosi	Roberto Napoli	José Luis Berrueta
Oscar Pamio	Carlos Chávez Aguilera	Guadalupe González
Luis E. Arroyave	Carlos Carillo Soberón	Luis Romero Rwgús
Joaquín Redig	Francisco García Noriega	Luis Sierra Campusano
Iván Espín	Jesús Virchez	Sergio Sotelo A.
Luz Marina Gómez S.	Anne E. Madrid G.	Feliz Fernández
José Antonio Gallardo F.	Raúl Eguila Nalo	Fernando Shutz
M. M de las Heras Polanco	Miguel A. Martínez	Ricardo R. De Tarsio
Miguel Marín P.	Fco Manel Lazo	Nelly Toledo
Anamaria de Moraes	Guillermo Sicard	Patricia Guizar Reyes
Gui Bonsiepe	Enrique Román Quintanar	Claudio Rodríguez
Rodrigo Walker	Walter Oehler de la Mora	Carlos R. Cadena
Francisco Masjuan	Carlos M. Caballero L.	Edgar Peregrina Marroquín
Ricardo Blanco	Francisco José Soto U.	Luis Soto Walls
Francisco J. Santos Z.	Jairo R. Acero	Manuel Ignacio Mier
Basilio Uribe	Gabriel Bernal Ruiz	Carlos E. Kohler
Dolores Ortíz	Ingo Werk	Luis Fernando Zapata
Jesús López Veloz	José M. Rodríguez	José Luis Alegría
Cecilia Durán	Sergio Rivera Conde	Rómulo Polo Flórez
Jaime González Yapor	Francisco Manuel L.	Enrique Camargo
Andrés Hayus du Tilly	Michael Weiis	Julio Colmenero
Alfredo Fernández	Jorge Vila Ortíz	Jesús Gámez
Santiago Tizón	Valeria London	Guido Díaz

Source: Opening minutes of ALADI (1980).

Several in this group are founders of academic programmes, many others are professors, and most are practitioners of the 'nascent' field of graphic and goods design in the region.

order to end cultural dependency. It was the demand to break free from those who did not wish for Latin America to create its own reality, as asserted historically by Oscar Pamio (1981). Self-governance to design based on the circumstances and for the circumstances, a dream, a utopia, a promise: such was the size of the task that the founders of ALADI envisioned for design in Latin America.

A long comet

Since the beginning of the republican policies in Latin America and primarily motivated by the difficult and violent processes of independence in countries of the Spanish empire, a long line of intellectuals began to advocate for cultural autonomy beginning in the early nineteenth century. The poverty and extreme poverty present throughout the territory caused the majority of Latin American intellectuals to think about how to overcome this scourge, making it the top priority above implementing any policy of a social nature (Cancelli, 2003).

Simultaneously, the expansionist policy of the United States began to threaten processes of independence in the countries in the region. The 'Monroe Doctrine' of 1823; the Mexican-American War in which North America took possession of old Mexican territories in the 1850s (what is now Texas, California, New Mexico, Nevada, Arizona, Utah, parts of Colorado, Wyoming, Kansas and Oklahoma); perceived US support for the pirate William Walker in Central America in the same decade; the so-called Pan-American policy promoted by the United States in the 1880s; and the US invasion of Cuba in 1898, among other things, caused some Latin American intellectuals to revisit some of the warnings of US imperialism in the region issued by Simón Bolívar beginning in 1820.[8]

Sensing this hegemonic threat, the emergence of the new republics would forge an imagined community with a common history, religion and language. The idea of not an Anglo-Saxon land but a Latin land was conceived of as an idea for the Americas. Some historians attribute this concept to the Colombian writer José María Torres Caicedo in 1857. Brazil would be included in this image in 1875. Mónica Quijada (1998) asserts that beyond reproducing European cultural events, Latin America would be seen as an image that was differentiated from what lay north of the Rio Grande (Mexico's northern border with the United States) and was configured with the purpose of defending itself from assault by expansionist policies. Let us recall that the independence processes of the former Spanish

---

[8] Two annotations are necessary. These matters are explored by Quijada (1998), Ayerbe (2012) and Betancourt (2013); Gilman (1999), Martin (2011) and Concha (2011); Schwartz (2013), Lucena (2012, 2015) and Pini (2008); Bayón (2011); and Eric Hobsbawm (2010, 2018) and in the compilations by Leslie Bethel (2011), Marco Palacios and Gregorio Weinberg (2008), José Luis Reyna (1995), Evelina Dagnino et al. (2010) and Gonzalo de la Massa and Carlos Ochsenius (2010). Second, the writings by Bolívar were organized by Manuel Pérez (2009) and made available online by Fundación Ayacucho in Venezuela.

colonies were long, bloody and painful, and hence it was necessary to defend them against any imperialist gesture.

This construction was an essentialist gesture of identity linked to the configuration of the concept of the nation; in part, a formula that would invite identification among those who did not share the same experiences around the idea of opposing a 'common enemy', as asserted by Manheim (1987).

Since that time, a large quantity of Latin American intellectuals, either consciously or unconsciously, reasserted the principle of essentialist identity and the regional autonomy extending from that. Modern ways of seeing and evaluating reality, critical economics, the upsetting of political populism and Marxist contributions to social critique, among other factors, lent a certain particularity and colour to the subject, making that reassertion, dating back to the nineteenth century, dense and complex as it intersected with Latin American conditions in the twentieth century. Several recently cited studies provide indications of this complex genealogy.

Philosophers, bishops and priests; poets, writers and musicians; scientists, politicians, economists and journalists; visual artists, engineers, architects and designers, all of them bringing the discourse up to date were committed to reclaiming the basis of that essentialist argument from the early decades of the nineteenth century through the final decades of the twentieth century. It was nearly 150 years of a Latin Americanist discourse that vigorously ploughed through the decades, producing illusions and intoxicating generations, a discourse that was exhausted by the early 1980s – ironically – at the precise moment at which ALADI began to configure itself around it.[9]

Along its path, one of the hues this argument acquired – present in an enormous variety of discourses – consisted of technology as the most efficient way to be independent from the Centre.[10] At a time when Latin America was questioning its participation in the International Trade System, the challenges of Latin American industrialization began to be discussed in countries such as Argentina and Ecuador in the 1920s, emerging as a relatively widespread purpose after 1940 (Love, 2011). Both in discourse and the material sense, the technological domain was essential for achieving autonomy. The different agencies tasked with studying the topic, particularly ECLAC (the Economic Commission for Latin America), saw in external technology a factor of dependency that had to be broken in the interest of social and economic development.

The desire to solve the scourge of poverty and extreme poverty caused Latin Americanists to reflect constantly on the idea of creating under the circumstances

---

[9] The Latin Americanist discourse did not disappear. The strength of its advocates gave way as of 1980 to the brutal onslaught of neoliberalism, which undid the bonds of identity and sent gestures of solidarity and cooperation down the drain.

[10] In this respect, the reflections of Oswaldo Sunkel (1970, 1995) within the ECLAC are notable, as are those of scientists such as the Argentine Oscar Varsavsky (Galafassi, 2004).

and for the circumstances, which intersects with part of the interest in local technology, favouring the needs and deficiencies expressed by people marginalized by the process of development. These arguments had been defended with clarity since the 1940s, a decade during which the effects of the modernization processes begun in countries in the region were made visible. Cities in the region would grow exponentially in the following years, producing belts of extreme poverty along their peripheries, given the asymmetry brought by industrialization. The pace of migration and informal settlements was more rapid than that of industrialization and job creation (Cavarozzi, 1995; Sunkel, 1995; Weffort, 1995; Puyana, 2008; Love, 2011).

Without entering into the economic, social and political debate it produced, these phenomena made poverty and extreme poverty visible, physically bringing it to the cities. If, before these flows, there were some critical thoughts about these problems and about the sizeable human settlements on the edges of Latin American cities, they had clearly become a pressing concern for the nascent urban generations that were more or less committed to progress and relatively aligned with the principles of equity and shared well-being. The principles of social change and the debate about national development presented arguments and political opinions that demanded to be understood in the realities of each one of the countries in the region. With their respective proportions, such discursive combustions stimulated generations that took sides based on their experiences, social status and cultural capital.

To create under the circumstances and for the circumstances thus became the motto of a manifesto in which all *aesthetic ecstasy* must be experienced to resolve the needs of others, but primarily those marginalized by the process of national development, as defended in the founding arguments of ALADI in 1980 noted in the previous pages.[11] It is noteworthy that at least two conceptions were intertwined in a complex way in that motto. On the one hand was an *ethos* that went along with the ideologies of Modern Architecture that struggled with the neoclassical practice in place in Latin American universities since the 1930s. On the other hand was a conception of 'the people' in a very Latin American sense, conceived of fundamentally by Catholicism in the region and that would end up being termed 'Liberation Theology' in the late 1960s.[12] The former de-individualized architectural creation (Buitrago, 2012; Buitrago & Braga 2013). The latter exposed several generations of Latin Americans to the living conditions of 'the others', mobilizing the possibility of Catholic mercy in frank articulation with what Sennett (2012) calls 'cooperation'. It is in the merging of these two genealogical lines that a sense of intervention in the lives of the defenceless is sparked: homes that were essential for settling the poor, technological systems

---

[11] A separate chapter expands on some of these relationships (Buitrago & Braga, 2015).
[12] On this last point, review the genealogy by Soledad Loaeza (2008).

that would provide them access to the conditions of modernity in their daily lives. A professional achievement would be manifested in Modern Architecture, hand in hand with a secular calling that made them intervene in the living conditions of people abandoned by the process of economic and social development. This was a reality that was present every day before the eyes of a generation of young dreamers – like most ALADI founders, a generation that ostensibly believed in social change and was intoxicated by the Cuban Revolution in 1959: a group of rebels that stood up to US imperialism in Havana. It was as if all of the promises begun with independence from Spain and Portugal in the early nineteenth century were finally materializing.

The events of the 1960s would strengthen these Latin Americanist ideas in the imaginations of the young (Jaramillo, 2007). The counterculture in Latin America seems to be expressed in a way in which the discourse demanding autonomy and coming from the previous century is united with the economic and political critiques of national elites, theories of social change, the achievement of prosperity, and in general, the longing for national strengthening and the integration of sister republics that identify secularly with the same problems and visualize a common enemy.[13] Communist critique, progressivism and anarchism; social Catholicism; modernism in literature and the arts in general; the liberal policies of modern societies; and the conservative strongholds that oppose them: everything seems to gradually adhere to that Latin Americanist discursive notion handed down through the decades. Circumstantialism merges with romantic essentialism and together they multiply with a latent and vigorous anti-imperialism.

An essentialist search for Bolivarian unity emerged from the ideology of Simón Bolívar during the first few decades of the nineteenth century. A cultural cry of that Latin Americanism. Our needs … our problems … our pride. From the linguistic revindication made by the Argentine artist Xul Solar in the 1920s in its 'neocreole' system or even paintings such as 'Drago' in 1927, through the graphic revindication of the territory in the famous painting '*América invertida*' by Uruguay's Joaquín Torres García in 1943 and the anti-imperialist denunciations of Ecuador's Osvaldo Guayasamín in paintings such as his 1970 '*Reunión en el Pentágono*', as well as the circulation of these ideas within 'the popular', when, for example, they were transformed into metaphors for songs. It is interesting to see how the discourse justifying the existence of Latin American design rests on common sentiments among regional intellectuals such as those mentioned.

---

[13] In a modernist gesture, these Latin Americans defend a weighty idea of nation that is simultaneously a paradoxical expression of loyalty and rejection of the past. The mechanism goes beyond the territorial, arguing that the very complex societies comprising the region share images of the world, histories, outlooks, scenarios, events, and rituals, as well as the sense of losses, triumphs, and disasters. In the vast territory of Latin America and its heterogeneous cultural configuration, this is a true illusion. Stuart Hall (2008, 2015) explains masterfully how these contradictions are expressed in the conceptions of identity of subjects in the effort to navigate modernity.

Symptomatic of this is the fact that Jesús Gámez decided to create a symbol for the first congress of ALADI in which Latin American unity is conquered and the territory is being closed against intrusion by any outsider, primarily – as seen in the upper curve of the symbol – the United States (see Figure 6.1).

Therefore, the cultural assertions regarding autonomy in relation to the exercise of design, although they are new in its epistemology, come from a critical framework that was 130 or 150 years old at the time they were enunciated. They reflected an anxious search for an essentialist identity; a latent problematization of circumstantialism; a determined attack against imperialism. The integration of the region's nascent republics was an objective ingrained in the thinking of a long line of intellectuals. The most different intellectual efforts hardly escaped that nineteenth-century goal. In this sense, ALADI would be no exception.

FIGURE 6.1 Black and White version of the ALADI logo, c. 1980. Designed by Jesús Gámez. Digital reproduction by the author. Personal collection of the author.

A 24-month awakening

Although it was officially founded in Colombia in November 1980, ALADI was in fact created in October 1978, in the context of an 'Interdesign' workshop organized in Mexico.[14] From that time forward, there were important moments in which people interested in the policy gradually joined. Of these, perhaps the most important event in size and even dissemination occurred during the 11th Congress of the ICSID (International Council of Societies of Industrial Design) organized in Mexico City in October 1979, a year after Interdesign '78 and a year before the founding of ALADI in Bogotá in 1980. At that event, a certain number of Latin American designers created a spontaneous parallel congress in which the proposal for ALADI was presented and worked on for four days. There, a special commission was chosen to define the basis for ALADI, assigning Colombia the

FIGURE 6.2 Presentation of the proposal for ALADI at the 11th Congress of ISCID, Mexico City, October 1979. From left to right: Rómulo Polo (Colombia), Basílio Uribe (Argentina), Gui Bonsiepe (Germany-Argentina), Roberto Napoli (Argentina) and Mario Mariño (Argentina). Taken from the book 'Crónicas del Diseño Industrial en la Argentina' [Chronicle of Industrial Design in Argentina] by Ricardo Blanco (2005). Fundación IDA, Investigación en Diseño Argentino. Fondo: Blanco, Ricardo

---

[14] At least three documents confirm this: the reconstruction in the 'Carreta del Diseño' (Polo, Gámez & Lozano, 1980a, pp. 17–18), the presentation in the Mexican report by Interdesign (Martínez & Gallardo, 1978, p. 26) and the documents drafted by the founding group during the event (Polo, 1978). This information can be triangulated with the memories of some of the attendees at Interdesign, particularly those of Rómulo Polo (2014), Luiz Blank (2014) and Oscar Hagerman (2016).

responsibility of organizing the first congress and the founding assembly.[15] The commission consisted of Anamaría de Morais of Brazil, Nelly Toledo of Puerto Rico, Claudio Rodríguez of Mexico, Roberto Napoli of Argentina, Gui Bonsiepe of Argentina, Iván Espín of Cuba, Rodrigo Walker of Chile, Oscar Pamio of Costa

TABLE 6.3 Signatories for the proposal to form ALADI, Mexico City, 1979

Signatories of the ALADI proposal at the 11th ICSID Congress in Mexico City, 1979		
Ricardo Blanco	Magdalena de las Heras	Jorge Vila Ortíz
Francisco J. Santos Z.	Jose Luis Alegria	Carlos E. Kohler
Basilio Uribe	Miguel Marin P.	Luis Fernando Zapata
Roberto Napoli	Dolores Ortiz	Juan Gómez Gallardo
Carlos Chavez Aguilera	Jesus López Veloz	Rómulo Polo Flórez
Carlos Carillo Soberón	Enrique Camargo	Ricardo R. G. de Tarsio
Francisco García Noriega	Andrés Hayaux du Tilly	Olicio C. Pelosi
Enrique Roman Quintanar Olivo	Adriana Canales	Franca Rosi
Walter Oehler de la Mora	Enrique Camargo C.	Oscar Pamio
Carlos M. Caballero L.	Miguel A. Martínez	Luis E. Arroyave
Francisco Jose Soto Curiel	Fco. Manuel Lazo	Joaquim Redig
Carlos Daniel Soto Curiel	Guillermo Sicard Montejo	Iván Espín
Jose Luis Berrueta Alvarez	Jesús Virchez Alanis	Ana Maria de Morais
Guadalupe González	Anne E. Madrid Gowd	Gui Bonsiepe
Luis Romero Regús	Raúl Eguia Malo	Rodrigo Walker
Luis Sierra Campuzano	Jairo R. Acero	Francisco Masjuan
Sergio Sotelo Aren	Gabriel Bernal Ruiz	Luz María Gómez S.
Felix Fernández G.	Ingo Werk	José Antonio Gallardo
Patricia Guizar Reyes	Jose M. Rodríguez	M.M de las Heras
Luis Soto Walls	Sergio Rivera Conde	Manuel Mier y Terán
Carlos R. Cadena	Michael Weiss	Jaime González Yapor
Edgar Peregrina Marroquín	Fernando Shutz	Cecilia Durán

Sources: Journal 'La Carreta del Diseño' (Polo, Gámez & Lozano, 1980b, pp. 20–2); Journal 'Módulo' (Pamio, 1980, pp. 30–2).

---

[15] The event is recorded in at least five articles: one published in the in Costa Rican journal 'Módulo' (Pamio, 1980, pp. 30–2); another in Colombia in the 'Carreta del Diseño' (Polo, Gámez & Lozano, 1980b, pp. 20–2); two more in Brazil (Morais, 1980; Redig, 1980) and a fifth in the Argentine newspaper 'La Nación' (ALADI: among Latin American industrial designers, 1979). Similarly, the event is present in the memories of at least seven attendees: the Argentineans Ricardo Blanco (2016) and Roberto Napoli (2016); the Mexican Claudio Rodríguez (2016); the Chilean Fernando Shultz (2016); the Italian Franca Rosi (2016); the Colombians Jairo Acero (2016) and Rómulo Polo (2014) and the Brazilian Joaquim Redig (2013).

Rica and Rómulo Polo of Colombia; a total of sixty-six designers from ten Latin American countries signed the document drafted in Mexico City. Figure 6.2 shows part of the group meeting in Mexico.

By June 1979, some national groups had already discussed the idea of founding ALADI. One of these meetings took place in Colombia, where some members of the national association of designers agreed with the idea and made some proposals. Figure 6.3 shows a copy of the manifesto. They discussed agreements drafted in India in 1979 – which we describe further below – as well as the manifesto proposed at Valle de Bravo, Mexico, in November 1978.[16] While the author does not have documentation of them, it appears that meetings such as this were carried out in Buenos Aires and Rio de Janeiro in those same months.

Five months before these meetings, in January 1979, Rómulo Polo from Colombia met José Abramovitz of Brazil and Basilio Uribe of Argentina at the 'Meeting for Development' organized in India between ICSID and UNIDO (United Nations Industrial Development Organization). In private, they discussed the 'Valle de Bravo Manifesto' and reinforced the idea of creating ALADI. There, they wrote what was called the 'Proposal in India for the creation of ALADI' whose copy can be seen in Figure 6.4. Based on the documents (Abramovitz, Polo & Uribe, 1980) and discussions with Polo (2014) and Abramovitz (2013), it was an executive meeting that addressed some logistical matters and what could be debated about the idea – it was a very short meeting.

Exoticism and identity

In terms of the growing awareness and membership of ALADI, 1979 was an important year for the process of creating ALADI. As noted, however, the process began in October 1978 in Mexico.[17]

Two years before the founding in Bogotá and one year before the aforementioned 1979 Congress, a number of Latin American designers became acquainted. The context was an ICSID-Interdesign workshop organized in Mexico. Sponsored by UNIDO and organized with assistance from CODIGRAM (*Colegio de Diseñadores Industriales y Gráficos de México* or the Mexican College of Industrial and Graphic Designers), the ICSID proposed a workshop to intervene in rural problems related to the production of alternative energy in San Miguel de Tzinacapan, an

---

[16] Both the document written in Colombia (Gutiérrez et al., 1980, p. 19) and in India (Abramovitz, Polo & Uribe, 1980, p. 18) were published in the journal 'La Carreta del Diseño'. Rey also transcribes part of the latter (2009, p. 400).

[17] José Rey (2009) states that this happened in 1974 and some Colombians in 1972 (ACD-Secretaria de organización, 1979, p. 3). The goal of each case was to create a regional body of a lager one (ICSID o US Council of Designers [sic]-), that was very different from the axiom that governs ALADI. Messell (2018, p. 11) describes a letter written by several Latin Americans in 1968 in Buenos Aires, that would coincide with this principle. It would be the antecedent of ALADI.

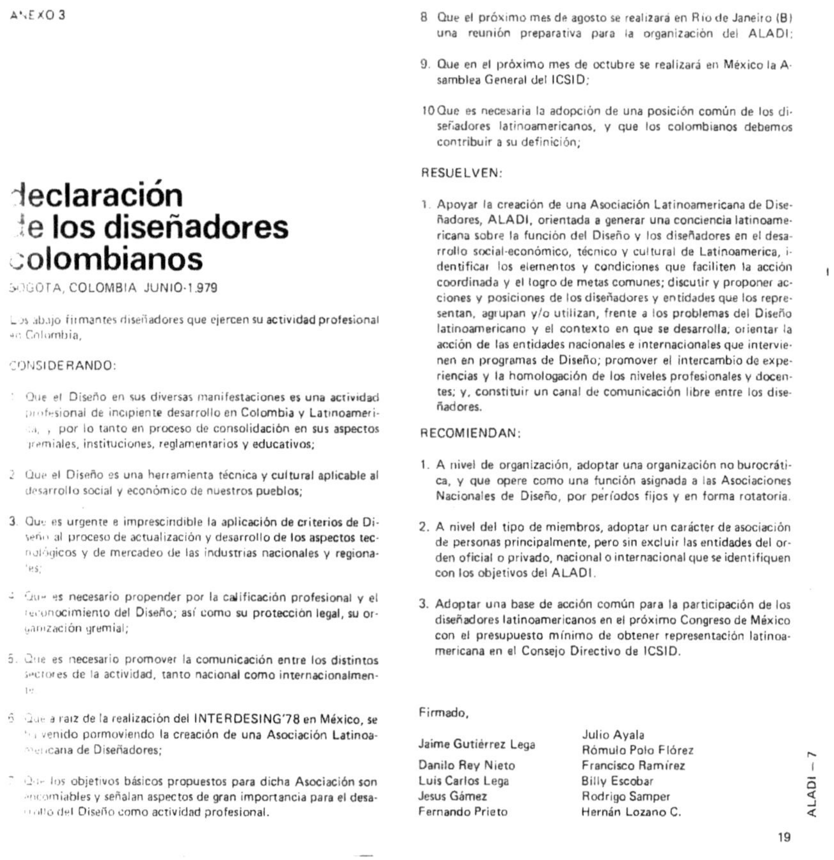

FIGURE 6.3 Statement by the Colombian designers. Document drafted and signed in Bogotá in June 1979. Taken from the journal *La Carreta del Diseño no. 3* (Gutiérrez et al., 1980, p. 19). Personal collection of Rómulo Polo, Bogotá, Colombia

indigenous community located 230 km from Mexico City (Martínez & Gallardo, 1978; Polo, 1978; Auböck, 1979; Polo, Gámez & Lozano, 1980a, pp. 17–18).

The workshop lasted 15 days and was divided into two major phases, according to the available documentation (Martínez & Gallardo, 1978; Auböck, 1979) and the recollections of some of the attendees, such as Luiz Blank (2014), Rómulo Polo of Colombia (2014) and Óscar Hagerman of Mexico (2016). The first phase comprised a series of conferences. The documentation generously provided by Blank confirms that these conferences discussed technical matters related to alternative energy production, methodological proposals for resolving community problems and the theory of social intervention based on appropriate technologies. These sessions took up the first 5 days and were carried out in Mexico City (CODIGRAM et al., 1978).

The second phase began on day 6 and lasted through day 14. This part was the workshop itself. The organizers of the event planned to move the attendees to a

ANEXO 2

propuesta para la formación de aladi

(Asociación Latinoamericana de Diseñadores Industriales)

BOMBAY, INDIA, ENERO-1.979

En la reunión sobre Diseño para el Desarrollo realizada en Ahmedabad y Bombay, India, los representantes de Argentina, Brasil y Colombia proponen la creación de una Asociación Latinoamericana de Diseño Industrial - ALADI con el fin de fortalecer la cooperación técnica entre los países en desarrollo. Dichos participantes darán los pasos necesarios para institucionalizar esta propuesta en sus respectivos países, invitando a los miembros de otras naciones latinoamericanas a tomar parte en estas actividades.

Entre sus objetivos mencionamos las siguientes proposiciones:

1. ALADI ayudará a establecer una corriente de comunicación entre personas e instituciones que se desenvuelven en el área del Diseño Industrial.

2. ALADI establecerá las bases comunes para la participación de Latinoamerica en eventos de Diseño Industrial.

3. ALADI informará sobre los programas de Diseño Industrial en Latinoamerica a las organizaciones internacionales.

4. ALADI ayudará a establecer un perfil profesional del Diseño Industrial en los países que la forman.

5. Establecerá bases comunes para la formación de diseñadores industriales y para la práctica profesionales en los países que integran ALADI.

6. Establecerá un banco de datos del Diseño Industrial en Latinoamerica.

7. Promoverá la inclusión del Diseño Industrial como factor de desarrollo en los programas de los gobiernos y organizaciones internacionales.

Firmado:
Basilio Uribe, Argentina
José Abramovitz, Brasil
Rómulo Polo Flórez, Colombia
Bombay, 23 de enero de 1979

FIGURE 6.4 Proposal for the formation of ALADI. Bombay, January, 1979. Taken from the journal *La Carreta del Diseño no. 3* (Abramovitz, Polo & Uribe, 1980, p. 18). Personal collection of Rómulo Polo, Bogotá, Colombia

convent in Valle de Bravo, a municipality 30 kilometres east of Mexico City. There, a daily programme was organized that was as rigorous as monastic life. In those eight days, organized into groups, the different attendees worked on proposals regarding alternative energy production for the indigenous community of San Miguel Tzinacapan. Each day, they followed a strict schedule that predetermined certain phases of the design process, the feedback sessions and presentations on daily progress.

These being days of collective work that was very intense and exclusively dedicated to the task, it could hardly be expected that the attendees would establish weak personal connections. From the curiosity to share experiences regarding the different ways in which design was understood in each place, to more general cultural exchanges, the time, interactions and similarities forged bonds that were even expressed as ties of identity and friendship. They noted that they shared the same values and concerns; that they coincided in their critical approach to their social and political realities; and had a very similar perception of the functions and meanings of design within the socio-economic conditions of their respective countries (Polo, 1978). Several of the Latin American participants began to express the hope of a professional identity that was infused by a firm ideological and political conception and that would activate Latin American linguistic and territorial identification – coming from the nineteenth century.

As a catalyst, over the course of these days, some of the designers began to meet and express disagreement with the meaning of the workshop's proposal, with its imposed methodology, and primarily what several of them understood as the way in which some members of ICSID underestimated Mexican and Latin American matters. As if refreshing the old threats of danger expressed by generations of Latin Americans since the nineteenth century, the dissent triggered a strong sense of identification in them, making it clear that there was an 'us' configured in opposition to a 'them'. Thus, the agglutinative Latin Americanism would provide a foundation on which to stand.[18]

TABLE 6.4 Schedule at Valle de Bravo from 22 to 29 November

Time	Activity
8h00–9h00	Breakfast
9h00–13h30	Morning work session
13h30–15h30	Lunch
15h30–18h30	Afternoon work session
18h30–19h30	Evaluation
19h30–21h00	Dinner
21h00–…	Presentation of progress

Sources: CODIGRAM report on Interdesign '78 (Martínez & Gallardo, 1978) and *Working Programme*, given to participants by the organizers (CODIGRAM et al., 1978).

---

[18] It seems inappropriate to state that there is 'a Latin Americanism' that remains intact in its development. There is an 'essence' that has been configured since the era of Bolívar (1812 or even before), upon which meanings have been added and defined over the decades as varied challenges arise. In an almost unconscious way, the categories upon which that Latin Americanism is established take root amid the particular circumstances. This category functions nearly akin to a 'collective unconscious' in the sense of Carl Jung (2014).

These Latin American designers studied architecture and/or design between 1957 and 1965 in the turbulent universities of the region. They were young students in those years in which cultural, economic and technological vindication was reinforced in the discourses of several intellectuals in the region. From the critical perspective promoted by circumstantialist philosophy through the economic critiques of development made at ECLAC, the pointing out of national elites as part of the historical drain to which Latin American was subjected in the International Trade System (an argument constructed by heterodox communism), Liberation Theology, dependency theory of course, the triumph of the Cuban Revolution in 1959: all of this was under debate from the 1940s through the 1980s, nourishing and being nourished by that Latin Americanism that reasserted autonomy and was the nucleus of the intellectual setting of the 1970s, when these individuals were studying architecture and design in Latin America.

With critical views of their reality, they had also acquired experience in the field of design – some of them as much as 15 years at that point – working on development projects for their respective governments in which they had to relate to people living in conditions very similar to those indigenous and peasants in Mexico who were the object of the workshop.[19]

Thus, when the ICSID designers came to Latin America to tell them how to do things, it could be said that two historical and cultural realities were colliding. One was based on a liberalism in the sense of Appiah (1998), that understands everything based on prefabricated categories and deems its counterpart – if it sees them – as wrong and confused, a 'zero point hubris', in the words of Castro-Gómez (2010). The other emerged in a context in which the idea of dignity was necessary for achieving autonomy and liberty. There was a need for professional respect mixed with an old notion of cultural identity. At the same time, a battle for professional prestige and Latin American cultural pride was being waged.

Meeting one another, these Latin American designers shared experiences, noted the similarity in their ways of seeing reality, dreamed about it for the future and primarily became friends. Excited, they decided to write a letter, which led to the path of founding ALADI. Figure 6.5 shows the first page of that document.[20]

---

[19] It is possible to affirm this after systematizing the in-depth interviews carried out with thirty of those involved in ALADI and who, among other things, were trying to trace their personal and professional trajectories.

[20] As stated in certain documents (Polo, 1978; Polo, Gámez & Lozano, 1980a, pp. 17–18) and corroborated in the reporting of Blank (2014) and Polo (2014), Rómulo Polo of Colombia led this process, who drafted the letter based on the discussions held during those days and subsequently sent it to Luis Blank in Río de Janeiro and Adriana Adams in São Paulo; Francisco López in Buenos Aires; María Elvira Udawaga in Asunción; Alberto Chiquillo in El Salvador; Alberto Rabat in Lima; and Fernando Ortiz and Sergio Rivera in Mexico City and Pablo Robles in Guadalajara.

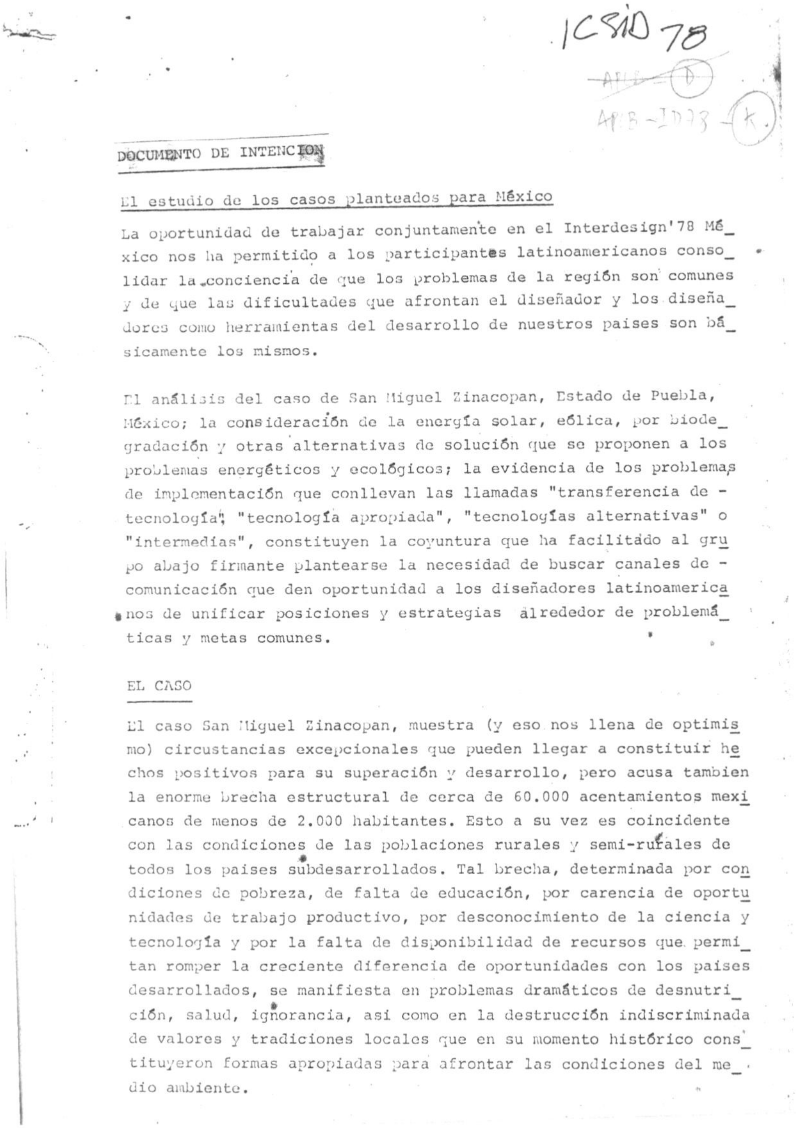

> DOCUMENTO DE INTENCION
>
> El estudio de los casos planteados para México
>
> La oportunidad de trabajar conjuntamente en el Interdesign'78 México nos ha permitido a los participantes latinoamericanos consolidar la conciencia de que los problemas de la región son comunes y de que las dificultades que afrontan el diseñador y los diseñadores como herramientas del desarrollo de nuestros paises son básicamente los mismos.
>
> El análisis del caso de San Miguel Zinacopan, Estado de Puebla, México; la consideración de la energía solar, eólica, por biodegradación y otras alternativas de solución que se proponen a los problemas energéticos y ecológicos; la evidencia de los problemas de implementación que conllevan las llamadas "transferencia de tecnología", "tecnología apropiada", "tecnologías alternativas" o "intermedias", constituyen la coyuntura que ha facilitado al grupo abajo firmante plantearse la necesidad de buscar canales de comunicación que den oportunidad a los diseñadores latinoamericanos de unificar posiciones y estrategias alrededor de problemáticas y metas comunes.
>
> EL CASO
>
> El caso San Miguel Zinacopan, muestra (y eso nos llena de optimismo) circunstancias excepcionales que pueden llegar a constituir hechos positivos para su superación y desarrollo, pero acusa tambien la enorme brecha estructural de cerca de 60.000 acentamientos mexicanos de menos de 2.000 habitantes. Esto a su vez es coincidente con las condiciones de las poblaciones rurales y semi-rurales de todos los paises subdesarrollados. Tal brecha, determinada por condiciones de pobreza, de falta de educación, por carencia de oportunidades de trabajo productivo, por desconocimiento de la ciencia y tecnología y por la falta de disponibilidad de recursos que permitan romper la creciente diferencia de oportunidades con los paises desarrollados, se manifiesta en problemas dramáticos de desnutrición, salud, ignorancia, asi como en la destrucción indiscriminada de valores y tradiciones locales que en su momento histórico constituyeron formas apropiadas para afrontar las condiciones del medio ambiente.

FIGURE 6.5 The first page of the 'Document of intent' Conceived of in Mexico in November 1978 and drafted by Rómulo Polo. Personal collection of Luiz Blank, Rio de Janeiro, Brazil

From Latin America and for Latin America

Thus, ALADI's founding discourse makes design accountable to the expectations of social change, whether these concern the economic development of states, the urgency to reduce poverty or to support the link between technology, dependence and underdevelopment.

The structure of this discourse is based on Latin American critique. By validating this discourse with the expectation that this critique establishes for technology, design enabled the creation of circumstances that would satisfy the needs of the people marginalized by development, recognizing and recovering their cultural differences and resisting the imperialist siege that had affected the entire region. It is an image of Latin American identity that feeds the representation of design as the way to achieve autonomy and sovereignty. In this context, ALADI – the largest associative design project operated in Latin America – is the institutional body of a Latin American far-reaching desire.[21]

References

Abramovitz, J. (4 November 2013). ALADI. *Interview of 1h 29m in duration* (J. Buitrago, interviewer) Rio de Janeiro, Brazil.

Abramovitz, J., Polo, R. & Uribe, B. (1980). Propuesta para la formación de ALADI. *La Carreta del Diseño 3*, 18. Rómulo Polo Personal Archive, Bogotá, Colombia (APRP).

ACD-Secretaria de organización. (1979). *ALADI, Asociación Latinoamericana de Diseño Industrial. Propuesta ACD.* Asociación Colombiana de Diseñadores (ACD). Bogotá: Unpublished – Personal collection of Jesús Gámez, Cali, Colombia (APJG).

Acero, J. (1 March 2016). Volvernos más fuertes, que en el camino nos econtramos. *Interview of 2h 8m in duration* (J. Buitrago, interviewer) Bogotá, Colombia.

'ALADI: ente latinoamericano de diseñadores industriales' (1979). *La Nación*, 7 November: Secc. 2º – Page unreadable.

ALADI (1980). *Acta de constitución de la Asociación Latinoamericana de Diseño Industrial, ALADI.* Bogotá: Inédito – Marcos Braga Personal Archive, São Paulo, Brasil (APMB).

ALADI. (1984). *Ata da 3ª Assembléia geral ALADI.* Petrópolis: Inédito – Instituto Superior de Diseño Industrial Library, Havana, Cuba (BISDI).

ALADI. (1995). *Séptima ALADI. Argentina' 95.* Buenos Aires: Inédito – Instituto Superior de Diseño Industrial Library, Havana (BISDI).

Appiah, A. (1998). Cosmopolitan Patriots. In Cheah, P. & Robbins, B. (eds), *Cosmopolitics Thinking and Feeling beyond the Nation.* Minneapolis: University of Minnesota Press, 91–114.

Auböck, C. (1979). *ICSID UNIDO Interdesign Mexico 1978.* Brigthon: Unpublished – University of Brigthon Design Archives (UBDA).

Ayerbe, L. (2012). *Los Estados Unidos y la América Latina. La construcción de la hegemonía.* La Habana: Fondo Editorial Casa de las Américas.

Barragán et al. (1993). *Sexta ALADI. Colombia 93.* Manizales: Inédito – Instituto Superior de Diseño Industrial Library, Havana, Cuba (BISDI).

Bayón, D. (2011). A Arte e a Arquitetura Latino-Americanas, c. 1920–c. 1990. In Bethell, L. (ed.), *Historia da América Latina. A América Latina após 1930: ideias, cultura e sociedade (vol. VIII).* São Paulo: EdUSP, 551–610.

Betancourt, A. (2013). La perspectiva continental: entre la unidad nacional y la unidad de América Latina. *Historia Crítica* (49), 135–57.

Bethell, L. (2011). *A América Latina após 1930: ideias, cultura e sociedade.* São Paulo: EdUSP.

Blanco, R. (2005). *Crónicas del Diseño Industrial en la Argentina.* Buenos Aires: Ediciones FADU.

---

[21] Nicolás Shumway (2008), would call such a 'ficción directriz (fictional directive)'.

Blanco, R. (31 August 2016). Una referencia universal. *Interview of 2h 15m in duration* (J. Buitrago, interviewer) Buenos Aires, Argentina.

Bloch, M. (2002). *Apologia da história. Ou o ofício do historiador*. Rio de Janeiro: Zahar.

Blank, L. (6 June 2014). Tudo nasce de uma conversa. *Interview of 4h 33m in duration* (J. Buitrago, interviewer) Rio de Janeiro, Brazil.

Bolivar, S. (2009 [1815]). Contestación de un Americano Meridional a un caballero de esta isla 'Carta de Jamaica' (Kingston 6 de septiembre de 1815). In Pérez, M. *Simón Bolívar. Doctrina del libertador*. Caracas: Biblioteca de Ayacucho, 66–87.

Bolívar, S. (2009). Al señor coronel Patric Campbell, encargado de negocios de Su Majestad Británica 'Carta Campbell' (Guayaquil, 5 August 1829). In Perez, M. (ed.), *Simón Bolívar. Doctrina del libertador*. Caracas: Biblioteca de Ayacucho, 354–6.

Buitrago, J. (2012). *Creatividad social. La profesionalización del Diseño Industrial en Colombia*. Cali: Programa Editorial de la Universidad del Valle.

Buitrago, J. (2017). *ALADI. Da libertação de nossos povos às leis do mercado*. São Paulo: Universidade de São Paulo, Faculdade de Arquitetura e Urbanismo. Submitted in Partial Fulfillment of the Requirements for Degree of Doctor of Design and Arquitecture, Minor: History and Theory of Design – Unpublished.

Buitrago, J. (forthcoming). *De la creatividad social a la liberación de nuestros pueblos. Diseño, Latinoamericanismo y autonomía cultural*. In press.

Buitrago-Trujillo, J.-C. (2020). Diseño en Sociedad. Una epistemología del Diseño en Colombia. In Devalle, V. & Garone, M. (eds), *Diseño latinoamericano: diez miradas a una historia en construcción*. Bogotá: Universidad Jorge Tadeo Lozano, Universidad Santo Tomás, Politécnico Grancolombiano, 95–143.

Buitrago, J. & Braga, M. (2013). De la Arquitectura Moderna al Diseño Industrial: algunas ideas sobre una tentativa migración de la utopía del proyecto moderno en América Latina. *Annales del IAA* (43), 169–87.

Buitrago, J. & Braga, M. (2015). Da América Latina para a América Latina: o design como ferramenta para o desenvolvimento econômico e cultural. In Patrocinio, G. & Nunes, J. (eds), *Design & Desenvolvimento: 40 anos depois*. São Paulo: Blucher, 83–109.

Buitrago, J. & Braga, M. (2019). From Latin America to Latin America: Design As a Tool For Economic and Cultural Development. In Patrocinio, G. & Nunes, J. (eds), *Design and Development. Leveraging Social and Economic Growth Through Design Policies*. São Paulo: Blücher, 209–76.

Cancelli, E. (2003). América del deseo: pesadilla, exotismo y sueño. *Estudios sociológicos*, 21 (1), 55–74.

Castro-Gómez, S. (2010). *La hybris del punto cer. Ciencia, raza e ilustración en la Nueva Granada (1750–1816)*. Bogotá: Editorial Pontificia Universidad Javeriana.

Cavarozzi, M. (1995). Más allá de las transiciones a la democracia en América Latina. In Reyna, J. L. (eds), *América Latina a finales de siglo*. Ciudad de México: Fondo de Cultura Económica, 460–85.

CODIGRAM et al. (1978). *Interdesign 78/Working Programme*. México: Inédito – Luiz Blank Personal Archive, Rio de Janeiro (APLB).

Chomsky, A. (2015). *História da revolução cubana*. São Paulo: Editora Veneta.

Concha, J. (2011). A poesía Latino-Americana, c. 1920–1950. In Bethell, L. (eds), *Historia da América Latina. A América Latina após 1930: ideias, cultura e sociedade (vol. VIII)*. São Paulo: EdUSP, 425–60.

Dagnino, E. et al.(2010). *La disputa por la construcción democrática en América Latina*. Ciudad de México: CIESAS and Fondo de Cultura Económica.

Delamaza, G. & Ochsenius, C. (2010). Trayectorias, redes y poder: sociedad civil y política en la transformación democrática chilena. In Dagnino, E. et al. (eds), *La disputa por la construcción democrática en América Latina*. Ciudad de México: CIESAS and Fondo de Cultura Económica, 450–500.

Espín, I. (1980). Hacia la institucionalización del Diseño en Cuba (Conferencia dictada como representante de Cuba, en el Congreso de ALADI en Bogotá en 1980). Encuentro Latinoamericano de Diseño. La Habana: Inédito – Universidad Nacional Library, Medellín (BUNM).

Espín, I. et al. (1989). *Memorias ALADI'89 Cuba*. La Habana: Unpublished – Instituto Superior de Diseño Industrial Library, Havana, Cuba (BISDI).

Fernández, L. (2005). Modernity and Postmodernity from Cuba. Journal of Design History, 18 (3), 245–55.

Fernández, L. (2012). Una isla de diseño. *Revolución y Cultura*, 2, 8–18.

Freidson, E. (1983). The Theory of Professions: State of the Art. In Dingwall, R. & Lewis, P. (eds), *The Sociology of the Professions: Lawyers, Doctors and Others*. New York: St. Martins, 19–37.

Freidson, E. (1998). The Theory of Professions: State of the Art. In Dingwall, R. & Lewis, P (eds), *The Sociology of the Professions: Lawyers, Doctors and Others*. New York: St. Martins, 19–37.

Freidson, E. (2001). *Professionalism. The Third Logic*. Great Britain: The University of Chicago Press.

Galafassi, G. (2004). A propósito de 'Ciencia, política y cientifismo' de Oscar Varsavsky. *Revista Theomai*, (9), 17–34.

García Márquez, G. (1982). *Gabriel García Márquez Nobel Lecture 1982*. At The Nobel Prize. https://www.nobelprize.org/prizes/literature/1982/marquez/lecture/ [accessed 26 October 2014].

Gilman, C. (1999). El intelectual como problema. La eclosión del antiintelectualismo latinoamericano de los sesenta y setenta. *Prismas. Revista de historia intelectual* 3 (3), 73–93.

Gruzinski, S. (2012). *Que horas são … lá, no outro lado?: América e o Islã no limiar da época moderna*. Belo Horizonte: Autêntica.

Gutiérrez, J. et al.(1980). Declaración de los diseñadores colombianos. *La Carreta del Diseño* 3, 19.

Hagerman, O. (12 May 2016). Lo originario, lo latinoamericano. *Interview of 1h 42m in Duration*. (J. Buitrago, interviewer) Mexico City.

Hall, S. (2008). *Da diáspora. Identidades e mediações culturais*. Belo Horizonte: UFMG.

Hall, S. (2015). *A identidade cultural na pôs-modernidade*. Rio de Janeiro: Lamparinha editora.

Hobsbawm, E. (2010). Nacionalismo y nacionalidad en América Latina. In Sandoval, P. (eds), *Repensanso la subalternidad. Miradas críticas desde/sobre América Latina*. Lima: Envión Editores, 311–26.

Hobsbawm, E. (2018). *¡Viva la revolución!* Buenos Aires: Crítica.

Jaramillo, J. (2007). *Jaime Jaramillo Uribe. Memorias intelectuales*. Bogotá: Taurus.

Jung, C. G. (2014). *Os arquétipos e o inconsciente coletivo*. Petrópolis: Editora Vozes Ltda.

Lévi-Strauss, C. (1992). *Tristes trópicos*. Barcelona: Paidós.

Loaeza, S. (2008). La Iglesia Católica en América Latina en la segunda mitad del siglo XX. In Palacios, M. & Weinberg, G. (eds), *Historia general de América Latina. Volúmen VIII, América Latina desde 1930*. Paris: UNESCO/Gráficas Verona, 411–34.

Lobato et al. (1982). *ALADI 2. Congreso Asociación Latinoamericana de Diseño Industrial (selección de ponencias)*. La Habana: Unpublished – Instituto Superior de Diseño Industrial Library, Havana, Cuba (BISDI).

Love, J. (2011). Ideias e ideologias econômicas na América Latina. In Bethell, L. *Historia da América Latina. A América Latina após 1930: ideias, cultura e sociedade (vol. VIII)*. São Paulo: EdUSP, 161–242.

Lucena, D. (2012). Arte y revolución. Sobre los fotomontajes olvidados de Tomás Maldonado. *Izquierdas*, (13), 18–28.

Lucena, D. (2015). *Contaminación artísitica. Vanguardia concreta, comunismo y peronismo en los años 40*. Buenos Aires: Biblos.

Manheim, K. (1987). *Ideología y utopía*. México: Fondo de Cultura Económica.

Martin, G. (2011). A narrativa Latino-Americana, c. 1920–c.1990. In Bethell, L. (ed.), *Historia da América Latina. A América Latina após 1930: ideias, cultura e sociedade (vol. VIII)*. São Paulo: EdUSP, 329–424.

Martínez, J., & Gallardo, J. (1978). *Interdesign 78/Mexico Report*. Mexico City: Unpublished – Oscar Salinas Personal Archive, Mexico City (APOS).

Messell, T. (2016). International Norms and Local Design Research: ICSID and the Promotion of Industrial Design in Latin America, 1970–1979. *Design, Research, Society. Future Focused Thinking. 50th Anniversary Conference*, 2739–54.

Messell, T. (2018). Globalization and Design Institutionalization: ICSID´s XIth Congress and the Formation of ALADI, 1979. *Journal of Design History*, 1–17.

Modulo. (1981). ALADI. Asociación Latinoamericana de Diseño Industrial. *Módulo* (2), 3–5. Rómulo Polo Personal Archive, Bogotá (APRP).

Morais, A. (1980). Meditações à sombra das pirámides sob o sol tropical', *Journal APDINS/RJ*, May: Page unreadable. Marcos Braga Personal Archive, São Paulo (APMB).

Napoli, R. (6 September 2016). Un ICSID para Latinoamérica. *Interview of 2h in duration* (J. Buitrago, interviewer), Buenos Aires, Argentina.

Pamio, O. (1980). ALADI. Documento presentado en el XI Congreso ICSID. *Módulo* (1), 30–2. Jesús Gámez Personal Archive, Cali (APJG).

Pamio, O. (1981). Hacia un Diseño Independiente. *Módulo* (2), 1–2. Rómulo Polo Personal Archive, Bogotá (APRP).

Palacios, M. & Weinberg, G. (2008). Historia general de América Latina. Volúmen VIII, América Latina desde 1930. Paris: UNESCO/Gráficas Verona.

Perez, M. (2009). *Simón Bolivar. Doctrina del libertador*. Caracas: Biblioteca de Ayacucho.

Pini, I. (2008). Arte latinoamericano desde 1930 hasta la actualidad. In Palacios, M. & Weinberg, G. (eds), *Historia general de América Latina. Volúmen VIII, América Latina desde 1930*. Paris: UNESCO/Gráficas Verona, 501–20.

Polo, R. (1978). *Documento de intención*. Bogotá: Unpublished – Luiz Blank Personal Archive, Rio de Janeiro (APLB).

Polo, R. (24 February 2014). Investigar para diseñar. *Interview of 2h 25m in duration* (J. Buitrago, interviewer) Bogotá, Colombia.

Polo, R., Gámez, J. & Lozano, H. (1980). Interdiseño'78, Valle de Bravo, México. Documento de intención (noviembre de 1978). *La Carreta del Diseño*, (3), 17–18. Rómulo Polo Personal Archive, Bogotá (APRP).

Polo, R., Gámez, J. & Lozano, H. (1980). Propuesta para la creación de la Asociación Latinoamericana de Diseño Industrial 'ALADI' (Ciudad de México, octubre de 1979). *La Carreta del Diseño*, (3), 20–2. Rómulo Polo Personal Archive, Bogotá (APRP).

Puyana, A. (2008). La industrialización de América Latina y el Caribe. In Palacios, M, & Weinberg, G. (eds), *Historia general de América Latina. Volúmen VIII, América Latina desde 1930*. Paris: UNESCO/Gráficas Verona, 79–104.

Quijada, M. (1998). Sobre el origen y difusión del nombre 'América Latina' (O una variación heterodoxa en torno al tema de la construcción social de la verdad). *Revista de Indias, LVIII*, 58, (214), 596–616.

Redig, J. (1980). XI Congresso do ICSID, México, Outubro 79. Os Designers do mundo, pela 11ª vez, se reúnem. Os Designers latino-americanos pela 1ª vez, se organizam.

Journal da APDINS/RJ, (1), 4–5. Marcos Braga Personal Archive, São Paulo (APMB).
Redig, J. (16 October; 1 November 2013). Uma semente. *Interview of 2h 45m in duration* (J. Buitrago, interviewer) São Paulo and Rio de Janeiro, Brazil.
Rey, J. (2009). *Historia del CIDI. Un impulso de diseño en la industria argentina*. Buenos Aires: Red Amigos CMD.
Reyna, J. (1995). *América Latina a finales de siglo*. Ciudad de México: Fondo de Cultura Económica.
Rivera et al. (1991). *Quinta ALADI. Diseño y desarrollo para América Latina. V Congreso internacional de Diseño*. México D.F: Unpublished – Instituto Superior de Diseño Industrial Library, Havana, Cuba (BISDI).
Rodríguez, C. (27 May 2016). El diseño para el desarrollo 1. *Interview of 1h 10m in duration* (J. Buitrago, interviewer). Mexico City.
Rosi, F. (22 October 2016). Identidad y memoria histórica. *Interview of 1h 36m in duration* (J. Buitrago, interviewer) Montevideo, Uruguay.
Said, E. (1996). *Cultura e imperialismo*. Barcelona: Anagrama.
Schwartz, J. (2013). *O fervor das vanguardas*. São Paulo: Companhia das letras.
Sennett, R. (2012). *Juntos. Os rituais, os prazeres e a politica de cooperação*. Rio de Janeiro: Record.
Sevcenko, N. (2005). *Virando séculos. A corrida para o século XXI. No loop da montanha-russa*. São Paulo: Companhia das Letras.
Shultz, F. (3 June 2016). Una idea de producción para América Latina. *Interview of 2h 59m in duration* (J. Buitrago, interviewer) Mexico City.
Shumway, N. (2008). *A invenção da Argentina. História de uma ideia*. São Paulo: EdUSP.
Souza Dias, D. (2018a). International Design Organizations and the Study of Transnational Interactions: The Case of ICOGRADALatinoamérica 80. *Journal of Design History*. https://doi-org.bd.univalle.edu.co/10.1093/jdh/epy038, 1–19.
Souza Dias, D. (2018b). 'The Winds of Change:' Cosmopolitanism and Geopolitical Identities in the Context of Icograda. *ICDHS 10th+1 Barcelona 2018 Conference Proceedings*. Barcelona: Universitat de Barcelona, 426–30.
Sunkel, O. (1970). La universidad Latinoamericana ante el avance científico y técnico: algunas reflexiones. *Estudios internacionales*, 4 (13), 60–89.
Sunkel, O. (1995). Del desarrollo hacia adentro al desarrollo desde dentro. Un enfoque neoestructuralista para América Latina. In Reyna, J. (ed.), *América Latina a finales de siglo*. Ciudad de México: Fondo de Cultura Económica, 15–60.
Ugarte, M. (1976). *La Nación Latinoamericana*. Caracas: Biblioteca de Ayacucho.
Weffort, F. (1995). La América equivocada. Apuntes sobre la democracia y la modernidad en la crisis de América Latina. In Reyna, J. L. (ed.), *América Latina a finales de siglo*. Ciudad de México: Fondo de Cultura Económica, 399–431.

7 INTERNATIONALIZING JAPANESE GRAPHIC DESIGN: FROM THE PRE-WAR PERIOD TO TODAY

Yasuko Suga

Introduction

The history of modern Japanese graphic design begins when the nation opened to the West in the mid-nineteenth century. Based on the technique of traditional woodblock printing, mass advertising rapidly developed. Japanese engravers and printers saw the art of the Western advertising posters, and quickly learned the trends and styles. By the turn of the century, many masterpieces were designed for the new palace of consumerism – departmental stores, by representative figures such as the designers Hisui Sugiura (1876–1965) and Goyo Hashiguchi (1881–1921).[1]

The international art magazine *The Studio* already had some influence upon Japanese artists by the end of the nineteenth century, its readers including the design-conscious novelist Soseki Natsume and Mingei artist Kenkichi Tomimoto. In the twentieth century, when periodicals dedicated to graphic design appeared such as *Commercial Art*, *Modern Publicity* and *Gebrauchsgraphik*, Japanese designers enthusiastically inhaled the modern graphic spirit. They realized what they fatally lacked: professional organizations for graphic designers, a periodical focused on graphic design in Japan and a proactive international presence.

The chapter overviews how Japanese graphic designers constructed international liaisons before the Second World War and analyses the post-war formations and activities of two major graphic design professional groups – the Japan Advertising Artists' Club (JAAC, 1951–1970) and Japan Graphic Design Association (JAGDA, 1978–) – to consider how they balanced or failed to balance their international experiences, such as the coming of the World Design Conference and the formation of International Conference of Graphic Design

---

[1] Ritsuko Endo and Michio Miyazaki, 'Book Design in the Meiji Era: Changes of Book Design in Relation to Printing and Other Techniques(1)', *Bulletin of Japanese Society for the Science of Design* 53, no. 5 (2007): 69–78.

Associations (ICOGRADA), with their domestic issues and social contexts. This, in turn, sheds light upon understanding some issues still persistent in Japanese graphic design today.

Pre-war actions towards internationalization

Before the war, internationalization of Japanese graphic design proceeded around two core figures: Sugiura, who studied in Europe from 1922 to 1924, and Munetsugu Satomi (1904–1996), the first Japanese student to graduate from the École nationale supérieure des Beaux-Arts in Paris.

The social status of designers was not firmly established in pre-war Japan. For instance, a designer once confessed how he did not even know the word 'copy writer' or 'design' as late as 1924[2] but things then began to move forward. Global liaisons were first brought about by Sugiura, who while in Europe was much influenced by 'Die Six', the German commercial artists' association founded in Munich in 1914. When he returned home to Tokyo he organized 'Shichinin-sha (The Seven)', with Iwao Koike (1902–1979) and other graphic artists.[3] The first exhibition was held in 1926, and the annual exhibitions continued for about a decade. *The Studio* seems to be the first publication to introduce contemporary Japanese graphic design to the West, as it introduced Shichinin-sha's second exhibition as 'Modern Japanese Posters'.[4]

The term 'shogyo bijutsu' (commercial art) was coined by the graphic designer and critic, Masuji Hamada (1892–1938) in 1926 when he and another artist Hokuu Tada (1889–1948) started Shogyo Bijutsu Kyokai (the Commercial Art Association), one of the first professional designers' groups, whose periodical *Shogyo Bijutsu* was dedicated to graphic design. The formation of professional groups followed, such as the Research Institute of Commercial Art, the Central Designers Group, the New Design Institution, the New Designers Group, the Tokyo Printing Artists Group and the Tokyo Advertising Artists Club (1932), which appeared not only in Tokyo but also in Osaka and in Kyushu Island. There was even a short-lived avant-garde group influenced by the Russian Constructivists, called MAVO.[5] Also important was Nippon Kobo (Japan Workshop, 1933–45), led by Yosuke Natori

---

[2] Reika Sawa, 'Natsukashiki Keshohin Kokoku', in *Nihon Dezain Sho-shi Henshu Dojin, Nihon Dezain Shoshi* [*Small Design History of Japan*], ed. Nippon Dezain Shoshi Henshu Dojin (Tokyo: Daviddo-sha, 1970), 69.

[3] Other six were Izumi Arai, Yoshiro Kubo, Hiroshi Suyama, Mansuke Hara, Hideo Kishi and Noboru Nomura.

[4] Harada was a writer for Mainichi Newspaper Company received a commission to send art-related information to The Studio Company in the UK.

[5] See Toshiharu Omuka, *Nippon no Abangyarudo Geijutsu – MAVO to sono jidai* [*Japanese Avant-garde Art: MAVO and Its Age*] (Tokyo: Seido-sha, 2001).

(1910–1962), Ken Domon (1909–1990), Ayao Yamane (1897–1980), Hiromu Hara (1903–1986), Tadashi Kono (1906–1999) and Yusaku Kamekura (1915–1997), all the influential designers. This group promoted pictorial journalism in Japan, and published a pictorial magazine called *NIPPON* in different languages. As Yamana recalled, while the Meiji (1868–1912) and Taisho (1912–1925) eras were the 'time of individual creative activities', the Showa (1926–1989) era 'suddenly started to witness fountains of collective activities'.[6]

It is clear that the platform for debates and criticism on graphic design developed rapidly. In 1926, *Kokoku-kai* (Advertising World) was inaugurated. In its pages, contributors argued how advertising could improve the Japanese society until it ceased publication in 1941 because of the Second World War. In 1927, a poster magazine, *Afisshu*, named phonetically after the French word for posters, was inaugurated (1927– 1930), again from the initiative of Sugiura. His aim was not simply to follow the new trends from the West, but also to globally claim a position for the Japanese graphic designers.[7] In the first issue, posters by Antoine Girard for the 1925 Paris Exposition Internationale des Arts Décoratifs et Industrielles, Eno's Fruit Salt posters by Edward McKnight Kauffer and some Russian Constructivist posters, as well as the Moulin de la Galette poster by Tsuguharu Foujita, active in Paris, were introduced. Later volumes carried a number of introductory articles on Herbert Bayer, Bernard Leach, Man Ray, Laszlo Moholy-Nagy and Saul Bass. Comparison with overseas works must have given them confidence in their works as well as international knowledge: from 1929, they decided to 'leave the introduction of foreign posters to the foreign magazines' and dedicate the magazine more to 'establish the creative attitude of ourselves'.[8]

The first direct global encounter was with France, brought about by Satomi who was active in Paris. His personal connection with poster artists Paul Colin, Jean Carlu and Charles Repo made it possible to hold an exhibition entitled 'Kokusai Shogyo Bijutsu Kokan Kai (Exhibition of International Exchange in Commercial Art)' in Tokyo in 1934. The motive of the exhibition was to connect many domestic design groups and individuals, as well as directly liaise with international artists. Satomi was a good bridge on both sides because of his extensive personal connections. In Europe, the German monthly magazine *Gebrauchsgraphik* carried an article on Satomi in 1936, and this possibly encouraged another article on Japanese graphic design in 1938. Both old and new graphic designs, from ukiyo-e prints to posters advertising department stores, exhibitions and tourist destinations, including Satomi's work, were reviewed. It was remarked that Japanese graphic design was 'on its way to developing a style peculiar to itself'[9] (Figure 7.1).

---

[6] Iwao Yamana, *Taikenteki Dezain-shi* [*Design History as Experienced*] (Tokyo: Seibun-do, 2015), 110–11. Yamana is known for his design for the cosmetic company, Shiseido.
[7] Yamana, op.cit., 184.
[8] Hisui Sugiura, 'Saikan No Goaisatsu', *Affishes* 2, no. 1 (1929): 1.
[9] 'Japanese Advertising Art', *Gebrauchsgraphik* 15, no. 11, pp. 2–15. Satomi who was individually introduced in 1936 (vol. 13, no. 5, pp. 59–61)was again mentioned in this article.

FIGURE 7.1 Satomi's poster (Gebrauchsgraphik, vol. 11, 1938). Author's collection

Towards the end of the 1930s, further organizations were formed, such as the Zen Nihon Shogyo Bijutsu Renmei (Japan National Commercial Art League, est. 1937) and the Advertising Artists Gathering (est. 1938). But these as well as the various organization that had been established in the preceding years were either dissolved or put into different use when the Second World War broke out. Nippon Kobo, for example, was forced to rename itself, placed under the Japan's Army Intelligence Service and made to concentrate on cultural work towards the war effort, and issued propagandic photo journals such as *Shanghai* and *Canton*. Paradoxically, the diversion to working for official causes secured the consistent platform for active design practice even during the war, providing continuity and practically paving the way for a significant breakthrough for Japanese graphic design in the post-war years.

From the birth of JAAC to WoDeCo

After the Second World War, Japan rapidly made a recovery from the bombed-out barrenness. New products were designed, manufactured, advertised and sold for homes in the domestic market and sent abroad as a means for gaining foreign currency. As part of this reconstruction, graphic designers moved quickly to establish themselves. Much before the San Francisco Peace Treaty established Japan as a sovereign nation in 1951, already the Japan Designers Association was organized in occupied Japan in 1946 by those from the former Nippon Kobo. This became the seed for the future Nippon Senden Bijutsu Kyokai (Japan Advertising Artists Club, JAAC).[10] The Nippon Kokoku-kai (Japan Advertising Club), a body consisting of advertisers and advertising agencies in Tokyo, was also formed in 1947, led by Ado Niwatari.

In the winter of 1950, the first post-war meeting of the Advertising Artists Gathering was held in Tokyo with Ayao Yamana, Takashi Kono, Yusaku Kamekura, Ado Niwatari and some others. Following some more frequent meetings, in June 1951 the Founding General Meeting of the JAAC, the first professional organization for graphic designers, was organized, attracting about fifty designers. Kamekura, later known for the 1964 Tokyo Olympics posters, acted as the chair.

In 1951, the Prospectus printed in the first volume of the JAAC's official organ stated the Club's aim as

> to state what our profession is, to fix the understanding of advertising art, to protect all the rights concerning our work, to connect each other for the sake of our mutual benefit and happiness, to link with every sector of society, to beautify the world, to make it pleasant, and to participate in the cutting-edge art movements in of the world.[11]

Hara recalled its establishment, 'When I participated with the founding of JAAC in 1951, for the very first time I had a real feeling that I was part of a professional group of designers.'[12]

---

[10] *Nihon Dezain Sho-shi*, 209.
[11] 'Nippon Senden Bijutsukai Setsuritsu no Shushi'[Prospect of JAAC], *JAAC*, no. 1 (1951), quoted in Seki, Tanaka and Sano eds., *The Epoch of the Japan Advertising Artists Club* (Tokyo: TransArt, 2000), 154.
[12] Hiromu Hara, 'Dezain Hoko' [Notes on Design], in *Nihon Dezain Sho-shi*, 89.

The body grew fast. When the first exhibition was held in Tokyo in May there were eighty-eight works, of which nine were invited from already established designers. As Kamekura was much influenced by renowned French poster artist Raymond Savignac, who started the idea of 'non-commissioned posters' and introduced free ideas in poster design, the JAAC poster exhibitions had the same nature of non-commissioned works. Soon the exhibition programme spread to local commercial cities and, by September the same year, a regional exhibition was held in Osaka, where 129 works were exhibited.[13] In January 1952, they held the Fukuoka Regional Exhibition, and in May the Second JAAC Exhibition opened in Tokyo before travelling nationwide to Nagoya, Osaka, Kobe and other local cities. For the third exhibition in 1953, JAAC introduced an open call for public participation, receiving 669 applications, out of which 487 posters were shown, including 18 invited works. The initial membership grew rapidly from 150 to 300 in four years, which was described as an 'un-heard-of size with designers gathered for the single purpose' from major commercial and industrial cities.[14]

At the same time, international connections were being actively built up. In 1952, JAAC sent 105 posters to *Graphis* the leading international magazine. Hiroshi Ohchi (1908–1974), JAAC member and the translator of Johannes Itten's *Color Theory* into Japanese, was central in the selection. The collection was introduced in an article by Georgine Oeri on 'Japanese Advertising', with works by Yoshiro Hayakawa (1917–2009), Hiroshi Ohchi, Takashi Kono, Ado Niwatari, Yusaku Kamekura, among other designers. Oeri commented how she was impressed by how their productions reflected 'something like a national decision to make the best of an unavoidable development and to assimilate the Western element' which itself was 'typically Japanese'[15] (Figure 7.2).

In the article, JAAC was introduced as a professional organization which had 'deepened their understanding for each other while increasing outside prestige'.[16] International demonstrations and appeals followed. From 1954 the annual *Modern Publicity* also began to include Japanese advertising posters, sent by JAAC. The Club committee also sent 260 posters to Australia, held their own exhibition at the Museum of the City of Linz in Austria, and also submitted 197 examples of package design for a special issue of *Graphis*. Domestically, too, in 1955 an International Graphic Exhibition was held by the central members of JAAC in Tokyo, with the American renowned designer Paul Rand, thus strengthening its global bonds. In 1957, JAAC played an initiative role in proceeding with the establishment of Nippon Dezain Kaunshiru (the Japan Design Council) to make connection across the different fields of design in Japan, and by the introduction

---

[13] Yoshio Itabashi, 'Nissenbi Soritsu Zengo' [At the formation of JAAC], in *Nihon Dezain Sho-shi*, 283–4. 48 works were from Tokyo.
[14] Hiromu Hara, 'Nissenbi no Ayumi' [History of JAAC], *Living Design*, September 1955, no. 9.
[15] Georine Oeri, 'Japanese Advertising', *Graphis* 9, no. 46 (1953): 86.
[16] Oeri, op.cit., 90.

FIGURE 7.2A Poster announcing the 3rd Exhibition of JAAC (Modern Publicity, vol. 24, 1954–1955). Author's collection

FIGURE 7.2B Posters sent from JAAC to Graphis (Graphis, 1953). Author's collection

of the G Mark system (the Good Design Products Selection System), the symbol was designed by Kamekura.

Thanks to the synergistic effect of JAAC's activities, local and global design debates were much promoted in the print media. Publications such as the bi-monthly Japanese design magazine *IDEA*, inaugurated in 1953, began to include subtitles in English under the heading 'International Advertising Art and Selling' and the editorial content also became bilingual from the following year. A further step in this direction, in 1959, the Japanese-English bilingual magazine *Graphic Design* was inaugurated by Masaru Katsumi (1909–1983), the art and design critic who later acted as the art director for the 1964 Tokyo Olympics.

The year 1960 marked a turning point for Japan in many ways. At a time of high economic growth, colour TV was introduced that year and symbols of the rise in consumer expectations included ownership of a car, a cooler (air conditioner) and a colour television, together called the 3Cs. This was accompanied by wider social recognition that design mattered in everyday life and for the national economy. Moreover, the population was becoming more globally minded and outward-facing, in part prompted by the planning for the 1964 Tokyo Olympics.

Coinciding with all of these changes, 1960 was the year of World Design Conference in Tokyo. As design historian Toshino Iguchi has suggested, the event worked to 'raise awareness regarding international design organizations for the public as well as for individual designers'.[17] This was considered by the Japanese designers as 'comparable to host the Tokyo Olympics' – an international stage to promote national prestige. WoDeCo marked the first major occasion to bring together international creators and design critics in Japan. JAAC played a pivotal role in the preparations for WoDeCo. Preparatory discussions took place from 1958 through the Central Committee of JAAC. The following year, the Japan Executive Committee of WoDeCo was established with the representatives from various fields of design. JAAC planned for the keynote lecture by Herbert Bayer, and Saul Bass, Bruno Munari, Louis Kahn, among others, participated from the world. This was all the more enthusiastically because the year could be used to mark the 10th anniversary of the JAAC's foundation. The organizers hoped that the discussion of international design issues during the event would in turn stimulate the consideration of domestic issues[18] (Figure 7.3).

FIGURE 7.3 WoDeCo exhibition sites (Dezain no. 9, 1960). Author's collection

---

[17] Toshino Iguchi, 'Reconsideration of the World Design Conference 1960 in Tokyo and the World Industrial Design Conference 1973 in Kyoto: transformation of design theory', *The Proceedings of IASDR2013* (2013): 4.

[18] Editor, 'Dezain Kaigi ni Kitai suru' [Let's hope for WoDeCo], *Design* (Japanese magazine), no. 5 (1960): 2.

TABLE 7.1 The rise in applicants to the JAAC exhibition. Table by Yasuko Suga

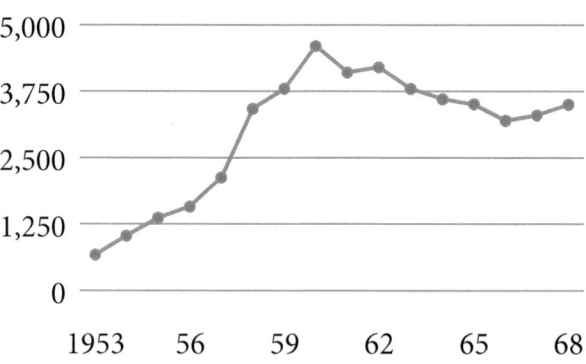

Reflecting the rapid growth of interest in design, the number of applicants for JAAC exhibition peaked in 1960 with 4,623 applicants solely from Japan. Influenced by the WoDeCo's main theme of 'visual communication', the tenth exhibition complemented this emphasis on communication design[19] (Table 7.1). In the following years they continued to receive around 4,500 submissions to their annual exhibitions. Alongside this significant increase in interest, the number of design schools in Japan increased especially between 1959 and 1965, and by 1969 amounted to nearly 100, reflecting the popularity of design as a future profession among young people.[20]

Internationally, Japanese graphic designers had more presence than during the previous decade. Besides *Graphic Design*, JAAC's own organ became bilingual from the late 1963.ABroad, *Graphis* covered the JAAC's exhibitions[21] and individual designers were also more widely featured. For the 1st International Poster Biennale held in 1966, Kazumasa Nagai (1929–) received a prize, and the 2nd Brno Graphic Art Biennale, Yoshio Hayakawa and Shigeo Fukuda (1932–2009) were represented. At home, when the 'Persona' Exhibition was held in 1965, ten years since the Graphic 1955, international designers like Paul Davis, Louis Dorfsman, Jan Lenica and Karl Gerstner were invited. This exhibition was positively reviewed as 'an artistic happening'.[22]

---

[19] Noboru Kawazoe, 'Kiro ni tatsu Nissenbi no Mondaiten' [Issues of JAAC in stray], *Bijutsu Techo*, October 1960, 11–19.
[20] Sadayuki Ando, *Dezainaa no Sekai* [*The World of Designers*] (Tokyo: Daiamondo-sha, 1969), 106.
[21] *Graphis* (no. 117, 1965). It introduced JAAC in no. 111 as well.
[22] Yusuke Kaji, 'Perusona ten to 11nin no gurafikku dezainaa tachi' [Persona Exhibition and 11 graphic designers], *Design*, no. 79 (1966): 13–15.

Considering all the achievements, it is a wonder why JAAC did not apply to become a full member of ICOGRADA on the Council's formation in 1964. The reason might reveal the internal issues JAAC was confronting: discordance induced by the political climate and growing authoritarianism in Japanese graphic design.

Design for whose sake?: The demise of JAAC

In 1964, ICOGRADA's *News Bulletin* reported that 'so far little or no news' from Japan had been received.[23] Throughout the rest of the decade, Katsumi was the only correspondent from Japan. Formally assigned as the Icograda Correspondent in 1965, he acted in the role until 1981. Therefore, when Katsumi gave a lecture on the design policy for Tokyo Olympic 1964, for the 2nd General Meeting of ICOGRADA in 1966, and ICOGRADA's 1st International Student Seminar on Graphic Design in 1966 as a speaker, he did so on an individual basis. This begs the question why had JAAC's collective action not come to the fore after the Tokyo WoDeCo?

One answer was because of the specific political climate. The year 1960 was the year of the renewal of the US-Japan Security Treaty that allowed the continued presence of US military bases in Japan, despite fierce counter-arguments that arose in pursuit of true independence. Okinawa and some other islands remained occupied even after the earlier San Francisco Treaty which ended the US occupation. Japan paid for the expense of US Army bases in the country and many citizens felt that the dignity of a sovereign state was made light of by this arrangement. Hostility towards the United States could be seen as one element in attacking American-oriented commercialism. Advertising was a good prey for the activists, many of whom were university students fighting against the renewal of the US-Japan Security Treaty. Throughout the 1960s, criticism of JAAC rose from art university students for the organization's reigning over the world of advertising.

In such a situation, WoDeCo's theme of 'visual communication', and the understanding of graphic design as 'visual design' which has a public role in society, encouraged designers and would-be designers to think of ethical issues and to align their creative activities with social actuality. Keywords such as 'social' or 'public' and 'against commercialism' were much more keenly noticed, and the trend was crystallized in more 'public posters' dealing with political and social

---

[23] ICOGRADA, *News Bulletin*, no. 1, February 1964, Design Archives, The University of Brighton.

issues like population growth, world peace, generational problems, poverty, among others. Furthermore, JAAC's 10th Exhibition reflected this tendency for designers to take up more of a social role and responsibility[24] (Figure 7.4).

JAAC, as an organization, took a non-political attitude, not intervening with political beliefs of each individual member. Besides, it was too busy with the internal problem based on the central-local conflicts: if a locally selected work was dropped at the central selection, a strong petition would come from the local branch and sometimes resulted in unfairness (to which the

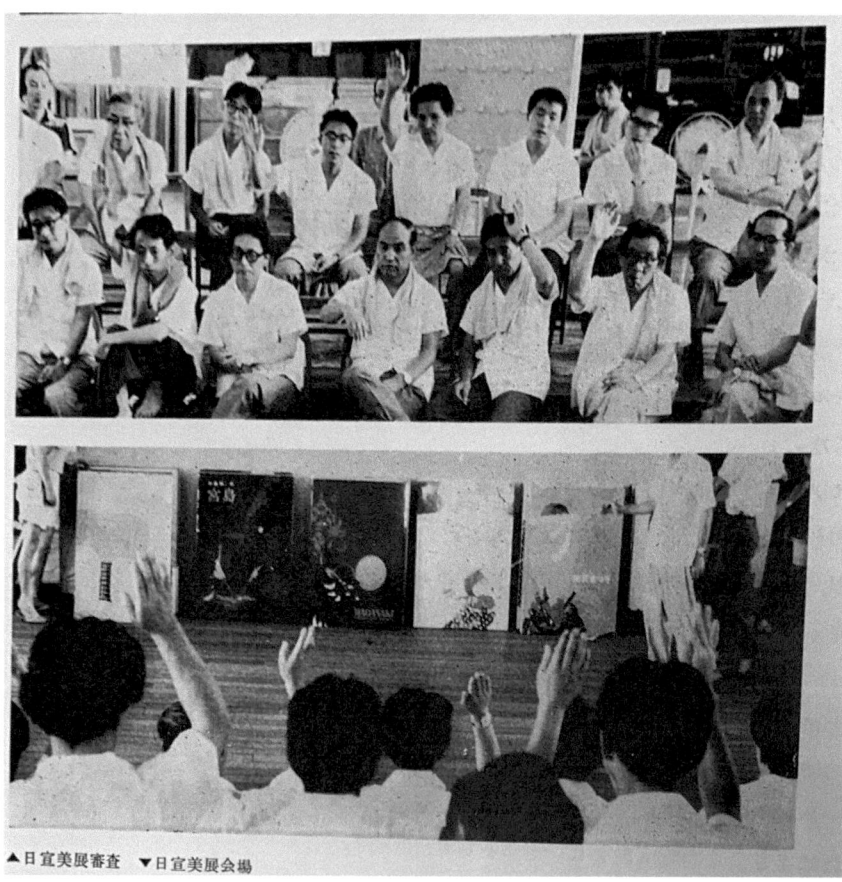

FIGURE 7.4 Judging scenes at JAAC (Dezain no. 13, 1960). Author's collection

---

[24] 'Gurafikku Dezainaa ni Nozomu: Renzoku zadankai 7' [What we hope for the graphic designers: Discussion series 7], *Design*, no. 13 (1960): 6–7.

younger members were naturally furious).²⁵ But to some members it seemed the political position was not taken seriously enough by JAAC. A critic who reviewed the exhibition of the JAAC, Michio Sugi asked, 'design for whose sake?'²⁶ Kiyoshi Awazu, the graphic designer who formed the avant-garde artists' and architects' group 'Metabolism', pointed out that while in the streets and at JAAC exhibitions public posters were increasingly seen, they were mostly meaningless or 'dead' because they were simply left there 'almost devoid of real everyday effort to tackle the issues'.²⁷ Katsumi, while reviewing the memorial 10th JAAC exhibition, also expressed his concern with JAAC's too 'exhibition-centric' attitude, that somehow the industry world and designers did not mesh and that designers were not reaching to the wider society.²⁸ It was just at this time of confusion that ICOGRADA came into existence, with its message that designers needed to 'face up, internationally, to the social and moral responsibilities implicit in their activity'.²⁹

More specifically, JAAC as a design organization had two major problems, its growing élitism and apparent stagnation of creativity. It grew authoritative because becoming a JAAC member was now a measure for the designer's success. It was said that compared with a Japanese designer, the US designer had the annual income of from three to thirteen times as much, and Kamekura once remarked, 'a rich son should be a designer' because otherwise it was usually hard to live by the profession.³⁰ In contrast, if a designer was selected twice for the JAAC exhibitions in a row he would be called the 'élite designers' of JAAC, and would be able to earn about 200,000 yen per month whereas a freelance designer would earn less than half.³¹

But was this selective 'authority' given in a considerate setting, besides central/local conflict? The actual judging time for each submitted work was only 6.5 seconds. Young designers would work for three or four months on end, spending as much as 50,000 yen or even more for the production of a poster for the purpose of selection by the jury alone and not for the actual use. In 1969, Tadanori Yokoo (1936–), a selected JAAC member at the 8th exhibition

---

[25] JAAC Newsletter (October 1959), quoted in Ando, op.cit., 129. In 1966, JAAC's national general meeting was held for reorganization. There were five large local committee and the central committee, but as the local committees pushed to have as many posters selected as possible from one's own locality, they decided to have the central committee only. Only three new central committee members were added: Iwao Hosoya, Mitsuo Katsui, and Tadashi Ohashi, but the others (Kamekura, Tanaka, Hayakawa, Hara, Kono, Nagai, Yamagi, Awazu, Itabashi, Ito etc) remained, consequently bringing little change.
[26] Michio Sugi, "'63 Nissenbi Tenpyou Dezain ha Dareno Monoka?' [Exhibition Review for JAAC: Design problem for whom?], *Bijutsu Techo* (October 1963):23, 25.
[27] Kiyoshi Awazu, 'KouKyou Posutaa' [public posters], *Design*, no. 9 (1960): 21.
[28] Masaru Katsumi, 'Nissenbi 10 nen no Seisou Sayou' [10 years of JAAC], *Design*, no. 10 (1960): 4.
[29] *ICOGRADA the first five years*, 5.
[30] Ando, op.cit., 96–9.
[31] Ando, op.cit., 42–4.

who had published an elegiac verse criticizing JAAC by explaining vividly how the submitted works were chosen and how the process thoroughly disillusioned him.[32] A few years before, Yokoo was one of the judges, and there was a work that looked like a picture book editorial with a clear slogan: 'Go to Hell JAAC', thus urging the higher-ups to face the injustice caused by its organizational operation. Eight approvals out of fifteen judges were necessary for passing the work, but although seven raised their hands, others complained of its colour or form with nobody touching on the fundamental moral theme capsuled in the work. The whole process took a few seconds only. Yokoo concluded that the 'JAAC must move towards dissolution'. When he exposed this problem in the media, there was even an appeal to expel Yokoo from the JAAC.

Stylistically, too, there was a problem of mannerism. In order to attract the judges' attention, works tended to develop a similar approach. This led to the forging of a 'JAAC style' visible in the works selected. One of the judges, Awazu commented in 1967 that the judges' preference was recognizable.[33] Yokoo analysed that this tended towards the 'amalgamation of Bauhaus and commercialist advertising design which was born out of the American capitalism'.[34]

Through such perspectives, JAAC had come to embody the 'Ancient Regime' of design. Yokoo mentioned how the members of JAAC acted as judges for other design prizes:

> When JAAC members leave JAAC to get involved with the rest of all design movements, extremely speaking, The whole design society in Japan is within the organized system. Without us noticing, a style of modern design called JAAC style creates lesions in our society. Therefore it makes very good sense to talk about criminality of design, the matter which All-Campus Struggle League for Crushing JAAC prosecute.[35]

As the next renewal of Japan-US Security Treaty of 1970 approached, criticism of the JAAC became more violent both from within and without.

On 2 August 1969, the first day of judging the public applications, the All-Campus Struggle League for Crushing JAAC made up of over forty art university students gushed into the judging venue and questioned the necessity

---

[32] Tadanori Yokoo, 'Genten kara Genten he – 5' [From the origin to the origin 5], *Design*, no. 12 (1969): 10–13.
[33] Kiyoshi Awazu, *Design*, no. 102, October 1967.
[34] Tadanori Yokoo, 'Genten kara Genten he – 5', *Design*, no. 12 (1969): 12. He got weary of the style as well as the world-wide trend of ISOTYPE and too much BAUHAUS everywhere, and began to discard 'good design' in the modernist form.
[35] Tadanori Yokoo, 'Genten kara Genten he – 5', *Design*, no. 12 (1969): 12. As he sympathized with the All-Campus Stroll League, Yokoo felt deeply guilty about his participating in Osaka Expo'70 project.

of holding an exhibition specifically for the fifteen judges for over 6 hours. They claimed that the General Meeting should be publicly open, and they wanted the suspension of the exhibition and the dissolution of JAAC. They fingerpointed the bad effect of exhibitions as a gateway for young designers, and condemned what it had achieved as a body since WoDeCo. In response, JAAC held an emergency general meeting on 5 August, where Kamekura made a heated speech defending the continuation of the exhibition, which was agreed. However, a week later, when the Struggle League and JAAC and the potential exhibitors were to meet to hold an open public meeting, JAAC decided not to attend. The Struggle League pressed the JAAC to answer 'what can design do for society?', to which it could not give a clear statement as a collective body in reply[36] (Figure 7.5).

FIGURE 7.5 A notice made by All-Campus Struggle League for Crushing JAAC (Dezain no. 126, 1969). Author's collection

---

[36] 'Kiroku' [The Record], *Design*, no. 126 (1970): 70. This issue was a Special issue on JAAC.

If JAAC began life as a professional union aimed to be inclusive, it grew to become too prestigious. If it was to exist as a creative group, over time there was no solid or shared vision for its existence. On 30 June 1970, in the middle of Japan World Exposition, Osaka 1970, JAAC's disbandment was announced. Katsumi sent a report on its demise to ICOGRADA, reporting the cause as related to the conflicts at WoDeCo and that since 'the issues raised at the Conference have not been pursued'.[37]

The art and literary critic Ichiro Hariu (1925–2010) summarized the dissolution as follows:

> We must take this into consideration that in such a historical turning point, anonymity and co-ownership which were placed at the outset of design are now reconsidered once more. For example, it is necessary to consider that on the socialist Utopia of William Morris is being shed a new light by the British New Left. At any rate, design of the Enlightenment period which simply aimed at modernization, is now producing design pollution ubiquitously linked with industrial pollutions. How to overcome the situation will be the starting point for post-Expo.[38]

The JAAC's sudden dissolution had given the graphic designers a deep traumatic shock. After its demise, there were several years without any institutionalising power to unite graphic designers and Japan missed an organizational presence on the international scene.

Formation of JAGDA and liaising with ICOGRADA

In the 1970s, overcoming the oil crisis and experiencing the end of high economic growth, Japan established itself as an industrial and technological power in the world. Opportunities for deeper design discussions were found in the ICSID (International Council of Societies of Industrial Design) General Meeting which was held in Kyoto in 1973 and the Design Year for Japan in the following year.[39] As for graphic design, the 1st Asian Typography Professionals Meeting was held in Tokyo in 1974.[40] As society changed, so did the nature of advertising: in 1975 the cost of TV advertising was overtaken by that of newspaper advertising.[41] At

---

[37] ICOGRADA, 'JAPAN', *News Bulletin*, no. 10 (1969): 4.
[38] 'Nipon sendenbijutsukai kaisann' [Demise of JAAC], *Design*, no. 126 (1969): 30.
[39] See, Iguchi, *op.cit.*
[40] *Graphic Design*, no. 53, 1974, 67.
[41] Akiko Moriyama et al., *Nihon Dezain-shi* [*Japanese Design History*] (Tokyo: Bijutsu-shuppan-sha, 2003), 124.

the same time, the awareness of the negative aspects of industry and consumerism such as pollution and deceptive advertising grew in society. One important step was taken in 1974, when the Japan Advertising Review Organization was established to protect the consumer from exaggerated advertising.[42]

In such a cautious mood and learning from past experience, the reorganization of graphic design slowly began when a few people from Tokyo Commercial Artists Association started discussing the establishment of a joint group. By 1977, several design organizations with overlapping interests in commercial art and design were finally linked within a horizontal shared affiliation of interests. These included the Tokyo Art Directors Club (est. 1952), the Tokyo Commercial Artist Association (est. 1952), the Japan Sign Design Association (est. 1965), the Japan Typography Association (est. 1971, and after Japan Lettering Designer Association established in 1964), the Japan Display Design Association (est. 1974, combining the display design organizations of Tokyo and Osaka), and the Japan Package Design Association (est. 1960). Together, they formed under the title of the Nippon Advertising Artists Council (NAAC). The art director Susumu Sakane acted as the chair of executive committee and the copy writer Seiichiro Arai, who had been an inaugural member of Tokyo Art Directors Club in 1952, was the first president.

In the same year, the 1st NAAC Exhibition was held, following an open-call application. As many as 1,462 applicants sent in their works with 80% in the category of poster art. One hundred and forty-six were selected from the total by 31 judges, including Ikko Tanaka (1930–2002), Nagai and Makoto Nakamura who was a Tokyo Art Directors Club member. The quality of the works however was criticized by the established designers for not showing much difference from the time of the JAAC. Nakamura lamented that 'during the eight years, Japanese designers seem to have lost much in terms of conceptual rather than technical, advancement'. He went on: 'It seems to me that an after-effect of the discontinuance has been disclosed in this exhibition'. He concluded by hoping that the exhibition could be a 'new soil of, and a new target for, young advertising artists'[43] (Figure 7.6).

Indeed, growing generations had to be given a new place for their creation. This was obvious in the large number again for the second NAAC then, which attracted 1,818 applications from which 171 were selected. The popularity of the NAAC, after some years of lack of a suitable competition platform, confirmed that the younger generation continued to grow. But the sad fate of JAAC had to be avoided. Art Critic Segi observed:

---

[42] See Japan Advertising Review Organization, 'History', https://www.jaro.or.jp/english/ [accessed 15 March 2021].

[43] Makoto Nakamura, 'Keisan sareta umasato anteishita Gijutsu' [Calculated dexterity and stable technique], *IDEA* 145 (1977): 116.

FIGURE 7.6 Scenes from 1st NAAC Exhibition (IDEA, no. 146, 1978). Author's collection

Some of those in their 20s may not know about JAAC. The condition of post-JAAC is totally different, and in parallel, this competition style is completely different, too …. The members should be very careful at least not to make it an authoritarian body. 'Post-JAAC' must mean not simply 'after JAAC' but 'out of JAAC'.[44]

More care for a designer as a worker was needed. Indeed, the biggest change was its attitude to the applicants as the judges returned unselected works to each applicant accompanied by their comments and reviews.

---

[44] Shin-ichi Segi, 'The 2nd NAAC Exhibition', *IDEA* 152 (1979): 72.

So, if a future collective action was to be taken for graphic designers at all, it was necessary to be different from the JAAC. When on 26 August 1978, the Japan Graphic Designers Association was formed (JAGDA, incorporated entity from 1984), once more chaired by Kamekura, its aim was to act as a professional 'union'. This involved addressing the systematization of design fees, copyright, welfare, insurance, information for and engagement with the local regions to balance any differences between the central Tokyo and regional locality. It thus continued JAAC policies while trying not to avoid its mistakes. Those whose primary profession was graphic design with the exception of students were entitled to join for the monthly membership fee of 1,500 yen, a modest sum, aimed to attract younger generations. The original membership of 705 designers rose to 1,000 in its first year[45] and the Association survives today with around 3,000 members.

The Association's main *raison d'etre* is education and globalization. In the field of education, the Association has published design textbooks, and held various competitions for design students. It also awards prizes, such as the Best New-Talent Award, the Kamekura Yusaku Award, and JAGDA Award, the accumulation of entries for these becomes a significant design archive in itself. Also in 1981, the annual publication *Graphic Design in Japan* was introduced, aimed to compile the culmination of a year's graphic works in one volume.

Deepening international relations was raised as an aim from the beginning of the Association, and sending the representatives to the world's design conferences was considered to have good appeal.[46] Extending its global reach, finally, an organizational link was officially made between Japan and overseas. ICOGRADA's *News Bulletin* in 1980 reported that JAGDA became 'a provisional Full Member'. Katsumi happily reported that until then he was compelled to be a 'lazy' correspondent but finally he was 'happy that JAGDA is going on its own way and has decided to join Icograda by its own choice', and that joining at this time was with 'unanimous consent and very natural, just like the apple that ripens and falls'.[47] In 1981, JAGDA formally joined ICOGRADA.

As a full member, JAGDA could begin its contribution to the global networking of graphic designers. In 1989, the Pan-Pacific Design Congress was held by ICOGRADA-JAGDA leadership in Tokyo on the theme of 'Communication in Design; its variation and potentiality', proposed by JAGDA and received by ICOGRADA as 'a very important milestone in the history of ICOGRADA'.[48] One novelty JAGDA

---

[45] 'About 30% were in their 20s, and 43.8% were in their 30s, and 25.2% were in their 40s. Ito, 'JAGDA no haikei to sono kadai' [Background of JAGDA and Issues it faces], *Senden Kaigi*, no. 328 (1978): 29.
[46] Ito, 'JAGDA no haikei to sono kadai' [Background of JAGDA and Issues it faces], *Senden Kaigi*, no. 328 (1978): 20.
[47] ICOGRADA, 'ICOGRADA membership grows', *News Bulletin*: 1.
[48] Mary V. Mullin, Secretary General of ICOGRADA to Kamekura Yusaku, 26 September 1989, ICOGRADA Archives, University of Brighton.

introduced was the system of the 'Friend of ICOGRADA'. In 1991, during a meeting at the Council's headquarters in Montreal, JAGDA and ICOGRADA agreed to set up a form of individual membership or 'Friend' for supporting ICOGRADA financially. The original idea came from Kojitani, vice-president of JAGDA, and he invited JAGDA members to join the Founder Friends to initiate the worldwide scheme, hoping that other countries might follow the Japanese initiative.[49]

In the late 1990s, it was confirmed that the ICOGRADA World Design Congress was to be held in Nagoya in 2003, a city that had already hosted the meetings for ICSID and the International Federation of Interior Architects (IFI). A total of 3,800 people gathered from all over the world to discuss the theme of 'Visualogue' (Figure 7.7). JAGDA has developed as a pivotal body for international liaising of graphic designers.

FIGURE 7.7A ICOGRADA-JAGDA Pan-Pacific Design Congress '89 Tokyo, pamphlet cover. Courtesy of University of Brighton Design Archives

---

[49] Correspondences between Jagda and ICOGRADA, September to November 1991, ICOGRADA Archives, University of Brighton.

FIGURE 7.7B ICOGRADA 'Visualogue', pamphlet cover. Courtesy of University of Brighton Design Archives

Conclusion: Again, 'design for whose sake?'

While it can be said that JAAC's annual poster exhibitions helped to establish graphic design as a profession and to talent-spot the young stars at the early important stage of its development, JAGDA expanded ambitions by helping to encourage internationalization on an organizational level to the benefit of Japanese graphic designers. Still, one must note that the possibility of an emerging 'Ancient Regime' of graphic design in the twenty-first century Japan is not quite zero, but still lingers, as the recent 2020 Tokyo Olympics official logo scandal has disclosed.

When the originally chosen logo design in 2015 was withdrawn following allegations of plagiarism,[50] the Select Committee was harshly accused by the general public for domestic exclusivism.[51] This was because the chair of the select

---

[50] It was accused of being too similar to the logo mark for Théâtre de Liège in Belgium created by Olivier Debie in 2013.
[51] JAGDA, 'Tokyo 2020 Orinpikku Pararinpikku Kyogitaikai Enburemu Dai1kai Sekkei kyougi nitsuite' (JAGDA kenkai ni kansuru tsuiki), 30 March 2017, downloaded from JAGDA's official HP.

committee, Kazumasa Nagai (JAGDA chair 1994–2000), had only invited eight designers to enter the competition. Among the original eight judges was Katsumi Asaba (JAGDA chair 2012–2018). Furthermore, those entitled to apply required at least two of several designated awards, among which were the Kamekura Yusaku Award and JAGDA Newcomers Award. In spite of all that, JAGDA officially made a public claim that it had no responsibility for the decision. These procedures prompted the public and the critics to ask whether this was a responsible attitude both domestically and internationally.

A competition was hurriedly reorganized for the following year. Twenty judges were appointed including some university professors and a lawyer, and still including JAGDA-related members, including Mitsuo Katsui (former JAGDA chair, 2009–2012). Out of a total of 14,599 entries, a design called 'Harmonized Checkered Emblem' designed to convey a message of 'unity in diversity', designed by Asao Tokoro, was selected. Some criticisms remained that JAGDA still had too much power in the selecting process and that some famous public figures added to the final selection (like a baseball player and a tennis player) seemed for the sake of populism.[52]

What is continuously needed is a voice to constantly ask 'design for whose sake?' and to check whether JAGDA fulfils the high-sounding activities it declares: most notably, 'appealing to the broader public' and 'becoming a base point for a world-wide network'. At least, thanks to the logo scandal the public has become more aware of the power structure in the field of design.

---

[52] Nikkan Gendai Digital, 'Shinsain ni "senpan" no kage: Shin-5rin enburemu mata dekire-su kenen', https://www.nikkan-gendai.com/articles/view/news/178914, revised 17 October 2016 [accessed 30 March 2020].

8 SHAPING NATIONAL AND INTERNATIONAL DESIGN POLICIES: THE TRANSNATIONAL TRAJECTORY OF THE BELGIAN POLICYMAKER JOSINE DES CRESSONNIÈRES (1926–1985)

Katarina Serulus

Introduction

A photograph taken in October 1973 shows a crowd of people watching a traditional Japanese musical performance at the gala dinner of the Eighth Congress of the International Council of Societies of Industrial Design (ICSID).[1] Central in the image is a woman in an elegant white evening dress, standing out against the mass of black tuxedos (see Figure 8.1). This woman is the Belgian design policymaker Josine des Cressonnières (1926–1985). As the picture suggests, Josine des Cressonnières was one of the few women to occupy a central role in the postwar institutionalization of industrial design. In Belgium, she was effective for more than 30 years in ensuring design was on the government's agenda. Starting out in 1956 as Secretary General of the Signe d'Or Benelux design prize, from 1961 des Cressonnières held the same position at the Institute of Industrial Design for Belgium and the Grand Duchy of Luxembourg, and was appointed director of the Brussels Design Centre from its opening in 1964 until her death in 1985. In addition to her work in the Belgian context, she was extremely influential in shaping and disseminating certain models of design promotion on an international scale. For 16 years, from 1961 until 1977, she occupied a powerful position at the heart of the international design community as Secretary General of ICSID. At the time that this picture was taken, she had just succeeded in preventing the move of the ICSID Secretariat from Brussels to London after a vicious attack by its former

---

[1] Throughout this article, all references preceded by the initials 'ICD' indicate materials that are held at the University of Brighton Design Archives, ICSID Archive. ICD, 8-3-3.

FIGURE 8.1 Josine des Cressonnières at the 8th ICSID Congress in Kyoto, 1973.
Source: ICSID Archive, University of Brighton Design Archives

President, Henri Viénot. This success served to reinforce her power position within international design networks.

Des Cressonnières's influence is also illustrated by numerous performances as speaker, jury member and design consultant for several governments and private companies. For example, she established missions in Brazil and Colombia to advise local governments on setting up design policies and education, organized the first ICSID seminar in Bruges on 'The Education of Industrial Designers', with UNESCO support, and was for several years Belgian correspondent for Raymond Loewy's design office.[2] She was affiliated to several prestigious initiatives, such as the Rosenthal collection 'Studio-Linie' and the Biennial of Industrial Design in Ljubljana, both as part of the international jury. She also was lady-in-waiting for the Belgian Queen Fabiola for several national and international excursions and was well acquainted with the nobility.[3] Her outstanding diplomatic skills and the international scope of her work are illustrated by her impressive network

---

[2] Throughout this article, all references preceded by the initials 'AJJS' indicate materials that are held at the Collection of the Flanders Architecture Institute – Collection Flemish Community, Archive Jean-Jacques Stiefenhofer (1943–2013), Box 24.2: Josines des Cressonnières, 'Rapport concernant la mission effectuee au bresil par mme des cressonnières, 4–30 avril 1973'; Box 22.1: 'The education of Industrial Designers, Bruges, 21–24 March 1964'; United States, Wilmington, Hagley Museum and Library, Raymond Loewy Collections (Accession 2251), Box 2, Des Cressonnières.

[3] Brussels, Archive of the Royal Palace, Secretary Queen Fabiola, Ladies-in-waiting; Baudouin D'hoore (archivist Archive of the Royal Palace), email message to the author and the archivist, 3 September 2015.

that included, among others, industrialists, members of royal families in Europe, government officials, and of course many designers such as Eliot Noyes in the United States, Kenji Ekuan in Japan, Yuri Soloviev in the Soviet Union, Roger Tallon in France, Tomás Maldonado in Ulm, and many others.

Her exceptional position – transcending national borders and design scenes – provides a unique insight into the national and transnational complexity of design cultures.[4] Although most design policies, exchanges, promotional activities and exhibitions in the post-war period were set up according to the logic of nationalism,[5] the case of Josine des Cressonnières offers a perspective that highlights the many offshoots beyond the borders of the nation-state and the transnational dynamics at work in the creation of these national design cultures. A close look at her professional trajectory reveals the interesting intersections where national, transnational and international forces meet and the 'permeability of the nation-state' – as historian Daniel Rodgers calls it – becomes visible.[6]

This chapter analyses the significance of Josine des Cressonnières' career by studying her transnational network, her intellectual trajectory and her impact on design policies in Belgium and abroad. Des Cressonnières' position as a pivotal intermediary point between different design networks offers a valuable lens through which it's possible to study intertwining local, national, transnational, supranational and global design narratives in more detail, ranging from that of a very personal story of a woman in a powerful position in a male-dominated design world to one of national interests and geo-political tensions, touching upon the role of design in the Cold War politics and diplomacy.

Promoting design 'as a prestigious discipline in the international stream of taste'

Josine des Cressonnières – her maiden name was Naus – was born in the interwar years into an upper-class French-speaking Catholic family in the Brussels area. After graduating in art history and archaeology at the Institut Supérieur d'Histoire de l'Art et d'Archéologie at the Brussels Royal Museums of Fine Arts, des Cressonnières married and moved with her husband to the Belgian Congo.[7]

---

[4] These insights into the transnational dynamics in the creation of national design cultures are developed together with Joana Ozorio de Almeida Meroz in the following book chapter: Joana Ozorio de Almeida Meroz and Katarina Serulus, 'A Theoretical Straddle: Locating Design Cultures between National Structures and Transnational Networks', in *Design Culture: Objects and Approaches*, ed. G. Julier, A. Munch, M. Foklmann, N. Skou and H-C. Jensen (London: Bloomsbury, 2019), 203–13.
[5] Gimeno-Martínez, 'The Role of the Creative Industries in the Construction of Regional/European Identities (1975–2002)' (PhD diss., KU Leuven, 2006), 38.
[6] Daniel T. Rodgers, *Atlantic Crossings. Social Politics in a Progressive Age* (Cambridge, MA/London: The Belknap Press of Harvard University Press, 1998), 2.
[7] Interview by the author with Geraldine des Cressonnières on 8 November 2013.

His sudden death shortly after this made her, at the age of 26, a young widow with a small daughter. Back in Belgium, she started a job as the reportedly 'first' stylist of the department store A l'Innovation in Brussels, where she was introduced to the emerging discipline of industrial design.[8] In the department store's magazine, she was called '*La pionnière de la pêche aux nouveautés*' (the pioneer in search of newness). In this position, she maintained close relations with the head of the purchasing departments, her French colleagues from the Galeries Lafayette and those from other foreign department stores. Des Cressonnières claimed that it was travelling to a wide range of countries to observe new design trends that had developed her natural '*goût esthétique*'.[9] She attributes to this position her knowledge of the Belgian and international markets, and the problems of distribution and creation. She later explained that, faced with the lack of taste and creativity in Belgian industry, she was shocked and felt forced to do something.[10]

Around the same time, the institutionalization of design took off slowly in Belgium and was – as in the rest of Europe – largely directed by government-backed initiatives.[11] Against the backdrop of European liberalization and Cold War tensions, the Belgian government showed an interest in industrial design as a tool to stimulate the dynamics of the national economy and as an instrument of modernization.[12] The first figure to formulate a firm design policy for Belgium was the Minister of Economy, Jean Rey (1902–1983). In 1954 he organized the first exhibitions of Belgian industrial design in Liège and at the X Triennale of Milan, and in 1956 founded two new design bodies: the Institute for Industrial Design and the Signe d'Or prize.[13] Rey considered industrial design to be a close ally in addressing the challenge of the new post-war economic order. The national economy was considered to be under threat from strong foreign competition in the increasingly liberalized markets. Moreover, after its post-war 'miracle' years, the Belgian economy was suddenly declining, mainly due to outdated infrastructure. In addition, there was the prospect of the 1958 Brussels World's Fair (Expo 58), the organization of which was entrusted to the Belgian Ministry of Economic Affairs. This world's fair was the first to be organized after the Second World War, and

---

[8] Interview by the author with Geraldine des Cressonnières (daughter of Josine des Cressonnières) on 8 November 2013, Coutisse; 'La pionnière de la pêche aux nouveautés', *Entre Nous. Le Magazin de l'Inno* 32 (1954).
[9] 'Mevrouw des Cressonnières, wie bent U?', *Distributie*, no. juni–juli (1977): 15.
[10] Ibid.
[11] Javier Gimeno-Martínez, 'The Signe d'Or Award Scheme from 1956 to 1960: The Economic Reasons for "Good Design"', *Konsthistorisk Tidskrift/Journal of Art History* 79, no. 3 (2010): 127; Jonathan M. Woodham, *Twentieth-Century Design* (Oxford/New York: Oxford University Press, 1997), 171–7; Woodham, 'Formulating National Design Policies in the United States: Recycling the "Emperor's New Clothes"?', *Design Issues* 26, no. 2 (2010); Penny Sparke, *An Introduction to Design and Culture, 1900 to the Present*, 2nd ed. (London/New York: Routledge, 2004), 198–206.
[12] For more information on the public promotion of industrial design in post-war Belgium, see Katarina Serulus, *Design and Politics: The Public Promotion of Industrial Design in Postwar Belgium (1950–1986)* (Leuven: University Press Leuven, 2018).
[13] Serulus, *Design and Politics*, 33–99.

FIGURE 8.2 Josine des Cressonnières, Secretary of the Signe d'Or. Source: Private archive Geraldine des Cressonnières

was consequently considered an extraordinary international event – especially in the light of growing tensions between the two Cold War superpowers, the United States and the Soviet Union.

Des Cressonnières was involved in these early stages of Belgium's design institutionalization as one of the founding members of the Institute for Industrial Design and, more importantly, as the first Secretary General of the Signe d'Or prize (see Figure 8.2).[14] From 1957 until 1960, this annual award was granted to products from Benelux that met the 'triple criterion of quality, reasonable prices and aesthetics'.[15] Promoting so-called good design, in line with high Modernist discourse, it followed the lead of its foreign counterparts, such as the Swiss Die Gute Form/La Forme Utile (1952), the French Beauté-France (1953), the Italian Compasso d'Oro (1954) and Edgar Kaufmann's design exhibitions at MoMA (1950–1955).

Most of Signe d'Or's founding members had found success in the Brussels interwar cultural world and had a background in art history, film-making, art or architecture. It was Josine des Cressonnières in particular, however, the youngest

FIGURE 8.3 The first Signe d'Or jury in 1957. From left to right: M. Stoffel, Robert Giron, Alberto Rosselli, Jaap Penraat, Josine des Cressonnières, Peter Muller-Munk and Louis Desamory. Source: Private archive Geraldine des Cressonnières

---

[14] Josine Des Cressonnières was a founding member of the Association Belge des Industrial Designers that was established in Liège in 1954. That same year the latter merged with the Industrial Design Institute into the Institute for Industrial Design for Belgium and the Grand Duchy of Luxembourg (Institut d'Esthétique Industrielle pour la Belgique et le Grand-Duché de Luxembourg/Instituut voor industriële vormgeving voor België en G.-H. Luxemburg). See N. 1044. Attachment to the Belgian Official Journal. Non-profit Organizations and Public Utility Foundations, 10 March 1956, pp. 369–71.
[15] 'L'association a pour but, en dehors de tout esprit de lucre, de promouvoir la fabrication et l'expansion commerciale d'objects usuels, produits en grande ou petite série, et répondant au triple critère de qualité, de prix adéquat et d'esthétique.' See N. 3919. Attachment to the Belgian Official Journal. Not-for profit Organizations and Public Utility Foundations, 2, 3 and 4 November 1956, pp. 1601–2.

and only female board member, who would take the lead in establishing industrial design, in her own words, 'as a prestigious discipline in the international stream of taste', and who would engage with the design community in Belgium and abroad.[16] This aspiration was especially apparent in the key design personalities des Cressonnières invited to sit on the international juries of the Signe d'Or award from 1957 to 1960. Among these were representatives of the recently established ICSID (Peter Müller-Munk, Misha Black, Pierre Vago, Sigvard Bernadotte, Enrico Peressutti), the Milan Triennale (Alberto Roselli), several foreign design organizations (Jaap Penraat from the Netherlands, Ake Huldt from Sweden, Mia Seeger from Germany, Raymond Loewy from the US), and independent designers (Eliot Noyes, Friso Kramer, Tapio Wirkkalla and Nanny Still) (see Figure 8.3).[17] Des Cressonnières's influential position was affirmed in 1960 when, at the request of the Ministry of Economic Affairs, the Institute and the Signe d'Or merged their activities. The two bodies remained separate legal entities, but shared a secretariat headed by des Cressonnières.

Belgian design policies: The siren call of Europe

The two design organizations des Cressonnières headed as Secretary General were, curiously enough, not only concerned with reinforcing the national image, but were also marked by a supranational and international scope.[18] This is explained by des Cressonnières's experiences abroad, the outward-facing approach she developed as a stylist at A l'Innovation and the political context in which these design bodies were founded. For example, in contrast to many other Western European countries, Belgium's official design promotion was not restricted to Belgian territory but reflected the latest political agreements that would eventually lead to European unification. The Institute for Industrial Design encompassed the territory of Belgium and the Grand Duchy of Luxembourg, reflecting the Belgo-Luxembourg Economic Union (BLEU), founded in 1922 and seen as the forerunner of Benelux. The Signe d'Or, on the other hand, was a Benelux prize, awarding products from Belgium, the Grand Duchy of Luxembourg and the

---

[16] '[…] comme une discipline de prestige dans le courant international du goût.' Léon-Louis Sosset, 'Aux Beaux-Arts, Exposition des oeuvres sélectionnées pour "Le Signe d'Or" label de qualité pour le style industriel.' *Les Beaux-Arts. Hebdomadaire d'Information Artistique* 21, no. 778 (1957): 14. See also her intense correspondence with the first ICSID board: ICD, 09-11-1: Correspondence (1957–1959), Belgium.

[17] For a complete list of the international jury of the Signe d'Or, see Gimeno-Martínez, 'The Signe d'Or Award Scheme from 1956 to 1960: The Economic Reasons for "Good Design"'.

[18] Katarina Serulus, 'Caught between National Interests and European Ambitions. Design Promotion in Belgium in the 1960s', in *Design Frontiers. Territories, Concepts, Technologies*, ed. P. L. Farias and P. Atkinson (Mexico City: Editorial Designio, 2014): 195–210; Serulus, *Design and Politics*, 103–29.

Netherlands. Benelux was an economic union between these three neighbouring countries that came into operation in 1948 and is seen as the predecessor of, and a great example for, the European Economic Community. Important to note is that the supranational character of the first Belgian design bodies had its limitations: the organization, funding and administration were purely Belgian, and one of the reasons to include foreign products was that they were considered to have the potential to stimulate the Belgian design industry.[19]

This leaning towards supranationalism is related to Belgium's position as one of the driving forces behind European unification. In 1957, 'the Six' – Belgium, France, Germany, Luxembourg, the Netherlands and Italy – signed the Treaty of Rome, which proposed, in a three-phase plan intended to last for twelve years, the establishment of a free trade area between the members, the creation of a European customs union and eventually a political union.[20] Brussels took on the role of Europe's unofficial capital, crystallizing in the 1958 Brussels World's Fair, and became the diplomatic and symbolic heart of Europe, positioned between the Cold War protagonists, the United States and the Soviet Union.[21] Given this context, it is then hardly surprising, then, that the early promotion of Belgian design was characterized by transnational and European initiatives. In this light, it is also worth noting that Jean Rey, who played a crucial role as Belgian Minister of Economy (1954–1958) in the early days of Belgian design institutionalization, became European Commissioner (1958–1967) and even President of the European Commission (1967–1970). Moreover, the famous Belgian politician Paul-Henri Spaak, one of the founding fathers of the European Union, was a good friend and nephew of Robert Giron, President of the Benelux Signe d'Or award.

Under des Cressonnières's leadership the Brussels-based design bodies aimed to expand to a European and international scale and connect with the growing international design community.[22] Most striking was the shifting ambition of the Signe d'Or. After four editions it was decided that it should evolve from a Benelux-focused award into a European design award. The Signe d'Or organization felt that the

---

[19] Gimeno-Martínez argues in the context of the Signe d'Or award that this 'international, altruistic ambition' can be interpreted as a gesture to put Belgian design at the centre of attention. See Gimeno-Martínez, 'The Signe d'Or Award Scheme from 1956 to 1960: The Economic Reasons for "Good Design"', 141.

[20] Rik Coolsaet, *België en zijn buitenlandse politiek 1830–2000*, 3rd ed. (Leuven: Van Halewyck, 2001): 449–70; Els Witte, Jan Craeybeckx, and Alain Meynen, *Politieke geschiedenis van België. Van 1830 tot heden* (Antwerpen: Standaard, 2005).

[21] Michael Ryckewaert, *Building the Economic Backbone of the Belgian Welfare State. Infrastructure, Planning and Architecture 1945–1973* (Rotterdam: nai 010, 2011): 175–97; Carola Hein, *The Capital of Europe: Architecture and Urban Planning for the European Union* (Westport, CN/London: Praeger, 2004): 136–59.

[22] See Arthur J. Pulos, *The American Design Adventure, 1940–1975* (Cambridge, MA: MIT Press, 1988), 209–21. For more information on the ICSID, see Tania Messell, 'Constructing a "United Nations of Industrial Design": ICSID and the Professionalisation of Design on the World Stage, 1957–1980' (PhD diss., University of Brighton, 2018).

Benelux award had 'skimmed off' the best examples of Belgian design production.[23] The conclusion was that the rhythm of an annual selection was too exhausting, and it advanced its aspiration to offer a selection of European design products.[24]

Driven by its intention to organize a European design award, des Cressonnières, the Signe d'Or Secretary General, set up a network to contact the award's international counterparts and investigate possibilities.[25] Contact was strengthened on the occasion of the 1960 International Industrial Design Exhibition at the Brussels store Au Bon Marché, where Des Cressonnières worked together with the first ICSID board to gather the best national products from fourteen different countries by collaborating with seventeen different design bodies. By February 1961, this whole endeavour, with the right ingredients in place – a strong international network, combined with Signe d'Or's European ambitions and its forced reorientation – resulted in the establishment of the Liaison Committee for Industrial Design in the Common Market.[26] Not only was a European award centrally positioned in the programme; a broader aim was also espoused: the exchange of objects and ideas, collective commercial effort, and the construction of a European design canon as a third way alongside capitalist US design and communist Soviet models. As well as the Belgo-Luxembourg involvement, the Liaison Committee consisted of four more institutions: the German Rat für Formgebung, the French Institut d'Esthétique Industrielle, the Dutch Raad voor Industriële Vormgeving and the Italian Associazione per il Disegno Industriale. Its composition – limited to the design bodies from 'Europe des Six' – reflected the political and economic developments it aimed to anticipate, namely the creation of the European Common Market.

Unfortunately, this initiative to create and disseminate a European design canon failed. While the event was announced with great pomp in 1961 and 1962, archival documents and design magazines make no mention of it whatsoever in 1963. Moreover, the committee was never again mentioned in reports. The 'European' design plan formulated by the Belgian design bodies in the 1960s remained a fantasy, and was never translated into reality. One can only speculate on the reasons for this failure. Obvious possibilities are the financial and organizational aspects and national interests. However, another interesting hypothesis is the conflicting interests of the Liaison Committee for Industrial Design in the Common Market and ICSID. While Josine des Cressonnières instigated the former in February

---

[23] Throughout this article, all references preceded by the initials 'ABKM' indicate materials that are held at the State Archives Beveren (Belgium), BKM collection (Archives of the Department of Fine Arts and Museums, Ministry of the Flemish Community/Transfer 2005 [1945–2004]): BKM 2013. ABKM, *Compte-rendu de l'activité du Signe d'Or pendant l'année 1960* (mars 61) fol. 83r.

[24] ABKM, *Commission 'Design'. Réunion 1. Du 18-10-60*, fol. 106r.

[25] ABKM, *Previsions d'activité du Signe d'Or pour 1961* (mars) fol. 88r.

[26] The name of the organization varied in different publications from 'Comité de Liaison pour l'Industrial Design dans la C.E.E.' to 'Comité de Liaison pour l'Industrial Design dans les Pays du Marché Commun.' See Serulus, *Design and Politics*, 268.

1961, she became Secretary General of the latter only seven months later, in September 1961. The memberships of both organizations partly overlapped: Liaison Committee members were all ICSID members. So it may have no longer been convenient for her to invest in this European branch.

At the heart of the international design community

Des Cressonnières' many international contacts, set up within the framework of the Signe d'Or award, provided her with an influential position at the heart of the international design community. This became especially apparent in 1961, when she was elected Secretary General of ICSID, succeeding her German colleague Mia Seeger.[27] She held this important position for sixteen years, during which time she was the only woman on the board. Design historian Tania Messell characterizes her as one of ICSID's most influential executive board members.[28]

Industrial design at that time has been described as a 'male preserve'.[29] Accordingly, some have described ICSID atmosphere as 'macho', and, judging from the composition of the executive boards, ICSID was indeed a male-dominated environment (see Figure 8.4).[30] During her sixteen years as Secretary General, for example, des Cressonnières was the only woman in the board. As one of the few women to hold a position of power in this network, she was faced with several prejudices concerning her gender. ICSID President Henri Viénot, for example, contested her role as ICSID's main spokesperson in 1973 because her style was not 'virile' enough. He complained that her style was 'half smiling, half crying, half begging, a hundred per cent scouting', and considered that 'it is time that we had someone who can express ICSID in a virile way'.[31] He even suggested moving the Secretariat to another city in order to limit des Cressonnières' influence.[32] The

---

[27] See ICD, 3-1-1 Minutes of the IInd G.A.: *Second General Assembly. Venice, Italy: 14 to 16 September 1961* (December 1961), 2, 5.
[28] Messell, 'Constructing a "United Nations of Industrial Design"', 84.
[29] Libby Sellers, Women Design. Pioneers in Architecture, Industrial, Graphic and Digital Design from the Twentieth Century to the Present Day (London: Frances Lincoln, 2017).
[30] Interview by the author with Geraldine des Cressonnières on 8 November 2013, Coutisse; Interview by the author with Françoise Jollant on 29 August 2015, Paris; Interview by the author with Hélène de Callatay on 27 July 2015, Brussels. See also: Rixt Hoekstra, 'Women and Power in the History of Modern Architecture: The Case of the CIAM Women', in *MoMoWo. Women Designers, Craftswomen, Architects and Engineers between 1918 and 1945*, ed. Marjan Groot, Helena Seražin, Caterina Franchini and Emilia Garda (Ljubljana: Založba ZRC, 2017): 132–45.
[31] ICD, 04-2 Board meeting 1971–1974: 'Minutes Restricted Board Meeting n° 9 – Brussels 8/9 September 1973'.
[32] ICD, 04-2 Board meeting 1971–1974: Josine des Cressonnières, 'Note for the consideration by the executive board' (23 March 1973); 04-2 Board meeting 1971–1974: 'Recapitulation of opinions exchanged during the Executive Board meeting in Milan (13–17 July 1973) concerning the proposition of moving ICSID Secretariat to London'.

previous ICSID president, John Reid, who was British, took up this suggestion and proposed to move it to Nash House in London's Mayfair.[33] As a result of these insulting controversies with Henry Viénot, des Cressonnières handed in her resignation as Secretary General.[34] After pressure from the rest of the board, however, she resumed her activities ten days later.[35] The tide turned in 1974, when

FIGURE 8.4 Josine des Cressonnières at the Second ICSID Seminar on The Teaching of Industrial Design in Ulm, together with Arthur Pulos (US), Roger Tallon (France), André De Poerck (Belgium), Misha Black (UK), Zvonimir Radic (Yugoslavia), Tomàs Maldonado (West Germany), Shinji Koioke (Japan), Nathan Shapira (US), Basilio Urbine (Argentina), Gino Valle (Italy), Manuel Villazón Vázquez (Mexico) and Alexandre Wollner (Brazil), 1965. Source: Ulm, HfG-Archiv Ulm

[33] Ibid.
[34] ICD, 04-2 Board meeting 1971–1974: Josine des Cressonnières, 'to all members of the executive board', 16 March 1973.
[35] ICD, 04-7: 'Board meeting 1968–1975 (Cahiers): Full board Meeting n° 4 – Louvain-la-neuve (Belgium) 23–26 March 1973'.

Carl Aubock was chosen as the new ICSID president at the General Assembly in Kyoto. Under his chairmanship, Josine des Cressonières could pursue her ambition and expand the Secretariat as its leader, which served to strengthen her connections to the heart of the international design community. Accommodated in a new office and equipped with a full-time staff of three, it became more and more an entity on its own, alongside the executive board.[36]

Her position as a woman in this man's world was broached most explicitly in 1977 when she agreed to the request of the former ICSID board, headed by Kenji Ekuan, to stand for the role of president.[37] Des Cressonnières' many years' service bore fruit, and as the board's choice she easily found support for her candidacy from Spain, France, Belgium, Germany, the United States and Japan, and estimated that she could also count on Italy, South Africa, Brazil, Canada, India, the Netherlands and Switzerland. However, she was well aware that many were against her candidature. During the congress in Dublin, shortly before the voting, the name of the Russian designer Yuri Soloviev was added to the list at the last minute. This disturbed ICSID circles as it was seen as a strategic move by the anglophone camp to maintain control of ICSID.[38] Correspondence reveals that it was the British members Paul Reilly, John Reid and Misha Black, in particular, who opposed her candidature.[39] They formulated several arguments against her nomination by the board.[40]

The Cold War context was one of the factors that played a role in the friction around des Cressonnières' candidature for the ICSID presidency. Misha Black – well aware of the tensions between East and West, as a Russian-born British designer – argued in a letter he wrote three months before he died that the simultaneous candidatures of Josine des Cressonnières and Yuri Soloviev were inevitably perceived as a showdown between the West and East. He worried that 'any votes against Yuri could well be interpreted as anti-Soviet'.[41] Because the connection between the West and East was, after all, considered to be one of the

---

[36] ICD, 04-2 Board meeting 1971–1974: 'Minutes Newly Elected Executive Board Meeting – Kyoto 13 October 1973'; 04-2 Board meeting 1971–1974: 'Minutes Full Board Meeting n°2 – Brussels (Belgium) 1–2 December 1973'.
[37] ICD, 03-9-8 Nominations: 'List of nominees for the election of the ICSID Executive Board 1977–1979'; 04-4 Board meeting 1977–1979: des Cressonnières, Josine, *statement of intent* [first draft] (June 1977).
[38] ICD, 08-3-3 Cressonnieres, Josine des (1972–1977) some photos: Hollerith, Richard, [Letter to Josine des Cressonnières] (19 January 1976). For a more detailed description of this incident, see Messell 174–5.
[39] ICD, 08-3-3 Cressonnieres, Josine des (1972–1977) some photos: des Cressonnières, Josine, [Letter to Kenji Ekuan] (20 June 1977).
[40] ICD, 08-3-3 Cressonnieres, Josine des (1972–1977) some photos: Black, Misha, [Letter to Josine des Cressonnières] (12 July 1977); 08-3-3 Cressonnieres, Josine des (1972–1977) some photos: Reid, John, [Letter to Josine des Cressonnières] (13 June 1977); 08-3-3 Cressonnieres, Josine des (1972–1977) some photos: Reilly, Paul, [Letter to Kenji Ekuan] (17 May 1977).
[41] ICD, 08-3-3: Cressonnieres, Josine des (1972–1977) some photos: Black, Misha, [Letter to Josine des Cressonnières] (12 July 1977).

strengths of ICSID, Black feared that the election of des Cressonnières would tear ICSID apart.

Yuri Soloviev himself implied to des Cressonnières that she might have problems in relation to the socialist countries due to her gender. He understood that there was a 'strong movement for women in the West', but claimed that the socialist countries did not value women as leaders.[42] Looking at the successful career of the Polish female architect Helena Syrkus in international architectural organizations, Soloviev's argument can, however, be questioned. In a letter to Paul Reilly, one of those opposed to her candidacy, it seems that des Cressonnières was well aware of this glass ceiling for women in ICSID when she wryly remarked that 'quite a number of nominations and support came in – and it seems that, in spite of the irretrievable fact that I am a woman, I might be accepted'.[43]

The main argument against her nomination was that she was not a professional designer but a design promotion member.[44] Her lack of any practical experience in the field of design whatsoever was especially held against her. Paul Reilly considered that a non-designer at the head of ICSID would 'demote the profession'.[45] He repeated this controversial statement in public before voting took place, repeating that 'ICSID, being a professional body, should always have at its head as its President a professional designer, not a promotion official'.[46] This public statement was received unfavourably by some of the design promotion members. Des Cressonnières responded to this criticism with two counterarguments.[47] First, she reasoned that ICSID did include both professional as well as design promotion organizations. Thus, according to democratic principle, design promotion members should also be eligible to become president. Moreover, she claimed that 'designers are rarely the best promoters for their own profession'.[48] Secondly, there was a precedent: Henri Viénot. Although she did not have a particularly good relationship with Viénot, des Cressonnières used him as an example of a non-designer elected with no problem in 1971 as ICSID president. In her final public speech before the vote, she called on the authority of Eliot Noyes as a final

---

[42] ICD, 08-3-3 Cressonnieres, Josine des (1972–1977) some photos: des Cressonnières, Josine, [Letter to Kenji Ekuan] (20 June 1977).
[43] ICD, 08-3-3: Cressonnieres, Josine des (1972–1977) some photos: des Cressonnières, Josine, [Letter to Paul Reilly] (s.d.).
[44] Gui Bonsiepe also considers now in retrospect that 'The weak point that hindered her election for heading a professional design organization, was that she was not considered a design professional, but mainly a design promoter.' See Bonsiepe, Gui, [E-mail to the author] (29 June 2015).
[45] ICD, 08-3-3 Cressonnières, Josine des (1972–1977) some photos: Reilly, Paul, [Letter to Kenji Ekuan], 17 May 1977.
[46] ICD, 03-9-16 Minutes: 'ICSID Xth General Assembly 23–24 September 1977 Dublin Ireland'.
[47] Her counter-arguments were formulated in a long letter to Paul Reilly, but also at the General Assembly in Dublin where she rose to speak immediately before the voting: ICD, 08-3-3 Cressonnieres, Josine des (1972–1977) some photos: des Cressonnières, Josine, [Letter to Paul Reilly] (s.d.); 03-9-16 Minutes: 'ICSID Xth General Assembly 23–24 September 1977 Dublin Ireland'.
[48] ICD, 08-3-3 Cressonnieres, Josine des (1972–1977) some photos: des Cressonnières, Josine, [Letter to Paul Reilly] (s.d.).

argument. Just before he died, he apparently approved her candidacy, advising that her experience as a design promotion member would be useful in undertaking the job because ICSID's role was to promote design, opening doors for all designers and widening their potential, activity and influence.[49]

Whether it was the result of gender issues, Cold War politics or des Cressonnières' lack of design experience, the voting at the 1977 General Assembly in Dublin went against her. After sixteen years of service Josine des Cressonnières withdrew from the ICSID board.[50] This was a turning point, not only in des Cressonnières' career, but also for ICSID. Messell observes that the whole incident left a definite mark, as 'ICSID's ambivalent ethics and political neutrality were brought to light, which must have further affected its reputation both within and beyond the Council'.[51]

The Brussels Design Centre and the malleability of the national category

In parallel with her international career, Josine des Cressonnières was one of the key women in the drafting of Belgian design policies. In 1962, one year after her appointment as ICSID Secretary General, she was one of the three founding members of the new Brussels Design Centre, and was its director until her death in 1985. The design policies drafted by des Cressonnières for Belgian design bodies not only existed within a national context: they were also the product of her transnational exchanges and responded to international design frameworks.

The Brussels Design Centre was a non-profit organization set up in 1962 with the support of the Belgian Foreign Trade Office and the Ministry of Economic Affairs to promote Belgian design, especially in the international market.[52] The export business was at the time one of the Belgian government's top priorities. Belgian officials observed that a favourable national image was a trump card in the increasingly liberalized markets. At the same time, informed by des Cressonnières' transnational network, the centre established itself within an international tradition of design promotion.[53] Belgium was, after all, not the first to establish a design centre. According to designer Arthur Pulos, the specific format prevailed in virtually every 'country – from Argentina to the Soviet Union – that could

---

[49] ICD, 03-9-16 Minutes: ICSID Xth General Assembly 23–24 September 1977 Dublin Ireland.
[50] She did not completely withdraw from ICSID but stayed active in some commissions. In 1981, she was, for example, appointed as administrator of the new committee 'ICSID/UNESCO.' 'News. Berichten,' *Design News* 7, no. 0381 (1981).
[51] Messell, 'Constructing a "United Nations of Industrial Design"', 175.
[52] *Design and Politics*, 155–86. The Design Centre was established by the trio of Pol Provost (1907–1990), Frans Wildiers (1905–1986) and Josine des Cressonnières (1926–1985).
[53] At the suggestion of the ICSID President Peter Muller-Munk, Josine des Cressonnières put forward a proposal to take the Signe d'Or closer to the British example and set up a Design Centre. See ICD, 09-11-1 Correspondence (1957–1959): Muller-Munk, Peter, [Letter addressed to Josine des Cressonnières] (22 January 1959).

lay claim to being industrialized' and should be understood in the light of the emergence of a global design scene.⁵⁴ Most of these centres were modelled on the CoID's well-known Design Centre in London, established in 1956 and probably the first of its kind. The format for the Centre consisted of a permanent exhibition of jury-selected products that changed every three months, supplemented by temporary themed exhibitions, a library and a design index. Adopting this British format, most importantly, meant becoming part of an international community of design centres, sharing experience through correspondence, exhibitions and meetings. Under des Cressonnières' directorship, the Brussels Design Centre was one of the longest-lasting of its kind, and advised on the setting up of many centres elsewhere.⁵⁵

The vision of the Brussels Design Centre was equally inspired by the design philosophy prevailing at the Ulm School of Design (HfG), which was characterized by an extreme rational and scientific approach and occupied a central position in the industry. The Argentinian design authority Tomás Maldonado, Rector of the Ulm School of Design, was a close friend of des Cressonnières. The Brussels Design Centre went on to adopt Maldonado's definition of design that he developed in 1964 at the first ICSID Seminar, 'The Education of Industrial Designers' in Bruges, supported by UNESCO and organized by des Cressonnières.⁵⁶ Informed by the Ulm approach, the Brussels Design Centre prided itself on being the first design centre in the world to move away from a concept of design that was limited to consumer goods for domestic use: from the outset it presented capital goods, engineering and professional instruments such as industrial milking and milling machines.⁵⁷ The Brussels Design Centre even fitted out part of its exhibition space with a concrete floor to be able to display heavy machinery.

Immediately after the Brussels Design Centre opened its doors in 1964, Belgian objects were sent to their counterparts in Japan, Finland, the Netherlands, Germany and elsewhere. In return, design objects from around the world set off on long trips to be shown in Brussels. This kind of exchange was the result not only of the global success of the design profession and des Cressonnières' impressive network, but also of the national agenda of the Brussels organization, namely to provide Belgium with a positive image in the arena of international trade and politics. Many of these international design exchanges were thus paired with

---

⁵⁴ Pulos, *The American Design Adventure, 1940–1975*, 210.
⁵⁵ Josine des Cressonnières and Jean-Jacques Stiefenhofer, 'Dossier: Het Design Centre: Tien jaar onderweg', *A+*, no. 9/10 (1974): 18. Not all Design Centres were as active or well situated in the network: see, for example, the short-lived Greek Design Centre: Artemis Yagou, 'Unwanted Innovation. The Athens Design Centre (1961–1963)', *Journal of Design History* 18, no. 3 (2005). Belgium, Brussels, State Archives, BE ARA. BDOP (510-2227), I504, no. 1081: *Rapport d'activités 1969*, 6; AJJS, Box 24.2: Josines des Cressonnières, *Rapport concernant la mission effectuee au bresil par mme des cressonnières, 4–30 avril 1973*.
⁵⁶ For the definition, see Messell, 'Constructing a "United Nations of Industrial Design"', 237.
⁵⁷ Serulus, *Design and Politics*, 161–9.

FIGURE 8.5 Josine des Cressonnières and Prince Albert at the opening of the Design Centre, 1964. Source: Private archive Geraldine des Cressonnières

commercial, diplomatic or economic missions within the framework of the Cold War. Members of royalty, ambassadors, ministers and other officials were thus mobilized to formally inaugurate these politically motivated design events (see Figure 8.5). Des Cressonnières' transnational network and favourable access to the heart of the international design community were often capitalized on by Belgian officials in these situations for national political and diplomatic purposes.[58]

Des Cressonnières' own motivation for these exchanges was somewhat different; in 1964 she explained the outward-looking attitude of the Brussels Design Centre in a promotional brochure as a kind of logical step in the modern project towards globalization:

> To those who fear that the multiplication of these exchanges [exchanges with foreign initiatives] will give birth to uniformity, we can say that the old regional values will inevitably dissolve into a civilization that is becoming global, but

---

[58] A remarkable case is the exchange with the Soviet design organization VNIITE (Russian All-Union Research Institute of Technical Aesthetics) in the early 1970s. See Katarina Serulus, '"Well-Designed Relations": Cold War Design Exchanges between Brussels and Moscow in the Early 1970s', *Design and Culture* 9, no. 2 (2017): 147–65.

that the folklore can be replaced by man, not by man alone, but man in a team, in a firm, in a design studio.⁵⁹

The quote leaves much room for interpretation, since it is not very clear exactly what des Cressonnières means by 'man in a design studio'. However, it is clear that her words appeal to a humanistic belief in design's universal character that would eventually erase national specificity, and that expressions of 'folklore' were only a transitional phase in the modern project. Soon after the opening of the Brussels Design Centre, des Cressonnières even advocated the expansion of the Brussels Design Centre to a European level in the light of the rapid internationalization of the markets.⁶⁰ The problem was that some of the products of Belgian companies were partly created in other countries and consequently could not be promoted by this national design body. She even concluded, after five years of heading the Brussels Design Centre, that 'the national character [of the centre] is no longer adapted to future economic structures'.⁶¹ However, there was no option to deviate from the national scope since the Centre was financially supported by the Belgian Foreign Trade Office, and the board of directors decided it should remain a tool of national promotion and progress. The same ambitions and vision were also reflected in des Cressonnières' comments on the ICSID debates on the role of design centres. Around 1967, ICSID was looking for a sound definition of a design centre in order to be able to grant them official recognition. During the drafting of this definition, des Cressonnières, who was by then also Secretary General of ICSID, suggested providing for the possibility of an 'international' design centre in the definition.⁶² This suggestion, although not included in the final ICSID version, illustrates des Cressonnières' willingness to elevate this national format to an international level.

This constraint continued to be considered an enduring obstacle.⁶³ The difficulties caused by the national approach, in combination with the new economic climate, however, forced the Brussels Design Centre to rethink the question of national identity with regard to products. While it had earlier defined its scope on the basis of where products were created, the evolution of the market led to the emergence of new selection criteria and definitions of what was, and was not, 'Belgian'. Trying to change tack, des Cressonnièrs stated in 1974 that the new role of the Brussels Design Centre was no longer the promotion of 'Belgian' products

---

⁵⁹ 'A ceux qui craignent qu'une uniformité ne naisse de la multiplication de ces échanges, on peut répondre que les anciennes valeurs régionales tendront inéluctablement à se fondre dans une civilisation qui devient planétaire, mais que le folklore peut être remplacé par l'homme, non pas l'homme seul, mais l'homme dans l'équipe, dans l'entreprise, dans le bureau de design.' See Josine des Cressonnières, 'La Signification d'un Design Centre', *Industrie* 19, no. 1 (1965): 30–1.
⁶⁰ Serulus, *Design and Politics*, 125–9.
⁶¹ Josine des Cressonnières, 'La Signification d'un Design Centre', *Industrie* 19, no. 1 (1965): 30–1.
⁶² ICD, 9-12-2: *Definition of a Design Centre*.
⁶³ Guy Rouckaerts, '15 jaar Design-promotie. Design Centre: Lukse of noodzaak?', *Komunikatief* 1979.

but the protection of 'Belgian' creativity.[64] However, this did not prevent the liberalized market, in combination with the prevailing national bias, from causing some occasionally absurd situations concerning national labelling, revealing the malleability of the term 'national'. For example, furniture by Artifort, a Dutch company with a production plant in the Belgian city of Lanaken, was included in the 1979 retrospective exhibition 'Furniture from Belgium: From Henry van de Velde until Now'.[65] The same 'Belgian' Artifort furniture was shown some years later as a 'Dutch' product at the Brussels Design Centre in the 1981 touring exhibition 'Design from the Netherlands', organized by Gijs Bakker for the Dutch Ministry of Culture's Visual Arts Office for Abroad.[66]

Social change by design

One of des Cressonnières' main concerns, evident throughout her career, was her belief in the contribution of design to social need and the responsibility of public authorities to create a human-friendly environment. International organizations and networks acted as important platforms for des Cressonnières to develop her design discourses. She first expressed her ideas on this topic as Secretary General of ICSID. In the 1960s, ICSID expanded its focus from solely professional interests to a more socially engaged vision of design in order to raise its status and address an expanding young public beyond the professional realm.[67] Messell considers des Cressonnières to be central to this 'social' turn by ICSID.[68] For the 1965 ICSID conference in Vienna, des Cressonnières proposed the conference theme 'Equipment for the Community', including the responsibility of the public authorities as one of industry's largest customers.[69] The aim was to bridge the Iron Curtain and include designers and government officials from Soviet countries. She argued that the theme would 'be attractive to Eastern countries and would give an opportunity to underline that DESIGN is not solely a matter for individual equipment but is also necessary to basic public equipment in every country'.[70] This was closely related to des Cressonnières' aim to make governments aware of industrial design in order to enable real change in people's everyday environment.

---

[64] des Cressonnières and Stiefenhofer, 'Dossier: Het Design Centre: Tien jaar onderweg'.
[65] *Meubelen uit België. Van Henry van de Velde tot heden/Mobilier de Belgique de Henry van de Velde à nos jours*, ed. Design Centre (Brussels, 1978).
[66] *Design uit Nederland*, ed. Visual Arts Office for Abroad (Amsterdam: Visual Arts Office for Abroad, 1980); Joana Ozorio de Almeida Meroz, 'The International as National: The Role of International Cultural Policy in the Construction of Dutch Design as Conceptual' (paper presented at the 9th International Committee Design History and Design Studies. Tradition, transition, trajectories: major or minor influences?, Aveiro, 2014).
[67] Messell, 'Constructing a "United Nations of Industrial Design"', 78–116.
[68] Ibid., 79, 83, 86.
[69] Ibid., 80, 107.
[70] ICD, 04-1 Board meeting 1962–1970: 'Minutes of the Executive Board Meeting held in Brussels on 20 February 1964'.

Her interest in human and social need was also noticeable in her attention to the ecological issues that had surfaced by the 1970s. In her ICSID notes of May 1970, she wrote that 'there exists a clear slide towards ecology', and that one of the emerging essential tasks of the day was the preservation of the environment.[71] She clearly alluded to the developing design discourse that was characterized by a new ecological and activist mindset.[72] In this context, the closure of the famous Ulm School of Design in 1968, at the height of student protests all over Europe, was telling. In its place, a smaller Institute of Environmental Studies was established as its successor in 1971.[73] Also, Maldonado's extreme scientific Modernist stance changed to a focus on 'the human environment'. In 1970 he published his book *Nature and Revolution: Toward a Critical Ecology*.[74] That same year activist student groups hijacked the well-established International Design Conference in Aspen on the theme 'Environment by Design' and left the Modernist design elite totally bewildered.[75]

The seventh ICSID conference in Ibiza in 1971 was able to avert such flagrant disruption by responding to the leftist critiques expressed in Aspen on the outdated non-participatory format of conferences. Accordingly, the conference in Ibiza, on 'Design in a Changing Society', was meant, according to its Secretary General, to be a 'congress revolution': no keynotes, no programme, but instead completely directed towards personal exchanges between participants.[76] That same year, Victor Papanek's book *Design for the Real World* (1971) kindled a strong debate on the future of design and its moral and social duties. In 1972, the Club of Rome published its widely read report *The Limits to Growth*, which served to intensify this message and warned about the exhaustion of natural resources on earth, particularly oil. Its message grew stronger when the oil crisis hit the following year, and car-free Sundays were organized. Drawn from the new environmental

---

[71] ICD, 04-7 Board meeting 1968–1975 (Cahiers): *Notes by Josine des Cressonnières* (May 1970); Messell, 'Constructing a "United Nations of Industrial Design"', 155.

[72] Alison J. Clarke, '"Actions Speak Louder": Victor Papanek and the Legacy of Design Activism', *Design and Culture* 5, no. 2 (2013); Pauline Madge, 'Design, Ecology, Technology: A Historiographical Review', *Journal of Design History* 6, no. 3 (1993); Javier Gimeno-Martínez, 'Redefining Social Design in 1970s Belgium: Affordable Design vs. Elite Design', *Interiors* 2, no. 2 (2011); Alison J. Clarke, 'Design for Development, ICSID and UNIDO: The Anthropological Turn in 1970s Design', *Journal of Design History* (2015).

[73] Paul Betts, *The Authority of Everyday Objects: A Cultural History of West German Industrial Design* (Berkeley, CA: University of California Press, 2004), 249–64.

[74] Tomas Maldonado, *Design, Nature and Revolution: Toward a Critical Ecology*, trans. Mario Domandi (New York: Harper & Row, 1972). The first edition was published in 1970 in Italian (*La Speranza Progettuale*) and the second revised version was translated in 1972 into English, French, German and Spanish.

[75] Alice Twemlow, 'I Can't Talk to You if You Say That: An Ideological Collision at the International Design Conference at Aspen, 1970', *Design and Culture* 1, no. 1 (2009).

[76] Throughout this article, all references preceded by the initials 'ADC' indicate materials that are held at State Archives Brussels (Belgium-, BE-A0545/Fic 2000, Archive Design Centre. ADC, 20: Josine des Cressonnières, L'industrial design dans le monde et en Belgique [undated article published in the magazine *Europe 13*].

awareness she observed, des Cressonnières expanded the Brussels Design Centre's scope from highlighting single industrial products to representing the 'product environment' that included architectural, urban, ecological and social issues.[77] In 1970 a new criterion for the selection of its exhibited products was added: their influence on the environment.

Des Cressonnières most explicitly developed these design strategies during the late 1970s. In her 1977 statement of intent as a nominee for ICSID presidency, she considered that the only way 'to contribute to change in our Society [sic] and to the transformation of this economic and political structure' was to introduce industrial designers into powerful milieus – understood by her as national governments, but also including large industries, management levels and non-governmental organizations – located at national and international levels.[78] In 1978 she submitted a proposal for a fellowship at the Woodrow Wilson International Center for Scholars in Washington, where she elaborated on the subject of a global policy of industrial design for public authorities.[79] She observed that a key problem of her time was the dysfunctional relationship between industry, products and people: 'The distortion between an economic system that still rests on growth and profit, and a totally new social consciousness, has been felt so keenly by the public that it has generated a sort of rejection of the enterprise by the young generation.'[80] According to her, design's essential contribution is 'to restore MAN, in all his dimensions, as the ultimate standard of production.'[81] The goals of the project – which was not eventually accepted – were to collect examples of national design policies from around the world and to formulate ideas for the future.[82]

In 1980, she even gave a short amusing demonstration at Le Centre de Création Industrielle (CCI) in Paris on how to implement these policies. In a lecture entitled '5 Minutes to Convince' she gave a playful example of how to introduce design into 'decision-making spheres' by capitalizing on the patriotic desire by government ministers to set up a stronger national economy, export trade and image.[83] The

---

[77] Serulus, Design and Politics, 203–8.
[78] ICD, 03-9-8 Nominations: des Cressonnières, Josine, *Statement of Intent*.
[79] Belgium, Coutisse, Private archives des Cressonnières: des Cressonnières, Josine, *Proposal for a fellowship to the Woodrow Wilson International Center for Scholars. September 78 (Washington). 'Design and Public Authorities' A proposal for a global policy of industrial design*.
[80] Ibid., 10.
[81] Ibid., 3.
[82] This plan was reminiscent of the actions of one of the ICSID working groups on design promotion – of which des Cressonnières was a member – that compiled a collection of national case histories in the early 1970s. The subject of state policy on design was well explored within ICSID. One of the sessions at the Kyoto conference in 1973 was devoted to this theme. The 1975 conference in Moscou even took 'Design as a state policy' as its main theme. See ICD, 03, 06-6bis Working Group VI: Promotion, des Cressonnières, Josine, *Minutes of Meeting Berlin, December 16 to 17, 1974, Session on 'Design as a State Policy'* (6 January 1975).
[83] ADC, 898: des Cressonnières, Josine, *'5 minutes pour convaincre', prononcé au CCI paris lors de l'assemblé général du ICSID du février 1980*.

trick was to first win them over on the topic of design. Des Cressonnières suggests starting as follows:

> Dear Minister.
>
> You have said – or written – that it is essential for our country to invest in innovation and creativity – (whether he actually said it or not is of no importance, he will agree to be credited with it) – creativity and innovation being some of the most precious assets which can compensate, on the internal markets, for the cost of our workforce, our strikes, our lifestyle, our growing social changes, etc. …[84]

Des Cressonnières suggested that to introduce 'design' was a way to get the best results in the short term. She explained that there were several ways to introduce design. One could start by inviting the minister to declare in public the importance of design. One could go further and propose more fundamental input: for example, to include design as one of the criteria for public contracts. But one could go even further … and suggest insisting on the employment of designers on public commissions. As such, the state itself would become the motor of innovation. She instructed the audience to finish on a nationalistic note:

> This policy is expected to have an additional effect: a new image for our country, a possible quality for our export capacity. Think, for example, how much the image of Japan has changed on our markets in the past twenty years! One last point, dear minister, there is no other country in the world where there exists today a complete and coherent Industrial Design policy. Why shouldn't we be the first?[85]

Design Commission

The most concrete result of des Cressonnières' focus on introducing design policies at a state level was the establishment in 1977 of the Inter-ministerial Design Commission – in short, the Design Commission. It became one of

---

[84] 'Monsieur le Ministre. Vous avez dit – écrit – qu'il est essentiel pour notre pays d'investir dans l'innovation et la créativité (qu'il l'ait dit ou non, c'est sans importance, il sera d'accord pour qu'on le lui attribue) – la créativité et l'innovation étant des plus précieux atouts qui puissent compenser, sur les marchés internes, le coût de notre main-d'oevre, de nos grèves, de notre train de vie, de nos charges sociales croissantes etc … ' See Ibid.
[85] 'On peut attendre un résultat supplémentaire de cette politique: une nouvelle image du pays, qualité éventuelle pour notre pouvoir à l'exportation. Que l'on pense par exemple combine l'image du Japon a changé en 20 ans sur nos marches! Un dernier point, Monsieur le Ministre, il n'y a aucun pays au monde où il existe à ce jour une politique complète et cohérente d'Industrial Design. Pourquoi ne serions-nous pas les premiers?' See Ibid.

des Cressonnières' main projects after her resignation from ICSID.[86] The commission was set up under the aegis of the Belgian Ministry of Public Works, and was headed by its Secretary General, Robert De Paepe. The Design Centre in Brussels served as the Secretariat. The Commission's aim was to standardize all public equipment. More concretely, it described its responsibility as 'design coordination' between governmental agencies and ministries. If one ministry, for example, needed street signs and the other streetlights, the Commission would address the potential for overlaps, omissions or cooperation. Therefore, the Commission included not only officials from the Ministry of Public Works, but also representatives from the Ministries of Transport, Postal Services, Education and Public Health.

The establishment of the Commission coincided with turbulent years in Belgian politics, as the first steps towards a federalized Belgium were taken in the 1970s.[87] Regions were increasingly asking for more political and cultural autonomy. Thus, one of the key premises of the Brussels Design Centre's activities was challenged: its national scope.[88] However, Belgium's federalization process did not hinder des Cressonnières' mission. On the contrary, she considered the newly created governments rather as excellent clients for design, since public commissions for graphic identity, public transport and urban furniture were considered important design opportunities. She pitched design as a way to make the 'state' – whether federal, regional, provincial, municipal – tangible for its citizens.

Along with its role as 'design coordinator' for governments, the Commission also proposed pilot projects for public services prompted by current debates or needs. One of these was a totally new concept for urban equipment by designer Bruno Stoppa, who designed a modular system based on an aluminium pole.[89] The whole range included traffic lights, road signs, bus stops, kiosks and telephone booths. The Commission's ultimate aspiration was to include design criteria and methods in purchasing orders from the Belgian state and, as such, to introduce a consistent design policy at state level. After all, as the Design Commission reasoned, the amount of equipment which the state bought represented more than a quarter of the national production – and as such there was great potential for design to humanize the everyday public environment.

---

[86] This Commission was established on 5 April 1977 under the presidency of Robert De Paepe (1927–2011), General Secretary of the Ministry of Public Works. The Commission was under the protection of Louis Olivier, the Minister of Public Works. ADC, 67: *Interministeriële Designcommissie* (October 1981); Louis Olivier, *Design: pour l'État, voor de Staat, für den Staat, for the State*, ed. Design Centre and Interministerial Design Commission (Brussels1983). See also: Serulus, *Design and Politics*, 209–13.
[87] Vincent Dujardin et al., eds., *Nieuwe geschiedenis van België. 1950-Heden*, vol. 3 (Tielt: Lannoo, 2009), 1443; Els Witte, Jan Craeybeckx, and Alain Meynen, *Politieke geschiedenis van België. Van 1830 tot heden* (Antwerpen: Standaard, 2005), 437–40.
[88] See also: Serulus, *Design and Politics*, 194–201.
[89] ADC, 251. Dossier inzake 'Stadsmeubilering: 16 bedrijven en een designer ontwerpen een innoverende uitrusting' (22 januari 1982–3 maart 1982).

FIGURE 8.6 Kenji Ekuan at the Brussels Design Centre exhibition 'Design for the State'. In front a model of a pilot boat made by a temporary association of the shipbuilding yards 'Langerbrugge' and 'Fulton Marine'. Source: Belgium, Brussels, State Archives, BE- A0545/Fic 2000, Archive Design Centre, 263

The Design Commission's initiatives resulted in a number of Design Centre exhibitions and publications: *Rest Areas along Motorways* (1978), *Design and Equipment of Public Spaces in the City Center* (1980) and *Furnishing the City* (1982).[90] But the absolute zenith was the 1983 'Design and the State' exhibition.[91] The show presented an overview of the Design Commission's achievements and was paired with an international symposium on the same subject. The prestigious event included lectures by Josine des Cressonnières, Jens Nielsen from Denmark, Jean François Grunfeld from France and two of the leading ICSID figures, Loek van der Sande from the Netherlands and Kenji Ekuan from Japan (see Figure 8.6).[92] Each speaker presented a national example of 'design for the state' for comparison. The exhibition itself presented pilot projects for urban furniture, school furniture, graphic design for public transport, and other objects developed by designers for public services at all levels in the federalizing Belgian state.[93]

---

[90] ADC, 220, 251; John Dassesse and Christine Smout, '*Inrichting en uitrusting van openbare ruimten in stadscentra* (Brussel: Design Kommissie / Ministerie van Openbare Werken, 1980).
[91] ADC, 263: Dossier inzake 'Design voor de staat' (10 November 1983–1 Februari 1984).
[92] ADC, 898.
[93] The exhibition was on show in the Design Centre from 10 November 1983 until 1 February 1984 under the patronage of the King Baudouin Foundation, ICSID, and the Belgian Ministry of Public Works. Louis Olivier, *Design: pour l'État, voor de Staat, für den Staat, for the State*, ed. Design Centre and Interministerial Design Commission (Brussels, 1983).

Conclusion

The case of Josine des Cressonnières offers insights into the transnational networks at play in the creation of national and international design policies. Rather than enclosed spheres that are often studied separately as well-defined topics, the career trajectory of Josine des Cressonnières actually documents the intense dynamics between these national, international and transnational frameworks where design cultures are shaped. The design policies drafted by des Cressonnières for Belgian design bodies not only existed within national logic and the Cold War politics, but were also the product of transnational exchanges and answered to international design frameworks. Platforms such as ICSID gave des Cressonnières the opportunity to develop and enrich her discourses on social and human design. The unique position as Secretary General for 16 years gave her access to information and contacts that were crucial to expand her knowledge, skills and network on this subject. At the same time, the ideas she exchanged and developed within the international design networks were informed by her experience at national and local levels. Des Cressonnières could moreover test the rather abstract concepts she developed within ICSID in the Belgian context, as she did with the establishment of a 'Design Commission' that was meant to coordinate the design of public equipment.

The huge amount of practical and intellectual work des Cressonnières achieved behind the facades of design bodies ran in parallel with her personal ambitions and struggles. She advanced her career within institutional frameworks of design but was also keen on expanding her business opportunities as a private consultant, working for commercial companies such as Raymond Loewy. As a single mother, and one of the few women to hold a position of power in the male-dominated discipline of industrial design, des Cressonnières was faced with prejudices concerning her gender and was confronted with a glass ceiling when applying for the role of ICSID President. It was thanks to her diplomatic skills, her organizational talents and her exceptional skills of navigating institutional and official structures that she was able to gain an influential position at the heart of the international design community.

PART THREE

DESIGN DEFINITIONS – EPISTEMOLOGIES – DIFFERENCES

9 NEGOTIATING GRAPHIC DESIGN BETWEEN NATIONAL AND INTERNATIONAL DESIGN ORGANIZATIONS: THE CASE OF THE ASSOCIAZIONE PER IL DESIGN INDUSTRIALE IN MILAN

Chiara Barbieri

The ADI, Associazione per il Design Industriale (Association for Industrial Design), was founded in Milan in 1956 to promote the professional status and raise standards of industrial design in Italy.[1] As one of the first members of ICSID (International Council of Societies of Industrial Design), an international organization formed in 1957 to bring together such professional associations, the ADI also promoted its agenda transnationally. In December 1962, the readers of *ICSID News Bulletin* could read the following news about the Italian member society: 'ITALY: … the ADI is … planning to form the first Italian Group of Visual Designers.'[2] At first glance, a distracted reader was likely to dismiss the news as yet another domestic matter with no relevance beyond Italian national borders. After all, on the same page of *ICSID News Bulletin*, the Verband Deutscher Industrie Designer (Association of German Industrial Designers) disclosed the names of the newly elected council members, the Netherlands reported the opening of the Dutch Design Center, and the Pakistan Council of Industrial Design announced the intention of setting up an Institute of Industrial Design and Graphic Art. Yet a more curious reader might have wondered: why was the ADI, an industrial design association, planning to form a graphic design branch? Was this really the first, or were there other groups locally representing the practice of graphic design? If so, why did the ADI feel the need to set up an alternative? An attentive and informed reader might even have drawn comparisons with the state of graphic design

---

[1] Renato De Fusco, *Una storia dell'ADI: 50* (Milan: Franco Angeli Editore, 2010).
[2] *ICSID News Bulletin*, no. 2 (December 1962): 3.

practice in other geographies. Readers could also have been able to contextualize the domestic news within the contemporary articulation of new thinking in visual communication that was shared by an international community clustered around international design organizations.

The ADI graphic design division is the starting point of this chapter that goes on to explore the articulation of graphic design in Italy by looking at changes in organizational strategies during the 1960s. Design practices are here understood as 'social practices, enacted, performed and negotiated through media, public institutions and professional organizations'.[3] Drawing from a wide literature on professional organizations, they are seen as important stages in the process of professionalism[4] and approached as 'internally structured groups that are located in complex networks of intergroups relations characterized by power, status, and prestige differentials'.[5] Organizational strategies are here explored as processes of self-categorization during which members identify themselves with an in-group and draw comparisons between this and relevant out-groups from which they differentiate themselves on valued dimensions of comparison.[6] This view of practices as ever-evolving social constructs, whose understanding is temporally and spatially specific, suggests that practitioners' collective identity is under constant renegotiation between and across different groups, including neighbouring practices, industry and the broader public, to address socio-cultural, political and economic changes, as well as reflect changing design discourse.[7] In line with this approach, the chapter identifies the 1960s as a moment of self-reflection and transition for the practice of graphic design in Italy. It argues that the tension between advertising and design constitutes a central and enduring feature in its professionalization, forming the basis for internal and external conflicts, alliances and compromise positions, which are the focus of this chapter.

---

[3] Armstrong, Leah and Felice McDowell, 'Introduction: Fashioning Professionals: History, Theory and Methods', in *Fashioning Professionals: Identity and Representation at Work in the Creative Industries*, ed. Armstrong, Leah and Felice McDowell (London: Bloomsbury, 2018), 1.

[4] Geoffrey Millerson, *The Qualifying Associations: A Study in Professionalization* (London: Routledge & Kegan Paul, 1964); Eliot Freidson, *Professional Powers: A Study of the Institutionalization of Formal Knowledge* (Chicago; London: University of Chicago Press, 1986), 196–9; Andrew Abbott, *The System of Professions: An Essay on the Division of Expert Labour* (Chicago; London: The University of Chicago Press, 1988), 79–83.

[5] Michael A. Hogg and Deborah J. Terry, 'Social Identity and Self-Categorization Processes in Organizational Contexts', *The Academy of Management Review* 25, no. 1 (2000): 121. See also Michael A. Hogg and Deborah J. Terry, 'Social Identity and Organizational Processes', in *Social Identity Processes in Organizational Contexts*, ed. Michael A. Hogg and Deborah J. Terry (London: Taylor and Francis Group, 2001), 1–12.

[6] Stephen Reicher, 'The Context of Social Identity: Domination, Resistance, and Change', *Political Psychology* 25, no. 6 (2004): 921–45; Stephen Worchel, Jonathan Iuzzini, Dawna Coutant and Manuela Ivaldi, 'A Multidimensional Model of Identity: Relating Individual and Group Identities to Intergroup Behaviour', in *Social Identity Processes: Trends in Theory and Research*, ed. Dora Capozza and Rupert Brown (London; Thousand Oaks; New Delhi: SAGE Publications, 2000), 15–32.

[7] Valérie Fournier, 'The Appeal to "Professionalism" as a Disciplinary Mechanism', *Social Review* 47, no. 2 (1999): 280–307.

The changing organizational strategies of graphic designers in Italy are situated within a network of national professional bodies and international design organizations, and contextualized within transnational discourses around graphics, design and advertising. In exploring the professionalization of graphic design as a transnational phenomenon that took distinctive characteristics within different local scenes, the chapter aims to answer the call 'to produce internationally situated investigations in which national design histories are understood within international contexts'.[8] For more than two decades, design historians have been advocating research on international design organizations as a means to broaden the geography of design history and explore the multidirectional exchange between different scales of focus: local, regional, national and global.[9] In line with this scholarship, the chapter explores how international design organizations offered Milan's graphic designers the opportunity to be part of an international community, formulate common strategies and contribute to a transnational graphic design discourse. All in all, it argues that a transnational gaze and a comparative approach afford a better understanding and a more comprehensive picture of the articulation of graphic design in Italy.

The ADI and the Aiap

The founding of the ADI graphic design division can be read as a reaction to internal power dynamics between the different in-groups that structured the industrial design association. Indeed, the ADI membership was heterogeneous from the outset. Alongside industrial designers, the association welcomed members among architects, graphic designers, industrialists and intellectuals. The heterogeneous membership suggests a wide recognition of the ADI and support for its agenda. Yet this diversity was a potential weakness that exposed the association to internal conflicts between in-groups with different access to power, status and prestige, as the following pages will demonstrate.

Despite being a minority group, key figures of Italian graphic design participated in the ADI from the beginning. Marcello Nizzoli, Giovanni Pintori, Albe Steiner and the Milan-based Swiss designer Max Huber attended the preliminary meeting in January 1956; Michele Provinciali and Bruno Munari joined the association straight after.[10] Steiner, best known for his work for major clients such as La

---

[8] Kjetil Fallan and Grace Lees-Maffei, 'Real Imagined Communities: National Narratives and the Globalization of Design History', *Design Issues* 32, no. 1 (2016): 12.
[9] Jonathan M. Woodham, 'Local, National and Global: Redrawing the Design Historical Map', *Journal of Design History* 18, no. 3 (2005): 257–67; Anna Calvera, 'Local, Regional, National, Global and Feedback: Several Issues to be Faced with Constructing Regional Narratives', *Journal of Design History* 18, no. 4 (2005): 371–83; Daniel J. Huppatz, 'Globalizing Design History and Global Design History', *Journal of Design History* 28, no. 2 (2015): 182–202.
[10] 'Riunione del 7 Febbraio 1956, per l'Associazione del Disegno Industriale', meeting minutes, Milan, Politecnico di Milano, Archivio Albe e Lica Steiner (AALS), Db. 14 fasc. 7.

Rinascente, Olivetti and Pirelli, and in the publishing sector, was elected a member of the first directive committee alongside the architect Enrico Peressutti and the industrialists Giulio Castelli and Antonio Pellizzari. Almost all of the successive directive committees included a graphic designer. Their involvement suggests an associative environment that was likely to act upon or at least acknowledge issues of visual communication.

Graphic designers' membership in an industrial design association is open to interpretation. Practitioners like Nizzoli and Munari were active in both fields of graphic and product design. The crossover between design practices may explain why graphic designers wished to be members of the ADI. However, a comment on Steiner's involvement in the ADI by the design critic Gillo Dorfles hints at a rather different and more compelling interpretation. According to Dorfles, an ADI member himself, Steiner was in fact driven by 'the opportunity to include the graphics – that is *graphic design* – within the sphere of industrial design [and] confer the "status" of industrial design not only to the three-dimensional graphic design but also to two-dimensional one, as long as this complied with a programmatic whole'.[11] Dorfles's point of view suggests that graphic designers might have used the ADI as an institutional stage towards affirming their identity and to stake claims for recognition as an independent practice, re-categorized within the design domain. Indeed, the ADI organizational context offered graphic designers the opportunity to articulate their professional identity in relation to a dominant in-group of industrial designers. But industrial designers were not the only group that the ADI graphic designers could compare themselves to and negotiate their practice with. Further evidence in support of graphic designers' strategic involvement in the ADI emerges when considering alternative memberships that were available to graphic designers in Italy at the time.

By contrast to the announcement in *ICSID News Bulletin*, the ADI was neither the only nor the first association for graphic designers in Italy. Since 1955, they could in fact also become members of another professional body, the Aiap, Associazione Italiana Artisti Pubblicitari (Italian Association of Advertising Artists).[12] Whereas the membership of the ADI was heterogeneous, the membership of the Aiap was limited to those defined as 'advertising artists'. Encompassing poster artists, illustrators, commercial artists and graphic practitioners, the advertising artists were in charge of the conception of all types of promotional printed matter. Their practice had been slowly emerging since the interwar period in relation to another figure with a key role in the advertising industry, the advertising technician.[13] In line with an American-inspired approach to advertising that had gradually taken

---

[11] Gillo Dorfles, in *Albe Steiner: Comunicazione visiva* (Milan: Fratelli Alinari, 1977), 11.

[12] Lorenzo Grazzani and Francesco E. Guida, *AIAP 70x70: Eventi, personaggi e materiali di una storia associativa* (Milan: Edizioni Aiap, 2015).

[13] Adam Arvidsson, 'Between Fascism and the American Dream: Advertising in Interwar Italy', *Social Science History* 25, no. 2 (2001): 151–86.

root in Italy during the post-war years, the technicians considered advertising as a new branch of business administration and their work as science-based, following the principles of rationalization and efficiency. From its very name, the Aiap was evidence of the often-neglected relationship between graphic design and advertising:[14] a relationship that had come to play a problematic role in the ongoing definition of graphic design during the 1950s and 1960s.

Graphics, advertising and design

In order to better understand the differences between the ADI and the Aiap, it is necessary to contextualize graphic practitioners' flexible professional identities within contemporary debates about the position of graphic design at the intersection between two allegedly incompatible fields: advertising and graphic design. Contemporary debates in Italy addressed two main overarching questions: is advertising an art, or is it rather a science? And can graphics be part of design?

The first question, whether advertising is an art or a science, set advertising artists against the technicians. During the post-war period, the former group saw its jurisdiction over advertising gradually undermined by the arrival, establishment and takeover of American-inspired full-service advertising agencies, including CPV, Radar&Benson, J. Walter Thompson and McCann Erickson.[15] As design historians Simona De Iulio and Carlo Vinti observed, the Americanization of Italian advertising was a phenomenon of cultural transfer that took the form of cultural resistance, transformation and hybridization.[16] American-inspired agencies found in Italy's main industries what they considered to be an inadequate advertising system, often based on a close partnership between leading graphic designers and the in-house Advertising or Propaganda Departments.[17] Italian advertising communication that pre-existed the dissemination of American-inspired practices favoured the representation of industry and production over commerce and consumption, thereby emphasizing the company's identity rather than appealing to the consumers' desires. By contrast, the American approach was marketing-driven and consumer-oriented. It was based on a division of labour and specialization of tasks that downgraded the advertising artist from

---

[14] Steven Heller, 'Advertising Mother of Graphic Design', *Eye* 5, no. 17 (1995): 26–37.
[15] Adam Arvidsson, *Marketing Modernity: Italian Advertising from Fascism to Postmodernity* (London: Routledge, 2003); Carlo Vinti, 'Grafica e pubblicità in Italia: 1933–1970', in *TDM5: Grafica italiana*, ed. Giorgio Camuffo, Mario Piazza and Carlo Vinti (Mantua: Corraini, 2012), 217–28.
[16] Simona De Iulio and Carlo Vinti, 'La Publicité italienne et le modèle américain', *Vingtième Siècle. Revue d'Histoire*, no. 101 (2009): 61–80; Simona De Iulio and Carlo Vinti, 'The Americanization of Italian Advertising during the 1950s and the 1960s: Mediations, Conflicts and Appropriations', *Journal of Historical Research in Marketing* 1, no. 2 (2009): 270–94.
[17] Carlo Vinti, *Gli anni dello stile industriale (1948–1965): Immagine e politica culturale nella grande impresa italiana* (Venice: Marsilio, 2007).

main character to one of the many actors involved in the process.[18] American-inspired advertising experts contested the effectiveness of local approaches: they considered graphic designers' visual experimentations unintelligible and detached from the general public, hence ineffective as advertising material. In their defence, the Italian counterpart accused the agencies of being more concerned with market research and media-planning than with visual research and graphic invention. They criticized the ordinary visual communication based on market surveys that aimed at persuading the consumers instead of pursuing the cultural and aesthetic responsibilities towards the public that Italian graphics had previously taken on.

Despite attempts at mediation and compromise, by the early 1960s the gradual shift towards a more Americanized concept of advertising had put in jeopardy graphic designers' central role in advertising communication. While American-inspired full-service agencies were threatening to reduce graphic designers' field of action considerably, Italian graphics was leaning ever more decisively towards design. Italy was not the only target of American advertising agencies as the Americanization of advertising was affecting a number of European countries whose advertising cultures were affected by the expansion of American communication strategies and work models.[19]

Discussions on graphic design and advertising entered the pages of the design magazine and ADI house organ, *Stile Industria*. Alberto Rosselli, ADI president and editor of *Stile Industria*, became a vocal advocate of the inclusion of graphic practice within the design domain. In an article entitled 'Grafici e Industrial Design' (Graphic practitioners and Industrial Design) published in April 1962, Rosselli indirectly answered the question as to whether graphics was part of design by clarifying the circumstances under which it could be.

> In principle, graphic design can be considered part of industrial design, [but] the graphic expressions that mainly address advertising cannot be compared nor put on the same level with the methodologies of industrial design. ... The basis for the development of the graphic design profession is then a new method of problem solving, ... an attitude proper to the 'designer'.[20]

To be recategorized within design, graphic designers needed 'to release the focus of [their practice] from the field of mere advertising and increasingly insert [it] within the operative sector of modern industry'.[21] In other words, if graphics'

---

[18] Michele Galluzzo, 'I grafici sono sempre protagonisti? Pubblicità in Italia 1965–1985' (PhD thesis, IUAV, Venice, 2018), 53–96.

[19] Victoria De Grazia, *Irresistible Empire: America's Advance through Twentieth-century Europe* (Cambridge, MA: Harvard University Press, 2005); Stefan Schwarzkopf, 'From Fordist to Creative Economies: The De-Americanization of European Advertising Cultures since the 1960s', *European Review of History* 20, no. 5 (2013): 859–79.

[20] Alberto Rosselli, 'Grafici e Industrial Design', *Stile Industria* 9, no. 37 (April 1962): 13–14.

[21] Ibid., 14.

inclusion in the design domain was still on hold, its affinity with advertising was to blame. To overcome this obstacle, graphic designers were expected to shift the focus of their practice towards a more systematic approach to visual communication that favoured the design of a comprehensive communication system over sporadic intervention. Design coordination and corporate image were indicated, in accordance with the guidelines of the so-called International Style, as one of the most relevant and appropriate outcomes of design approaches applied to visual communication. Indeed, they provided graphic designers with a chance 'to be redeemed from the subordinate role … and be actively assimilated in the production process'.[22]

This shifting agenda of Italian graphic designers intersected with the articulation of a transnational graphic design discourse that was emerging during the period. International design conferences provided opportunities for transnational encounters, therefore occasions for the construction of networks, information exchange and collective discourse articulation. This was the case with the 1960 World Design Conference (WoDeCo) in Tokyo.[23] The conference brought together exponents of the international design community from twenty-six countries to discuss, among a variety of topics, issues of graphic design. One of the core issues debated at WoDeCo under the general theme 'Our Century: The Total Image – What Designers Can Contribute to the Human Environment of the Coming Age' was the idea of design as a social service, hence designer's responsibility towards the society. The Argentinian design theorist and educator Tomás Maldonado opened the session on visual communication. 'Visual communication has become the object of scientific research', he explained, 'however the majority of designers still think that the most important aspect of communication media is the artistic creation'.[24] He then directly criticized 'the bad habit of explaining communication by restricting it to the field of advertising' and identified this misunderstanding as the cause of graphic designers' undervalued intellectual and professional status.[25]

Alberto Rosselli, Bruno Munari and Max Huber represented Italy at WoDeCo, talking on design production, designers' personality and social responsibilities respectively. In his presentation, Huber called for graphic designers' commitment to their public by offering informative and easily readable visual representations that would appeal to rationality rather than provoke emotional reactions. Emphasis was to be put on the clarity of design in communicating complex

---

[22] Raffaele Baldini, 'Grafica nella produzione', *Stile Industria* 9, no. 38 (June 1962): 33.
[23] Rem Koolhass and Hans Ulrich Obrist, *Project Japan: Metabolism Talk* (Köln: Taschen, 2011); Jilly Traganou, *Designing the Olympics: Representation, Participation, Contestation* (New York: Routledge, 2016), 77–9; Toshino Iguchi, 'Reconsideration of the World Design Conference 1960 in Tokyo and the World Industrial Design Conference 1973 in Kyoto: Transformation of Design Theory'. Available online: http://design-cu.jp/iasdr2013/papers/1183-1b.pdf [accessed 21 February 2020].
[24] Tomás Maldonado in Alberto Rosselli, 'World Design Conference 1960', *Stile Industria* 7, no. 28 (August 1960): xix.
[25] Ibid.

information to an ever more international audience rather than on designers' self-expression. In line with the principles of International Style, this approach to visual communication was visually translated into a preference for asymmetrical and geometrical compositions, grid layout, standardized design systems and long-term planning over subjectivity and one-off interventions and the exclusive use of sans-serif typefaces and photographic images. Together with design coordination and corporate image, also the design of wayfinding systems and infographics were indicated as appropriate outcomes of a systematic approach to visual communication: they were the antidotes that could redeem graphic design by distancing it from advertising.

The ADI graphic design division

The contemporary debates around graphics, advertising and design provided a backdrop for changes in the organizational strategies of graphic designers in Italy. They are evidence of the gradual distancing from the commercial sector towards design. Debates resonate in the words of Alberto Rosselli in which he disclosed the forthcoming foundation of the ADI graphic design division to the readers of the April 1962 issue of *Stile Industria*: 'A section of Italian graphics has already expressed on several occasions, and recently again in the ADI, the desire to go beyond the conventional status of the profession and develop their practice towards industrial design.'[26] Minutes of the founding meeting of the division on 8 May 1962 clearly state its ambitions: graphic designers in the ADI 'felt the need to constitute an ADI graphic design division in order to bring forward initiatives within this sector to be included in the ADI general agenda' and they asked for 'the official (not only formal or accidental) recognition' of the graphic design practice within the ADI and the design community at large.[27] In the light of the still ambiguous perception of graphic design and the challenges that the practice faced in both the fields of advertising and industrial design in the early 1960s, the ADI graphic design division offers insights into more than the mere association's policy. Its significance becomes evident once the organizational strategies of graphic designers in the ADI are set within a network of dynamic intergroups relationships between the in-group of industrial designers and the out-group of advertising artists.

Before claiming 'official recognition', graphic designers in the ADI had to clarify, define and agree among themselves what was their own collective identity. Despite the general uncertainty, members of the ADI graphic design division

---

[26] Rosselli, 'Grafici e Industrial Design': 13.
[27] '1a Riunione della Sezione Grafici della A.D.I.', meeting minute, 8 May 1962, Milan, Politecnico di Milano, AALS, Db. 14 fasc. 7: 1.

were able to agree on a vaguely common understanding of their practice, which was defined in comparative terms. In particular, they made a distinction between graphic practitioners and graphic designers: a graphic designer was a graphic practitioner, but not all graphic practitioners were graphic designers, hence not all of them could be admitted in the ADI. The distinction was contingent upon the types of artefacts produced and the kinds of methodologies adopted. For instance, packaging was deemed more appropriate than advertising as it embedded the graphic practice within industrial production. This did not mean that advertising was banned. It was in fact indicated as one of the expressions of graphic design, together with editorial design, signage design, infographics, exhibition design, moving image design, corporate image and many others.[28] Graphic designers were also not industrial designers, and the design practice was only a portion of their field of action. Nevertheless, graphic and industrial designers shared a similar approach and were both concerned with industrial production. As Michele Provinciali put it, graphic designers '[had left] a phase based on sketches and [had entered] a phase based on methodology'.[29]

During the founding meeting, the idea of establishing a new professional body restricted to graphic designers was taken into consideration, but it was concluded that it was actually in the interest of the practice to remain in the ADI together with the industrial designers. The ADI membership and the collaboration with fellow members were deemed instrumental if graphic designers were to become an integral part of the design process. The Aiap was neither suggested as an alternative professional body, nor mentioned at all. The silence speaks volumes and indicates that members of the ADI graphic design division did not recognize themselves in the agenda of the Aiap. While the ADI membership was a means of distancing graphic design from advertising, to be portrayed as advertising artists must have felt counterproductive to their demand for an official status in the design field. However, some members of the ADI graphic design division were actually members of both associations. Indeed, graphic designers Erberto Carboni, Franco Grignani, Pino Tovaglia and Ezio Bonini had subscribed to the Aiap since its early years. On the one hand, their twofold membership reinforced the idea that the ADI and the Aiap represented diametrically opposite aspects of the same practice whose boundaries, caught between the domains of advertising and design, were still blurry. On the other hand, their multiple collective identities suggested that there must have been some similarities between the ADI graphic design division and the Aiap, thereby hinting to a certain flexibility of behaviours between the two groups depending on context.

---

[28] 'Riunione del 7 Febbraio 1967', archival document, Milan, Politecnico di Milano, AALS, Db. 14 fasc. 7.
[29] '1a Riunione della Sezione Grafici della A.D.I.': 2.

The AGI and Icograda

The emphasis on readability, clarity, objectivity and functionality aligned the ADI graphic design division with new thinking in visual communication that was meanwhile emerging within the international design community. Membership of international design organizations enabled Milan's graphic designers to take part in and contribute to this design change. Indeed, international design organizations like the AGI (Alliance Graphic Internationale) and Icograda (International Council of Graphic Design Associations) promoted multidirectional exchanges between different local scenes by facilitating transnational connections among groups and individuals with common interests and problems.

One indication of this can be found in the AGI statute in the folder of the ADI graphic design division in Albe and Lica Steiner's archive.[30] This suggests that graphic designers in the ADI looked abroad for similar out-groups in an attempt to emancipate the practice from advertising and access the design domain. Founded in 1952, the AGI is an international association that unites world-leading graphic designers. By the end of the 1960s, Italian or Milan-based members included Erberto Carboni, Franco Grignani, Bruno Munari, Giovanni Pintori (1952), Albe Steiner (1955), Max Huber (1958), Riccardo Manzi (1956), Massimo Vignelli (1965), Bob Noorda (1966), Giulio Confalonieri and Pino Tovaglia (1967).[31] All but Manzi were members of the ADI graphic design division as well.

During the first two decades, the AGI followed a pattern that closely mirrored the Italian graphic design scene as it slowly but steadily distanced itself from advertising and poster art. AGI members periodically met at annual exhibitions and conferences that could be considered as 'field-configuring events' contributing to the emergence and gradual articulation of their practice.[32] Held at the Louvre in Paris in 1955, the first AGI exhibition stressed advertising in its very title: 'Art et Publicité dans le Monde' (Worldwide Art and Advertising). The commercial art poster remained the dominant medium of the following two exhibitions. The fourth AGI annual exhibition was held at the Galleria d'Arte Moderna in Milan in 1961. Despite having a title that was similar to the Parisian exhibition, 'Grafica e Pubblicità nel Mondo' (Worldwide Graphics and Advertising) focused on design coordination programmes rather than individual posters and favoured informative over persuasive messages. The following exhibition – 'Graphic Design for the Community: Print Around the Clock' – at the Stedelijk Museum in Amsterdam in

---

[30] 'Codice dell'A.G.I.', archival document, Milan, Politecnico di Milano, AALS, Db. 14 fasc. 7.
[31] Antonio Boggeri and Eugenio Carmi also are listed as AGI members since 1955 in F. H. K. Henrion, *AGI Annals* (Zürich: Alliance Graphique Internationale, 1989), 299. However, their membership is not confirmed in the AGI websites: https://a-g-i.org/members/ [accessed 24 January 2020].
[32] Joseph Lampel and Alan D. Meyer, 'Introduction: Field-Configuring Events as Structuring Mechanisms: How Conferences, Ceremonies, and Trade Shows Constitute New Technologies Industries, and Markets', *Journal of Management Studies* 45, no. 6 (2008): 1025–35.

1962 illustrated how graphic design was ingrained in everyday life by featuring the printed materials encountered during an ordinary twenty-four-hour day.

The AGI annual congresses during the first half of the 1960s further demonstrated changes in the understanding of graphic design. In 1960 the AGI members met in St-Germain-en-Laye to debate around the question as to 'whether [they] should be equated with the free artist or with the scientist, who is entrusted with finding the solution for a given problem'.[33] Four years later at the 1964 AGI congress in Alpbach, the Italian but London-based graphic designer Germano Facetti, best known as art director of Penguin Books, declared that visual communication had nothing to do with self-expression, persuasion and marketing, but rather was concerned with technology and information theory.[34] In his presentation, Facetti proposed an alternative view of the purpose of graphic design, thereby setting new tasks, priorities and professional standards. It was time for graphic designers to adopt a problem-solving approach to visual communication, he argued and for them to learn new methods of research and analysis that would allow the efficient transmission of visual messages and achieve consistent long-term planning.

The year before, in 1963 another international actor entered the transnational network of graphic design, namely Icograda. The brainchild of two members of the British SIA (Society of Industrial Artists), the illustrator Peter Kneebone and the graphic designer Willy de Majo, Icograda was intended as the graphic design equivalent of ICSID. The first decade of the international council reflected the so-far investigated articulation of graphic design practice: its estrangement from commercial art and shift towards design. According to Kneebone, Icograda First Secretary, the early 1960s were 'exactly the right moment in the history of the profession, [when] "commercial artists" discovered that they were really "graphic designers"'.[35] While the participants to the first congress in Zurich in 1964 were yet again asking themselves whether they were 'Commercial Artist or Graphic Designer', they doubtless defined themselves as 'graphic designers' at the 1966 Icograda congress in Bled.[36] As was the case with the AGI, the pattern of Icograda shows that by the mid-1960s graphic design had become a matter of research, methodology, information handling, effective communication, long-term planning and design coordination.

Attracted to Icograda as a body bringing together graphic design associations, the AGI and the Aiap were among the first twenty-four subscribers from eighteen countries. By contrast, the ADI declined the invitation but asked to be kept

---

[33] Fritz Bühler (AGI President), in Henrion, *AGI Annals*, 102.
[34] Germano Facetti, in *AGI: Graphic Design since 1950*, ed. Ben Bos and Elly Bos (London: Thames and Hudson, 2007), 121.
[35] Peter Kneebone, in *Graphic Design World Views: A Celebration of Icograda's 25th Anniversary*, ed. Jorge Frascara (Tokyo; New York: Kodansha, 1990), 13.
[36] *2nd General Assembly and Congress Icograda – International Council of Graphic Design Associations*, conference proceedings, 1966.

informed.³⁷ The ADI graphic designers were nevertheless represented in Icograda because of their AGI and/or Aiap membership. Representatives of the Aiap took part in congresses and general assemblies of Icograda. Updates on Icograda featured in the association's house organ, and news on the Aiap was included in *Icograda News Bulletin*. Yet the Aiap resigned a couple of years later, in 1969, due to difficulties in meeting the membership fee. After the resignation, Icograda lacked an Italian member association until the mid-1980s when both the Aiap and the ADI were granted membership.³⁸ By that time the ADI graphic design division had disbanded, but in 1991 one of its founding members, Giancarlo Iliprandi, was elected president of the international council.

Evidence so far suggests that the ADI graphic design division can be seen as a response to the local and transnational articulation of a different approach to graphic design. But what about the Aiap? Was the association indifferent or did the emergence of a new thinking in visual communication have an effect on it as well? The impact of graphic designers' attempt to emancipate the practice from advertising was also felt within the Aiap. Indeed, the association changed its name in 1964 and was retitled Associazione Italiana Artisti e Grafici Pubblicitari (Italian Association of Advertising Artists and Graphics) but kept the original acronym. Although the term 'advertising' was still prominent, the addition of the term 'graphics' was evidence of the association's change of direction. The name change of the Aiap was duly recorded in three issues of the house organ of Icograda. *Icograda News Bulletin* no. 2, 3 and 6 informed readers that the Executive Council of the Aiap was set to propose to change the name of the association into Associazione Artisti Grafici Pubblicitari Italiani (Association of Italian Advertising Graphic Artists), a proposition that was to be rejected in favour of Associazione Italiana Artisti e Grafici Pubblicitari.³⁹ The difference was significant. Indeed, the addition of the conjunction 'e' (and) turned 'grafici' from an adjective (graphic) that qualified the noun 'artisti' (artists) into a noun (graphics). As such, the revision of the name change officially diversified the Aiap membership by establishing a difference between advertising artists and graphics. As was the case with the issue of *ICSID News Bulletin* announcing the foundation of the ADI graphic design division in December 1962, the readers of *Icograda News Bulletin* could draw parallels between other member associations and thus contextualize the local event within transnational design discourses.

---

[37] 'Icograda Inaugural Meeting London April 26th–28th 1963', archival document, 26-28 April 1963, Brighton, University of Brighton Design Archives, Icograda Archive, ICO/1/1/2: 3.
[38] Letter from Marijke Singer (Icograda) to Giotto Stoppino (ADI), 20 June 1984, Brighton, University of Brighton Design Archives, Icograda Archive, ICO/2/2/1; letter from Marijke Singer (Icograda) to Valeriano Piozzi (Aiap), 2 October 1984, Brighton, University of Brighton Design Archives, Icograda Archive, ICO/5/4/69.
[39] *ICOGRADA News Bulletin*, no. 2 (1964): n.p.; *Icograda News Bulletin*, no. 3 (1964): 4; *Icograda News Bulletin*, no. 6 (1966): 6.

SIA-D and D&AD

A similar response to the tensions underlying the terms and definitions in graphic design can be detected in other countries at this time. Britain was a case in point here. In the same page of *Icograda News Bulletin* no. 2 where the Aiap announced the change of its name for the first time, readers were notified of the publication in full by the SIA of 'the graphic design manifesto written by Ken Garland and signed by 22 designers'.[40] This was Garland's *First Things First* manifesto. With it, the British graphic designer set out new priorities and standards for the practice: whereas until then advertising had been seen as 'the most lucrative, effective and desirable means of using [graphic designers'] talents', the manifesto proposed a 'reversal of priorities in favour of the more useful and more lasting forms of communication'.[41] Although it is only possible to speculate, there is reason to believe that Garland's manifesto became well known within the Italian graphic design scene. It achieved a wide international circulation, and it was signed by Germano Facetti, who was well acquainted with most of the members of the ADI graphic design division.

First Things First was the expression of a younger generation which was then entering the profession. They did not identify itself with contemporary professional bodies in Britain – the SIA in particular – and took a political stance against the purely commercial graphics used to communicate values they disagreed with.[42] By the early 1960s, the SIA was experiencing a membership crisis. It was in response to a meeting entitled 'Why you should join the SIA?' in December 1962 that Garland, not a SIA member, read out a first draft of his manifesto. At the time of its publication, the Society of Industrial Artists had just recently changed its name and become the SIAD, the Society of Industrial Artists and Designers. As design historian Jonathan M. Woodham argued, the use of changeable terms such as advertising artist, commercial artist, graphic practitioner or graphic designer 'can lend insights into the changing politics of professional validation'.[43] Commenting on the name change of the SIA-D, he observed that the addition of the 'D' in 1963 was a reaction to the 'growing unease about the term "Artist" as an appropriate descriptor for a profession which sought recognition for itself as a par with

---

[40] Ibid.
[41] Ken Garland, *First Things First Manifesto* (London: Ken Garland, 1964), n.p., published in Leah Armstrong, 'Steering a Course Between Professionalism and Commercialism: The Society of Industrial Artists and the Code of Conduct for the professional Designer 1945–1975', *Journal of Design History* 29, no. 2 (2016): 167.
[42] Armstrong, 'Steering a Course Between Professionalism and Commercialism': 167–9; *Communicate: Independent British Graphic Design since the Sixties*, ed. Rick Poynor (London: Laurence King, 2014), 22.
[43] Jonathan M. Woodham, *Twentieth Century Design* (Oxford; New York: Oxford University Press, 1997), 167.

engineers, lawyers, doctors and architects'.[44] In line with this argument, the almost simultaneous name change of the SIA-D and the Aiap, with the addition of the words 'designers' and 'graphics' respectively, is evidence of an international shift in the identity and representation of design.

In 1962, the interests of British graphic design and advertising coincided as they came together under the banner of British Design and Art Direction (later Design and Art Direction, D&AD). The new professional body was founded by a group of London-based advertising creatives and designers in an attempt to gain recognition, define and improve standards and encourage understanding and commissioning of what they considered to be good design and art direction.[45] Its foundation has been read as a signal of 'a profound shift in the cultural-economic orientation of actors that constituted the advertising industry' at the time.[46] This shift in the balance of power between different specialists working in the advertising agencies was a consequence of the impact of a new approach to advertising that championed creativity above market research and the science of selling as measures of good advertising.[47] A new generation of graphic designers joined forces with art directors in order to promote and celebrate creativity and effectiveness in commercial communication in opposition to market researchers' approach to advertising. Under this new guise, advertising gained a renewed appeal that made an impact on Milan's graphic designers.

The Art Directors Club Milano

The paths of the D&AD and Milan's graphic designers were soon to cross. On 3 November 1967 the exhibition 'Today's Italian Publicity and Graphic Design' opened its doors at Reed House, on Piccadilly Circus in London. This was organized by the Aiap under the sponsorship of the D&AD. As reported in the D&AD annual publication, it was 'the very first time that [the association] sponsored an exhibition of European graphics'.[48] By supporting it, the D&AD was returning a favour to the Aiap, which had hosted an exhibition by the London-based association in Milan in 1965.[49] In the pamphlet accompanying

---

[44] Jonathan M. Woodham, *A Dictionary of Modern Design* (Oxford/New York: Oxford University Press, 2004), 76.
[45] Jeremy Myerson and Graham Vickers, *Rewind: Forty Years of Design & Advertising* (London/New York: Phaidon, 2002); *D&AD 50*, ed. Rod Stanley (Köln: Taschen, 2012); Beryl McAlhone, 'Twenty-One Years Ago, D&AD was a Gleam in Bob Brooks' Eye', *Design &Art Direction* (June 1983): 10–7.
[46] Schwarzkopf, 'From Fordist to Creative Economies': 867.
[47] Sean Nixon, 'Looking Westwards and Worshipping: The New York "Creative Revolution" and British Advertising, 1956–1980', *Journal of Consumer Culture* 17, no. 2 (2015): 147–66; Poynor, *Communicate*, 17–22.
[48] D&AD, *Design and Art Direction '67: The Annual of the Fifth Exhibition of the Designers and Art Directors Association of London Limited* (London: Studio Vista, 1967), 10.
[49] Nixon, 'Looking Westwards and Worshipping': 158.

the London exhibition, the Italian association presented itself as a 'promoter of international exchanges and exhibitions'.[50] As the author of a review published in the Italian advertising magazine *Sipradue* put it, the London exhibition was part of 'a framework of broad cultural exchanges between European countries' and contributed to the country's broader economic policies as demonstrated by the support of the Ministry of Foreign Trade and the Italian Institute for Foreign Trade.[51] Exhibitions like 'Today's Italian Publicity and Graphic Design'

Mr. Booth-Clibborn, Presidente del Designers and Art Direction:
« ... anche la grafica pubblicitaria dimostra che non c'è tanta differenza tra i nostri due popoli se nel concepire un messaggio che nel decifrarlo usiamo un linguaggio grafico che ci riesce reciprocamente comprensibile ».

metri quadrati di pubblicità in confronto dei chilometri quadrati di immagini che si producono ogni anno in Italia?
Un turista inglese che venga in vacanza a Rimini o un commerciante inglese che venga alla Fiera di Milano incontrerà ben poca di questa pubblicità esemplare; riporterà invece a casa un'immagine assai più deludende della pubblicità italiana.
La verità è che su dieci manifesti attaccati sui nostri muri ce n'è forse uno all'altezza di quelli che si sono visti esposti a Londra. Così sfogliando un giornale o una rivista, osservando uno stand o semplicemente guardando le vetrine il visitatore inglese ha tutto il diritto di giudicarci pubblicitariamente sottosviluppati. Confusione e dilettantismo vanno a braccetto. La « tecnica pubblicitaria » è per ora riuscita ad affermarsi più come terminologia ed è servita a mettere un po' di fascinosa modernità in certe trattative d'affari di pubblicità, in pratica siamo ancora alla pretesa di fare le nozze con i fichi secchi del giovanetto tanto promet-

FIGURE 9.1 One page from *Poliedro* no. 5 (January–April 1968). In the picture (from left to right), the Aiap president Franco Mosca visits the exhibition 'Today's Italian Publicity and Graphic Design' with the Italian ambassador to the UK Gastone Guidotti and the chairman of the D&AD Edward Booth-Clibborn. Courtesy of Aiap CDPG, Centro di Documentazione sul Progetto Grafico, Milan

---

[50] 'Aiap: Today's Italian publicity and graphic design', exhibition pamphlet, Autumn 1967, Milan, Aiap – Centro di Documentazione sul Progetto Grafico (CDPG).
[51] 'Novanta grafici italiani alla conquista di Londra', *Sipradue*, no. 12 (December 1967): 67.

were intended as vehicles of design exchange and exemplified the soft power of design diplomacy (Figure 9.1). After London, the exhibition was reinstalled at the Salford Technical College in Manchester and, in the following year, at the Haus Industrieform in Essen and at the École Estienne in Paris.[52]

A closer look at the ninety participants in the London exhibition provides further information on the organizational strategies of graphic designers in Italy that show the way in which relationships between and across groups, in particular between the Aiap and members of the ADI graphic design division, changed over time. Although eligibility criteria restricted participation to Aiap members, organizers decided to make an exception: graphic designers Enrico Ciuti, Giancarlo Iliprandi, Remo Muratore, Ilio Negri, Cecco (Francesco) Re and Albe Steiner were among the non-members included in the London exhibition. Together with Aiap members – Ezio Bonini, Erberto Carboni, Franco Grignani, Giovanni Pintori and Pino Tovaglia – they were representatives of the ADI graphic design division. This exception to the rule was the 'evidence of the generosity and maturity [of the association and] a kind demonstration of open-mindedness … On the occasion of presenting abroad an entire professional category, the Aiap proved to be aware of its official national duties'.[53] From the point of view of the Aiap, the representation of the practice as a whole benefitted from the inclusion of ADI members. Through this, the exhibition could count on several AGI members, that is, the so-called élite of international graphic design. However, why did members of the ADI graphic design division join in? Their personal interest in being exhibited abroad in an institutional context might have prevailed over their scepticism towards the Aiap and their reluctance to be compared with advertising artists. Yet pragmatic personal interests offer only a partial explanation of the ADI graphic designers' change of attitude towards the Aiap. Alternative explanations come to the fore when taking graphic designers' flexible professional identities and multiple memberships into account.

ADI graphic designers' change of behaviour towards the Aiap and their decision to join in the London exhibition showed that there was a margin for mediation and that the international setting offered a neutral space for intergroup alliances. From its very title, 'Today's Italian Publicity and Graphic Design' made a clear distinction between advertising and graphic design, but at the same time it also implied the possibility of coexistence and interaction between the two fields. As such, it reflected the contemporary reconciliation between graphic designers and advertising. By the second half of the 1960s, graphic designers had found a new

---

[52] Benca (Carlo Benedetti), 'Gli artisti grafici italiani Aiap a Londra: Una manifestazione di prestigio per la grafica italiana che ha avuto una appendice anche a Manchester', *Linea Grafica* 19, no. 6 (November–December 1967): 401–2; Anon., 'Notiziario. Londra: Mostra di Grafica Pubblicitaria Italiana', *Bollettino del Centro Studi Grafici* 21, no. 227 (November 1967): 5.

[53] Benca (Carlo Benedetti), 'La migliore pubblicità potrebbe essere italiana', *Poliedro*, no. 5 (January–April 1968): 10.

entry point into the advertising agency as part of the creative team. Using their experience as coordinators of complex systems of visual communication, they contributed to the team's effort to articulate advertising as a coherent discourse that was seen as an integral part of the coordinated image of a company.

The support of the D&AD acquired a particular appeal for a group of Milan's graphic designers and advertising creatives included in 'Today's Italian Publicity and Graphic Design' who had contributed to the foundation of a new professional body in December 1966: the Art Directors Club Milano (ADCM). Like the D&AD in London, the ADCM brought together art directors, advertising creatives and graphic designers. Significantly, the ADCM was tightly entangled with the ADI graphic design division and indirectly with the ADI itself: not only were three out of the five founding members – Giancarlo Iliprandi, Till Neuburg and Pino Tovaglia – also members of the ADI graphic design division, but many others joined soon after and the first meetings of the newly founded club were held at the ADI headquarters.[54] Membership of the one organization did not exclude the other but was favoured according to the specific situation and network the practice was set in. In the context of 'Today's Italian Publicity and Graphic Design', the ADCM membership was more salient than the ADI. As members of the ADCM, the ADI graphic designers could then have their work exhibited in the same room as Aiap members without feelings of ambivalence or a perceived threat to their status.

An open-ended negotiation

Keeping a foot in each camp – advertising and design – graphic designers held an ambiguous and uncertain position during the 1950s and 1960s in Italy. As this chapter demonstrates, it is only by taking into account graphic designers' multiple professional identities and fields of practice that one can attempt to understand their changing organizational strategies. By focusing on conflicts, exchanges and alliances between the different groups, set within a complex and mutually relevant network of national and international organizations, the chapter investigated graphic designers' constant negotiation of their discipline's boundaries and its adaptation to shifting design discourses. Practices are in a constant state of formation and professional bodies play a key role in this process. International design organizations, in particular, offered graphic designers a platform for transnational exchange through congresses, exhibitions and printed publications, all arenas for information exchange and shared discourse.

The analysis of the ADI graphic design division through a transnational gaze offers insights into more than the association's history. It shows how its foundation was not simply a domestic matter without relevance or implications outside Italy.

---

[54] Galluzzo, 'I grafici sono sempre protagonisti?', 173–219.

The division was, rather, evidence of a moment of self-reflection and crisis that the practice of graphic design underwent in the 1960s, both within and beyond Italy. The comparative analysis of national and international debates shows that graphic designers from many countries were facing similar issues, sharing related experiences and adopting comparable solutions. Thus, as a case study, the ADI graphic design division shows how a focus on the simultaneous local and transnational situation is key for a design historical analysis of the negotiation of design practices and articulation of design discourses.

10 *TÖÖSTUSKUNSTI KOMITEE*: A CASE STUDY OF AN INVISIBLE DESIGN ORGANIZATION IN SOVIET ESTONIA

Triin Jerlei

> *Because truth was far. Truth was in Moscow.*[1]

This sentence was written by Kaljo-Olev Veskimägi in his book on the Central Committee of the Communist Party of Estonia. Veskimägi's study highlights the difficult, obscure and near-Kafkaesque relationship between the Central Committee of the Communist Party and its Estonian branch, a system where the governing structures and their decisions were often contradictory and thus peripheral organizations struggled to understand the 'truth'. Similar processes took place elsewhere in the governing structures: this chapter focuses on one particular Soviet Estonian design organization, *Tööstuskunsti komitee* (Industrial Art Committee, in short TKK), established in 1967. The committee differed from major Western mid-century design organizations, as its front figure was female, a glass designer Ingi Vaher. Compared to many other similar organizations, the committee had little visibility both locally and globally and is currently absent from any regional design histories. To address this, this chapter analyses the functioning of this committee to determine the practices and processes that characterized Soviet design organizations in the 'peripheries' and their relationship with the central power. This research aims to challenge the traditional Moscow-centred narrative in the research of the Soviet Union, demonstrating the possibilities of regional autonomy in this field and the ultimate problems of attempts to exercise that autonomy.

In recent years, several scholars have expanded the understanding of Soviet design organization with fascinating subversive histories. Tom Cubbin has studied the history of the Experimental and Educational Studio of the Soviet Union

---

[1] Kaljo-Olev Veskimägi, *Kuidas valitseti Eesti NSV-d [How Soviet Estonia was governed]* (Tallinn: Varrak, 2005), 14.

of Artists, known as Senezh Studio.[2] Initiatives by local Artists' Unions have also been considered increasingly fascinating by scholars: Karolina Jakaitė has researched the Lithuanian pavilion of the Soviet exhibition in London, 1968, as an aesthetically revolutionary phenomenon in its time,[3] and in Estonian context, Mari Laanemets has analysed the struggle towards a more humane living environment in the 1960s and 1970s.[4] However, the functioning of less revolutionary Soviet design organizations in Western borderlands has received less attention. Thus, this research is dedicated to an organization that was probably not unique in the world or in the Soviet Union. It made no significant direct contributions to international design. However, its study allows to broaden the understanding of 'peripheral' design organizations in general and the methodological challenges posed by the study of institutions considered insignificant or even invisible. The Industrial Art Committee differs from most major international design organizations of the mid-twentieth century because of its gender focus. Throughout its entire existence it was led by a woman, Ingi Vaher.[5] Therefore, this research also contributes to the study of female designers whose role in the twentieth-century design organizations has often been overlooked or has remained invisible.

This chapter aims to avoid a simplified view of the interrelations between 'power' and 'people' in Soviet Union. As Susan Gal and Gail Kligman have stated: 'Rather than any clear-cut "us" versus "them" or "private" versus "public", there was a ubiquitous self-embedding or interweaving of these categories.'[6] Especially members of bureaucratic institutions often did not see their role as a part of the Soviet system but had other motivations besides loyalty towards the Soviet regime to be working in higher positions. In late 1980s and 1990s, Alexei Yurchak conducted a number of interviews with higher Soviet officials to define their relationship with Soviet ideology, where his interviewees differentiated two types of Komsomol practice: 'ideological shell' and 'work with meaning', which they 'found important and enjoyable, and often organised on his own initiative'.[7] Similarly, many designers were forced to learn to function within the Soviet practices and to manipulate these processes in order to perform 'work with meaning'. Local design organizations could have never functioned without the skilful manipulation of

---

[2] Tom Cubbin, 'Postmodern Propaganda? Semiotics, environment and the historical turn in Soviet design 1972–1985', *Journal of Design History* 30, no 1 (2017): 16–32; Tom Cubbin, *Soviet critical design: Senezh studio and the communist surround* (London: Bloomsbury, 2018).

[3] Karolina Jakaitė, Šaltojo karo kapsulė. Lietuvos dizainas Londone 1968 [Cold War capsule. Lithuanian design in London 1968] (Vilnius: Lapas, 2019).

[4] Mari Laanemets, 'In Search of a Humane Environment: Environment, Identity, and Design in the 1960s–70s'. *Rethinking Marxism* 29, no. 1 (2017): 65–95.

[5] Estonian National Archives. ERA.R-1906.1.478; ERA.R-1906.1.593; ERA.R-1906.1.626a; ERA.R-1906.1.746; ERA.R-1906.1.824.

[6] Susan Gal and Gail Kligman, *The Politics of Gender after Socialism: A Comparative-Historical Essay* (Princeton, NJ: Princeton University Press, 2000).

[7] Alexei Yurchak, 'Soviet Hegemony of Form: Everything Was Forever, until It Was No More', *Comparative Studies in Society and* History 45, no. 3 (2003): 498.

the Soviet system. Therefore, the practices of TKK are not labelled as dissent or collaboration, but as mechanisms of survival.

This research is based on the discovery of a partial set of preserved TKK archives at the Estonian National Archives, which form the core body of primary sources used.[8] The documents demonstrate an engagement with international styles and issues, thus invoking a fascination with the activities of the organization. As my research into this subject started, I had a predetermined narrative in my mind, a seemingly simple and convenient story: a story of globalization and resistance, of Western influences behind the Iron Curtain and of a reclamation of global modernism. However, as the research progressed, I found cracks in this tale. Thus this chapter demonstrates the fallacy of approaching the Soviet system through a narrative of polarity.

VNIITE, the most visible Soviet design organization

The most visible of Soviet design organizations was VNIITE, *Vsesoyuzny Nauchno-Issledovatelsky Institut Teknicheskoy Estetiki* (All-Union Scientific Research Institute of Technical Aesthetics), established in 1962. Already in 1964, the research of Raymond Hutchings introduced this institution and its functioning mechanisms to English-language audiences, culminating in a detailed manuscript in 1976.[9] VNIITE also belonged to ICSID from 1965 and, as stated by Yulia Karpova, was actively engaging with Western design specialists already in the 1960s.[10] As Dmitry Azrikan has argued, 'The goal of VNIITE was the creation of a system of industrial design through the research of design theory, setting up the design principles and methodology, and developing the design concepts for the most important products.'[11]

In a global context the establishment of VNIITE came relatively late. Larger Western European countries had already established local design organizations and ICSID had been founded in 1957.[12] Even several members of the European Socialist Bloc were ahead of the Soviet Union: Czechoslovakia had opened a design centre in 1947, Poland in 1950, German Democratic Republic at the beginning of 1950s and Hungary in 1954.[13] Thus, evidence suggests that the organization of

---

[8] ERA.R-1906.1.478, ERA.R-1906.1.824, ERA.R-1906.1.593, ERA.R-1906.1.626a, ERA.R-1906.1.746.
[9] Raymond Hutchings, *Soviet Science, Technology, Design* (London: Oxford University Press, 1976).
[10] Yulia Karpova, 'Accommodating "design": Introducing the Western Concept into Soviet Art Theory in the 1950s–60s', *European Review of History: Revue européenne d'histoire* 20, no. 4 (2013): 627–47.
[11] Dmitry Azrikan, 'VNIITE, Dinosaur of Totalitarianism or Plato's Academy of Design?', *Design Issues* 15, no. 3 (1999): 49.
[12] Tania Messell, 'Globalization and Design Institutionalization: ICSID's XIth Congress and the Formation of ALADI, 1979', *Journal of Design History* 32, no. 1 (2018): 88.
[13] Hutchings, *Soviet Science, Technology, Design*, 150–1.

design in the Soviet Union was dictated not only by the need for better quality consumer objects, but also by global pressure. Timing was significant: Stalinist production had concentrated on heavy industry and advancing the space program and thus the arrival of VNIITE might be considered as a turn towards consumer objects – as visible in the preserved archives of VNIITE Vilnius branch, the first listed task of the office was the development of consumer products for the purpose of improving the quality of industrial design.[14] Nevertheless, as this chapter proves, the scope and understanding of Soviet 'design' was fairly narrow, concentrating mainly on consumer technology.

An important task for VNIITE was establishing the concept of design itself in the Soviet context, while balancing the tensions of the Cold War. Where the slogans and terminology did not yet exist, it was extremely important to invent words that sounded ideologically correct. As shrewdly phrased by Dmitry Azrikan: 'If they could not ban something, they at least gave it another name.' He remarked that for bureaucratic purposes, the word 'artistic engineering' was adopted.[15] However, Victor Buchli stated that in certain contexts, the word *'dizain'* was used and propagated already during the Thaw.[16] Raymond Hutchings sees the problem from a different angle, claiming that the English words 'design' and 'designer' were imported to fill a void, as the Russian words 'constructor', 'form-giver' and 'artistic modelling' were not clear enough.[17] Similar problems of terminology can also be seen in other languages of the Soviet Union. As mentioned above, VNIITE was officially named the institute of 'technical aesthetics'. However, this research has chosen to use the contemporary notion of design synonymously, as de facto, the designers of VNIITE worked with similar problems and methods as their colleagues in the West. Similarly, 'industrial art', *tööstuskunst*, was used for the design of small household objects, for example in the name of the organization this study focuses on, although effectively the activity should be identified as 'design' in its broad meaning.

Even though the central structures of VNIITE have been thoroughly researched and described by both Raymond Hutchings as an eminent political historian and Dmitry Azrikan as a designer with personal experience of working within the organization, the relationships between VNIITE and 'peripheries' have received less attention. There are several practical reasons for this oversight, most commonly the loss of archives during the collapse of the Soviet Union. However, Dmitry Azrikan named branches in Leningrad (current St Petersburg), Kiev and Kharkov in Ukraine, Minsk in Belarus, Sverdlovsk (current Yekaterinburg) in Siberia, Khabarovsk in Far East Russia, Tbilisi in Georgia, Yerevan in Armenia,

---

[14] RGANTD 281/P-688.3–6.187, 29.
[15] Azrikan, 'VNIITE, Dinosaur of Totalitarianism', 48–9.
[16] Victor Buchli, 'Khrushchev, Modernism, and the Fight against "Petit-Bourgeois" Consciousness in the Soviet Home', *Journal of Design History* 10, no. 2 (1997): 162.
[17] Hutchings, *Soviet Science, Technology, Design*, 145–7.

Baku in Azerbaijan and Vilnius in Lithuania. As he emphasizes, regional branches could only collaborate under Moscow's supervision and, while regional projects were presented during an All-Union meeting annually, the work of designers employed in Moscow was not discussed.[18]

Interestingly, the branch in Vilnius was the only one in Baltic republics: neither Estonia nor Latvia had a separate branch. It remains unclear whether the branch in Vilnius was originally intended to undertake research in the entirety of Baltic region. In a letter written on 19 October 1984, architect G. Ruuben wrote that Estonian designers visited the branches of Moscow, Leningrad and Vilnius to learn more about the studies in ergonomics and other contemporaneous issues in industrial design; similarly the specialists responsible for manufacture often visited mentioned branches for expert evaluation in the field of ergonomics.[19] One is also able to identify several Estonian specialists on the photographs from the archives of the Moscow branch, published recently by the Moscow Design Museum.[20] Thus local designers were definitely informed of the research undertaken in VNIITE.

Tööstuskunsti nõukogu and the beginning of a local design culture

There had been no professional design organization in Estonia prior to the Soviet rule, even though certain enterprises and factories already employed professional artists whose task was to design consumer products: for example Langebraun porcelain factory, ceramics company Savi, Voldemar Alterman furniture factory and Roman Tavast's precious metalwork factory.[21] However, the years immediately after the Second World War were a difficult time for mass production. Under Stalinist centralization, many objects were based on models sent from Moscow or Leningrad.[22] The first time the need for local designers was publicly voiced was in 1955 at the 'Baltic applied arts exhibition', where the Artists' Unions of the three countries issued a joint statement demanding, among other issues, for industrial artists to be employed in factories.[23] The relative advances made in industrial design by the Baltic republics, compared to the rest of the Soviet Union, are illustrated by

---

[18] Azrikan, 'VNIITE, Dinosaur of Totalitarianism', 60–1.
[19] ERA.R-1.17.2707, 8.
[20] Olga Druzhinina and Alexandra Sankova, *VNIITE: Discovering Utopia – Lost Archives of Soviet Design* (London: Unit Editions, 2016).
[21] Kai Lobjakas, 'Creators of a New Environment: Employment Opportunities for Applied Arts Graduates of the State School of Arts and Crafts in the 1920s and 1930s'. In *From the School of Arts and Crafts to the Academy of Arts. 100 Years of Art Education in Tallinn*, ed. Mart Kalm (Tallinn: Eesti Kunstiakadeemia, 2014).
[22] Interview with Maie-Ann Raun, 2012.
[23] ERA.R-1665.2.159.

the fact that these demands took place half a year before Khrushchev's decree to focus on the mass production of consumer objects in 1954.[24]

The Department of Industrial Art at Estonian State Institute of Art was founded only in 1966[25] and thus the few designers working for Estonian factories had graduated relevant applied arts programs: for example the designers of glass factory Tarbeklaas had trained in glass art. Thus the early products of numerous factories were often of poor quality due to the lack of local professionals. As commented by an engineer working for the metal factory Norma as late as 1965, the designs of the 1950s and early 1960s were often conceived by engineers, not artists, and based on foreign products. Often, this practice meant that factories were producing low-quality copies of Western products that were a few years out of date.[26] Elsewhere, artists with no knowledge of the issues surrounding industrial production were employed. Thus arose the need for organizing and institutionalizing local design.

Even in the early 1960s there was still little research and organization in the local design industries. For example, in a letter addressed to Estonian Academy of Sciences on October 15 in 1962, the chief editor of a local cultural newspaper *Sirp ja Vasar* [*Hammer and Sickle*], published by the Communist Party, expressed his concern that matters of industrial design are not studied in Estonia and asked if the department of art history plans to rectify that. The head of art history replied that two researchers were working on the subject and hopefully the newspaper would agree to publish some of their relevant articles.[27] The fact that the newspaper editor chose to approach art history department illustrates firstly the absence of local design professionals, but also the perceived link between design and applied arts and therefore arts in general. Even later, the distinction between applied arts and design often remained unclear. Industrial and unique products were often displayed at same exhibitions and discussed in the same articles. An excellent example was an article published in 1972 in magazine *Kunst* [*Art*], comparing the quality of works of different Estonian glass artists without distinguishing between mass production and unique objects.[28]

There was one organization that to some extent united local designers and other professionals, *Tööstuskunsti nõukogu* (Council of Industrial Art). In the USSR, each product or work of art had to receive a favourable assessment from a council of professionals before being produced. The main task of the Council, established in 1966,[29] was to oversee all new products and, if necessary, suggest changes or

---

[24] Buchli, 'Khrushchev, Modernism, and the Fight'.
[25] Virve Sarapik, 'The beginnings of the Department of Design: A Seeping Utopia' in *From the School of Arts and Crafts to the Academy of Arts. 100 Years of Art Education in Tallinn*, ed. Mart Kalm (Tallinn: Eesti Kunstiakadeemia, 2014), 332–63.
[26] J. Vaher, 'Kunstilise Konstrueerimise Probleemidest [About the Problems of Artistic Construction]', *Kohalik tööstus: informatsiooniseeria [Local Industry: Information Series]* Spring (1967): 6–8.
[27] ERA.R-2343.2.264.
[28] Eda Liin, 'Kaasaja Eesti Klaasist [on Contemporary Estonian Glass]', *Kunst* 14, no. 1 (1971): 34–7.
[29] A.-M. Laev, 'Klaasi Ajaloost Ja Klaasikunstnikest [About the History of Glass and Glass Artists]', *Kohalik tööstus: informatsiooniseeria [Local Industry: Information Series]*, November (1974): 14.

reject them. However, as demonstrated by the archives of *Tööstuskunsti nõukogu*, as design activities undertaken in Estonia diversified, the work of the organization became increasingly complex. For example, in 1966 the duties of the council ranged from organizing major exhibitions of Estonian design to advertising the new products on state television and radio, as well as organizing the evaluations of new products and hosting informative seminars to industrial artists.[30] Many of these activities were not in reality the responsibilities of the council. The same year, Helen Sirel, the senior secretary of the Soviet Estonian Ministry of Things, identified the main tasks of the council as follows:

1. Organizing the evaluation of products;
2. Verifying that the approved objects would fit the requirements set by mass production;
3. Observing that industrial artists would be employed in factories to suitable positions;
4. Organizing experimental groups in enterprises for the modernization of produce;
5. Observing the qualification of industrial artists.[31]

Based on the response from the council, Sirel's reiteration was intended as a reproach towards the council for diverging from their main duties. Thus, there was a need for an organization that would take over some of these 'extracurricular activities'. It is unclear if the founding members of the Committee had any specific examples in mind. However, as this chapter will further demonstrate, it is probable that Ingi Vaher would have been aware of the major design organizations in both socialist and capitalist world.

During a meeting of the Council of Industrial Art on 13 May in 1967, a question of founding a professional organization for industrial designers was raised.[32] The minutes outlined the current situation of industrial design in Estonia. There were around 268 active artists working in the industries, who had very different levels of education. Not all of them were actively participating in art exhibitions, which was the key criterion for joining the Artists' Union. The council had sent out questionnaires to active industrial artists and factories to determine their main expectations; by the time of the meeting, replies had come from twenty different sources. Those most interested in the future organization were designers working outside Tallinn, as they were less able to access specialist information and training.[33]

---

[30] ERA.R-1.17.1904, 20.
[31] Ibid., 16.
[32] ERA.R-1.17.1947, 17.
[33] Ibid., 17.

The meeting where a new organization was discussed and which all active industrial designers were expected to attend took place on 7 December 1967.[34] The newly founded committee was technically a subgroup of *Eesti Vabariiklik Teaduslik-tehniliste ühingute nõukogu* in Estonia (Estonian State Council of Scientific-Technological Organisations, ETTÜN);[35] thus its position was similar to VNIITE, which was under the jurisdiction of the State Committee of Science and Technology.[36] The minutes of the previous meeting on 13 May also reveal the reason for this perhaps surprising decision: 'An independent organisation of industrial artists would not have been possible due to the lack of a similar All-Union organisation.'[37] We can only speculate why there are no traces in the records of anyone proposing a local branch of VNIITE. Possibly, this idea had already been previously denied by the central administration in Moscow. However, the most likely reason was the wish to avoid being submitted to the central structures of VNIITE. This is further supported by the use of the phrase 'independent organisation of industrial artists', revealing the rigidity of the Soviet regional structures. It was necessary at this point for any organization to be under the supervision of an appropriate All-Soviet establishment.

Ingi Vaher – A professional designer for industry

The two organizations, committee and council, were led by the same person, Ingi Vaher (1930–1999). In 1955, Ingi had been appointed as the first professional designer in the influential local glass factory Tarbeklaas.[38] Although trained as a glass artist, the numerous articles that she published already as a factory designer demonstrate her interest in the problems of local design in general, not just glass as a material. Vaher had since the beginning of her career been interested in international design. Her former co-workers recall that her relatives who had emigrated to Sweden would send her design magazines that she would also share with her colleagues.[39] After leaving the factory in 1965 she started working at the Estonian Council of Ministers, where she stayed until 1989 (see Figure 10.1). In 1965–1969 Vaher was additionally undertaking doctoral research at the Leningrad Vera Mukhina Higher School of Art and Design.[40]

---

[34] Ibid., 20.
[35] Ibid., 17.
[36] Azrikan, 'VNIITE, Dinosaur of Totalitarianism', 49.
[37] ERA.R-1.17.1947, 17.
[38] Kai Lobjakas, *Kunsti ja tööstuse vahel. Kunstitoodete kombinaat = Between Art and Industry. The Art Products Factory* (Tallinn: Eesti Tarbekunsti- ja Disainimuuseum [Estonian Museum of Applied Art and Design], 2014).
[39] Interview with Maie-Ann Raun, 2012.
[40] Kai Lobjakas and Kristi Paap, *Kohalik ilu. Tarbeklaas = Local Beauty. Glass Factory Tarbeklaas* (Tallinn: Eesti Tarbekunsti- ja Disainimuuseum [Estonian Museum of Applied Art and Design], 2016), 186.

FIGURE 10.1 Ingi Vaher, head of the Council of Industrial Art and the Industrial Art Committee. Photo by: Oskar Juhani, April 1969. Estonian National Archives, EFA.252.0.71275

Her appointment to the role as the head of TKK was probably related to her skills in managing the Soviet bureaucracy. Vaher was familiar with the functioning of all-Union structures in Moscow, as well as the people behind the organizations (see Figure 10.2). However, the fact that she was leading two organizations that were different in their structure and aims, but both dedicated to industrial art, has complicated research into the field. Records show that the two organizations, although located in different fields – one of them founded simply as an

FIGURE 10.2 Ingi Vaher (third from right) with colleagues at the evaluation of Olympic souvenirs. Photo by: Arnold Moskalik, April 1977. Estonian National Archives, EFA.311.0.156386

administrative body, the other a scientific institution – functioned collaboratively. Very often one can find references to activities carried out by the other organization in the meeting briefs. Designers interviewed for this research simply remember things that 'Ingi was organising',[41] but do not actually remember which activities took part under which name. As one interviewee, a former furniture designer, recalls: 'There were so many committees!'[42] The general bureaucratization of the Soviet context renders it difficult to define or recognize the different organizations. Effectively, committee was a design organization without a visual identity: for example, the letterhead used in official documents is the same as used by ETTÜN, without any mention of the specific committee.

The foundation of the TKK

The regulations governing the committee were approved on 29 December 1967. The aim of TKK was to unite the 'industrial artists' and other specialists of the field to coordinate creative work and develop creative activities and initiatives, which would enhance the aesthetic level of industrial produce (see Figure 10.3). For every 100 artists ten members were to be elected. The committee was to

---

[41] Interview with Pilvi Ojamaa, 2017.
[42] Interview with Teno Velbri, 2017.

disseminate information about design in the Soviet Union and foreign countries and to inform of contemporaneous issues in industrial art and aesthetics, which signals the international aspirations of the proposed organization.[43] Nevertheless, even after the establishment of TKK, the Council still organized lectures and seminars to bring together industrial artists, for example, this task still existed in the work plan of 1970.[44] This fact illustrates the overlapping in the structures and aims of the two organizations.

The first meeting of TKK took place earlier, before the regulations had even been approved, on 7 December 1967 at the Worker's Club of the Tallinn Plywood and Furniture Factory.[45] The location symbolically tied the new organization to the local pre-Soviet past and its global aspirations. The Plywood and Furniture Factory was nothing less than the nationalized Luther Plywood Factory, renowned in the 1930s for supplying the furniture company Isokon and several other influential factories around the world with plywood.[46] However, it is unlikely that this connection was intentional. The minutes show the following schedule:

1. 'Organisational questions' by Ingi Vaher
2. Main presentation 'Artist and machine' by art historian Leo Gens
3. Speeches
4. Lunch break 13.00–14.00
5. Electing the committee of industrial artists
6. Analysis of advertising films
7. Discussion on the regulations of the committee

The schedule was also translated into Russian, although synopses of presentations and speeches were omitted.[47] Most subsequent meetings were translated as well, although it is unclear if they served to inform the central government in Moscow or ETTÜN as the directly superior organization. The participant lists do not include any visitors from Russian central institutions and all public presentations were held in Estonian.

As the surviving meeting minutes demonstrate, the committee strived towards a wider importance on the Estonian design landscape. At the first meeting, it was proposed to form four different sections: clothing, interiors, souvenirs and toys and advertising.[48] Clothing and advertising sections had four members each,

---

[43] ERA.R-1906.1.478, 1.
[44] ERA.R-1.17.2126, 9.
[45] ERA.R-1906.1.478, 5.
[46] Jüri Kermik, *Lutheri vabrik: vineer ja mööbel = The Luther Factory: Plywood and Furniture: 1877–1940* (Tallinn: Eesti Arhitektuurimuuseum, 2018).
[47] ERA.R-1906.1.478, 9.
[48] ERA.R-1906.1.478, 9.

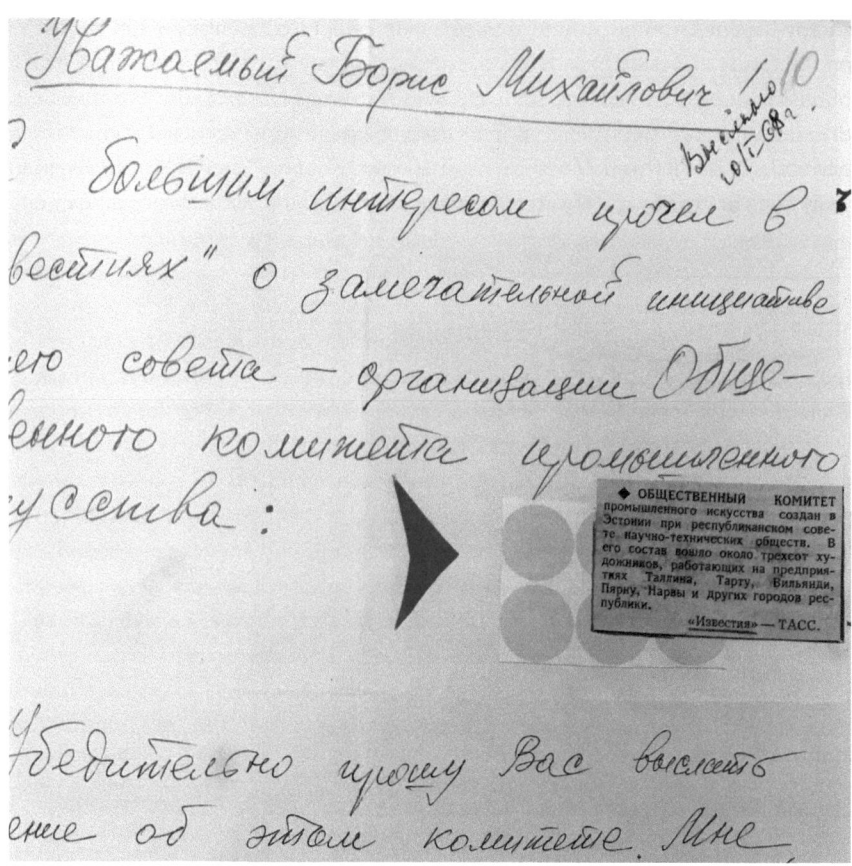

FIGURE 10.3 Fragment from the archives, a short article from Russian newspapers *Izvestija*, announcing the establishment of the committee. The reason for the graphic design still remains unclear – certain pages of minutes are decorated in a haphazard manner. ERA.R-1906.1.478, p. 10

souvenirs and toys three members, whereas the interiors section consisted of eleven industrial artists. The committee approached the idea of interiors in a wider sense: in addition to furniture designers the division also included artists working for glass and home textile factories, among others. Thus, the task of the interiors section was designing the home environment instead of simply furnishing.

In the late 1960s the committee appears to have held some administrative power to shape local industrial design. As visible from a discussion on graphic design of drink labels on April 4 in 1969, the initial idea seems to be that the committee would have had jurisdiction over the industrial art councils and the right to work out trends based on which the councils would have evaluated the designs.[49] Through the links to the Council, which had a direct power to decide

---

[49] ERA.R-1906.1.478, 32.

which objects could be produced in Estonia, the committee was able to shape the design of local material culture, at least to some extent. In accord with Jonathan M. Woodham's statements of the Council of Industrial Design in post-war Britain, the Committee strongly believed in its aesthetic hegemony, yet, whereas its British counterpart could mainly function through promoting and facilitating, the right to 'veto' designs that were considered unsuitable for local taste through the Council of Industrial Art gave TKK more direct tools for shaping local design.[50]

Here, an interesting question arises: to what extent would Ingi Vaher have been aware of the work of the Council of Industrial Design in the UK, or any other significant Western design organizations other than ICSID? Once again, the problematics of studying Soviet design complicate or even prohibit finding an answer to this question. Although information on Western consumer products was available even in publications intended for general audiences, this research failed to find any articles in general media that would have discussed foreign design organizations in detail. Neither are any design organizations mentioned in the preserved minutes of the meetings, which in the Soviet system might be attributed either to the absence of these topics in discussions or to the need to censor discussions to some extent. It is probable that through Vaher's contacts in Sweden she would have received information regarding Scandinavian design organizations and that she was also aware of the Council of Industrial Design. Preserved archives of VNIITE in Moscow prove that by 1968 both Vilnius and Leningrad branches kept numerous foreign design journals,[51] including British magazine *Industrial Design*.[52] As Ingi Vaher would have visited Leningrad often between 1965 and 1969 for doctoral studies, she was probably also familiar with the foreign magazines kept in Leningrad branch. *Industrial Design* specifically is, along with West German *Schöner Wohnen* and Italian *Domus*, named by several Estonian designers as a magazine they were also able to access in Tallinn.[53] However, this research was unable to determine whether those magazines would have been accessible to most designers in Estonia already by the founding of TKK or if their existence here was directly or indirectly the result of Ingi Vaher's work. Oral history, otherwise a valuable source of information omitted from official documents, often proves to be unreliable for determining precise time periods.

TKK was mostly concerned with the practical and utilitarian aspects of design. In the minutes of the very first meeting held on 7 December 1967, several issues regarding the quality of local design are approached. Vaher herself states that the work of artists and engineers should be connected better. The representative of Estonian Ministry of Light Industry, 'comrade' Kässu, mentioned that artists

---

[50] Jonathan M. Woodham, 'Managing British Design Reform I: Fresh Perspectives on the Early Years of the Council of Industrial Design', *Journal of Design History* 9, no. 1 (1996): 55–65.
[51] To be precise, Vilnius office received 13 foreign magazines and Leningrad 16.
[52] RGANTD 281/P-688.3–6.64.
[53] Interview with Leonardo Meigas, 2012; Matti Õunapuu, 2012.

need to have a better understanding of machinery involved in production and unification of different products should be encouraged. In the main lecture of the day, 'Artist and machine', art historian Leo Gens phrased a somewhat cryptic idea that artists should not lose respect towards past and present and 'Must not change fashion and style!' Although secretary Tiiu Kreis has written in her remarks that Gens's speech was 'interesting and useful to all participants', these few sentences are all that she wrote down.[54] In an article published in 1969 Gens has spoken against 'kitsch' and 'carnival', praising practical design[55] and thus we may assume

FIGURE 10.4 Ingi Vaher. Vases produced by Tarbeklaas in early 1960s. Photo credit: Estonian Museum of Applied Arts and Design

[54] ERA.R-1906.1.478, 5–6.
[55] Leo Gens, 'Inimene, Ese, Keskkond [Human, Artefact, Environment],' *Rahva Hääl*, 12/10/1969.

that Gens's message not to change style referred to the modern style preferred by the few professional designers employed in factories. For example Ingi Vaher's own designs (see Figure 10.4) reveal her preference towards Scandinavian modernism, as confirmed in an interview by her friend, glass artist and professor Maie-Ann Raun.[56] In different evaluations of products there are distinctions between 'pleasant' and 'unpleasant' colours: for example, dark blue and purple on leather products were 'unpleasant'.[57] In 1973 Meissen porcelain and glass from Moser and Iittala factories were mentioned as well-designed products.[58]

Among other activities, industrial artists had an opportunity to read professional foreign magazines twice a week.[59] An essential part of dissemination was presentations by artists or designers who had visited foreign countries. As visible from the chosen subjects, the committee was oriented towards culture outside of the Soviet Union. While Czechoslovakia and Poland were sometimes discussed, Russia or other Soviet states do not seem to be the focus of any specific talk. Sadly, the notes on these presentations have not been preserved, but, for example, in 1968[60] artist H. Sorgi talked about visiting the United States,[61] while on 22 November 1968 a lecture 'Remarks from the Soviet industrial exhibition in London' was given by artists who had participated at the exhibition.[62] Karolina Jakaitė has researched the importance of said exhibition within the Baltic region and the modern appearance and culture of especially Lithuanian pavilion, which demonstrated the openness of local design culture to international influences.[63]

Especially in the 1970s, the scope of the presentations grew increasingly global, embracing several non-European countries. For example, in 1979 these presentations discussed Indonesia, Singapore, Mexico and Peru and included photographs and viewings of local souvenirs.[64] Many presentations coincided with international exhibitions. Topics of lectures do not appear to be prescribed by any higher authorities, but instead, due to the difficulties of foreign travel, TKK selected the presentations based on the activities of their members. Thus, in spite of the control the committee was presumably subjected to, there are no reasons to assume that the central power structures in Moscow or ETTÜN were influencing local talks.

However, the topics of lectures mirror the Cold War geopolitics. Since 1965 Soviet Union had attempted to increase their power in Southeast Asia to advance

---

[56] Interview with Maie-Ann Raun, 2012.
[57] ERA.R-1906.1.478, 42.
[58] ERA.R-1906.1.626a, 11.
[59] ERA.R-1906.1.593, 4.
[60] Exact date unknown.
[61] ERA.R-1906.1.478, 25.
[62] ERA.R-1906.1.478, 52.
[63] Jakaitė, *Šaltojo karo kapsulė*.
[64] ERA.R-1906.1.824, 4

international socialism around North Vietnam.[65] In Peru, there had been a strong Marxist party which had received financial support from the Soviet Union in the 1960s.[66] Here, it is interesting to note how the international ambitions of the Soviet Union paradoxically allowed Soviet citizens to access the culture of non-Western world significantly easier than was possible for an average Western European or American. The same idea has been noted by Eleonor Gilburd in regard to literature and cinematography: 'But in the late Soviet decades, an abundance of cultural material was imported, displayed in museums, translated, and dubbed. By contrast, a modest share of the world's literary traffic consisted of translations into English, and the ostensibly open American society was notoriously inaccessible to foreign films.'[67]

However, compared to VNIITE the committee was still isolationist in its activities. There are no records of any international activities taking place or any foreign design specialists visiting the organization. The geographical focus of TKK steps outside of the traditional paradigms of Western hegemony in design, instead appreciating alternative cultural exchanges. This unique focus was to a large extent caused by the regional nature of TKK, as the lack of affiliation with any major design organizations hindered the development of traditional centre-periphery traditions. Tania Messell has analysed the centre-periphery relations in the case of Latin America and ICSID and the lack of interest in regional design issues often demonstrated by ICSID in their 'development initiatives'.[68] While the isolationist nature of TKK hindered the functioning of the organization and the development of design discourse, its detachment from both communist and capitalist design organizations changed the mechanisms behind the colonization of local design.

International aspirations are to a degree also illustrated by an interest in souvenir production. As already mentioned, souvenirs were highlighted as a key theme in one of the sections established at the very first meeting. Later, the committee compiled several reports on the contemporary souvenir production in Estonia. For example, in 1974 a thirteen-page-report was disseminated, which emphasized the role of the souvenir 'as a cultural ambassador behind the border'.[69] It went on to criticize how 'our shops often hold not only useless, but also pointless and absurd items that somehow are labelled souvenirs'.[70] This tone was not unusual in the committee's reports: often these contained strongly worded disapproval of contemporaneous Estonian produce, highlighting issues with both the design and production quality. The report stressed that to the industry the main aspect

---

[65] Muthiah Alagappa, 'Soviet Policy in Southeast Asia: Towards Constructive Engagement,' *Pacific Affairs* 63, no. 3 (1990): 321–50.
[66] Paul Navarro, 'A Maoist Counterpoint: Peruvian Maoism beyond Sendero Luminoso', *Latin American Perspectives* 37, no. 1 (2010): 157.
[67] Eleonor Gilburd, *To See Paris and Die* (Cambridge: Harvard University Press, 2018), 334.
[68] Messell, 'Globalization and Design Institutionalization'.
[69] ERA.R-1906.1.626a, 10.
[70] Ibid., 12.

was the financial profit gained from the sale of souvenirs, thus illustrating the growing aspirations of catering to foreign tourists.[71] In 1977, a special report was issued based on the evaluation of Olympic souvenirs.[72] Unfortunately the evaluation does not include any discussion on the aesthetics or quality of the souvenirs, only recommendations which factories should contribute more to designing new objects.

As an illustration to the committee's activities and their popularity, in 1977 the public lectures were: 'Functions of art' with 16 participants, 'Problems in design' with 12 participants, 'Seminar on clothing in 1978' with 48 participants, 'Problems of design in England: overview of a trip' with 14 participants, 'Textile art exhibition' with 150 participants, 'Seminar on fashion' with 103 participants, 'Impressions of an exhibition in Izmir, Turkey' with 48 participants and 'Discussion-exhibition on souvenirs' with 30 participants.[73] Fashion and textiles were generally a key issue in the work of the committee, as textile production had an important role in Estonian economy. Fashion lectures attracted the largest crowds and their transcripts have been retained in the archives. However, the transcripts only include texts, thus it is unknown if the audience was also shown illustrative materials or objects. For example, the lecture 'Fashion and textiles in 1977' held in 1976 started with a reiteration of the fashions approved by the colourists of socialist states at a meeting in Weimar, which is then followed by advice found in the magazines *Habit* and *International Textile*. There were comparisons between South European and Nordic colour schemes and French, Swedish, German, British and American fashion trends are separately described in detail.[74] Interestingly there were no mentions of fashions of other Soviet states, which suggests that Western countries were instead seen as the main source for identifying contemporaneous trends.

In time local design culture increasingly internationalized. Estonia was opening to Western influences during the 1970s, especially in connection to the Moscow Olympics of 1980 and its sailing regatta that was held in Tallinn. The number of tourists increased significantly and information on international design became more frequent in local media. On 31 May 1974 an interview with two Estonian interior designers, Toivo Gans and Mait Summatavet, was published in a major newspaper *Sirp ja Vasar*. Not only were they freely discussing their visit to EXPO'74 in the United States, but they even praised American exhibition the most.[75] Therefore, this research also assumes that the initial educative mission of the committee was becoming redundant, as relevant information was increasingly available to interested specialists.

---

[71] Ibid., 12.
[72] ERA.R-1906.1.746, 8.
[73] ERA.R-1906.1.746, 7.
[74] ERA.R-1906.1.746, 13–20.
[75] J. Mamers, 'Maailmanäituse Ja Ameerika Juttu Meie Sisearhitektidega [Discussing Expo and USA with Our Interior Architects],' *Sirp ja Vasar*, 35, 31/05/1974: 8.

The final years of TKK

The last records in the archives date from 1981. However, in 1983 the details of the committee and the contacts of Ingi Vaher and the secretary Tiiu Kreis are still listed in the information brochure of the Council of Scientific-technological Associations.[76] It is therefore impossible to determine whether the committee functioned until the end of the Soviet Union or whether it was disbanded earlier, or indeed, the type of activities the committee might have been involved in during the 1980s. It seems reasonable to speculate that the committee's activities had more or less ceased in the 1980s, as already the files for the year 1981 demonstrate mainly disagreements between TKK and the organization they were governed by, ETTÜN.

Although both VNIITE and TKK focused on industrial design, their priorities differed. As demonstrated, the focus of TKK was mainly on fashion, souvenirs and other small consumer objects. VNIITE, on the other hand, concentrated mainly on industrial equipment, especially in its early days.[77] The lack of attention to fields related to engineering appears to have been one of the factors behind the demise of TKK. There are no records of the committee approaching any specific technical problems of design. Furthermore, already in 1970, ETTÜN reprimanded TKK for ignoring the questions of engineering and design of machinery and advised the committee to be more involved in interior design solutions of factories.[78] These recommendations were taken into consideration to some extent: for example, on 27 March 1974 TKK organized a lecture on the 'Design of industrial spaces'.[79] However, these subjects remained marginal within the committee. Similar reproaches were present in later evaluations as well: on 25 February 1977 another meeting of ETTÜN again suggested to focus more on machinery and metalwork.[80]

The small consumer objects that the committee focused on fall into what might be considered to be 'the feminine spheres of design'.[81] The same 'feminine' focus set TKK aside from other similar organizations. The committee was fronted by two women, Ingi Vaher and Tiiu Kreis, a leather artist who acted as the secretary. This was unusual in the scientific-technological field that was a typically a male dominion in Soviet Estonia. For example, in 1983 all eleven members of

---

[76] *Eesti Vabariikliku Teaduslik-Tehniliste Ühingute Nõukogu ja TTÜ Vabariiklike Juhatuste Telefonid [The Telephone Numbers of Estonian State Council of Scientific-Technological Associations and TTÜ State Boards]* (Tallinn: 1983).
[77] Azrikan, 'VNIITE, Dinosaur of Totalitarianism', 51.
[78] ERA.R-1906.1.478, 69.
[79] ERA.R-1906.1.593, 3.
[80] ERA.R-1906.1.746, 3.
[81] Grace Lees-Maffei, 'Introduction: Professionalization as a Focus in Interior Design History', *Journal of Design History* 21, no. 1 (2008): 1–18.

the presidium of ETTÜN were male.[82] Similarly, out of the forty-two scientific-technological organizations that belonged to the Council that year, only three were led by women: TKK by Ingi Vaher, the Scientific-Technological Association of Food Industry by Nadeshda Alexandrova and the Committee of Young Specialists by Ludmila Laanemäe.[83] This research suggests that the reason for the presence of several strong female figures, as well as the high number of women among factory designers in general, was the origin of industrial art in disciplines related to crafts and applied arts, traditionally popular among female students.

Meanwhile, as indirectly demonstrated by Dmitry Azrikan's article and the photo archives of VNIITE,[84] VNIITE and the engineering-oriented fields of product design in general were mainly a masculine domain, regardless of the specific types of appliances the designers might have been concentrating on. As stressed by Susan E. Reid, the scientific-technological innovations in the home sphere became an important subject in the Cold War, presenting another basis for competition between the Soviet Union and the United States.[85] However, this competition was to be mainly led by men and, according to Reid: 'Although the Marxist commitment to equality was a consistent theme in official rhetoric, the party operated in practice with unexamined stereotypes of women as irrational and resistant to socialization, along with, indeed because of, the kitchen in which a large proportion of their time and energy was still spent.'[86] Thus, women were to partake in the Scientific-Technological Revolution mainly as *objects*, not *subjects*, resulting in an opposition between the methodologies of the two sides of product design, the 'feminine' focus of TKK and the 'masculine' scientific research exemplified by VNIITE.

In an article published by a local newspaper in 1983, Ingi Vaher formulated the following idea:

> Why the artists designing interiors and their products cannot be integrated to an entity is a very difficult question, as the artists from different branches of industry, all involved in designing interiors, are in the jurisdiction of different ministries. So far there is no legal ground to coordinate their work.[87]

Although the article does not mention TKK directly, this quote perfectly illustrates both the initial idea of the committee, to coordinate the artists working in these different factories with various materials, and Vaher's disappointment in its failure

---

[82] *Eesti Vabariikliku.*
[83] *Eesti Vabariikliku.*
[84] Druzhinina and Sankova, *VNIITE: Discovering Utopia.*
[85] Susan E. Reid, 'The Khrushchev Kitchen: Domesticating the Scientific-Technological Revolution', *Journal of Contemporary History* 40, no. 2 (2005): 289–316.
[86] Reid, 'The Khrushchev Kitchen', 291.
[87] Eda Vool, 'Konjunktuurist, Maitsest, Tööstuskunstist [About Conjuncture, Taste, Industrial Art]', *Sirp ja Vasar [Hammer and Sickle]*, 09/08/1983: 7.

to achieve all its intended tasks. In 1983, seventeen years after the committee was established, the cooperation of different fields was still problematic. Thus the case study of TKK highlights the issues of centralization in Soviet design and the inefficiency of the resulting system.

Especially in the 1980s, debates emerged among Estonian designers concerning the need for a more scientific research into design. In 1984, the Art Products Factory ARS, which was in the jurisdiction of Soviet Estonian Art Fund, proposed a new institution called the State Creative Scientific Production Association. The industrial and applied artists of ARS were responsible for designing and manufacturing both unique objects and designs for mass production; the proposal would have added to the existing structure a design centre that would have coordinated work and research in the fields of industrial design and ergonomics and disseminated design information. Additionally, the proposed design centre would have been moved to be under the jurisdiction of Estonian Council of Ministers and thus would have been governed locally.[88]

The Soviet Estonian State Planning Committee replied on 31 January 1985 that the need for the organization was not demonstrated clearly enough and there was no support from the governing organ, the Soviet Estonian Art Fund.[89] The next day, the Estonian Ministry of Finances added that permission should be granted by the All-Soviet Art Fund instead of its local branch.[90] On 18 March 1985, the Soviet Estonian Art Fund sent a cold letter to ARS, stating that although the All-Soviet Art Fund supports the idea of the design centre, the fact that ARS first approached the Council of Ministers instead of the All-Soviet Art Fund was an incorrect and hasty action.[91] While the idea of a complete design centre never realized, ARS established an industrial design group led by Matti Õunapuu, which executed several notable industrial design products in both Estonia and elsewhere in the Soviet Union.[92] Thus, although the rigid and impenetrable structures of Soviet production hindered the establishment of appropriate institutions, the desired aims were eventually nevertheless achieved, albeit on a smaller scale. In 1986, the subject was approached again, this time with a complete drawing of the proposed systems.[93] However, once again the plan seems to have been stopped by the central administration.[94] The next association that was founded was the Designers' Union on July 7 in 1989, which was no longer obliged to acquire a permission from Moscow.

---

[88] ERA.R-1.15.2707, 3–4.
[89] ERA.R-1.15.2707, 13.
[90] ERA.R-1.15.2707, 14.
[91] ERA.R-1.15.2707, 16.
[92] Lobjakas, *Kunsti ja tööstuse vahel*.
[93] ERA.R-1.15.2713, 40.
[94] Ibid., 46.

Conclusion

The case study of the Industrial Art Committee in Estonia raises a question of visibility in the functioning of design organizations. I have argued that the Industrial Art Committee had, despite its lack of visibility in the public design debates and media, a significant role in disseminating information on international trends in the late 1960s and 1970s. Especially the debates on contemporary fashion and souvenirs were informed by international trends, yet focused on local contexts. Dmitry Azrikan has denounced the common practice of referring to the designs of VNIITE as 'paper design'; 'Sometimes a couple of projects that died on paper conveyed more influence to the design and engineering philosophy, as well as to the public attitude, than more than a hundred mass-produced mediocre artefacts.'[95] Similarly, although the efforts of the Industrial Art Committee might not have left a lasting visible and identifiable legacy, they shaped Estonian local design culture through debates and activities of dissemination.

As this chapter has shown, in the state-governed Soviet system, design organizations functioned differently from in the West. Any new organization had to fit in the existing system to ensure the approval of political supervision. Nevertheless, one should not overestimate the actual involvement of the Communist regime in the organization's operations. Evidence suggests that in spite of the suggestions and orders from the supervising organizations, the committee managed to disseminate relatively diverse information on global design and initiate debates on local design. Unfortunately, the committee was unable to fulfil all the needs that the rapidly transforming design systems of Soviet Estonia required. Nevertheless, in spite of the relative invisibility of the committee and its small size, its legacy in shaping the local understanding of design should not be underestimated.

References

Alagappa, Muthiah. 'Soviet Policy in Southeast Asia: Towards Constructive Engagement'. *Pacific Affairs* 63, no. 3 (1990): 321–50.
Azrikan, Dmitry. 'VNIITE, Dinosaur of Totalitarianism or Plato's Academy of Design?'. *Design Issues*, 15, no. 3 (1999): 45–77.
Buchli, Victor. 'Khrushchev, Modernism, and the Fight against "Petit-Bourgeois" Consciousness in the Soviet Home'. *Journal of Design History* 10, no. 2 (1997): 161–76.
Cubbin, Tom. 'Postmodern Propaganda? Semiotics, Environment and the Historical Turn in Soviet Design 1972–1985'. *Journal of Design History* 30, no. 1 (2017): 16–32.
Druzhinina, Olga and Sankova, Alexandra. *VNIITE: Discovering Utopia – Lost Archives of Soviet Design*. London: Unit Editions, 2016.

---

[95] Azrikan, 'VNIITE, Dinosaur of Totalitarianism', 68.

Eesti Vabariikliku Teaduslik-Tehniliste Ühingute Nõukogu ja TTÜ Vabariiklike Juhatuste Telefonid [The Telephone Numbers of Estonian State Council of Scientific-Technological Associations and TTÜ State Boards]. Tallinn, 1983.
Estonian National Archives. ERA.R-1.15.2713.
Estonian National Archives. ERA.R-1.17.1904.
Estonian National Archives. ERA.R-1.17.1947.
Estonian National Archives. ERA.R-1.17.2126.
Estonian National Archives. ERA.R-1.17.2707.
Estonian National Archives. ERA.R-1665.2.159.
Estonian National Archives. ERA.R-1906.1.478.
Estonian National Archives. ERA.R-1906.1.593.
Estonian National Archives. ERA.R-1906.1.626a.
Estonian National Archives. ERA.R-1906.1.746.
Estonian National Archives. ERA.R-1906.1.824.
Estonian National Archives. ERA.R-2343.2.264.
Gal, Susan and Kligman, Gail. *The Politics of Gender after Socialism: A Comparative-Historical Essay*. Princeton, NJ: Princeton University Press, 2000.
Gens, Leo. 'Inimene, Ese, Keskkond [Human, Artefact, Environment]'. *Rahva Hääl*, 12/10/1969.
Gilburd, Eleonor. *To See Paris and Die*. Cambridge: Harvard University Press, 2018.
Hutchings, Raymond. *Soviet Science, Technology, Design*. London: Oxford University Press, 1976.
Interview with Leonardo Meigas, 2012.
Interview with Maie-Ann Raun, 2012.
Interview with Matti Õunapuu, 2012.
Interview with Pilvi Ojamaa, 2017.
Interview with Teno Velbri, 2017.
Jakaitė, Karolina. *Šaltojo karo kapsulė. Lietuvos dizainas Londone 1968 [Cold War Capsule. Lithuanian Design in London 1968]*. Vilnius: Lapas, 2019.
Karpova, Yulia. 'Accommodating "Design": Introducing the Western Concept into Soviet art Theory in the 1950s–60s', *European Review of History: Revue européenne d'histoire* 20, no. 4 (2013): 627–47.
Kermik, Jüri. *Lutheri vabrik: vineer ja mööbel = The Luther Factory: Plywood and Furniture: 1877–1940*. Tallinn: Eesti Arhitektuurimuuseum, 2018.
Laanemets, Mari. 'In Search of a Humane Environment: Environment, Identity, and Design in the 1960s–70s'. *Rethinking Marxism* 29, no. 1 (2017): 65–95.
Laev, A.-M. 'Klaasi Ajaloost Ja Klaasikunstnikest [About the History of Glass and Glass Artists]'. *Kohalik tööstus: informatsiooniseeria [Local Industry: Information Series]*. November (1974): 14–15.
Lees-Maffei, Grace. 'Introduction: Professionalization as a Focus in Interior Design History'. *Journal of Design History* 21, no. 1 (2008): 1–18.
Liin, Eda. 'Kaasaja Eesti Klaasist [on Contemporary Estonian Glass]'. *Kunst*, no. 1 (1971): 34–6.
Lobjakas, Kai. *Kunsti ja tööstuse vahel. Kunstitoodete kombinaat = Between Art and Industry. The Art Products Factory*. Tallinn: Eesti Tarbekunsti- ja Disainimuuseum, 2014.
Lobjakas, Kai. 'Creators of a New Environment: Employment Opportunities for Applied Arts Graduates of the State School of Arts and Crafts in the 1920s and 1930s'. In *From the School of Arts and Crafts to the Academy of Arts. 100 Years of Art Education in Tallinn*, ed. Mart Kalm. Tallinn: Eesti Kunstiakadeemia, 2014, 136–52.
Lobjakas, Kai and Paap, Kristi. *Kohalik ilu. Tarbeklaas = Local Beauty. Glass Factory Tarbeklaas*. Tallinn: Eesti Tarbekunsti- ja Disainimuuseum, 2016.

Mamers, J. 'Maailmanäituse Ja Ameerika Juttu Meie Sisearhitektidega [Discussing Expo and USA with Our Interior Architects]'. *Sirp ja Vasar* 31/05/1974: 8.

Messell, Tania. 'Globalization and Design Institutionalization: ICSID's XIth Congress and the Formation of ALADI, 1979'. *Journal of Design History* 32, no. 1 (2018): 88–104.

Navarro, Paul. 'A Maoist Counterpoint: Peruvian Maoism beyond Sendero Luminoso'. *Latin American Perspectives* 37, no. 1 (2010): 153–71.

Reid, Susan E. 'The Khrushchev Kitchen: Domesticating the Scientific-Technological Revolution'. *Journal of Contemporary History* 40, no. 2 (2005): 289–316.

Russian State Archive of Scientific and Technical Documentation (1968). RGANTD 281/P-688.3-6.64.

Russian State Archive of Scientific and Technical Documentation (1971). RGANTD 281/P-688.3-6.187.

Sarapik, Virve. 'The Beginnings of the Department of Design: A Seeping Utopia'. In *From the School of Arts and Crafts to the Academy of Arts. 100 Years of Art Education in Tallinn*, ed. Mart Kalm. Tallinn: Eesti Kunstiakadeemia, 2014, 332–63.

Vaher, J. 'Kunstilise Konstrueerimise Probleemidest [About the Problems of Artistic Construction]', *Kohalik tööstus: informatsiooniseeria [Local Industry: information Series]*, Spring 1967: 6–8.

Veskimägi, Kaljo-Olev. *Kuidas valitseti Eesti NSV-d [How Soviet Estonia Was Governed]*. Tallinn: Varrak, 2005.

Vool, Eda. 'Konjunktuurist, Maitsest, Tööstuskunstist [About Conjuncture, Taste, Industrial Art]'. *Sirp ja Vasar [Hammer and Sickle]*, 09/09/1983.

Woodham, Jonathan. 'Managing British Design Reform I: Fresh Perspectives on the Early Years of the Council of Industrial Design'. *Journal of Design History* 9, no. 1 (1996): 55–65.

Yurchak, Alexei. 'Soviet Hegemony of Form: Everything Was Forever, until It Was No More'. *Comparative Studies in Society and History* 45, no. 3 (2003): 480–510.

11 DESIGN FOR DEVELOPMENT, ICSID AND UNIDO: THE ANTHROPOLOGICAL TURN IN 1970s DESIGN*

Alison J. Clarke

From the late 1960s to the close of the 1970s, anthropology and the social sciences coalesced with industrial design, transforming design from a practice whose aesthetic discourse was largely dominated by industrial rationalism, to one of critical intervention with a social agenda. First emerging as a grassroots 'alternative design' movement influenced by workers' unions, design student activists and user-based research methodologies, the coming together of social science (more specifically anthropology) and design by the late 1970s evolved into formal policy within the international industrial design profession. Incorporating previously unexplored documentation of the International Council of Societies of Industrial Design (ICSID) and the United Nations Industrial Development Organization (UNIDO), this chapter examines the crucial dispersion of anthropology within design, and its culmination in the 'Ahmedabad Declaration' in 1979. Launched at an ICSID/UNIDO congress under the title 'Design and Development', this formalized the emergence of a specific genre of 'development design' based on quasi-anthropological paradigms. The author considers how the informal 'alternative design' movement was incorporated into industrial design's role in 1970s entente Cold War politics; highlighting how anthropological methodologies and considerations were key to securing the design profession's prominence in newly emerging development policies and 'soft power' structures.

> In the century to come, the design professions, with industrial design in the vanguard, will rededicate their efforts toward the final emancipation of all humans from drudgery and social and economic subjugation […] human beings in a new Renaissance will, once again, become the masters of their environment as the race achieves, finally, that ultimate form of equilibrium known as peace.[1]

---

* © The Author [2015]. Published by Oxford University Press on behalf of The Design History Society. All rights reserved. Advance Access publication 1 August 2015.
[1] A. J. Pulos, 'The Profession of Industrial Design', Professors' Seminar at the Congress and Assembly of the International Council of Societies of Industrial Design Mexico City, 14–19 October 1979.

When Arthur J. Pulos, President of the International Council of Societies of Industrial Design (ICSID), delivered an opening speech entitled 'The Profession of Industrial Design' at the organization's congress in Mexico City, 14 October 1979, he made explicit reference to the design profession's overlap with a development agenda.[2] While the canon of design history is built largely on the study of design's role in challenging and shaping industrial production and concomitant models of political economy, from the nineteenth century through to the early twentieth century, design's critical role in underpinning global, postindustrial institutional development policy in 'peripheral economies' has largely escaped critical scrutiny. Conversely, theorists within the social sciences have increasingly recognized design's distinctive and politicized agency in the development paradigm.

In this context, anthropologist Arturo Escobar, whose contemporary research deals with post-neoliberal Latin American politics and political ecology, has recently turned his attention to the ways in which design culture might be understood in a 'cosmopolitical' context and as part of a broader historiography of development policies.[3] Observing contemporary design's move out of the studio, the blurring of distinctions between users/clients, experts and stakeholders vand the shift away from definitions of the classic design profession, he reconsiders the prescience of 1970s design critiques written 'as industrialism and US cultural, military and economic hegemony were coming to their peak', in terms of their legacy within development studies.[4] Echoing a seminal work of the 1970s, Victor Papanek's bestselling book *Design for the Real World: Human Ecology and Social Change* (1971), Escobar revisits the 'Design for the Real World' rhetoric in the context of post-development theory, adding the qualifying questions 'But which world? what design? what real?'[5] Drawing on current 'narratives of transition' as a means to moving towards a 'pluriverse', Escobar considers how transition discourses have emerged over the last decade as a response to contemporary environmental and political crises, 'from a multiplicity of sites, principally social movements, some civil society NGOs, and from intellectuals with significant connections to environmental and cultural struggles'.[6] Moving from a universe to a pluriverse, a post-development notion of 'a change of civilizationational model, or

---

[2] Within the history of twentieth-century design there are, of course, numerous examples of design's engagement with a social agenda, from the Arts and Crafts Movement to the Modernist socio-technological utopianism. However, the period discussed in this chapter highlights the design profession's formal incorporation of a holistic, culturally comparative and anthropologically underpinned understanding of the 'social' as applied to practice from social science paradigms.

[3] A. Escobar, 'Notes on the Ontology of Design', draft circulated for the panel 'Design for the Real World: But which World?', American Anthropological Association, San Francisco, 13–18 November 2012.

[4] Ibid., p. 2.

[5] V. Papanek, *Design for the Real World: Human Ecology and Social Change*, 2nd ed., completely revised (London: Thames & Hudson, 1984) (1971); Escobar, op. cit., p. 4; see the title of Papanek, op. cit., ch. 2, Part I.

[6] A. Escobar, 'Sustainability: Design for the Pluriverse', *Development* 54, no. 2 (2011): 138.

even the coming of an entirely new era beyond the modern dualist, reductionist, and economic age' challenges the post-war Western development paradigm of industrial domination and rationalization.[7]

Importantly, Escobar's work in establishing the historiography of development studies, in *Encountering Development: The Making and Unmaking of the Third World* (2012 [1995]), revealed the ways in which a hegemonic vision of the 'Third World' was forged in the post-war period through policies that held up the industrialized nations of North America and Europe as the appropriate models for imitation. By the close of the 1970s, the initial 'top-down' economic development theories of the 1950s had devolved into a 'basic human needs approach' that 'emphasized not only economic growth *per se* as in earlier decades but also the distribution of the benefits of growth', that appealed in particular to appropriate technology and design movements, and became concretized in Papanek's *Design for the Real World* polemic.[8] As criticism mounted regarding the false premise of established post-war development theory, that riches would eventually 'trickle down' to the poorest, a basic needs approach evolved embracing 'development policies [...] focused on the poorest people of society, rather than at a macro-level'.[9] Formalized by the support of the International Labour Organization and the World Bank, this shift in focus led to the review of models of design production, and 'greater research on labour-intensive production techniques that were appropriate for small scale activities'.[10] 'Grassroots' strategies, aimed at empowering people from underdeveloped nations, emerged as a concomitant aspect of this shift. Papanek and his contemporaries drew heavily on both the ideas of basic needs and on grassroots approaches, both of which signalled the necessity of anthropological methodologies aimed at understanding and interpreting the cultural specificity of 'needs'.

In stark contrast to the sanguine tone of Arthur Pulos' 1979 opening address to the ICSID congress in Mexico, a congress organized under the theme 'Industrial Design as a Factor', Papanek had famously condemned industrial design as a profession that 'put murder on a mass-production basis'.[11] Denouncing designers as 'a dangerous breed' whose ambitions needed to be re-imagined in the framework of a collective social conscience and cross-cultural sensitivity, a new design approach emerged that advocated ethnographic-style observation and a renewed respect for vernacular cultures. At the ICSID Mexico congress, Papanek presented a design for a 'food cooler' (with 'open combustion' and a

---

[7] Ibid.
[8] A. Escobar, *Encountering Development: The Making and Unmaking of the Third World* (Princeton, NJ: Princeton University Press, 2012) (1995), 5. For a thorough outline of what became known as the 'Basic Needs Approach' (BNA), see K. Willis, *Theories and Practices of Development* (Abingdon, Oxon: Routledge, 2005), 103–5.
[9] Willis, op. cit., p. 103.
[10] Ibid., p. 105.
[11] Papanek, op. cit., p. ix.

'solar-powered alternative') that epitomized this sensibility and placed it in contrast to a Westernized refrigerator and its politics of rationalized 'top-down' development. The objective was to create a prototype 'designed with cottage-level and village-level technology and materials in mind', a 'soft' technology aimed at decentralizing modes of production. Any design intervention into indigenous life, Papanek reiterated, 'should offer villagers the chance to participate by having surfaces that could be painted, decorated, carved, embellished or covered'.[12] With their call for relocalization, decentralization and 'local cosmopolitanism', design propositions such as this pre-empt contemporary transition narratives and current trends in areas such as design for social innovation and transition design.[13]

On the surface, asserts Escobar, little appears to have changed since Papanek's international intervention into the field of development and design: neoliberal economic policy has expanded, the commodity consumption Papanek and his contemporaries were pitted against thrives, the hegemonic culture of free market capitalism rather than social need continues to drive design innovation.

However, what has unequivocally transpired in the four decades since Papanek's discourse gained such currency in design is that the notion of the practice across disciplines has become ever more expanded, from biotechnology to the social sciences. As we move from conceptions of the rationality of modernity to 'understanding human practice in terms of ontological design', to quote Escobar, it has never been more timely for historians to turn their attention to the historiography and objects borne of the specifics of a design and development discourse.[14] A myopic design history approach focused almost exclusively on the objects of Western capitalism and formal design aesthetics eschews the fact that development politics and anthropology are inextricably bound to the history of industrial design.[15]

The anthropological turn within design

The 1970s ended, at least among the design industry's policy-makers, with unbridled optimism for the industrial design profession; poised at the centre of an interdisciplinary network of social sciences ranging from anthropology to epidemiology, the transformative potential of design's social agenda promised to lead humankind into a future beyond the bare-faced technocracy of Modernism.

---

[12] V. Papanek, 'LiBrA 1: A Food Cooler for Developing Countries powered by Open Combustion; LiBrA 2: Solar- Powered Alternative'. In *Industrial Design and Human Development*, ed. P. Ramirez and A. Margain (Amsterdam: Excerpta Medica, 1980), 78.
[13] See, for example, S. Yelavich and B. Adams, eds., *Design as Future-Making* (London: Bloomsbury, 2014).
[14] Escobar, 'Sustainability', op. cit., p. 139.
[15] This issue was addressed in September 2013 by the Design History Conference entitled 'Towards Global Histories of Design: Postcolonial Perspectives', National Institute of Design, Ahmedabad, India.

Think-tank style events, such as the series sponsored by the Ciba Foundation on 'Health and Industrial Growth', brought professors representing Britain's first national institute of development studies at Sussex University together with world-leading policy-makers and academics including medical scientists from India, representatives of the London Tavistock Institute of Human Relations and industry representatives. For the first time, design was lent equal disciplinary footing; figures at this particular event, including Papanek, addressed the topics of 'harmful side-effects of industrial development' and the 'socio-environmental consequences of designers'.[16]

At the start of the decade, design had been critiqued by commentators, social activists and theorists in Europe and the United States as a threat to local cultures, emerging economies and authentic social relations, cast as the handmaiden of wanton commercialism, corporate power and Western ethnocentrism.[17] This stance was coupled with a growing dissent towards development policies, and the concept of charitable aid as an extension of quasi-imperialism, an idea that was gathering momentum with widely read publications including *Aid as Imperialism* by Teresa Hayter (published in paperback by Penguin in 1971) and, in the area of economics, Fritz Schumacher's highly influential *Small Is Beautiful: A Study of Economics as if People Mattered* (1973). Schumacher's work, and his role as co-founder of the Intermediate Technology Development Group in 1966, was of particular relevance to designers keen to reject their acritical role in bolstering corporate technological developments and consumer culture in general.[18]

In his study of the incorporation of design as a form of 'soft power' in Cold War politicking, historian Greg Castillo identifies how from the 1960s onwards 'scholarly debate shifted to the notion of US cultural imperialism, defined as the exaltation and propagation of American values at the expense of native culture'.[19] While one version of development, most explicitly seen in Jawaharlal Nehru's modernization programme for India, advocated the incorporation of Western models of pedagogy (famously relying on Bauhaus and Ulm rational modernist design approaches), the 'basic need' grassroots approach became more commonly

---

[16] See Health and Industrial Growth: Ciba Foundation Symposium 32, Elsevier, Amsterdam, 1975.
[17] See R. Nader, *Unsafe at Any Speed* (New York: Grossman Publishers, 1965); V. Papanek, *Design for the Real World*, 1st ed. (New York: Pantheon, 1971); W. F. Haug, *Kritik der Warenaesthetik* (Frankfurt am Main: Suhrkamp, 1971). *Design for the Real World* has remained in print constantly since its first publication in English in 1971.
[18] T. Hayter, *Aid as Imperialism* (London: Pelican, 1971); E. F. Schumacher, *Small Is Beautiful: A Study of Economics as if People Mattered* (London: Blond & Briggs, 1973). In the preface to the second edition of *Design for the Real World*, Papanek observed: '*Design for the Real World* appeared in most European bookstores together with two other books, Alvin Toffler's *Future Shock* [Random House, New York, 1970] and my good friend Fritz Schumacher's *Small Is Beautiful*. There is an important communality among these three volumes.' Papanek, *Design for the Real World*, 2nd ed., op. cit., p. xvi.
[19] G. Castillo, *Cold War on the Home Front: The Soft Power of Design* (Minneapolis, MN: University of Minnesota Press, 2010), xiv.

inculcated in the policies of ICSID and the United Nations Industrial Development Organization (UNIDO).[20]

When, in 1979, the so-called Ahmedabad Declaration (discussed in greater detail later) brought together major leaders of industrial design to sign a policy document formalizing a proactive stance on 'Design for Development', a watershed moment emerged perfectly poised to offer a forum for the exploration of alternatives to straight modernizing development strategies. The ratification of the Ahmedabad Declaration, by representatives from nations as diverse as Pakistan and the USSR, followed a ten-day congress in India organized jointly by ICSID and UNIDO, bringing together specialists to discuss issues ranging from small-scale cottage industry production techniques to the protection of indigenous crafts. Pulos had justifiable reason for his optimism in viewing industrial design as a vanguard force set 'toward the final emancipation of all humans from drudgery and social and economic subjugation'.[21]

During the 1970s, the rhetoric of the international industrial design profession, as made apparent in the configuration of working parties and conference proceedings of ICSID, the leading professional body, began to question the overtly commercial role of the designer, addressing instead design as a tool for social change within a humanist paradigm that crossed both post-industrial and so-called developing nations. Within the European art and design schools, syllabi based on formalist aesthetics and technological functionalism were brought into question by the emergence of an 'alternative design' movement underpinned by theories of anthropology, intermediate technology, development studies and neo-Marxist critiques of Western consumer culture. Even within self-consciously 'designerly' movements – such as those in the Italian avant-garde – anthropological discourse, theories and methodologies moved prominently to the fore. The avant-garde Italian radical designers and the anti-design movement openly rejected an industrial capitalist mode of design in favour, in the case of the famous Global Tools consciousness-raising initiative, of a 'primordial type of design that was non-designed, primitive and handmade'.[22]

Testament to this shift, in 1976, was the controversial 'MAN transFORMS' exhibition at the Cooper Hewitt National Design Museum, New York, which featured leading international architects and industrial designers, exploring design as a dynamic, cross-cultural practice tied to the social processes of the everyday. The guest curator, Austrian architect Hans Hollein, challenged the primacy of the great American industrial design figures (including George Nelson and Charles and Ray

---

[20] See M. P. Ranjan, 'Lessons from Bauhaus, Ulm and NID: Role of Basic Design in PG Education', paper submitted for the DETM Conference at the National Institute of Design, Ahmedabad, March 2005.
[21] Pulos, op. cit.
[22] J. Grima et al., 'The Role of Radical Italian Magazines'. In *The Italian Avant-Garde 1968–1976*, ed. A. Coles and C. Rossi (Berlin: Steinberg Press, 2011), 9.

Eames, who failed in their own bids to curate the show) and notions of the auteur-maker, by including artefactual exhibits (workers' hammers, breads of the world) that self-consciously sought to expand the notion of design into the realm of the social. Even Italian designers, such as Ettore Sottsass, famed for their design of pop culture icons (in Sottsass' case the scarlet-coloured portable 'Valentine' typewriter), turned their approach to that of anthropological reflection. Rather than exhibiting his feted designs for glamorous consumer goods, Sottsass' contribution consisted of a series of ethereal black and white photographs showing *ad hoc* naturalistic design installations emerging from desolate landscapes around Milan and the Spanish Pyrenees, shot during a period when Sottsass purportedly considered abandoning formal design altogether.[23] The accompanying ethnographic-style prose, through which he reminisced over the lost rituals and material cultures of his rural childhood (much as an ethnologist might record the folklore of a culture in demise), invoked a design culture in crisis; it portrayed a collective searching for an antidote to an advanced state of alienation.[24] Significantly, Sottsass had also been a cofounder of the 1973 Global Tools initiative that brought together a group of radical Italian architects and designers who, in the context of Italian post-industrial economic crisis, advocated a return to consciousness-raising craft-production and the quasi-anthropological study of indigenous forms of material culture and ritual as a progressive design solution.[25]

The 1970s, then, marked the dispersal of design into the interdisciplinary realm of the social sciences, with emphasis placed on experiential contexts, social imperatives and user needs that extended to the furthest reaches of formal design practice. Anthropological-style discourse, with its focus on localized meanings, ritual context and human-centred methodologies, began to be embraced within strands of the mainstream design professions, resulting in a series of high profile conferences, policy initiatives and design projects that transformed the politics of 1970s design culture. The constructs and terminologies of 'First World' and 'Third World' were challenged, as was the role of industrial design within human development policies, and studies addressed cultures, material and social, beyond the Western paradigm.

Accusations of neocolonialism, that considered the intervention of Western designers in broader development areas as patronizing at best, deeply harmful at worst, featured in the leading design press. One illustrative example of this critique was a tense debate that emerged between Giu Bonsiepe (a former professor of the Ulm School of Design), and Victor Papanek in 1974 in the pages of the cutting-

---

[23] E. Sottsass and B. Radice, *Design Metaphors* (New York: Rizzoli, 1988), 9.
[24] E. Sottsass, 'When I Was Child'. In DESIGN: MAN transFORMS, ed. H. Hollein (Washington, DC: Cooper-Hewitt National Design Museum, Smithsonian Institution, 1976), 30.
[25] See A. J. Clarke, 'Anthropological Object in Design: From Victor Papanek to Superstudio'. In *Design Anthropology: Object Culture in the 21st Century*, ed. A. J. Clarke (Vienna & New York: Springer, 2011), 74–87. See also A. J. Clarke, 'Ettore Sottsass Jr.: The Design Ethnologist', in Coles & Rossi, op. cit., pp. 7–22.

edge Italian design and architectural (mouthpiece of the avant-garde) *Casabella*, in which Bonsiepe accused Papanek of peddling a poisonous new brand of neocolonialism, that was ignorant of a basic political understanding of power relations.[26] Despite these internal debates within the profession, 'anthropologized' design was generally understood as a tool operating outside the commodity culture and monolithic economic structures, with the aim of 'broadening constituencies'.[27]

How far, though, was the radicalism of the art and design school, keen to break down the hierarchies of applied art practices through the incorporation of social rather than aesthetic agendas, co-opted by a neocolonial agenda of 'design for development'? To what extent was design inculcated by the rhetoric and postcolonial policy of nations allied to the United States in the Cold War, underpinned by a transnational 'modernization theory' set on 'staging growth' through the export of modernization and economic development?[28]

'Design for Development': The Ahmedabad Congress 1979

From 14 to 24 January 1979, the National Institute of Design (NID), Ahmedabad, and the Institute of Technology, Bombay, hosted the ground-breaking 'Design for Development' congress following a series of working party discussions and initiatives led by the International Council of Societies of Industrial Design (ICSID) and the United Nations Industrial Development Organization (UNIDO) (see Figure 11.1). The spectacular event brought together 130 delegates (ninety-eight of whom were representatives of India) from twenty-five nations. It firmly positioned India at the centre of a design and development policy-making agenda; their self-proclaimed mission to address 'the role of industrial design in the development and diversification of a developing country's industrial production by designing new products and re-designing old ones', also identifying 'ways and means' of satisfying needs through 'co-operative and bilateral arrangements'.[29] Lasting a full ten days, the historic meeting was timed to coincide with the auspicious Hindu festival 'Makar

---

[26] For an expanded discussion of this debate, see A. J. Clarke, 'The Indigenous and the Autochthon: Design for the Real World meets Global Tools', in *Global Tools. 1973–1975: Towards an Ecology of Design*, ed. S. Franceschini, Salt, Istanbul, 2015. E-book accessible at http://saltonline.org/en#!/en/1195/sdfsdf/?books.

[27] For the notion of 'broadening constituencies', see V. Papanek, *Design for Human Scale* (New York: Van Nostrand Reinhold, 1983), 13. Useful overviews of the rise of social agendas in the 1970s are provided by P. Madge, 'Design, Ecology, Technology: A Historiographical Review', *Journal of Design History* 6, no. 3 (1993): 149–66, and N. Whiteley, *Design and Society* (London: Reaktion Books, 1993), in particular the chapter 'Responsible Design and Ethical Consuming', 94–133.

[28] For an extensive discussion of Cold War politics and development see D. C. Engerman, N. Gilman, M. Haefele and M. E. Latham, *Staging Growth: Modernization, Development, and the Global Cold War* (Amherst, MA: University of Massachusetts Press, 2003).

[29] 'Design in India: The Importance of the "Ahmedabad Declaration" Meeting for Promotion of Industrial Design in Developing Countries', aide-memoire, UNIDO archive, Vienna, id.78–5076, 3.

Sankranti', and Gujarat's cultural highlight, the dramatic and picturesque Kite Flying Festival that would be watched by an array of social policy experts, design leaders and NGO representatives. India acted as 'case example' of the opportunities for industrial design in the context of a mixed economy with particular attention paid to design education, skill upgrading for small and medium-scale industries and craft and village industries. Indeed the keynote address of the congress, titled 'Identity in Modernisation', was delivered by Romesh Thapar, left-leaning author of *India and Transition* (1956), outspoken critic of Nehru and member of the Club of Rome global think-tank that in 1972 published the renowned *Limits to Growth* report regarding sustainability and expansionism.[30] An aide-memoire, circulated within UNIDO, four months prior to the Ahmedabad Congress, stated clearly that the 'role of industrial design in related areas of social need, including design for the handicapped' would be clearly 'demonstrated'.[31]

Posited as a political showcase, the result of a decade-long series of working party meetings that had engaged with extensive issues of design in peripheral economies, the 'Design for Development' theme was preceded in 1977 by the signing of a 'memorandum of understanding' between UNIDO and ICSID, as well as in-depth discussions later that year at the tenth ICSID congress in Dublin, Ireland. The Dublin ICSID was of particular significance, as it was on this occasion that Ashoke Chatterjee, Executive Director of NID, purportedly challenged the ICSID membership, accusing it of exclusively representing the industrially advanced economies 'at a time when only few developing lands [had] felt the need for design as a motive force in their economic improvement'.[32] While Chatterjee's observation may have been well-founded, as early as 1971 the Development Working Party had in fact striven for worldwide representation with diverse range of design experts from Kenya, Ireland, Denmark, Yugoslavia, Hong Kong, Thailand, India, the Philippines and Brazil, for reasons of developmental strategy rather than ideals of social inclusion. By the late 1970s, surrounded by a design culture of growing dissent, with student uprisings at Aspen and critiques of the 'hands-off' suit-and-tie corporate engineers and designers that dominated professional design bodies, ICSID risked seeming anachronistic if they failed to act on the broad-ranging critique of design's apolitical role in a Western modernizing project.[33]

The 1979 Ahmedabad Congress, as the first industrial design congress to be held in a 'developing' country, was not simply a response to internal politics or

---

[30] R. Thapar, *India in Transition* (Bombay: Asia Publishing House, 1956); D. H. Meadows, D. L. Meadows, J. Randers and W. W. Behrens, *The Limits to Growth* (New York: Universe Books, 1972).
[31] UNIDO aide-memoire, op. cit., p. 3.
[32] S. Balaram, 'Design in India: The Importance of the Ahmedabad Declaration', *Design Issues* 25, no. 4 (2009): 54–79.
[33] See A. Twemlow, 'I Can't Talk to You If You Say That: An Ideological Collision at the International Design Conference at Aspen, 1970', *Design and Culture* no. 1 (2009): 23–50, and A. J. Clarke, 'Actions Speak Louder: Victor Papanek and the Legacy of Design Activism', *Design and Culture* 5, no. 2 (2013): 151–68.

FIGURE 11.1 Ahmedabad Congress, 1979. © University of Applied Arts Vienna, Victor J. Papanek Foundation. Reproduced with permission from University of Applied Arts Vienna

debates. Rather, it was the culmination of a series of policy meetings – the ICSID 'Design in Developing Countries Working Parties' – that had actually commenced as early as 1965, dovetailing with an overt and overarching Cold War agenda.

As a growing body of research attests, high and popular cultural forms, design and specific genres of goods, were instrumental in affecting 'soft power' in the Cold War period. As Castillo states in his study of the cultural diplomatic politics of Cold War mid-century design, 'from World War II through the 1960s, what US foreign policy analysts found problematic was not the rapid pace of worldwide Americanization but the lack thereof. In response, they called for aggressive overseas propaganda programs'.[34] The extent of Cold War soft power strategy extended beyond the wholesale marketing of the 'American Way of Life' through US commodities, as epitomized by the famous Khrushchev and Nixon 'Kitchen Debate', and in sponsored Museum of Modern Art (MoMA) travelling exhibits featuring ideal US domestic design, into the realm of the indigenous and handmade.[35] Historian Takuya Kida has documented, for example, how crafts

---

[34] Castillo, op. cit., p. xiv.
[35] See G. McDonald, 'The "Advance" of American Postwar Design in Europe: MoMA and the Design for Use, USA Exhibition 1951–1953', *Design Issues*, 24, no. 2 (2008): 15–27; G. McDonald, 'The Modern American Home as Soft Power: Finland, MoMA and the "American Home 1953" Exhibition', *Journal of Design History*, 23, no. 4 (2010): 387–408.

played a crucial role in the Japanese-US cultural exchange project of the 1950s, to the extent of having considerable impact on the established aesthetics and forms of traditional Japanese crafts.[36] Such models of political-cultural intervention into indigenous material culture were then already established as an integral component of 'soft' cultural policy by the early post-war period.

The astute selection of the National Institute of Design (NID) as the location for the ICSID 1979 Congress placed India at the forefront of the policy while drawing on the Cold War legacy of the West's cultural-political intervention in Nehru's modernizing agenda. In 1977, NID had been awarded the ICSID-Philips Award for industrial design in developing countries. The following year, a UNIDO pilot report conducted by John Reid, former President of ICSID, exploring *The State of Industrial Design in Developing Countries,* had confirmed India, and NID under the directorship of Chatterjee specifically, as the optimal venue for the commencement of the congress. Chatterjee himself had introduced Reid, acting as a UNIDO consultant, to the design culture of NID, and Gujarat more generally. Reid had presided over the ICSID executive board from 1969 to 1971, during a period in which affirmative action in recruiting a broader constituency outside developed countries was a priority for the society.[37] He began his report with a definition of design as a socially-bound practice: '[T]he development of industrial design [...] despite its enormous technical and scientific content, is an *art*, not a science. It is concerned with people – their hopes, needs and aspirations.'[38] While impressed by the efforts to be socially innovative through 'bringing students face to face with the realities of life in India', Reid also found mild amusement in a suggestion voiced at a meeting with the Ahmedabad Chamber of Commerce regarding the conservation of ethnic and vernacular material cultures: 'One person thought there should be a museum for pots!'[39] (This suggestion was realized soon after by the establishment of the Vechaar Utensils Museum in 1981.) This dialectic between preserving design as an embodiment of national identity and authenticity, and the explicit drive to innovate new designs fit for export to a Western market was a defining theme of the design development agenda. Early into the section of the report dealing with India, Reid encapsulated this search for the authentic, echoing the Eameses' fetishization of the 'lota' in their famed *India Report*.[40] 'It

---

[36] T. Kida, 'Japanese Crafts and Cultural Exchange with the USA in the 1950s: Soft Power and John D. Rockefeller III during the Cold War', *Journal of Design History* 25, no. 4 (2012): 379–99.

[37] 'The Motion to Set Up a Special Commission to Examine the Problems of Developing Countries Was Eagerly Greeted by the Sixth General Assembly of ICSID When It Sat at Nash House on 8–9 September', *Design Journal* no. 250 (October 1969): 16.

[38] J. Reid, 'The State of Industrial Design in Developing Countries 1978: A Report of the Pilot Mission to India, Pakistan, Egypt and Turkey', UNIDO archive, Vienna, id.78–7582, preface.

[39] Reid, op. cit. p. 27.

[40] C. Eames and R. Eames, *The India Report*, National Institute of Design, Ahmedabad, 1997 [April 1958], sourced from The National Institute of Design. http://nid.edu/Userfiles/ Eames___India_Report.pdf [accessed 25 August 2014].

is sad,' observed Reid, 'that the first chair I saw was of Scandinavian design in itself "derived" from an American original'.[41] A rather clumsy slogan, coined in the making of this UNIDO pilot report, summarized a freshly honed design and development agenda: 'Industrial Designing is About Caring For People'.[42]

Within design history and theory, the few existing discussions generally identify the Ahmedabad Declaration as a golden moment; a crucial turning point in the recognition of the social potential of industrial design in the 'Third World', 'developing' or 'peripheral economies'.[43] The Declaration is also most often represented as the culmination of a linear history; an extension of India's policy-making, rooted in Prime Minster Jawaharlal Nehru's post-Independence stance of national industrial development, in which design was viewed as an 'element to improve the quality of life'.[44] Such accounts, in some instances penned as academic articles by original attendees themselves, frame the Declaration in the context of the legacy of the Eameses' famed 1958 *India Report,* which led to the establishment of the National Institute of Design in 1961. Ahmedabad's unique claim to the national design heritage of India, as the site of Mahatma Gandhi's first *ashram* and the political legacy of the *swadeshi* policy, is also noted as the backdrop to the Declaration.

The rhetoric used to frame the Declaration asserts that following Independence in 1947, Nehru extended an invitation to Charles and Ray Eames, asking the couple to give their insight into the potential of design in India as part of the 'modernizing agenda of the postcolonial nation state'.[45] This relationship between Nehru's India and the Eameses as a design team was of course far more complex and politicized in nature, forming an integral part of a broader Cold War Indo-American public diplomacy and propaganda strategy.[46] Nehru had made his first official visit to the United States in October 1949, during a period of extensive Soviet public diplomacy activities and the Chinese Communist Revolution. During the Second World War the US Office of War Information (OWI) actively represented the United States to the Indian people as a 'champion of democracy', associating, according to diplomatic historian Sarah Ellen Graham, 'America's war aims with the cause of democracy worldwide'.[47]

---

[41] Reid, op. cit., p. 13.
[42] Ibid., p. 248.
[43] See, for example, A. Chatterjee, 'Design in India: The Experience of Transition', *Design Issues* 21, no. 4 (2003): 4–10; Balaram, op. cit., p. 54. Both authors analyse the Ahmedabad Declaration and Congress through incorporation of their perspectives as first-hand experience as an attendee, in the case of Balaram, and as leading delegate and Executive Director of NID, in the case of Chatterjee.
[44] See, for example, Balaram, op. cit., p. 54. Balaram is himself an industrial design and NID alumnus, and former recipient of an Indian Ford Foundation scholarship to study at the Royal College of Art London in the 1970s.
[45] S. Mathur, 'Charles and Ray Eames in India', *Art Journal*, 70, no. 1 (Spring 2011): 34–53.
[46] For an extensive discussion of the use of art and culture in US Cold War propaganda, see F. S. Saunders, *Who Paid the Piper? The CIA and the Cultural Cold War* (London: Granta, 1999).
[47] S. E. Graham, *Engaging India: Public Diplomacy and Indo-American Relations to 1957* (Los Angeles: Figueroa Press, 2012), 18.

The USSR was outspending the United States in terms of cultural diplomacy in India, and Washington was particularly sensitive to this fact in the light of China's turn to communism. To quote Graham: 'US analysts noted that the Indian public by and large supported Nehru's policy of neutrality, condemned racial segregation within the United States, and regarded Washington's anti-Communist foreign policy as a vehicle for neo-Colonialism'.[48] After the suspension of philanthropic activity during and immediately after the Second World War, the first prominent public diplomacy act in the Cold War was the commencement of the Fulbright scholar exchange programme, and from 1952 the Ford Foundation investment schemes between the United States and India. Winning over the Indian elite – intellectuals and cultural leaders – was seen as vital in assuaging suspicion of the USA.

As a growing body of research finds, it was within this context of Cold War diplomatic rivalry that the Ford Foundation arranged for the Eameses to make their five- month tour of India, and report upon the state and future of its design culture. In other words, Nehru did not simply 'invite' the Eames to offer their superior knowledge as Western industrial designers to a developing economy. Rather 'design [was viewed] as a catalyst for change, newness, and creativity for Indians' and for the USA an integral part of public diplomacy policy.[49] The Eameses' involvement in India, in itself the result of a decade of Cold War politicking, arguably fuelled the rhetoric of a modern democracy of design, underpinned by the neo-colonial Modernist pedagogy of Ulm school tutors and their ilk, the end of which was marked by the 1979 Ahmedabad Congress.

The Ahmedabad Congress took place after a period of considerable rupture in Indian politics that had unsettled pre-existing Cold War cultural diplomatic strategies. Following Nehru's death in 1964, Indira Gandhi's Congress Party had taken power. By 1979, the replacement coalition government of opposition parties established after the so-called Indian Emergency, in which Gandhi's party was accused of corruption, had collapsed. In the context of India's shifting domestic politics and an emergent 'basic-needs' rhetoric in international development, Ahmedabad is better understood as emerging from this disjuncture with the unrealized Nehruvian vision of design as a catalyst of change, rather than as a linear progression. It constituted a major diplomatic undertaking aimed at bolstering Western relations with India at a time of upheaval, with Indira Gandhi re-elected with a newly honed pro-foreign policy approach by 1980.[50]

---

[48] Graham, op. cit., p. 25.
[49] S. Mathur, *India by Design: Colonial History and Cultural Display* (Oakland, CA: University of California Press, 2007).
[50] See M. T. Kauffman, 'Mrs. Gandhi Making the Most of Foreign Policy Openings', *The New York Times*, 6 June 1982. http://www.nytimes.com/1982/06/06/weekinreview/ mrs-ghandi-making-the-most-of-foreign-policy-openings. html [accessed 24 August 2014].

Design dilemmas and quasi-anthropological solutions

The Ahmedabad Congress consolidated a post-colonial concept of design for social usefulness, epitomized by the emergence of what art historian Saloni Mathur has described as a 'design in an Indian idiom', with proposals for adapting indigenous forms from the tiffin lunch box to the automated rickshaw entering conventional professional design media.[51]

Published under the auspices of the UK government-backed Design Council, with the by-line 'India's Design Dilemma', the mainstream *DESIGN* journal illustrated designs from students of the National Institute of Design (NID), Ahmedabad, and the Royal College of Art (RCA), London, that were engineered specifically for 'Indian conditions'.[52] The author Allen Cobold, chief exhibition officer at the Commonwealth Institute, emphasized how members of NID 'reacted strongly against any "arranged marriages" between Indian and Western approaches in design'.[53] The Institution had, earlier on in its inception, been linked to the formalist teaching and design theories of the Ulm School of Design (Hochschule fur Gestaltung or HfG), widely renowned for its 'Ulm Model' of design teaching as indelibly Western in cultural heritage and attitude.[54]

This renunciation of 'Western approaches to ideas in design', reiterated in Thapar's Ahmedabad Congress keynote address, under the title 'Identity and Modernization', had called for a 'renewed offensive against "vulgarity"' and the upholding of traditional aesthetic values, thus marking a clear turning point in understanding the relations between design and development policy and the objects borne of this paradigm.[55] The designs featured in the *DESIGN* article including a 'new type of harvesting implement' [2, (1)], a bicycle customized to hold a torch [2, (2)] and a wheelchair aimed specifically at so-called generic 'Indian conditions' [2, (3)], consolidated modes of hybridized material culture

---

[51] Art historian Saloni Mathur (*India by Art journal*, op. cit., p. 39) describes the 1970s design magazines that the Eames had in their study collection as indicative of Nehru's notion of design as a catalyst for change, for newness and for creativity and 'to communicate the problem-solving spirit of the Nehruvian era'. However, this genre of hybridized 'design for development' that entered mainstream design discourse in the late 1970s was arguably a post- Nehruvian response to broader policy initiatives, including the Green Revolution.

[52] A. Cobold, 'India's Design Dilemma', *DESIGN*, no. 336 (June 1979): 70–3.

[53] Cobold, op. cit., p. 70. The author, Allen Cobold, presided over a future 'Design in India' exhibit, in 1982. In the same year as his article was published, 1979, British and Indian politicians began devising what would become the Festival of India in London – major museums and galleries took part in Design in India at the Commonwealth Institute. The Commonwealth Institute had a pre-existing permanent exhibit on industrial design devised by NID.

[54] For further context, see H. Alpay Er, 'Development Patterns of Industrial Design in the Third World: A Conceptual Model for Newly Industrialized Countries', *Journal of Design History* 10, no. 3 (1997): 293–307.

[55] Cobold, op. cit., p. 70.

desperate to forego formalist aesthetics in favour of the vernacular, and the guise of appropriate technology. The designer of the customized bicycle, Singanapalli Balaram (who would go on to be a prominent design theorist and educationalist in India), attended the RCA Master's course in industrial design through the support of a Ford Foundation Scholarship, an example of intra-cultural design transfer that could not have been a more perfect assertion of Cold War cultural diplomatic policy on design and development brought to fruition.

This design typology, generated within the parameters of the intermediate and appropriate technology ethos, had emerged in the 1970s to embody in material and visual form the dialectics of the development discourse, rather than, as Mathur has suggested 'the problem-solving spirit of the Nehruvian era'.[56] In fact, accusations of neo-colonialism had been aimed at designers from the earliest emergence of design and development discourse. The most populist version of this 'design for development' phenomenon was illustrated in Papanek's *Design for the Real World* (1971) and those of his design projects that utilized quasi-anthropological constructs such as a co-participatory 'tin can radio' design powered by dried cow dung and allowing the application of indigenous decoration. The reverse-side of the first English language edition of *Design for the Real World* featured a telling commendation by Finnish industrial designer Barbro Kulvik-Siltavuori: 'Today there is much controversy about design responsibility. And inevitably in discussions and articles Victor Papanek is mentioned. Some think he is too political, others that he is not political enough; some that he encourages neo-colonial exploitation.'[57]

In many respects Papanek had become the totem for design development by the 1970s, both in terms of its successes and its discontents.

Objects such as Papanek's tin can, dung-powered radio constructed from low-cost readily available materials, costing less than nine cents a unit, designed for UNESCO and aimed specifically at Indonesian users, evolved as archetypes of a design for development genre; a form of material culture that stood as shorthand for a broader set of ideological intents that sought to challenge the authoritarian logic of design as the 'central political technology of modernity'.[58] In *Design for the Real World,* Papanek lends his readers a telling anecdote regarding a visit in the mid-1960s to the Ulm School, where he took the occasion to show slides of his 'indigenous' tin-can radio replete with brightly coloured embroidered applique decoration, shells and sequins. The professors at the Hochschule fur Gestaltung at Ulm purportedly walked out of his lecture in protest at the tin can's lack of 'formal' aesthetic merit. Painted in muted grey, the Ulm contingent suggested, the design might be rendered acceptable. 'But painting it would have been wrong,' retorted Papanek, '[f]or one thing, it would have raised the price of each unit by maybe one

---

[56] Mathur, *India by Art journal*, op. cit., p. 39.
[57] Papanek, *Design for the Real World*, 1st ed., op. cit., inside dust jacket.
[58] Escobar, 'Notes', op. cit., p. 5.

FIGURE 11.2 A. Cobold, 'India's Design Dilemma', *DESIGN*, vol. 336, 1979, figs 1–5. Reproduced with permission from the Royal College of Art archive

twentieth of a penny each. [...] [M]uch more importantly, I feel that I have no right to make aesthetic or "good taste" decisions that will affect millions of people in Indonesia, who are members of a different culture'.[59] Considering the Ulm School's overtly Modernist agenda, and its enormous influence and complicity in Cold

---

[59] Papanek, *Design for the Real World*, 1st ed., op. cit., p. 164.

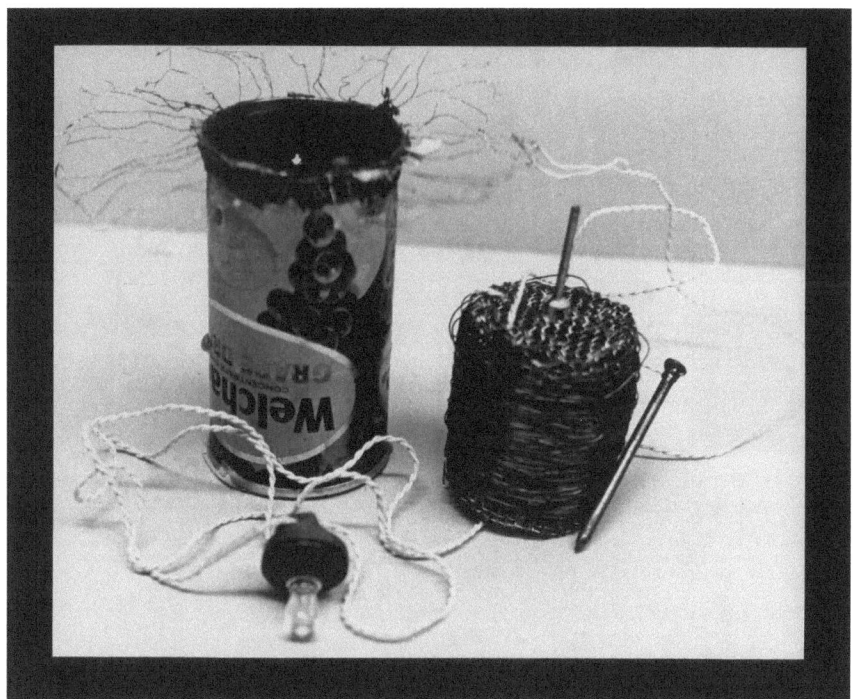

FIGURE 11.3 The Tin Can Radio: Designed by Victor Papanek and George Seeger at North Carolina State College for 'developing countries' using recycled and locally sourced materials. Courtesy of Fundación: UNESCO. © University of Applied Arts Vienna, Victor J. Papanek Foundation. Reproduced with permission from University of Applied Arts Vienna

War post-colonial cultural politics through pedagogic policy-making in schools such as India's NID, it is clear that Papanek and his contemporaries were eager to disassociate themselves from the Ulm School's brand of perceived neocolonialist positioning.

'Project Batta-Koya' typified a newly defined design thinking, uniting cultural anthropological sensitivity and a desire to address 'the real needs of the user'. Devised in 1973 as an intermediate teaching aid for 'under-developed' countries, it was sponsored by the Tanzanian and Nigerian Governments, under the auspices of UNESCO, the design credited to 'Victor Papanek and Mohammed Azali Bin Abdul Rahim of Malaysia in consultation with peoples from West Africa, Central Equatorial Africa and East Africa'.[60] Based on observations of 'oral story-telling traditions' in emerging nations ('Batta-Koya' means 'talking teacher' in the Chadic language Hausa), the design consisted of a customized cassette player, part of which could be housed in a calabash and bamboo case.

---

[60] V. Papanek, 'Project Batta-Koya', *Industrial Design* 22 (July–August 1975): 56–7.

The design, which received a UNESCO award, was underpinned by ethnographic research identifying the need to communicate orally with a disparate group of communities, using over 200 dialects, on vital issues such as public health and nutrition. The cassette tapes gave information in a range of tribal dialects with the progressive intent to bridge the gap between pre-literate and post-literate information systems and societies. The cassette player design was a simplified version of a Phillips 3302 battery-powered recorder, customized for educative and informational needs. A broader intention of the design was to decentralize government information through the use of dialects for localized consumption and the furtherance of community empowerment. The project left itself open to accusations of neo-colonial interventionism, and the question of how such apparently benign design projects could be appropriated for propaganda purposes. Following publication of his Batta-Koya project, Papanek complained that some social scientists 'in the West' would argue against the device, stating that it did not fit into the concept of indigenous authenticity, thus making it neo-colonial in intent. Papanek countered, 'To withhold it because of theoretical sociological minority reasons smells of professional imperialism, or bourgeois romanticism camouflaged behind revolutionary rhetoric', arguing instead that

FIGURE 11.4 Decorated Tin Can Radio: Designed by Victor Papanek and George Seeger at North Carolina State College for 'developing countries' using recycled and locally sourced materials. Courtesy of Fundación: UNESCO. © University of Applied Arts Vienna, Victor J. Papanek Foundation. Reproduced with permission from University of Applied Arts Vienna

'tools of this sort are by their very nature trans-national, culture- preserving and meta-political'.[61]

Conclusion

When, in 1979, Victor Papanek was invited to present the first international award for 'Design in Developing Countries' (sponsored by the Philips corporation) to the co-host National Institute of Design, Ahmedabad, at the UNIDO/ICSID conference, the dispersal of anthropology within design had become mainstream.[62]

Hybridized designs, emanating from pedagogic initiatives in progressive design school programmes, were redolent of the contradictions of the design and development agenda that the Ahmedabad Congress attempted to institutionalize as an extension of a Cold War cultural diplomacy and Western development strategy. Many anthropological methods and paradigms including theories of localization, authenticity and ethnographic observation were utilized informally, but when posited strategically as an extension of industrial design practice, they ultimately had far-reaching political consequences in maintaining a dualist, top-down approach to development. Histories of development studies tend towards the macro-level of discourse, emphasizing the agency of institutions and political organizations. This chapter attempts to move away from the macro-level and into a deeper consideration of the attempts to globalize vernacularity, with anthropology as the mediating force, as a project that simultaneously combined the grassroots objectives of design activists, and the broader legacies of Cold War political agendas.

By the late 1970s, development-thinking had extended from the economic theories of post-war US policies, evolving into a 'basic human needs approach' by which even those in disagreement with prevailing capitalist policies were, according to Escobar, 'obliged to couch their critique in terms of the need for development'; through concepts such as 'participatory development' and 'socialist development', development had achieved 'the status of a certainty in the social imaginary'.[63] The designed artefacts emerging through the 1970s idiom of 'design for development' (arising from educational courses, conferences and design activism) have remained excluded as objects of design history, museological display, or as documents in history-making. Yet the specificity of these designs, and the processes and ideological parameters in which they were produced, played a crucial part in the concretization process that forged development's impact as

---

[61] Ibid., p. 57.
[62] The full extent of the design for development discourse legacy is too expansive to deal with in this chapter, but initiatives such as 'Design for the Other 90%' at Cooper Hewitt Design Museum, NYC (2011), are direct descendants.
[63] Escobar, 'Notes', op. cit., p. 5.

'a certainty in the social imaginary' beyond the formalities of policy-making.[64] Design has been systematically under-represented in its role in 'making' the world, due to its assumed depoliticized status. As new configurations of design emerge, from transition design to design anthropology, and the notion of the social in design takes on a new significance in a contemporary cosmopolitical context, exploration of these objects and the related historiographies and political indices of such material culture becomes ever more salient.

Acknowledgements

The author wishes to thank the four anonymous reviewers for their insightful and helpful comments and to acknowledge the support of a fellowship award from the Botstiber Institute for Austrian-American Studies, USA, for related research. An outline version of the paper was presented in September 2013 at 'Towards Global Histories of Design: Postcolonial Perspectives', the Design History Conference of the National Institute of Design, Ahmedabad, India.

---

[64] Ibid.

12 NO GOOD (DESIGN) WOULD COME OF IT: THE INTERNATIONAL DESIGN CONFERENCE IN ASPEN, 1977–2004

Penelope Dean

For a time, the International Design Conference in Aspen (IDCA) provided the most open forum available for critical design discussion among leaders from design, business, government and academia. From the IDCA's inception in 1951 until its conclusion in 2004, the organization invited distinguished individuals from design offices, museums, universities, government agencies, business corporations, publishing houses and professional associations to convene from all over the world to explore the sources and influences of design.[1] These high-altitude events, held annually under a tent in a meadow at 8,000 feet, chronicled design priorities through post-war economic booms, activist outbreaks, environmental crises, politico-economic transformations and a digital revolution. If the annual conferences of other professional organizations were obligated to design's narrowing professionalization, the IDCA aspired to address vital questions about design's broader role, while upholding design itself as an international culture open to a 'convocation of amateurs'.[2]

That the IDCA survived for as long as it did is impressive. When it was conceived from a mid-century optimism to strengthen alliances between North American business and modern design, the IDCA embodied a union between a corporate and design elite at a moment when 'design was a subject not much discussed by

---

[1] The IDCA was founded by Container Corporation of America executive Walter Paepcke, typographer Egbert Jacobsen and Bauhaus artist Herbert Bayer. For the historical overview of circumstances leading to the IDCA's founding and incorporation, see James Sloan Allen, *The Romance of Commerce and Culture* (Chicago: University of Chicago Press, 1983), 269–78. For a selected anthology of conference papers and brief history of the IDCA between 1951 and 1973, see Reyner Banham, ed., *The Aspen Papers: Twenty Years of Design Theory from the International Design Conference in Aspen* (New York/Washington: Praeger Publishers Inc., 1974).
[2] Robert Campbell, 'Critique: After 50 Years, Does the Design World Still Need a Conference with Its Head in the Clouds?' *Architectural Record* (August 2001): 58.

anyone except designers'.³ This ambition for cultural reform, which was widely aspired to among corporate America, held sway for decades at the IDCA, as did the designer's entitlement to its sites of practical application despite periodic disagreements over the priorities. Yet halfway through the IDCA's duration, things started to break apart. The arc of this dissolution began in the late 1970s, as a New Economy emerged, and terminated in the early 2000s with the demise of the philanthropist-businessman and the ends of design. What began as a mission to align the ambitions of business and design in a milieu committed to integrating the arts and humanities, ended in a delta-like dissipation of different topics, design professions and special business interests, with everyone purportedly talking about design and the paradoxical realization that design had 'faded from the original conference idea'.⁴ After half a century, the IDCA's initial hope of collaboration culminated in a state of disintegration.

The political-economic context of the IDCA's end inverted the situation of its beginnings. While the organization's internal operations, organization (Board of Directors; Advisors to the Board) and corporate sponsorship endured as predominantly North American, the IDCA's *external* context became far less coherent over time.⁵ From the late 1970s onwards, North America entered an 'age of fracture' as socio-economic forces took design and business in opposite directions, fragmenting the design professions into specialized niches and prompting businesses to eschew sociocultural partnerships for more profitable opportunities.⁶ These transformations in value, which effected culture, practices and markets during this period, proved far more consequential to the IDCA's fate than the occasional activist challenge launched from the inside.⁷ The demands of a globalizing economy were at odds with the IDCA's mid-century sociocultural values. Moreover, the disconnect between a changing peripheral context and the

---

³ Ralph Caplan, 'International Design Conference in Aspen', brochure (undated), International Design Conference in Aspen Papers (hereafter cited as IDCA Papers) Box 3, Folder 37, Special Collections and University Archives, University of Illinois at Chicago.

⁴ John Hockenberry, 'Postcard from Aspen', *Metropolis* (November 2005): 119. There are numerous references to 'design integration' in early IDCA conferences. See, for example, R. Hunter Middleton and Alexander Ebin, 'Impressions from the Design Conference Held at Aspen, Colorado, June 28 through July 1, 1951', brochure, unpaginated. IDCA Papers, Box 15, Folder 734, Special Collections and University Archives, University of Illinois at Chicago.

⁵ The IDCA's Board of Directors largely comprised individuals based in the United States, although a substantial number of these members were European émigrés with international biographies. An Advisory Board to the Board of Directors was modestly international with non-Americans constituting, on average, between 20 and 30 per cent of board membership between 1977 and 2004.

⁶ For a history of this fracturing see Daniel T. Rodgers, *Age of Fracturing* (Cambridge: Harvard University Press, 2012).

⁷ Internal challenges to the IDCA ranged from activist flare ups (1963, 1970) to board member calls for the IDCA's redesign (1989, 1993). While Reyner Banham, for example, prematurely described the confrontations between student activists and the IDCA at the 1970 conference as near cataclysmic for the organization ('1970 marked the end of the road for the Aspen that most of us had known and valued') and contra to histories that have upheld that conference as the IDCA's most precarious, it was the transformed political economy that became the true threat to its survival.

IDCA's internal operations said more about the significance of the IDCA's corporate internationalism and financial sponsorship than it did about the accident of its geography or national identity. Silently and systematically, as political-economic

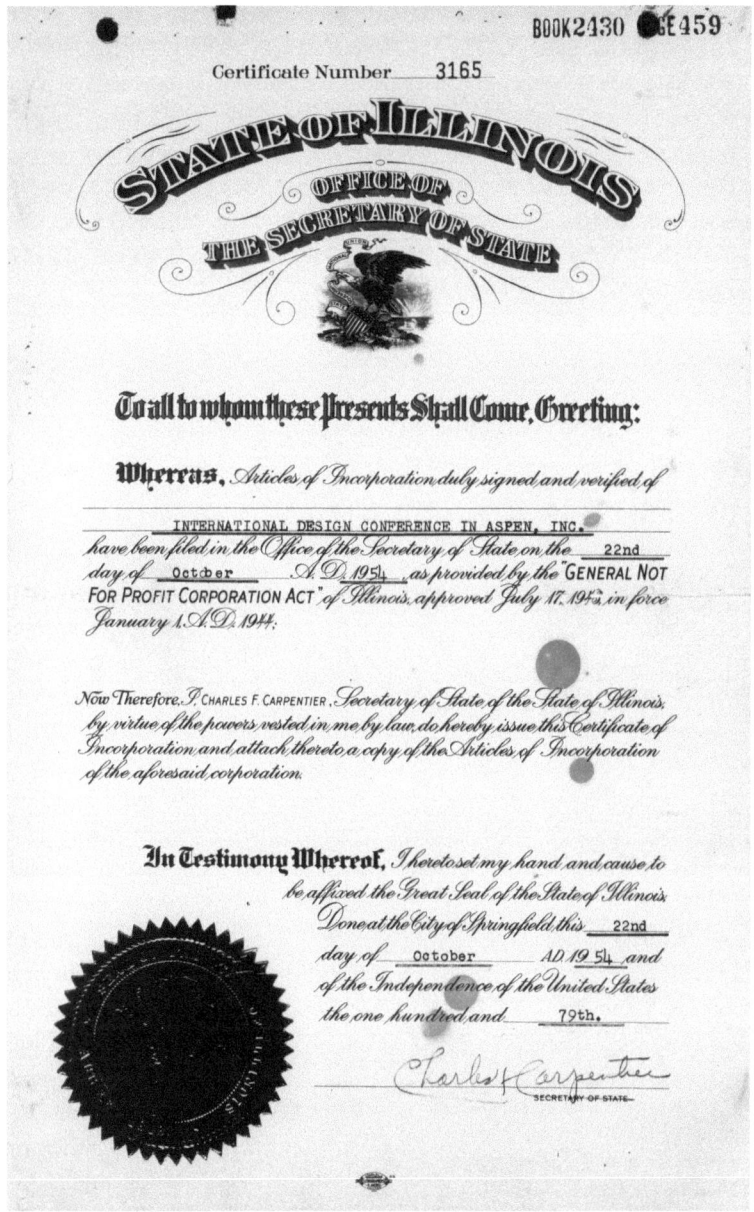

FIGURE 12.1 Certificate of Incorporation for the International Design Conference in Aspen, as provided by the 'General Not for Profit Corporation Act' in the State of Illinois, 22 October 1954. IDCA_0001_0014_032–1, International Design Conference in Aspen papers, Special Collections and University Archives, University of Illinois at Chicago

forces everywhere transformed ethical values into economic values, the IDCA both reflected a broader disintegration between design and business cultures, while practically manifesting its impact internally. As its original mission lost traction and annual conferences lost their specificity, the organization provided both a lens and a mirror to this post-1970s situation.

This essay examines the effects of these strains on the organization's values, identity and content from the late 1970s onwards, as well as the changed expectations of 'success' that came with them. As select board meeting minutes, annual conferences and their critical receptions show, the strength and weakness of the IDCA was both that its structure neither yielded to, nor fully responded to, the new expectations and paradigms of a transformed political economy.

Blurry and specific

From the outset, the IDCA's annual assembly evaded clear categorization. Legally, the organization was a not-for-profit corporation registered in the State of Illinois, headquartered in the City of Chicago (along with the Container Corporation of America demonstrating what mattered was a corporate locale), and established for the purposes of planning and holding conferences and meetings about the general subject of 'design'.[8] Conceptually, the IDCA remained specifically committed in its geographic scope (international), subject matter (design), format (conference) and place (Aspen), despite evolving definitions of what constituted 'international' and 'design', and periodic questionings of the Aspen location. But compositionally, its conference line-ups were blurry. On the one hand, they exhibited the characteristics of a think tank which, as historian Thomas Medvetz observed, always comprised a rotating cast of characters from a diverse range of institutions (private, public, academic, business, government, not-for-profits) who brought different resources, forms of expertise, network ties to government officials and journalists and the ability to raise money.[9] Like a think tank, the IDCA was defined by its *dependence* on other organizations for intellectual content,

---

[8] IDCA Articles of Incorporation, 21 October 1954. International Design Conference in Aspen Records (hereafter cited as IDCA Records) 2007.M.7, Box 101, Folder 7, Special Collections, The Getty Research Institute. The IDCA was registered as a not for profit corporation in 1954. Bylaws indicate that any person or corporation could become a member of the organization by paying an annual fee. The Board of Directors consisted of eighteen members, each on staggered, three-year terms. See 'Bylaw revisions', IDCA Papers, Box 2, Folder 21, Special Collections and University Archives, University of Illinois at Chicago.

[9] Think tanks emerged concurrently with the IDCA's founding during the 1950s. Both shared the ambition to provide services to business, albeit in different ways. For a comprehensive history of the North American think tank see Thomas Medvetz, *Think Tanks in America* (Chicago and London: The University of Chicago Press, 2012). For a description of what think tanks do, see John Goodman, 'What Are Think Tanks?' Goodman Institute for Public Policy Research. http://www.goodmaninstitute.org/how-we-think/what-is-a-think-tank/.

donations, services, audiences and advertising venues.[10] This dependence meant the IDCA was open to insiders and outsiders, its discursive content inclusive and interdisciplinary, its venues of critical reception diverse – e.g. *Domus, Casabella, The New York Times, The Aspen Times, Progressive Architecture* – and its annual content transferrable across knowledge domains. At the same time, it allowed the IDCA to be, as Michel Foucault wrote of heterotopias, 'endowed with the curious property of being in relation with all the others, but in such a way as to suspend, neutralize, or invert the set of relationships'.[11] This inverse relationship meant it could be an organization of the design establishment and a countercultural happening all at once.

Yet on the other hand, the IDCA's output differed from that of think tanks in important ways. Unlike a think tank, the IDCA was not commissioned to 'solve' particular problems. It did not yield 'deliverables'. It did not contract scholars to research specific topics.[12] Nor did it make policy recommendations, produce legal documents, bibliographies, or databases. Instead it produced ephemera and chatter, exquisite visuals and eloquent speech, graphic identity and verbal recordings in a carnivalesque-like atmosphere. Colourful brochures, fliers, schedules, postcards and posters, designed by a rotating cast of graphic designers, vividly communicated the personality of each conference (by contrast, think tank graphics were 'not visually pleasing'[13]). The central mode used by and characteristic of the IDCA was communication. It yielded marketable identity without the corporation, thinking without a tank, exchange without obligations of application.

As British critic Reyner Banham put it in 1974, the IDCA's critical discourse manifested itself with 'no particular vested interest to guard, no social position to defend' and in the 'lingering tradition of bohemianism' bringing 'attitudes of questioning open-mindedness that are proper to any organization that takes its intellectual activities seriously'.[14] Furthermore, temporarily encamped each

---

[10] Medvetz, *Think Tanks in America*, 29. The IDCA received funding from numerous North American corporations, foundations, government agencies and individuals throughout its tenure. Supporting corporations included the American Museum of Natural History, W. Braun Company, California College of Arts & Crafts, Coca-Cola Company, Container Corporation of America, Victor Gruen Associates, Ludlow Typograph Company, Herman Miller Furniture Co., Olivetti Corporation of America, Rand McNally, ARDCO, American Telephone and Telegraph Company, Ford Motor Company, IBM, Knoll International, Mobil Oil Company, Polaroid, Hallmark cards, Inc. and Siemens AG. In addition, the IDCA received donated goods (e.g. paper supplies for posters and brochures), professional services (e.g. typography, graphic design) and international advertising space (e.g. *Abitare, Architectural Record, Casabella, Contract Design, Domus, Graphis, Inland Architecture, I.D., Interiors, Metropolis, Print*).

[11] Michel Foucault, 'Of Other Spaces: Utopias and Heterotopias', in *Architecture Culture 1943–1968: A Documentary Anthology,* ed. Joan Ockman (New York: Rizzoli International Publications, Inc., 1993), 421–2. First published, in part, in *L'Architettura* 150 (April 1968): 822–3.

[12] Goodman, quoted in Medvetz, *Think Tanks in America*, 44.

[13] John Goodman, 'What Are Think Tanks?' Goodman Institute for Public Policy Research. http://www.goodmaninstitute.org/how-we-think/what-is-a-think-tank/. [accessed 4 October, 2019].

[14] Banham, *Aspen Papers,* 112.

June, the conferences were time-bound affairs in the tradition of architectural events ranging from 1933's *Congress International d'architecture modern* (CIAM), where architects had cruised the Mediterranean Sea from Marseille to Athens to discuss urban planning and produce the Athens Charter, to the *Delos Symposium* (1963–1975) that had sailed the Aegean Sea with an international group of interdisciplinary attendees to similarly address urban planning issues, to the *ANY*

FIGURE 12.2 Publicity poster, 27th International Design Conference in Aspen, 'Shop Talk', 1977. IDCA_0002_0023_010, International Design Conference in Aspen papers, Special Collections and University Archives, University of Illinois at Chicago

Conferences (1991–2001) where disparate academics and practitioners jet-setted to far-flung cities – Istanbul, Los Angeles, Yufuin – to discuss, on a high theoretical plane, the condition of architecture for reproduction in the *Any* proceedings. Between CIAM and ANY, the IDCA was design's Fitzcarraldo, having hauled a discursive model from the sea to the top of a mountain, without the baggage of a Charter or serial publication.

This Sisyphusian feat, with all its blurriness between domains, allowed for a wide variety of viewpoints without the business model of a bottom line or the obligation to deliver a specific product or professional service. It also provided a centre for design discourse. But as a new political economy imposed expectations of financial and professional accountability, the IDCA's historic inability or unwillingness to satisfy either of two narrowing agendas – the instrumental expectations of a think tank, and the critical discourse of academia – would leave it high and dry. When think tank culture exponentially took off in North America in the late 1970s through the unlikely convergence of counter-culture activists and technocratic experts into a new professional elite, and as academia increasingly professionalized, withdrawing into separated silos, the IDCA ran around, indifferent to impact or credential. One consequence of these changed conditions was that it welcomed new kinds of professionals into its orbit.

Ascending professionals

While the organization had always invited a range of professionals to its conferences for professional development purposes and tax deduction, this orientation generally did not compromise its 'amateur' contributions. From 1977 onwards, professionalism exerted pressure on the IDCA under conflicting circumstances. For example, in that year's 'Shop Talk', the IDCA's Board of Directors decided to wholly orient the conference towards the field of design after recent meetings had abandoned the subject, appointing themselves as speakers. The line-up of émigré-insiders, which included architects (Julian Beinart, Richard Saul Wurman, Moshe Safdie), graphic designers (Saul Bass, Ivan Chermayeff, Lou Dorfsman, Milton Glaser, Henry Wolf), industrial designers (Niels Diffrient, George Nelson, Ettore Sottsass) and design critics (Ralph Caplan, Reyner Banham) focused on the practicalities of design methods, practices and projects. The closed forum offered a portrait of design comprising distinct areas of aesthetic expertise performed by competent professionals. The line-up represented a consensus about what actually constituted design and who had the right to practise it.

Five years later, such clear-cut embraces of professionalism would be questioned by invited outsiders. In his keynote lecture delivered at 1982's 'The Prepared Professional' for example, historian Daniel Boorstin conversely cautioned against the perilous, and characteristically American, tendency of 'professionals to pay attention to their own interests rather than to those of a

FIGURE 12.3 Frame from proof sheet, Daniel Boorstin at lecture podium at the 32nd International Design Conference in Aspen, 'The Prepared Professional', 1982. International Design Conference in Aspen Record, 1949–2006. Getty Research Institute, Los Angeles (2007.M.7)

larger community'.[15] In its place, he called for an 'amateur spirit' – the attitude where one picks an assignment 'not because it is expected by profession, or by client, or is fashionable, or even respectable, but because he's fallen in love with it and can't help it'.[16] As an exemplar 'of the irrelevance of professionalism and

---

[15] Daniel Boorstin, 'Amateurs, Professionals, and the Quest for Lost Innocence', recorded audio, 1982. IDCA Papers, Box 7, Cassettes 421 and 422, Special Collections and University Archives, University of Illinois at Chicago. Transcribed by Darshan Shah and Stuart Shanks. The conference was chaired by George Nelson. *The Prepared Professional, International Design Conference in Aspen, June 13–18, '82*, conference catalogue. IDCA Papers, Box 16, Folder 751, Special Collections and University Archives, University of Illinois at Chicago.
[16] Ibid.

professional training' – i.e. a historian speaking at a design conference knowing little about design – Boorstin emphatically made a case for the outsider, for the leader who keeps a vision of naivete, for the amateur who keeps a 'sense of community with a vast world of nonprofessionals'. He endorsed the IDCA's amateur disposition, while presaging the design professional's contrary fate.

Over the next two decades, Booorstin's words would be echoed at the IDCA: no longer as critique, but as fact. Subsequent conference talks and speaker line-ups evidenced the rise of new kinds of design professionals – 'production designers, video designers, organization designers, communication designers, social designers, network designers, software designers, enterprise designers, and cyberspace designers'[17] – exploding alongside and between architects, interior designers, fashion designers, graphic designers and industrial designers, while laying claim to new niches. For design outsiders, the arrival of new professionals was used to incite a wake-up call for traditional designers who now needed to 'learn more about [their] future environment, instead of simply talking to [themselves]' – an inadvertent rebuke to the earlier 'Shop Talk'.[18] For some traditional designers, the new professionals lacking in art education devalued the quality of design. Debates intermittently erupted over the advantages and disadvantages of design's increasing professionalization and spoke to how the proliferation of new professionals was more than just a matter of degree: they broadened conceptions of design and repositioned traditional designers into a new equilibrium of competing professionals.

The apotheosis of this transformation was reached at the final IDCA conference 'Ambient: Interface' in 2004 where practitioners and academics hyphenated their bios to demonstrate their professional versatility – scientist *and* roboticist, media artist *and* designer, media historian *and* cultural theorist, design engineer *and* technoartist, designer *and* interface manager, object *and* media designer, motion *and* environmental designer – while embracing the minutiae of the digital medium in highly specialized interchanges.[19] If the IDCA's subject matter had become totalizing ('all design as interface design'), its professional acceptance was conversely narrowed ('they were just talking to themselves'; 'a conference of limited appeal'). After years of eschewing 'nuts and bolts' interchanges to 'break through the immense pressures of everyday details that seem to be swamping all of us', the IDCA had inadvertently conceded to techno-centric dialogue.[20] After prioritizing generalist discussions with the understanding that 'design was an international

---

[17] Richard Farson, 'Metadesign, Toward a Redefinition of Design', *Domus*, no. 772 (June 1995): 53–4.
[18] John Kao, 'IDCA – Overarching Themes, Guiding Questions', fax, 31 March 1995. IDCA Records, 2007.M.7, Box 91, Special Collections, The Getty Research Institute.
[19] Conference program, 'IDCA: 54', n.p. IDCA Records, 2007.M.7, Box 105, Folder 7, Special Collections, The Getty Research Institute.
[20] 'How the International Design Conference in Aspen Can Help Your Company' brochure, 1960. IDCA Papers, Box 3, Folder 37, Special Collections and University Archives, University of Illinois at Chicago.

language', it had surrendered design as a technical dialect.[21] The professionalism Boorstin had sought to admonish had now become the IDCA's identity.

The rise of new design professions was a by-product of specialization. North America's design's labour force had exponentially grown after 1970, yielding diverse kinds of designers in response to fracturing consumer markets.[22] This explosion of new designers paralleled a general rise of new professionals – e.g. management consultants, government advisors, authors of specialized reports. – everywhere. When new professional 'problems gave rise to new functions and to new specializations for dealing with them,' as Daniel Bell put it, specialization affected both knowledge *and* organizational structures.[23] Nowhere was this more evident than in graphic and industrial design, for example, where designers found themselves confounded with the problems of conceiving packaging, annual reports, corporate identity, electronic publishing, trade shows, product planning and software development, among other tasks, by the mid-1980s.[24] According to Bell, such high degrees of specialization bore 'a penultimate disjunction between the everyday world of fact and experience and the world of concepts and matter',[25] a separation that led individual arts to bifurcate on either technical or hermetic terms, the final IDCA conference reflecting one side of the disjunction in the sermons delivered by design technicians.

The explosion of design professionals also made visible a shift in values and expectations between two kinds of 'elite' associated with the IDCA. Initially, the IDCA emerged out of a strategic collaboration between what sociologist C. Wright Mills designated an 'American business elite' and a mid-century design establishment at a moment when there was a general investment in liberal arts for the masses in North America.[26] From the IDCA's inception, both sides of this elite – represented in the IDCA's Board of Directors, conference chairs, invited speakers and corporate sponsors – attempted to resolve their internal tensions 'between the imperatives of practicality and the ideals of

---

[21] Ibid.
[22] According to Jane Alexander, appointed NEA chair by President Clinton in 1992, North America's design labour force grew by 156 per cent between 1970 and 1990. See Jane Alexander, 'Redesigning the National Endowment for the Arts', in IDCA proceedings, *The New Business of Design* (New York: Allworth Press, 1996), 83. Numerous intellectuals observed the general rise of professionals in the West and non-Western world from the late 1970s onwards including Alvin W. Gouldner, *The Future of Intellectuals and the Rise of the New Class* (New York and Toronto: Oxford University Press, 1982), Daniel Bell, *The Cultural Contradictions of Capitalism* (New York: Basic Books, Inc. Publishers, 1978), Edward Said, *Representations of the Intellectual: The Reith Lectures* (London: Vintage, 1994), and Andy Merrifield, *The Amateur* (New York: Verso, 2018).
[23] Bell, *The Cultural Contradictions of Capitalism*, 94.
[24] See Larry Keeley, 'Demass Design', *STA Design Journal* (1987): 36–7.
[25] Bell, *The Cultural Contradictions of Capitalism*, 98.
[26] For a history of this elite, see C. Wright Mills's, 'The American Business Elite: A Collective Portrait', in *Power, Politics and People*, ed. Irving Louis Horowitz (New York: Oxford University Press, 1963): 110–39 and *The Power Elite* (Oxford: Oxford University Press, 1956).

cultural reform'.[27] As its 1960s promotional brochure 'How the International Design Conference in Aspen Can Help Your Company?' infers, the IDCA offered the place for differences to be reconciled, for progressive capitalists and established designers to bring their interests, resources and priorities into horizontal alignment with one another.[28]

Yet by late-century, as government began withdrawing support for the arts, Mills's version of the elite, with its shared aspiration for sociocultural reform, was displaced by another kind of elite comprising a much wider range of design

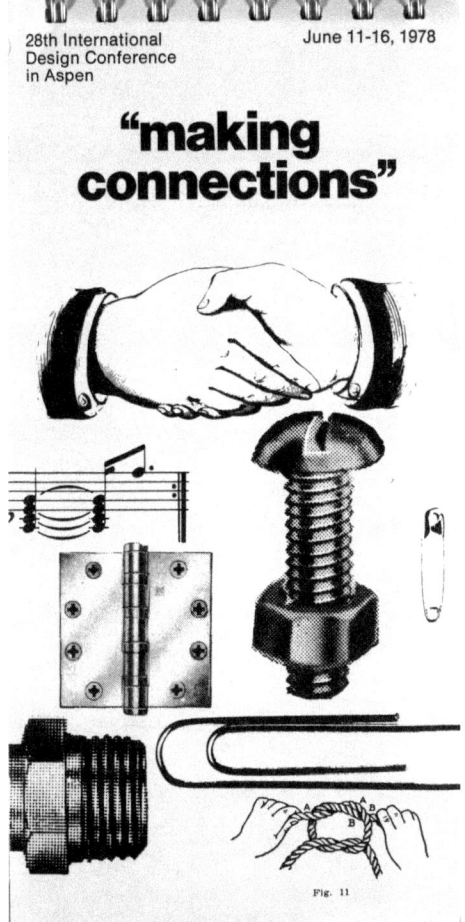

FIGURE 12.4 Program booklet cover, 28th International Design Conference in Aspen, 'Making Connections', 1978. Design by John Massey. Box 16, Folder 750, International Design Conference in Aspen papers, Special Collections and University Archives, University of Illinois at Chicago

---

[27] James Sloan Allen, *Romance of Commerce and Culture*, 274.
[28] See 'How The International Design Conference in Aspen Can Help Your Company' brochure, 1960. IDCA Papers, Box 3, Folder 37, Special Collections and University Archives, University of Illinois at Chicago.

professionals with more specialized objectives. Sociologist Alvin Gouldner had anticipated the ascendancy of a 'New Class' characterized by an ideology of professionalism with an internal tension 'between (technical) intelligentsia and (humanist) intellectuals'.[29] Instead of emphasizing the convergence between business and industry for greater ends, the new professional class pursued narrower interests, attracted niche-audiences and addressed smaller problems. One fallout of their increased specialization was the waning of a wider ambition for cultural reform between business and design, despite many members of the earlier design establishment remaining on the IDCA's board of directors until the early 2000s. Another consequence was that any consensus on what actually constituted design disintegrated.

Dividing design

A year after 1977's inward-focused 'Shop talk', the IDCA turned the thematic focus of its next conference outward. Indebted to the architectural thinking of Charles and Ray Eames, 1978's conference 'Making Connections' framed design as a relational activity reaching out to other fields – to physics, literature, television, social science and zoology, among others. As co-organizers Ralph Caplan and Andrea Bayes framed it: 'While design practice is chiefly the business of professional designers, design process, values, and consequences are too important to be left to the practitioners of any single discipline.'[30] This centrifugal outlook marked a turning point within the IDCA's history and made visible design's fracturing identity for the first time: from being understood as the terrain of architecture, graphic design, industrial design and the fine arts, to a more diverse obligation of a host of professions and practices; from being understood via products and services for customers, to its existence as a creative procedure exportable to other professions. In opening up design's 'process, values, and consequences' to a range of participants (including animals), the conference reflected the splintering of design itself.

Subsequent IDCA conferences reflected further splintering, but in less considered ways. Most notably, a wide-ranging proliferation of design 'topics' came to displace the IDCA's earlier sociocultural 'project'. For example, between 1979 and 1997, the category of place briefly overtook that of 'issue' as several conferences turned to examine design's site-specific instantiations in Mexico, Canada, the United States, Italy, Britain and Germany – a turn that paralleled the

---

[29] Gouldner, *The Future of Intellectuals and the Rise of the New Class*, 8. Despite the emergence of a New Class, perceptions of the IDCA being linked to an old class endured at Aspen, more often by critics and visitors outside the United States. See, for example, references to 'the design establishment' in 'How the doyens of UK design preserved standards in Aspen', *Campaign* (18 July 1986).

[30] Ralph Caplan, 'International Design Conference in Aspen', brochure (undated), 4. IDCA Papers, Box 3, Folder 37, Special Collections and University Archives, University of Illinois at Chicago.

FIGURE 12.5 Frame from proof sheet, participants in costume at the 28th International Design Conference in Aspen, 'Making Connections', 1978. Photograph by James O. Milmoe. International Design Conference in Aspen Record, 1949–2006. Getty Research Institute, Los Angeles (2007.M.7)

globalization being pursued in numerous design magazines at the time, rather than a move ahead of the curve.[31] Partially overlapping with the national focus, between 1990 and 2004 other conferences examined the role of design in relation to children, sport, the human body, government, religion, software.[32] Cumulatively, the annual diversifications in place and topic depicted design culture as globally ubiquitous, yet at the same time increasingly nichefied. Between highlighting geographic identity and reducing design's scope, the IDCA portrayed design's enlarging terrain in tandem with its narrowing fragmentation. The variegated picture had more in common with the structural characteristics of market culture than it did with the IDCA's mid-century conception of neatly demarcated aesthetic disciplines coming together for public 'good'.

In tandem, design's transformation provoked different reactions from within the IDCA. On the one hand, the changed nature of design provided reasons to challenge, undermine and reframe traditional conceptions of design. 'Is it still useful to talk about "a" design profession?', chair John Kao asked the IDCA's Board of Directors in a memo concerning the program for his forthcoming 'New Business

---

[31] During this period, several conferences focused on hot spots: Japan (1979), Italy (1981, 1989), Canada, Mexico and the USA (1984), Britain (1986), Germany (1996) and Hollywood (1997).

[32] During this period, conferences focused on design for kids (1990), government (1993), human body (1994), business (1995), sports (1998), digital environment (1999) and computer interface (2004).

of Design' conference in 1995.³³ 'We absolutely and resolutely do not base projects on traditional design "disciplines" such as graphic design, ceramics, illustration, or industrial design; nor are they based on traditional product sectors (furniture, books, fashion),' John Thackara – an Amsterdam-based think-tank leader – declared a few months later at the same conference.³⁴ At the height of a digital revolution and new information economy, traditional boundaries were meant to be ignored. Subsequently at 2001's 'Spirit of Design', program chair Rebecca Rickman declared 'this is not necessarily a design-specific conference,' and a year later at 2002's 'What Matters Now?', program co-chairs Lorraine Wild, Walter Hood and Michael Rotundi wrote: '[T]he role of design is to define and synthesize elements of uncertainty towards a more positive and optimistic future and to create paths and processes for achieving this.'³⁵ At the beginning of the twenty-first century, design was either vaguely considered or oriented towards instrumentality. In sum, the various reformulations demonstrated design's inherent unevenness, its capacity to reconfigure across time. According to 2002's publicity poster, it also heralded 'the end of design as we know it'.³⁶

Conversely, others saw design's mutability as symptomatic of IDCA's mission drift. Some Board members uncomfortably perceived a deterioration in the organization's goals and identity. The IDCA has been 'without a sense of purpose for a long time' observed Michael Crichton in a memo to the Board of Directors in 1989. Recent conferences 'have either been thinly disguised show-and-tell demos, or some rather special conceit of a chairman'.³⁷ Richard Farson and Julian Beinart subsequently wrote in 1993: 'The conference is often seen as marginal or irrelevant to the needs of designers, and to the needs of society. It lacks a clear focus or purpose.'³⁸ For them, the proliferation of design signified a loss of control and institutional paralysis. The 'open-mindedness' that Banham had earlier referred to as one of the IDCA's attributes was now considered a lack of focus.

Design critics similarly diagnosed design's reformist deficiencies and overgeneralization. Following 1984's 'USA, Mexico, Canada', the *Wall Street Journal* lamented the 'conference's inability to address serious design issues' and that some

---

[33] John Kao, 'IDCA–Overarching Themes, Guiding Questions', fax, 31 March 1995. IDCA Records, 2007.M.7, Box 91. Special Collections, The Getty Research Institute.

[34] John Thackara, 'Can We Count on Connectivity?' in IDCA, *The New Business of Design* (New York: Allworth Press, 1996): 97.

[35] See Rickman quoted in John Colson, 'Designing Our World', *The Aspen Times* (Saturday–Sunday, 17–18 June 2000): 13-A and IDCA, 'What Matters Now(?)' 21–24 August 2002, conference program, p. 5. IDCA Records, 2007.M.7, Box 104, Folder 7, Special Collections, The Getty Research Institute.

[36] IDCA, 'What Matters Now?' conference poster, IDCA Records, 2007.M.7, Box 166*, Folder 4, Special Collections, The Getty Research Institute.

[37] Memo from Michael Crichton to IDCA Board Re 'Future Planning', January 1989. IDCA Records, 2007.M.7, Box 104, Folder 5, Special Collections, The Getty Research Institute.

[38] Memo to IDCA Board of Directors and Advisors from Richard Farson and Julian Beinart, Re 'Long Range Plan', 3 November 1993. IDCA Records, 2007.M.7, Box 104, Folder 5, Special Collections, The Getty Research Institute.

conferees 'were disappointed and even angry at the lack of relevant substance'.[39] After 1987's 'Success and Failure', *Advertising Age* recalled conferences being 'more design-driven', and of 1988's 'Cutting Edge', *Architecture Minnesota* quoted a co-chair speculating that 'fueled by money and controlled by the bottom line, American design has reached a plateau'.[40] At 1990's 'Growing by Design', *The New York Times* observed the IDCA 'drifting into a single design' and in anticipation of 1993's 'Reconstruction Ahead', architecture critic Herbert Muschamp called on the IDCA to regain the sense of social mission it once stood for: '[F]or too long, the conference has been content to reflect the times instead of reform them.'[41] In 2000, *The Aspen Times* confirmed 'many different disciplines [... were] included under the vague label of "design,"' at that years 'Spirit of Design' and in 2001, *Architectural Record* conveyed that 'nobody worried about the meaning of the word *design* [... it] is generally believed [...] to mean just about anything you want it to mean'.[42]

According to the critics, the IDCA had fallen to pieces in the forty years since its launch. And with the organization, seemingly, so too had the foundations of design. Yet it was not that the world of design was completely in shambles, but rather that the idea of design had distorted: it was fragmented yet everywhere; it appeared to lack a sociocultural mission but was preoccupied with applicability; it could not hold in focus design's aggregated nature, but stood in for a hyper-specialized part. As IDCA president and architect Harry Teague eventually put it in 2001, 'design is more abundant than ever but may be harder to recognize'.[43] Indeed, the ascent of new design professionals, their increasing specialization and the marginalization of traditional design specializations rendered such an impression almost unavoidable. But there was more to the story than the judgements portrayed. The splintering and multiplication of *designs* at the IDCA were as symptomatic of nichefying markets and a dissolving distinction between business and design, as they were intentionally construed. For it was not just that design had mutated in definition theoretically and practically, but that business had evolved too, altering the orientation and identities of each. The awkward reality was that the IDCA was diverging from its mid-century ideals and objectives because the values of design were being replaced by new ones: those of business itself, now understood as a species of design.

---

[39] Stephen MacDonald, 'A Tax-Deductible Rocky Mountain High', *Wall Street Journal*, sec. 1, 6 July 1984.
[40] Jay Chiat, 'Rocky Mountain High', *Advertising Age*, 6 July 1987, C4 and Kira Obolensky, 'Aspen's Edge', *Architecture Minnesota* 14, no. 5 (September–October 1988): 19.
[41] See Theodore Sizer quoted in Carol Lawson, 'A Child's World, Bettered by Design', *The New York Times*, sec. C, 28 June 1990, and Herbert Muschamp, 'Rocky Mountain Low: Aspen's Design Conference', *The New York Times*, 16 May 1993.
[42] See Rickman quoted in John Colson, 'Designing Our World', *The Aspen Times* (Saturday-Sunday, 17–18 June 2000): 13-A and Campbell, 'After 50 Years', 57.
[43] Conference statement, 'The More Things Change ...' (6–9 June 2001), undated, n.p. IDCA Records, 2007.M.7, Box 98, Folder 1, Special Collections, The Getty Research Institute.

FIGURE 12.6 Tent interior at the 45th International Design Conference in Aspen, 'New Business of Design', 1995. International Design Conference in Aspen Record, 1949–2006. Getty Research Institute, Los Angeles (2007.M.7)

Minding your own business

It all came into focus at the IDCA's forty-fifth annual conference, 'New Business: Redefining the Idea of Design' in 1995. The event returned to look at design's role in relation to business with John Kao – business consultant and program chair of 'Enhancing Corporate Creativity' at Harvard University's Business School – serving as chair. Stacked with participants from business, speakers emphasized how design, now redefined as a process (i.e. a means rather than an end), might help companies plan for unknowable futures in a New Economy. This new 'idea of design' – which augured, in today's lingo, 'design thinking' and 'strategic design' – was premised on the understanding that design *techniques* were applicable to external domains, could be adapted for business's organizational needs, were independent of products and services and helped businesses do things faster.[44] The conference not only called into question traditional design's long-standing

---

[44] Michael Schrage, 'Design for Facilitation, Facilitation for Design: Managing Media to Manage Innovation', in IDCA, *New Business of Design*, 47. Design as strategy had been evolving in North America since the 1960s. For a historical account and indebtedness to 'design methods' see author's essay 'Strictly Business: A Working Definition of Chicago's Design, 1978–1997', in *Chicago Design: Histories and Narratives, Questions and Methods*, ed. Jonathan Mekinda (forthcoming).

assumptions, practices and values, but inverted the IDCA's founding design–business relationship: design began to appear in the *image of business*.

The conference theme coincided with escalating diagnoses and prognoses within the business world about the role of management as it transitioned from an old economy dependent on manufacturing – the kind that had sponsored the IDCA's beginnings – into a new economy emphasizing knowledge and information.[45] The shift from production to finance in the US economy, although typical of transformations elsewhere as well – Japan, Germany, the Netherlands, France, Italy, Sweden – along with the supplanting of national with global corporations and the arrival of digital technology, put enormous pressure on old businesses to reinvent themselves just as it gave rise to new, tech-savvy start-ups. From administration, to marketing, public relations, research and development, the new economy challenged many of the assumptions underlying organizational behaviour and provoked questions about the ways companies competed, managers managed and business was conducted. For many in business, including those invited to speak at the IDCA, the appropriation of design procedures for reimagining office collaborations, and even work flow itself, provided a novel antidote to address these demands. Design offered a way to optimize existing operations, a roadmap for managers to adapt and learn from the bottom up. As the editors of *Business Week* put it, 'design' was to the '90s what finance was to the '80s and marketing to the '70s: 'the corporate buzzword for the new decade'.[46] The IDCA's 'New Business' speakers expressed this buzz for design in business-speak – 'creativity' and 'innovation' – and in no uncertain terms: 'Design is the Trojan horse for bringing a renewed spirit of creativity in the corporation,' Kao proclaimed.[47] 'We tried to [...] create an environment in which to foster creativity and innovation,' Hatim Tyabi acknowledged.[48] Design should 'help companies, designers, and researchers improve their capacity for innovation', declared Thackara.[49] 'Businesses want innovation,' stated Dorothy Leonard-Barton.[50] Innovation, innovation, innovation.

If 'innovation' had been used in industrial design theory during a production economy to describe how products were brought into being through incremental refinement, by the new economy, innovation referred to the design

---

[45] See, for example, the list of books published on the topic between 1992 and 1993 in Alan M. Webber, 'What's So New about the New Economy?' in *Harvard Business Review* (January–February 1993): 26; Peter F. Drucker, 'The Coming of the New Organization', *Harvard Business Review* (January–February 1988): 45–53l and Peter F. Drucker, 'The Theory of the Business', *Harvard Business Review* (September–October, 1994): 95–104.

[46] Quoted in American Center for Design, 'Design Strategies in a Changing World', conference brochure, 1990. IDCA Records, 2007.M.7, Box 47, Folder 2, Special Collections, The Getty Research Institute.

[47] John Kao, 'New Business: Redefining the Idea of Design', in IDCA, *New Business of Design*, 9.

[48] Hatim Tyabi, 'Managing the Virtual Company', in IDCA, *New Business of Design*, 64.

[49] Thackara, 'Can We Count on Connectivity?' in IDCA, *New Business of Design*, 97.

[50] Dorothy Leonard-Barton, 'Designing with the Enemy: Creative Abrasion', in IDCA, *New Business of Design*, 130.

of an organization and its collaborative relationships between workforce and customers.[51] This shift evolved from two understandings of business. The first was that the mid-century conception of business as a patron (i.e. the commissioner of an independent designer) was replaced by business itself being conceived as a kind of designer. According to Michael Schrage, 'at the center of innovation was not just creative individuals, but creative relationships,' or as architecture critic Gordon Brown noted more divisively in his review of the 1995 conference for *Progressive Architecture,* 'in the design professions, the creative individual is a hallowed idol; in business, it's the work relationships in the organization that are seen as having to be creative.'[52] When businesses internalized design methods, design personalities were less necessary. This attitude was also evident in the British business context when representatives from the Department of Trade and Industry turned down the opportunity to attend the IDCA's 'Insight and Outlook: Views of British Design' conference in 1986, citing the impression that it was reserved for 'famous architects and designers' and therefore 'not relevant to our mainstream interests'.[53] At the time, those mainstream interests amounted to Margaret Thatcher's 'Design for Profit' campaign.

The second consequence of understanding innovation as a managerial operation was that it rendered the IDCA's long-held belief 'good design is good business' obsolete. In 1995, graphic designer Milton Glaser (the IDCA's paradoxical outsider that year) lamented the loss:

> When I first came to Aspen, the mantra, 'good design is good business,' was the guiding assumption of our professional lives. […] We were convinced that once business experienced 'beauty' (good design) a transformation would occur. Business would be enlightened and pay us to produce well-made objects for a waiting public. […] Society would be transformed and the world would be a better place. After 40 years, business now indeed believes that good design is good business.

The problem, Glaser continued, was that 'the relationship of graphic design to art and social reform has become largely irrelevant'[54] because business has 'recognized that its inherent value system, which is essentially capital accumulation and the pursuit of profit, is a worldly view of life that no longer has to accommodate itself

---

[51] For more on this translation see Peter Gorb, 'Design and the Control of Innovation', *STA Design Journal* (1986): 18–23, and Stan Davis, *Future Perfect*, 2nd ed. (Reading, MA: Addison-Wesley, 1996): 201.

[52] See Michael Schrage, 'Design for Facilitation, Facilitation for Design: Managing Media to Manage Innovation', in IDCA, *New Business of Design*, 48, and Gordon M. Brown, 'The Gulf between Business and Design', 49.

[53] See 'Aspen Conference' letters dated 31 October 1984 and 2 November 1984 in Design Council Archives, Box 48, University of Brighton Design Archives.

[54] Milton Glaser, 'Good Design Is Good Business', *Domus* 772 (June 1995), 58.

to any alternate views'.⁵⁵ Good design was no longer good enough as an end value, but only as a means to optimize corporate functioning. With the fall of good design, the IDCA found itself in the awkward position of having to defend the two things Banham saw the IDCA taking for granted: 'vested interest' and 'social position'.

Other designers, from the commercial side, conversely welcomed the demise of 'good design is good business', confirming Glaser's diagnosis from the avant-garde side. For example, Thackara gleefully declared its end in 1995⁵⁶ while design strategist Larry Keeley subsequently dismissed its relevance at the IDCA's 2001 conference:

> The idea that good design is good business is a ridiculous statement […] it's crazy for designers to have concern about articulating the relationship between design and business.⁵⁷ In this post-corporate time of change designers can no longer expect a business person to show up with a closet full of cash and ask them to do something astonishing. […] Let's update that goofy, wrong-headed notion that good design is good business. What would be good for business, is to be redesigned to be about people.⁵⁸

Instead of enlightened businessmen serving as patrons of good design, instrumental design was now tasked with enabling more business, more customers, more money. The reformist ambitions that had instigated a businessman's founding of IDCA in 1951 were being invalidated by a generation of designer-businessmen fifty years later.

Regardless of being condemned or celebrated, there is another way to look at the fall of good design in the IDCA context, namely that it was symptomatic of larger economizing tendencies. Political theorist Wendy Brown has conceded that economic conduct came to replace political conduct in every dimension of human life by this time. In *Undoing the Demos*, she argues that neoliberalism extends 'a specific formulation of economic values, practices, and metrics' to all fields, activities and individuals, remaking each through its own terms.⁵⁹ She contends 'all conduct is economic conduct; all spheres of existence are framed and measured by economic terms and metrics, even when those spheres are not directly monetized'.⁶⁰ As the market model radically transformed the purpose

---

⁵⁵ Milton Glaser, 'Roundtable Discussion: Reframing Design', in IDCA, *New Business of Design*, 166.
⁵⁶ John Thackara, 'Can We Count on Connectivity?' in IDCA, *New Business of Design*, 93.
⁵⁷ Larry Keeley, 'Facts, Forces, Fog', *Blueprint* (August 2001): 38.
⁵⁸ Ibid., 41.
⁵⁹ Wendy Brown, *Undoing the Demos* (New York: ZONE Books, 2015), 30. For Brown, neoliberalism understood as Michel Foucault conceived it: '[A]n order of normative reason that, when it becomes ascendant, takes shape as a governing rationality extending a specific formulation of economic values, practices, and metrics to every dimension of human life.'
⁶⁰ Brown, *Undoing the Demos*, 10.

and character of every sphere and the relations among them, even rationalities conceived in opposition to markets turned out to mirror certain aspects of them. The consequences of this conversion were being revealed in real time at the IDCA. As a new economy based on creativity and innovation replaced an earlier one driven by commodities and consumption, the design profession slowly comported with the business model.[61] If early IDCA conferences had focused on the designer's position in society with design as an instrument of social progress – a collaborator with business in service to the world – by 1995 design itself was conceived as a form of business in service of a market. The new code word in the business-design relationship was 'added value'. After business had absorbed the protocols of design, it was diluting them, redirecting them.

In tandem to all of this, the IDCA found itself sliding into its own business quagmire. Afflicted by declining attendance numbers, dwindling financial sponsorship and a stagnant organizational structure, the institution struggled to keep afloat. Despite the lessons and insights from its conferences, despite self-diagnoses of mission drift and despite warnings from external critics, the IDCA carried on as though there was no pressing need for change. In contrast to the speakers and chairs who explicitly affirmed or resisted the consequences of changing design and business cultures, the IDCA remained curiously indifferent to a changing economic context, neither accommodating nor rejecting the world outside, nor reassessing its own organizational assumptions. The inaction proved fatal.

Gauging 'impact'

Outdated. Imitative. Increasingly tired. This was how IDCA board member and futurist author Michael Crichton characterized the IDCA in 1989.[62] He saw an organization stuck in a time, unwilling to change, lacking in identity, and without a clear sense of purpose. 'Now that corporate America has the bejesus designed out of it, IDCA has become a structure without a function. An elegant structure; a prestigious structure; an ongoing structure; but a functionless structure nonetheless,' he wrote and one would expect the author of *Jurassic Park* to know something about extinction.[63] The problem was conceptual and administrative. While annual conferences aspired to be 'Vital' in outlook (i.e. address a particularly important or pressing conflict) they instead demonstrated a 'Hidden Agenda' (i.e. professionals network, swap business cards, find a job). Furthermore, the IDCA copied itself year after year. Crichton attributed the repetition to the

---

[61] Ibid., 65.
[62] Memo from Michael Crichton to IDCA Board Re 'Future Planning', January 1989. IDCA Records, 2007.M.7, Box 104, Folder 5, Special Collections, The Getty Research Institute.
[63] Ibid.

approach of the Board of Directors, which primarily acted to keep the institution going (focusing on fees, financial structures, scholarships and donations), rather than creating compelling conferences. Administratively, the IDCA's operational structure suffered from burdensome chairmanship, impoverished finances, excessive tradition and lack of publication: 'ours is an amateur conference – conceived in the '50s, and still clinging to an aging physical setting, a weeklong format, a minimum of professional staffing, and a basically charitable attitude to what it does, and asks others to do. Few conferences today operate so informally'.[64] Lacking an identity, sense of purpose and executive structure, the IDCA lived on 'as a kind of inexpensive Mom and Pop quasi-intellectual crypto-charity which offers little in the way of support to a prospective chairman'. It had 'long ago achieved its purpose'.[65] The IDCA's lack of commitment to internal management together with an ineffective board forewarned of imminent collapse.[66]

Nevertheless, Crichton's memo did set off suggestions for the IDCA's 'redesign'. The first came from Crichton himself. If it is to continue ('Why shouldn't IDCA close itself down?') it should exploit, rebuild and prioritize its image: Define a new mission. Cut through routine Board work. Redesign the Board structure. Give full attention to conceptual issues. Innovate. In other words, *professionalize* its business model. A second set of suggestions came from Richard Farson and Julian Beinart's more diplomatically worded memo. They too were optimistic that the organization could be redesigned. Despite a lost sense of mission ('marginal or irrelevant to the needs of designers, and to the needs of society'), murky program ('without clear objective'), narrow audience ('middle-aged, middle class, white people'), weary format ('has continued virtually unchanged for 43 years'), drained staff ('overworked and underpaid') and limited revenue ('reserves have been reduced almost to zero'), the IDCA could survive if 'board members […] apply the same creative, expansive, transformational, anticipatory design approaches that they follow in their professional lives to the design of the IDCA […] – one that is tuned to the 21st century'.[67] Finally the focus was outward. But it was not until the beginning of the twenty-first century that these suggestions would be taken up.

In 2001, the IDCA Board moved forward with a plan to reorganize under 'the imperative provided by the dramatic changes in design'.[68] New leadership,

---

[64] Ibid.
[65] Ibid.
[66] In the same year as Chrichton's diagnosis, management guru Peter F. Drucker noted of 'every single business failure of a large company in the last few decades, the board was the last to realize that things were going wrong'. See Peter F. Drucker, 'What Business Can Learn from Nonprofits', *Harvard Business Review* (July–August 1989): 90.
[67] Memo to IDCA Board of Directors and Advisors from Richard Farson and Julian Beinart, 'Long Range Plan', 3 November 1993. IDCA Records, 2007.M.7, Box 104, Folder 5, Special Collections, The Getty Research Institute.
[68] Letter from President Harry Teague to IDCA Board/Advisor member, 20 February 2001. IDCA Records, 2007.M.7, Box 101, Folder 4, Special Collections, The Getty Research Institute.

FIGURE 12.7 Half empty tent interior at the 51st International Design Conference in Aspen, 'The More Things Change', 2001. Photograph by Burnham W. Arndt. International Design Conference in Aspen Record, 1949–2006. Getty Research Institute, Los Angeles (2007.M.7)

management structure, transition team, publishing initiatives and smaller programs and residencies were discussed at a retreat held in Los Angeles where the board voted in favour of installing a new executive structure. It was installed by the end of the year after a conference of limited participation.

But to no avail: the eleventh-hour attempt to revitalize the IDCA failed to instil an impression of freshness. 'Has Aspen been around too long? [...] Is it now about the past, not the future?' architecture critic Robert Campbell asked of that year's conference, adding it 'felt dated'.[69] Two years after the restructuring, *Creative Review* noted the 'IDCA has struggled to maintain its relevance in recent years'. And when the curtain finally fell on the organization a year later, *Metropolis* magazine concluded, the 'Aspen conference has struggled to maintain an identity through all this'.[70] The makeover had come too late.

In their attempt to revive the organization, the IDCA's Board of Directors had finally recognized the changed political-economy under which they were operating. Yet the pressures that had been imposed on design culture and the

---

[69] Campbell, 'After 50 Years', 57.
[70] See Helen Walters, 'Playing Safe in Aspen', *Creative Review*, 1 October 2003, and Hockenberry, 'Postcard from Aspen', 119. IDCA attendance numbers dropped from over 1800 in 1988 to less than 700 in 2001. Conversely, registration fees almost doubled from between 1986 and 1997 to $750 in 2002.

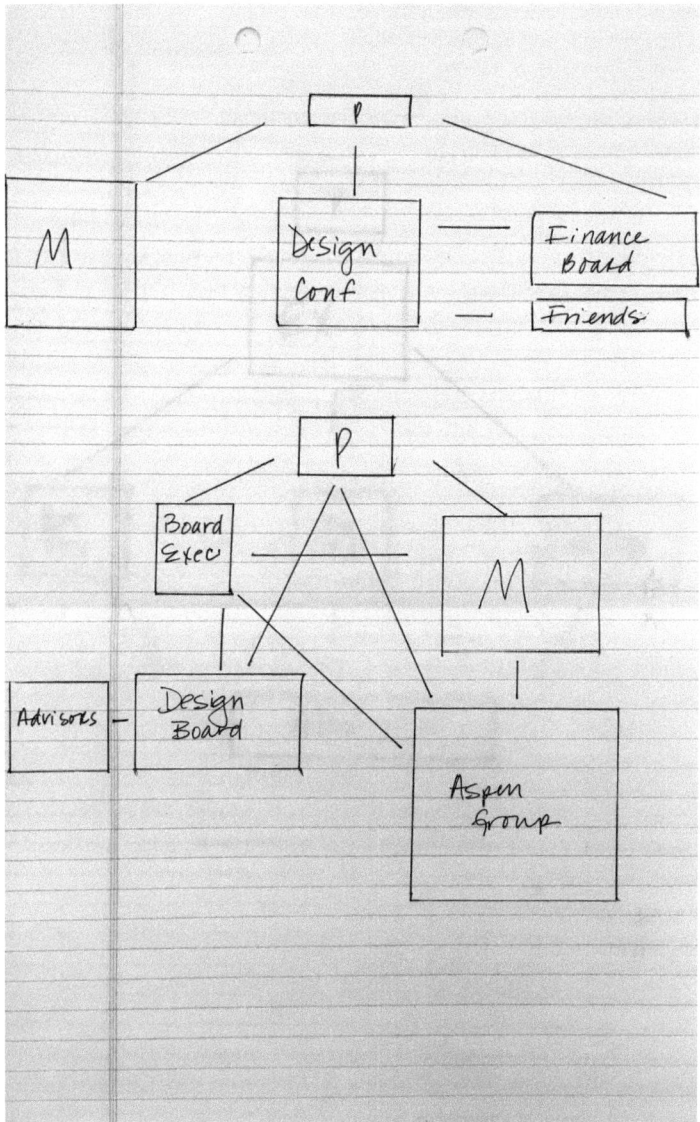

FIGURE 12.8 Organizational restructuring diagram for the International Design Conference in Aspen, 2001. International Design Conference in Aspen Record, 1949–2006. Getty Research Institute, Los Angeles (2007.M.7)

identity changes they had inflicted across a quarter of a century, had in many ways already eaten away at the organization's mission. As new design professionals proliferated, as traditional designers faded from an established elite into service providers, as design culture expanded and fragmented, as business culture globalized and absorbed design's methods, as sociocultural values were spawned and replaced by market values, the IDCA itself inevitably became subject to new measures of business success: metrics, professionalism, innovation, accountability. For an organization that had produced very little in terms of *measurable* impact, these new demands proved insurmountable. The IDCA's early success in injecting design culture into business, and in helping create a context for design as an area for academic study would thus culminate in partial defeat. Reaching a dead end, the organization had, in many ways, become unnecessary.

The IDCA's most enduring legacy, however, lies less with its inability to adapt to a changed political-economic context than with the *attitude* it managed to uphold for so long: conceptual blurriness, a commitment to design discourse, an amateur disposition. Such intellectual and cultural decadence had become extraneous in a profit-pursuing world where institutions replaced broader aspirations with mission-specific actions. It is perhaps neither coincidental nor surprising then that the absorption of the IDCA into the Aspen Design Summit under the aegis of the American Institute of Graphic Arts (AIGA) in 2005 – the professional organization of a single design specialization – saw the ambitions of the organization contract into those of a think tank with deliverables. The Summit sought to 'demonstrate the role of creativity', eschewed 'discussing big ideas and new approaches to old problems' and worked on 'practical solutions to certain problems', like 'educational innovation', 'sustainable community development', and 'social entrepreneurship'.[71] Such platitudes evidence the extent to which business speak had infiltrated design culture.[72] The typecasting of design after business had fully colonized it, was an outcome the IDCA could not possibly have foreseen fifty years earlier. Having remained committed to preserving (indeed, engendering) design as a discursive field open to a convocation of amateurs, it had not counted on the fact that the subject matters of design and the cultural aspirations of international business would liquidate, and that each sphere would inevitably transform the other. In the end, no 'good design' came of it. The IDCA proposed a bright future it was eventually unable to occupy.

---

[71] See https://www.aiga.org/aspen-design-summit. [accessed 12 December 2019] and John Colson, 'Redesigned Design Conference Debuts', *The Aspen Times*, 20 June 2006.
[72] Brown, *Undoing the Demos*, 27.

13 XIN, A MESSAGE WITH STRATEGIC VISION – AN ANALYSIS OF THE MEANING OF THE 2009 ICOGRADA BEIJING CONGRESS

Yun Wang

Introduction

In June 2009, Wang Min, the Dean of Central Academy of Fine Arts (CAFA) Design School and Academic Director of the 2009 Icograda Beijing Congress, realized that he was confronting a major challenge in his career. Two months earlier, he had been informed that Beijing-Hyundai Auto were cancelling 5 million CNY (447,675 GBP) of sponsorship for the congress due to the lack of approval from the Korean headquarters.[1] As the congress was to be held in about three months' time, many issues needed to be resolved. According to Wang Min, on the worst day, he received three telephone calls urging him to make payments, including one from China CYTS Tours Holding Co., Ltd (中青旅) and Gehua New Century (歌华开元大酒店), asking for 450,000 CNY (40,290 GBP), half of the cost of the flights for the speakers and the board members, as well as further hundreds of thousands for hotel reservation deposits, respectively.[2] Although this event was supported by the government, those payments were usually for a fixed purpose. Also, it took time to go through all the processes to receive the funds. Take for example, the 1 million CNY sponsorship CAFA promised from the Ministry of Education could only be used to buy equipment, such as projectors and hardware.[3] Meanwhile, the funds that the Gehua Group (歌华集团), the co-organizers of the congress, had gained from the

---

[1] Wang Min interview with the author, through WeChat, 27 July 2019; On Chinese Yuan and Sterling exchange rate, see 'Daily Spot Exchange Rates against Sterling – June 2009'. In *Bank of England / Database*. https://www.bankofengland.co.uk/boeapps/database/Rates.asp?TD=15&TM=Jun&TY=2009&into=GBP&rateview=D [accessed 2 August 2019].

[2] Wang Min interview with the author, through WeChat, 12 July 2019; On Chinese Yuan and Sterling exchange rate, see 'Daily Spot Exchange Rates against Sterling – June 2009'. In *Bank of England / Database*. https://www.bankofengland.co.uk/boeapps/database/Rates.asp?TD=15&TM=Jun&TY=2009&into=GBP&rateview=D [accessed 2 August 2019].

[3] Ibid.

Beijing Municipal Government were not in place yet.[4] In this urgent situation, Wang Min thought of asking for help from the other institutions. So he, together with his colleagues Tan Ping (谭平) and Xiao Yong (肖勇), began to contact other art and design institutions around China, communicating with them about the possibility of participating in the congress as cooperative institutions.[5] After a week, they had received 2.5 million CNY from about forty-five schools to resolve the 'crisis'.[6]

Wang Min's dramatic experience in the process of preparing for the 2009 Icograda Beijing Congress reflected the situation in which at that time neither the government nor the business community were fully aware of the value of design. This encouraged him and his colleagues to rethink the positioning and meaning of design in the local environment. As a result, the content of some of the events was adjusted to appeal to the public, as well as the decision-makers, the government.[7] They were trying to make changes.

This chapter examines the 2009 Icograda Beijing Congress, the international graphic design exchange that had a significant influence in China in the early 2000s. The narrative is based on the first-hand material I collected as a participant of the Congress. Drawing on previously unstudied materials in Yu Bingnan and Wang Min's personal archive, including the information about the exhibitions organized as part of the Congress, as well as reports about the events from local media, based on interviews I conducted with some of the Icograda members who came to participate in the congress, the chapter describes the interaction between the Icograda and Chinese graphic design circles from 1993, when Yu Bingnan first proposed to hold the congress in China. It demonstrates how Yu Bingnan and his Chinese colleagues, Wang Min and the CAFA team responsible for the organization of the Icograda Beijing Congress, interpreted and presented the theme of the congress locally.

The chapter makes a new claim about the 2009 Icograda Beijing Congress. More than has been previously understood, engagement with an international design organization was far more than mere communication within the professional field. It was the result of the joint action of multiple forces, including the achievements in economic development brought about by reform and opening up, the long-term evolution of the Chinese government's cultural policy, and the international design community's attention to Chinese design and the Chinese market due to these changes, as well as the persistent efforts made by key figures from the Chinese graphic design field. These complex factors have not been clarified in earlier research due to the fact that the purpose of most of the reports in China, either in online or paper media, was to promote the event, instead of providing in-depth analysis with reflective thinking.

---

[4] Ibid.
[5] Wang Min interview with the author, through WeChat, 6 July 2019.
[6] Ibid.
[7] Wang Min interview with the author, through WeChat, 27 July 2019.

In the 2000s, China was entering into a development-oriented society, which meant that the situation and tasks of reform and development were very different from those at the initial stage of reform and opening up. The mission of the new stage was to stimulate the creativity of the whole of society, to gradually realize fairness and justice and to promote the harmonious development of society.[8]

Xin with multiple meanings

FIGURES 13.1 AND 13.2 China National Centre for the Performing Arts; The banner of 2009 Icograda Beijing Congress inside the China National Centre for the Performing Arts, 26 October 2009 (© Arnold Schwartzman (photo on the top)/© Wang Min (photo on the bottom))

---

[8] Chi Fulin, *Starting Point – Thirty Years of China's Reform* (Beijing: China Economic Publishing House, 2007), 92.

In the afternoon of 26 October 2009, China National Centre for the Performing Arts looked quiet in the late autumn sunshine of Beijing (Figure 13.1). Newly completed and in use for just two years, the once controversial gigantic building designed by French architect Paul Andreu, with a hemispherical shape made up of metal and glass, was floating peacefully on the water. Once entering the building, this quietness was transformed into something dynamic with the huge banner of the 2009 Icograda Beijing Congress (Figure 13.2). The main elements of this were large, regular and irregular geometric blocks in black and white. On the right top corner of the banner was the name of the congress in both Chinese and English. 'Icograda World Design Congress 2009 Beijing', the English title, was presented in bold capital characters. Above this, the Chinese characters were presented in Heiti, a type style characterized by strokes of even thickness corresponding to sans serif styles in Western typography. In the left top corner, there was the Chinese

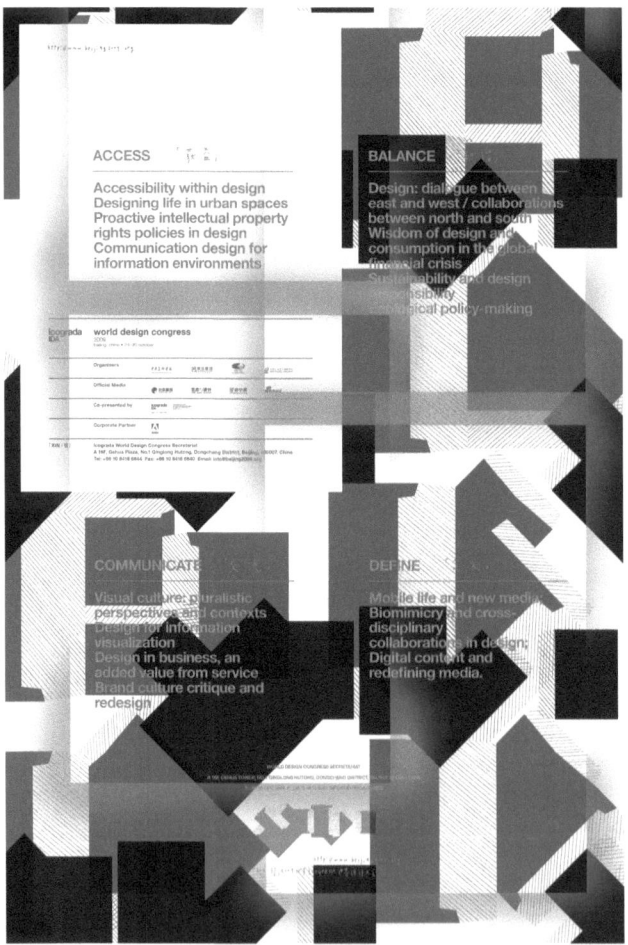

FIGURE 13.3 He Jun, 2009 Icograda Beijing Congress poster, 2009 (© Wang Min)

character 信, consisting of similar structures, that formed the main part of the banner. Its appearance conveyed a modern, powerful message through its size, visual elements and typeface. There were similar geometric forms in the poster design for the congress, also designed by He Jun, a faculty member from CAFA Design School (Figure 13.3).

But where is Xin — the theme of the 2009 Icograda Beijing Congress? Is it missing from the poster? If not, how was it presented? To find out, it would be helpful to first of all to understand the meaning of Xin and to trace the reason why it was selected as the theme of Beijing congress. The following is the text explaining the definition of Xin on 2009 Icograda Beijing Congress website.

> Literally meaning 'message' or 'letter', 「Xin-信」 represents a primitive means of communication. Today, however, it encompasses many more dimensions than ever before, as illustrated by words such as Xin-xi (information); Xin-nian (vision); Xin-ren (trust); Xin-yong (creditability) and Xin-xin (faith).[9]

The Chinese character 信 consists of two parts, 亻 and 言. 亻 has the meaning of people and 言 has the meaning of talking and speaking. Based on this, the meaning of 信 was expanded to an individual, human and society context, as well as communication, dialogue, contact, expression and a voice beyond boundaries, and so on. From a chart with the analysis of the word 'Xin', together with the multiple meanings derived from it, the thinking process of the Icograda CAFA curatorial team including Wang Min, Xu Ping (许平), Xiao Yong (肖勇) and Zheng Tao (郑涛), as well as Ron Newman, an Australia designer who had been active in the international design education field, the Icograda representative, can be seen clearly (Figure 13.4).[10] On the chart, the classification of the literal and extended meaning of Xin, for example, Xin as correspondence, the most basic meaning of the character to its abstract meaning as credit (symbol, sign, signal) and trust (confidence) is paralleled by an analysis of the structure of this character.

The analysis of the theme of the congress helps to decode its promotional materials. The basic element in the banner and poster designed by He Jun who tried to create a strong and dynamic atmosphere is an envelope, an image prompted by the literal meaning of Xin. Based on this element, He Jun created a series of colourful forms, as shown in the poster, or in black and white, in the huge banner on top of the glass facade discussed above, as well as the other places where related events took place. It was also applied to various promotional materials, such as the bag for each delegate and on the official congress website. Sometimes, they were presented as abstract forms and at others they make up the letters. Unlike the poster for 2004 AGI (Alliance Graphique Internationale) Beijing Congress,

---

[9] 2009 Icograda Beijing Congress, 'Theme'. In *Icograda Beijing 2009 Congress*. http://www.beijing2009.org/xin.htm [accessed 28 February 2019].
[10] Zheng Tao interview with the author, through email, 24 April 2017.

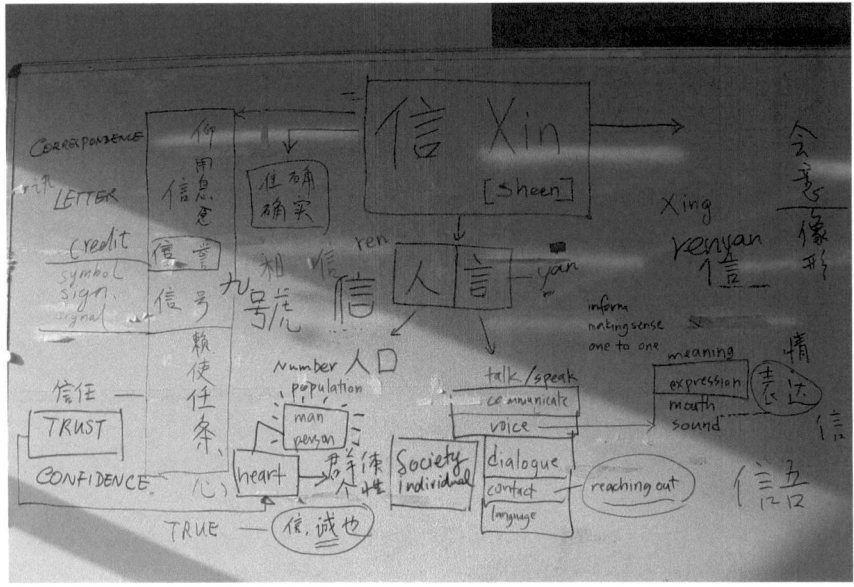

FIGURE 13.4 Brainstorm for the meaning of XIN, the theme of the 2009 Icograda Beijing Congress at CAFA Design School, 2007 (© Zheng Tao)

created by Zhao Jian from the Academy of Arts & Design, Tsinghua University, any obvious Chinese elements were invisible in this design. Take for example, the geometric structure forming the main part of the banner was the character XIN. It was not easy to identify, and the inner meaning seemed only to speak to the professional designers.[11] The abstract shapes made of envelopes displayed at different venues through different media became the visual identity of the 2009 Icograda Beijing Congress as a recurring pattern related to the congress.

At the age of thirty-two, having already received many important design awards, including the Excellence award for book design from the 2003 Tokyo Type Directors Club, He Jun seemed to be confident in developing his own style without having to worry about positioning himself as a Chinese designer.[12] Consisting of bright red, bright blue and white geometric blocks, as well as the grid of red blocks at a 45-degree angle, his poster design tries to convey a vibrant atmosphere. Layers of information are differentiated through the size and colour of the typeface. The four topics in the parallel sessions of the congress, including Access, Balance, Communicate and Define, together with their explanation, are in ochre yellow. Placed in the centre at bottom of the poster, the contact information for the

---

[11] 'Exclusive Interview with He Jun, GDC17 International July: Creation of Content and Form'. In *DesignLive*. http://www.sohu.com/a/208228824_556783 [accessed 14 June 2019].

[12] Zi Mo, 'Design Conversation: He Jun'. In *CCII 798 International Design Museum*. http://www.ccii.com.cn/cciinew/member/talk_1.html [accessed 13 June 2019].

Chinese office of the congress is of the same colour but in a much smaller typeface. The same size of typeface but in red is the information about organizers, official media and corporate partners, separated by red horizontal lines underneath the access explanation. Details of the Chinese office of the congress are presented here again. On the left top and at the bottom of the poster is the website addresses of the congress, in red and ochre yellow, respectively.

In addition to showing the designer's confidence, the poster also reflected He Jun's attitude. For him, design was a lifestyle, a way to enjoy life.[13] He was often inspired by everyday details and tried to deliver a 'simple and undemanding' atmosphere in his work.[14] Therefore, it was not difficult to understand the playfulness of the 'jigsaw puzzle' incorporating envelopes, as well as the childlike handwriting in the poster design. He Jun's understanding of design, as well as his approach to expressing his personal attitude, somehow reflected the more diversified status of contemporary Chinese graphic design in the early 2000s.[15] By this time, information about international design circles was much easier to access, due to the internet. Meanwhile, with the achievement brought about by the deepening of reform and opening up, establishing cultural self-confidence had become a matter of concern to the government, and this tendency was strengthened by the 2008 Beijing Olympic Games.[16] Under these circumstances, many designers of the younger generation began to think about their own position. In interview, He Jun tried to express his understanding about the value and position of the designer:

> (Designers) should not be satisfied with being an added value. Designers should have the right to speak … (designers) should not simply be an employer; instead, we should participate in the production process. Therefore, designers should take the initiative instead of remaining in a passive state.[17]

He Jun's enthusiasm and attitude towards design were reflected in his design for 2009 Icograda Beijing Congress, and this kind of dynamism was in parallel with the excitable atmosphere inside the fully packed venue of the China National Centre for the Performing Arts. Meanwhile, outside the venue, there were anxious students waiting from morning to afternoon for the opportunity to get access to the venue.

---

[13] Tu Zhichu (Associate Professor, Department of Design, Hubei Academy of Fine Arts), 'Designer He Jun: The Youngest Chinese AGI Member'. In *Tu Zhichu Blog*. http://blog.sina.com.cn/s/blog_4a63a4800100phz1.html [accessed 13 June 2019].
[14] ChinaVisual, 'He Jun: Inspiration Comes from Details, Design Is Not So Heavy'. In *Hanming Blog*. http://blog.sina.com.cn/s/blog_4b837cb7010005vd.html [accessed 14 June 2019].
[15] Jiang Hua, 'Independence and Collaboration – 30 Years of Pioneer Contemporary Chinese Graphic Design'. In *Documentary of the 20th Century Chinese Graphic Design*, ed. Xu, 434–6.
[16] Chang-Tai Huang, 'The Politics of National Celebrations in China'. In *The People's Republic of China at 60: An International Assessment*, ed. William C. Kirby, Barry R. Bloom, Timothy Cheek, Sheena Chestnut, Sheena Cohen, 357–72 (Cambridge, MA: Harvard University Press, 2011), 360.
[17] Tu, 'Designer He Jun: The Youngest Chinese AGI Member'.

They were specifically attracted here by Sol Sender, the American graphic designer known for his Obama 'O' logo, the first keynote speaker in the afternoon during day one of the Congress. I clearly remember how excited one student was when he finally obtained permission to enter the seminar room after hours of waiting, trying hard to persuade the teachers from CAFA to allow him in. I also heard these teachers complaining about all the student volunteers who were meant to be working at National Centre for the Performing Arts helping the participants with way-finding or answering their questions disappearing soon after the beginning of the seminar to listen to the presentations. Their 'complaining', however, was mixed with pride.

The situation at the China National Centre for the Performing Arts reflected the attraction of the Opening Ceremony and Keynote Presentations of the 2009 Icograda Beijing Congress, featuring well-known international and local speakers such as Sol Sender, Jan van Toorn, Lu Jingren (吕敬人) and Freeman Lau (刘小康), the strong media publicity, close cooperation with design schools all over China and the choice of venue.[18] The congress had forty-five cooperating media channels of different kinds. In addition to artron.com (雅昌艺术网), ChinaVisual (视觉中国), *Art and Design* (《艺术与设计》) and *Design 360°* (《设计360°》), the influential professional local design media that were often invited by art and design events in China, there were also many popular mass media channels such as Sina (新浪), *Morning Post* (《北京晨报》), *Beijing Youth Weekly* (《北青周刊》).[19] This clearly demonstrated the organizer's intention to position the congress as an event for the whole of society, instead of something limited to design circles. Besides, the congress also had a wide range of international media partners, including *Baseline* and *Creative Review* from the UK, *Communication Arts* from the United States, *novum* from Germany, *d[x]i Magazine* from Spain, *abcdesign* from Brazil, *DESIGN>In Formation* from South Africa and others.[20]

All these conveyed a strong message from the CAFA team about introducing the event to local audiences and international participants, emphasizing the contemporary context in which Chinese design had achieved great improvements, whether at the technical or conceptual level, instead of focusing on the legacy of ancient China. The choice of He Jun for the visual identity of the congress seemed to further confirm this idea. He was young but a frequently award-winning designer at international design competitions. When talking about his design, He Jun did not mention the influence of Chinese history or over-emphasize the impact of 'the West'. In many interviews, he specifically mentioned that his

---

[18] The information about the 2009 Icograda Beijing Congress and its close connection with design schools in China comes from David Berman interview with the author, through telephone call and email, 9 June 2019; On the information about venue during the congress, see 'Home'. In Icograda Beijing. http://www.beijing2009.org/index-eng.htm [accessed 11 June 2019].

[19] 'Media Partners'. In *Icograda Beijing*. http://www.beijing2009.org/mediapartner.htm [accessed 12 June 2019].

[20] Ibid.

inspiration came from everyday details.[21] This seemed to symbolize the signs that Chinese designers and international designers were competing on the same stage, a situation his predecessors such as Wang Min, the then Dean of CAFA Design School and Academic Director of Icograda Beijing Congress would not have thought about at He Jun's age. Wang Min once spoke of the ambition in an interview, clarifying the main aim in organizing the congress was 'the urge to help China to gain the right of speech in the international design community'.[22] For him, this was an opportunity to promote Chinese design. In the viewpoint of the congress local organizer represented by Wang Min, He Jun's floating black and white and colourful geometric forms, the elements that made up Xin, seemed to be a confident design vocabulary that created an 'ideal' facade for presenting contemporary Chinese graphic design in these circumstances.

Xin as strategy

On 27 October 2009, the second day of the congress, the venue moved to the campus of CAFA, where the four topics in the parallel sessions of the international conference on the theme 'Xin' began: Access (accessibility within design), Balance (the wisdom of design and consumption in the global financial crisis), Communicate (Design in business, an added value from service) and Define (biomimicry and cross-disciplinary collaborations in design).[23]

A view of these raised questions in my mind, such as these: was the theme of the 2009 Icograda Beijing Congress simply derived from the Chinese character 信? What about its connection with a contemporary international context? What was the value and thinking behind the theme? How was this kind of value and thinking presented and how did it function in a week's congress in 2009? To discuss these questions, it is important first of all to investigate how Chinese design circles reached Icograda.

Chinese design circles' first formal encounter with Icograda can be traced back to 1993. A year after introducing Yu Bingnan to AGI, Henry Steiner, an Austrian graphic designer based in Hong Kong, the first Chinese AGI member,[24] put Yu Bingnan in touch with Philippe Gentil, Icograda's then president to whom Yu Bingnan wrote a letter, asking for China to become a member. The reply was negative, however, since only national design associations could be considered as members of this organization.[25] At that time, the Chinese graphic design profession

---

[21] Zi, 'Design Conversation: He Jun'; Zhong Heyan, 'He Jun+Guang Yu+Liu Zhizhi=MeWe'. In *AD110*. http://www.ad110.com/hi/blogview.asp?logID=174 [accessed 17 June 2019].
[22] Ibid.
[23] 'Theme'. In *Icograda Beijing*. http://www.beijing2009.org/index-eng.htm [accessed 17 June 2019].
[24] 'Members'. In *Alliance Graphique Internationale*. https://a-g-i.org/members [accessed 25 February 2020].
[25] Jin Minhua, 'They Brought Icograda to China', *Shenzhen Business Daily*, 4 November 2009, p. C3.

had just started and there was no design organization on this scale. Therefore, Yu Bingnan was accepted as a communication member of Icograda to keep in touch with the organization.[26]

Six years later, in 1999, Yu Bingnan received an invitation to participate in the Icograda Sydney Congress from Leimei Julia Chiu, the Vice-President of Icograda, who was born in Taiwan and raised and educated in the United States and later in Japan.[27] According to Leimei Julia Chiu's analysis, China was a big country and it was difficult to set up a national association in a short period of time, so it would be more practical for Icograda to accept an emerging design association from a Chinese city or province. This suggestion was accepted by the committee later that year and the Shanghai Graphic Design Association was accepted as the first Chinese Icograda member.[28] In the following year, the Academy of Arts & Design, Tsinghua University, as well as Beijing CCII (Capital Corporation Image Institution (首都企业形象研究会)) joined the organization at the 2000 Icograda Seoul Congress.[29] According to Yu Bingnan, many delegates gathered together, calling for 'Oullim' ('great harmony') during the opening ceremony at the Seoul International Convention and Exhibition Centre. Deeply impressed by this experience, Yu Bingnan and his colleagues were determined to integrate China into this international community.[30]

In 2001, with a recommendation from the national design association of Japan and Korea, as well as the Beijing CCII, Yu Bingnan was elected to be the Vice-President of Icograda, a position he held for three years until 2003.[31] After that, Yu served as Icograda ambassador in China. During this time, he participated in eight Icograda congresses.[32] While actively participating in the international events organized by Icograda, Yu Bingnan and his colleagues were also trying to bring Icograda to China to strengthen mutual understanding. One year later in 2002, Robert L. Peters, a Canadian graphic designer and educator, the then Icograda president, was invited to visit China for the first time when he was impressed with the individual designers he met while at the same time being quite surprised by the fact that China had no national design association.[33]

---

[26] 'Professor Yu Bingnan's Speech at Preparatory meeting of the 2009 Icograda Beijing Congress Preparatory Committee'.
[27] ico-D, 'Leimei Julia Chiu Appointed Executive Director of JIDPO'. In *ico-D news*. https://www.ico-d.org/connect/index/post/1311.php [accessed 4 March 2019].
[28] 'Professor Yu Bingnan's Speech at Preparatory meeting of the 2009 Icograda Beijing Congress Preparatory Committee'.
[29] Ibid.
[30] Yu Bingnan interview with the author, in Beijing, 17 May 2017.
[31] Yu Bingnan interview with the author, through WeChat, 2 June 2019.
[32] 'Professor Yu Bingnan's Speech at Preparatory meeting of the 2009 Icograda Beijing Congress Preparatory Committee'.
[33] Robert L. Peters, 'Crumbling Walls, New Dawn'. In *Icograda Board Message*. http://www.robertlpeters.com/news/images/Icograda_BM12-02.pdf [accessed 10 June 2019]; On Robert L. Peters, see 'About'. In *Robert L. Peters*. http://www.robertlpeters.com [accessed 25 February 2020].

FIGURE 13.5 Lu Jingren, *Zhu Xi Bangshu Thousand-Character essay* (《朱熹榜书千字文》), 1999. (© Lu Jingren)

Was Robert L. Peters' trip to Beijing and Shanghai a direct result of Yu Bingnan and his colleagues' persistent efforts to bring Icograda to China? Was it simply a diplomatic protocol? Or did this action represent a profound transformation on Icograda's part? To answer these questions, it is important to view the issue in a global context.

Since the 1990s, Icograda had been going through a transformation from being Eurocentric to embracing a more global approach, which included developing countries.³⁴ Globalization and changes in communication technology, for example, the use of personal computers, the internet, email and digital data transfer, played a significant role in helping Icograda fulfil its broader vision and mandate as an international non-governmental organization for professional graphic design.³⁵ Asian names started to appear on the list of Icograda board members, which brought a change in its structure.³⁶ This brought a huge effect, especially when many design schools in Asia, particularly in China, Japan and Korean, joined in and their votes became powerful.³⁷

During this period, communication between Chinese, Japanese and Korean graphic designers became frequent. Lu Jingren, the influential Chinese book designer who went to Japan in 1989 to study with Kohei Sugiura started to pay attention to design, art and folk culture in China, Japan and Korea under the influence of his mentor.³⁸ He translated, edited and introduced a series of books on Japanese design after returning to China. Take, for example, *Nobuyoshi Kikuchi's Collected Works* (《菊地信义作品集》), *Japanese Contemporary Illustrations* (《日本当代插图集》), as well as *The Birth of the Plastic Arts* (《造型的诞生》) in 1992, 1994 and 1999, respectively. Meanwhile, he was connected with Ahn Sang-Soo through the recommendation of Kohei Sugiura.³⁹ From the early 2000s, these three had participated in and promoted a series of design exchange activities in China, Japan and Korea, with the idea of discussing and promulgating East Asian aesthetics through international activities and design practices (Figure 13.5).⁴⁰ Ahn Sang-Soo chaired Icograda's Millennium Congress, 'Oullim 2000'.⁴¹ Together with Leimei Julia Chiu, he was one of the two earliest Asian members to join in Icograda board in 1997.⁴² Like Ahn Sang-Soo, Leimei Julia Chiu, the Vice-President of Icograda from 1997–2001, was also influenced by Kohei Sugiura.⁴³ The communication between the two provided Leimei Julia Chiu with a different sense of her role in Icograda and that was, as she recalled in an interview with the author, to reach broader regions such as Africa, South America and Asia.⁴⁴Meanwhile, she was deeply influenced by Austrian designer and design educator Victor Papanek's *Design for the Real World*.⁴⁵ When describing her experience as

---

[34] 'Board History'. In *ico-D*. https://www.ico-d.org/about/history [accessed 17 June 2019].
[35] Robert L. Peters interview with the author, through email, 12 June 2019.
[36] Jin, p. C3.
[37] David Berman interview with the author, through email, 11 June 2019.
[38] Lu Jingren interview with the author, through WeChat, 28 July 2019.
[39] Ibid.
[40] Ibid.
[41] 'Ahn Sang-Soo to receive Icograda Education Award'. In *ico-D*. https://www.ico-d.org/connect/index/post/1346.php [accessed 7 July 2019].
[42] 'Board History'. In *ico-D*. https://www.ico-d.org/about/history/sb_expander_articles/19.php [accessed 7 July 2019].
[43] Leimei Julia Chiu interview with the author, through WeChat, 7 July 2019.
[44] Ibid.
[45] Jin, p. C3.

the vice-president of Icograda, Leimei Julia Chiu mentioned that during that time she visited many countries and areas in Africa, Cuba and South America where she encountered very different opinions on design. With an awareness of design for those in need and design for developing countries, she felt it was both her responsibility and her wish to bring China to Icograda.[46]

Robert L. Peters was also part of a younger group of leaders within Icograda who pushed for a better global distribution for Icograda. He did this

> for a broadening of the benefits for all of Icograda's members and members' members. This led us to actively develop contacts, programming, and events beyond the relatively narrow scope of Europe (and sometimes North America) — to include Asia (including India), Africa, Oceania, and South America.[47]

With a similar approach, Robert L. Peters wrote an article titled 'No Sleeping Dragon – the Dawn of Graphic Design in China' after his trip to China in September 2002 when he participated in the Icograda council meeting that took place in Beijing, followed by a series of events including 'The First Poster Exhibition of China Red Cross Society' and symposium, 'A Trip to Shanghai: International Visual Art Master Seminar' and so on.[48] The article was an introduction to China, including references to its history, culture, politics, economy, social transformation and philosophy, connections with Chinese art and design, as well as a comparison between Western and Chinese design. His understanding of Chinese design and close communication with Yu Bingnan, however, started one year before his first trip to China, when he and Karen Blincoe, the then vice-president of Icograda, helped Yu Bingnan with his communication with the other board members in English.[49] Take for example, Robert L. Peters translated Yu Bingnan's talk 'Review of Chinese Graphic Design' at Icograda Melbourne and the Oceania Regional Conference in Australia in 2001.[50] This kind of help was frequent during Yu Bingnan's tenure on the Icograda board from 2001 to 2003.[51]

In 2005, a Chinese delegation headed to Denmark to participate in the Icograda Copenhagen Congress.[52] At this point, Yu Bingnan had retired and handed the task of applying for the right to host the 2009 Icograda congress in Beijing to the CAFA team, including Wang Min, dean of CAFA Design School, as well as Xiao Yong (肖勇) and Wang Ziyuan (王子源), staff members from the CAFA Design

---

[46] Ibid.
[47] Robert L. Peters interview with the author, through email, 12 June 2019.
[48] Robert L. Peters, 'No Sleeping Dragon: The Dawn of Graphic Design in China', *Communication Art*, March/April, 2004, pp. 86–99.
[49] Yu Bingnan interview with the author, through email, 11 March 2018.
[50] Ibid.
[51] Ibid.
[52] 'China Wins the Right to Host the World Design Congress'. In *Sina.news*. http://news.sina.com.cn/c/2005-10-13/11317159524s.shtml [accessed 17 June 2019].

School.⁵³ The application was eventually approved after fierce competition on 30 September 2005, when Beijing defeated four other cities, Singapore, Montreal, Warsaw and Brussels.⁵⁴

> Recalling this experience, Peters, the past President of Icograda in 2005, declared that there was no doubt in my mind that Beijing was the best choice for 2009. China was making significant strides on the global stage to become more connected (and less withdrawn) than it had been for many decades, and the Icograda board was very conscious of the considerable potential that could flow from finally having a more open flow of ideas, work, and conversations with Chinese colleagues. We had a clear sense that Beijing would be a spectacular venue. In no small part, the world's focus on Beijing's 2008 Olympics would offer natural momentum to build on, and the experience this brought to China's expertise are: hosting international visitors, etc. was welcomed and evident.⁵⁵

If Peters's recognition for CAFA as the organizer of the 2009 Icograda Congress was based on years of communication with Yu Bingnan while both of them worked as Icograda Board members, and his trips to China, through which he saw the potential for Icograda to connect with design circles in China, then the support from Ron Newman, the Australia designer who travelled to the 2007 Cuba Icograda Congress as a voting member to ensure there was good support for Beijing was also connected with his long personal history of engagement with China.⁵⁶ Ron Newman's first trip to China was in 1980 as a practising industrial designer travelling by train from Hong Kong to Guangzhou to work with toolmakers who were producing production moulds for his company in Australia.⁵⁷ At that time, he still needed to apply for all permissions and was supervised during the whole visit.⁵⁸ From 2006 to 2008, he was a member of the Raffles Institute which at that time had campuses all over China.⁵⁹

Nearly 20 years of experience of working in China, as well as the working experience related to China based on substantial design projects, provided Newman

---

⁵³ 'Icograda General Assembly 21: Minutes, Copenhagen, Denmark, 29–30 September 2005', the document was provided to the author by Jacques Lange (Icograda President 2005–2007), through email, 23 June 2019. The document is situated in Jacques Lange's personal archive. Also see Xiao Yong Design Studio, '2009 World Design Conference Will be Held in Beijing'. In *VisionUnion*. http://www.visionunion.com/article.jsp?code=200510090039 [accessed 17 June 2019].
⁵⁴ Jacques Lange interview with the author, through email, 23 June 2019. Also see Lang Li and Wang Min, 'A New Discussion about Seventh Anniversary of Beijing Design Week and Design Drives Innovation Based on the View of User Experience', *Zhuangshi*, 9 (2016), 36–41 (36).
⁵⁵ Robert L. Peters interview with the author, through email, 12 June 2019.
⁵⁶ Ron Newman interview with the author, through email, 17 June 2019.
⁵⁷ Ibid.
⁵⁸ Ibid.
⁵⁹ 'Professor Ron Newman'. In *Virtu Institute*. http://www.virtuinstitute.edu.au/professor-ron-newman/ [accessed 19 June 2019].

with a more specific perspective on the design industry in China. Therefore, he was able to help the Icograda CAFA team with specific advice. He advised the team on what Western colleagues would understand or otherwise in the material, as well as the balance of speakers and topics; for example, he encouraged the use of Chinese characters in Congress materials design with explanations because in his view, these characters represented a real cultural experience for the congress guests.[60] This, however, contrasts with the approach of He Jun's. In his poster design for the Congress, the cultural and historical significance carried by Chinese characters were eliminated, which reflects the gap between the *modern* China the local organizer wanted to demonstrate and the culture experience Newman expected. Newman joined the CAFA team to brainstorm about Xin, the theme of the congress with an awareness of the importance of introducing the Icograda members to the 'true' culture of China, including its modernity, the professional drive, and the desire for outside contact and collaboration.[61] This kind of close international collaboration in an everyday work context seemed to provide the opportunity for mutual penetration for both sides at the conceptual and operational levels. As a result, Xin became the quality that spoke to multiple agents, including the Icograda team, who was concerned about access to the level and nature of design practice in an open and communicative context, as well as the CAFA team, who was eager to present qualities such as vision, trust, creditability and faith in contemporary Chinese design from an interpretation of this Chinese character.

Xin as an influence

FIGURE 13.6 The main entrance of the National Museum of China where Design as Productive Force, the sub-theme exhibition of the 2009 Icograda Beijing Congress was organized, 27 October 2009 (© Wang Min)

---

[60] Ron Newman interview with the author, through email, 17 June 2019.
[61] Ibid.

The Icograda Beijing Congress was held alongside the first Beijing Design Week from 24–30 October 2009.[62] During this period, various black and white or coloured geometric forms transformed from the shape of an envelope representing the theme of the congress appeared in different locations across the city, including the glass facade inside the China National Centre for the Performing Arts, the main entrance of The National Museum of China (中国美术馆) (Figure 13.6), the outer wall of the China Millennium Monument (中华世纪坛), and on the facade of various buildings inside the CAFA campus. More than a hundred scholars and designers of international reputation from six continents delivered nearly a hundred speeches, including seventy-eight keynote speeches under four main topics and in eighteen design education seminars.[63] Twenty-five exhibitions showing Chinese and international design works, as well as thirteen events related to design, were organized.[64] When recalling his experience helping to organize the congress, David Berman, the Canadian graphic designer, board member of Icograda from 2005 to 2011, described it as 'culturally unprecedented for me, and thus often mysterious, while often impressively dramatic' and he was 'humbled' when witnessing 'the non-Western design process in China, the non-Western decision-making process, the powerful way to bring people together rapidly towards a common goal'.[65] The dramatic and powerful feeling seems to have been reflected in many aspects of the congress, including the glamorous opening ceremony at the China National Centre for the Performing Arts, the presentation delivered by former politicians such as Long Yongtu (龙永图), former deputy minister of Foreign Trade and Economic Cooperation.[66] In addition, the Beijing Municipal People's Government, Ministry of Education and Ministry of Culture were all on the list as Congress' hosts. This was, even for local Chinese designers, something unique. Usually a design conference would and could not have such 'drama'.

So what were the reasons that made this congress special? What were the expectations of the sponsors and supporters? To search for answers to these questions, it is important to trace the trajectory of Icograda CAFA team's cooperation with the sponsors and supporters of the congress.

The preparation for the 2009 Icograda Beijing Congress started in the second half of 2006, soon after CAFA won the bid to host the congress in Copenhagen.[67]

---

[62] 'Gehua 20 Years | 2009 Beijing World Design Congress and the First Beijing Design Week'. In *Beijing Gehua Cultural Development Group*. http://www.gehua.com/html/2017/bigevent_0828/411.html [accessed 20 June 2018].
[63] 'Programme' and 'Exhibitions'. In *Icograda World Design Congress*. http://www.beijing2009.org/programme.htm [accessed 28 February 2019].
[64] 2009 Icograda Beijing Congress, 'Programme'. In *Icograda World Design Congress*. http://www.beijing2009.org/programme.htm [accessed 28 February 2019].
[65] David Berman interview with the author, through email, 11 June 2019.
[66] On Long Yongtu (龙永图), see 'Long Yongtu'. In *ICC (International Capital Conference)*. http://www.internationalcapitalconference.com/cn/speakers/long-yongtu [accessed 20 June 2019].
[67] Zheng Tao interview with the author, through WeChat, 6 March 2019.

Very quickly, however, Wang Min and his colleagues realized that it was very difficult for CAFA to independently take the responsibility of organizing an international congress on such a scale.[68] In their opinion, the conversations about design education and the design industry might not bring substantial results without governmental involvement and concern. Therefore, the original idea of establishing a platform for designers to discuss design issues was transformed into a much more urgent task, that of helping the government to understand the meaning and importance of design.

In these circumstances, the 2009 Icograda Beijing Congress CAFA team was trying to cooperate with local government to get support for the realization of their visions. Soon after, the theme of the congress 'Xin' was finalized in February 2006, the CAFA team submitted their proposal in the application for the Congress to the Beijing municipal government.[69] The Beijing Gehua Culture Development Group (北京歌华文化发展集团),[70] a large state-owned cultural business in Beijing committed to cultural services provision and the promotion of the cultural and creative industries, contacted the CAFA team for further communication after learning of the application. The involvement of Gehua provided support specifically for the fostering of an awareness of design through media campaigns.[71]

Meanwhile, in the letter inviting the Beijing Municipal Government and the Ministry of Education to jointly sponsor the 2009 Icograda Beijing Congress, the CAFA team emphasized the significance of organizing this event, including the opportunity to effectively promote Chinese design in the international arena, as well as to promote industrial transformation and the further development of cultural and creative industries in Beijing.[72] Also it would help to enhance Beijing's competitiveness as a candidate to compete for the title of World Design Capital. All this was consistent with the strategic decision of the Beijing municipal government to develop cultural and creative industries at that time.[73] After continuous communication, the CAFA team received approval from the Ministry of Education and Beijing municipal government to confirm them as joint organizers of the 2009 Icograda Beijing Congress in April and December 2008, respectively.[74] This also meant that the impact of the congress would go beyond the

---

[68] Zheng Juxin, Chen Yongyi and Yu Jiadi, 'Professor Wang Min, Dean of CAFA Design School Talks about the Comparison of the Design from the East and West'. The text was provided to the author by Wang Min, through email, 7 February 2017. The text is situated in Wang Min's personal archive.
[69] Zheng Tao interview with the author, through WeChat, 6 March 2019.
[70] On Gehua (歌华), see 'Beijing Gehua Cultural Development Group'. In *Beijing Gehua Cultural Development Group*. http://www.gehua.com/html/2017/bigevent_0828/411.html [accessed 20 June 2018].
[71] 'Organisers'. In *Icograda World Design Congress*. http://www.beijing2009.org/organizers.htm [accessed 20 June 2019].
[72] Zheng Tao interview with the author, through WeChat, 6 March 2019.
[73] 'Beijing Cultural and Creative Industry Development Plan during the Eleventh Five-Year Plan Period'. In *The People's Government of Beijing Municipality*. http://www.beijing.gov.cn/zfxxgk/110021/ndgzjh32/2015-05/29/content_6d05937dd17841ac9d8226159116212e.shtml [accessed 21 June 2019].
[74] Zheng Tao interview with the author, through WeChat, 6 March 2019.

scope of graphic design in terms of the topics and issues of concern and extended it to an area more closely related to government strategy.

There were various ways to achieve this goal, including the choice of keynote speakers, and communication during the seminar and exhibition with specific topics. In doing so, the importance of design, as well as the problems that needed to be dealt with, were highlighted. For example, the speeches by Sol Sender and Patrick Whitney were arranged for the same day of opening ceremony, enabled the representatives from Beijing Municipal Government, Ministry of Education and Ministry of Culture an opportunity to get a better understanding of how design could have an impact on politics, as well as how to build links between design and business strategy.[75] Meanwhile, to promote the idea of design as innovative economy, the exhibition 'Design as Productive Force' (设计·生产力), set up by the CAFA team in the National Museum of China, aimed to educate officials about how design could be used to increase the value of enterprise benefits with successful samples from the Netherlands, the United States, Japan and other countries.[76] It also explained the relationship between branding and the knowledge economy. In doing so, the organizers of the congress tried to raise the awareness of government and industry of the importance of design. The topics highlighted in the congress, including those about strategic thinking about the future of Chinese design, were still discussed in the design press after the congress, for example, the value of design, how to make design the driving force of economic development, and the ownership of the design industry by government agencies.[77]

Another important issue raised during the Congress was the advantage of having a national design association.[78] In the Chinese graphic design context, there was still no national association. There were only a few local associations: among them, the Shenzhen Graphic Design Association formed in 1995 was the most active.[79] The benefit of having a national design association was that it could discharge the functions and powers that the government could not perform. Without it, industry regulations and supervision could not be conducted. However, it was challenging to establish such an organization and to find a relevant ministry to take care of. There was only the Ministry of Industry and Information, which started to conduct an investigation into the development of the design industry in

---

[75] 'Programme' and 'Exhibitions'. In *Icograda World Design Congress*. http://www.beijing2009.org/programme.htm [accessed 28 February 2019].

[76] '2009 Beijing World Design Conference Special Exhibition: Design As Productive Force'. In *National Art Museum of China*. http://www.namoc.org/Videos/spzy/zlhd/2009/201304/t20130423_244286.htm [accessed 10 May 2018].

[77] Chen Yuan, 'Cultural Pulse: Design Is Not Only Culture, But Also Productivity'. In *cpcnews*. http://cpc.people.com.cn/n/2012/0929/c83083-19151025.html [accessed 10 April 2019].

[78] Zhu Shuai, 'What Can the Icograda Congress Bring to Us? A Conversation with Wang Min, Dean of CAFA Design School', *Art Observation*, 4 (2010), 26–27 (27).

[79] 'About SGDA'. In *Shenzhen Graphic Design Association*. http://www.sgda.cc/about.aspx [accessed 2 March 2020].

2009. The result of this situation was that even though the importance of design was frequently mentioned in design circles, there is no specific data to support it. Take for example, there was no documentation of design as a percentage of GDP, the number of the practitioners in design industry in the country as a whole, or how product sales figures and value would be improved by design.[80] Wang Min mentioned in an interview with *Art Observation* that at that time, among the issues in the design industry, the aspect he could address with government was design education, since he could explain that there were one million design students, which meant that there was a demand for designers in society.[81]

The Icograda Beijing Congress turned out to be a reflection and practice on the meaning of design caused by the specific difficulties – such as the shortage of funds – encountered by the CAFA team in the organization and preparation of the congress. The idea of 'design as productivity' was formally promoted with the exhibition at the National Museum of China. Meanwhile, Beijing Design Week, hosted by the Beijing Municipal Government and the Ministry of Culture, was retained and now happens annually, with the intention of promoting basic knowledge of design to the government, business enterprises and citizens, and to popularize the concept of 'design making life better' in a situation when the understanding of design was still very vague in China.[82, 83] Wang Yudong (王昱东), deputy director for the Office of the Organising Committee of Beijing Design Week, who originally thought design was a kind of artistic creation, mentioned in an interview that his own understanding about design went through a transformation through the organizational work for Beijing Design Week.[84] Although the Congress did not directly lead to the introduction of design-related policies, the promotion and popularization of design might eventually gradually shape government, industry and public's understanding about design. In the long run, this would be beneficial to create a context that is conducive to the development of design in China.

Conclusion

In the early 2000s, international exchanges in the field of graphic design in China became active. After years of observation, communication and cooperation on the periphery, some international graphic design organizations, including Icograda, started to work together with the leading Chinese art and design

---

[80] Ibid.
[81] Ibid.
[82] Wang Yudong interview with the author, through email, 11 September 2018.
[83] 'Summary of 2018 Beijing Design Week', in *2018 Beijing Design Week Theme Exhibition Guide Book: Design in China after 1978*, ed. Wang Min, Lin Cunzhen and Wang Yudong (Beijing: Beijing Design Week, 2018), unpaginated.
[84] Wang Yudong interview with the author, through email, 11 September 2018.

academies such as the Academy of Arts & Design, Tsinghua University and CAFA. Frequent international exchanges in the graphic design field and the attraction to international design circles reflected to some extent the achievement of China's social and economic development.

The chapter describes the influential graphic design international exchange, the 2009 Icograda Beijing Congress, as well as its significant meaning to Chinese design circle, which had rapid development since 1980s when the Communist Party of China made major decisions resulting in what was known as 'reform and opening up' in 1978. Before that, China pursued a strategy of isolationism, and the state control of imagery under Communism after 1948 led to a form of mass propaganda in which posters played a significant role.[85] It is after 1978, rapid expansion in China's relative economic size became the norm and in this context, graphic design field experienced a tremendous transformation, which provided a foundation for the large-scale international exchange activities such as the 2009 Icograda Beijing Congress to take place. The visual analysis of the promotional materials for the event exemplifies the development in the field of graphic design in China in the early 2000s, from emphasizing the tradition and glory of the Chinese literati spirit to an experimental style represented in a visual system combining a Chinese character with its contemporary interpretation.

---

[85] Jeremy Aynsley, *Nationalism and Internationalism Design in the 20th Century* (London: Victoria & Albert Museum, 1993), p. 159.

SELECT BIBLIOGRAPHY

Abbott, Andrew. *The System of Professions: An Essay on the Division of Expert Labour*, Chicago, IL/London: The University of Chicago Press, 1988.

Adamson, Glenn and Sarah Teasley and Giorgio Riello, Eds. *Global Design History*, London/New York: Routledge, 2011.

Akkach, Samer. 'Professional Identity and Social Responsibility'. In *Design in the Borderlands*, edited by Eleni Kalantidou and Tony Fry, 61–75. Abingdon/New York: Routledge.

Armstrong, Leah. 'Steering a Course between Professionalism and Commercialism: The Society of Industrial Artists and the Code of Conduct for the Professional Designer, 1945–1975'. *Journal of Design History* 29, no. 2 (2016): 161–79.

Armstrong, Leah and Felice McDowell, Eds. *Fashioning Professionals: Identity and Representation at Work in the Creative Industries*, London: Bloomsbury, 2018.

Aynsley, Jeremy. *Nationalism and Internationalism Design in the 20th Century*, London: Victoria & Albert Museum, 1993.

Azrikan, Dmitry. 'VNIITE, Dinosaur of Totalitarianism or Plato's Academy of Design?' *Design Issues* 15, no. 3 (1999): 45–77.

Balaram, Singanapalli. 'Design in India: The Importance of the Ahmedabad Declaration'. *Design Issues* 25, no. 4 (Autumn 2009): 54–79.

Bandeira Jerónimo, Miguel and José Pedro Monteiro, Eds. *Internationalism, Imperialism and the Formation of the Contemporary World*, Cham: Palgrave Macmillan, 2018.

Banham, Reyner, Ed. *The Aspen Papers: Twenty Years of Design Theory from the International Design Conference in Aspen*, London: Pall Mall Press, 1974.

Barbieri, Chiara. *Italian Graphic Design. Culture and practice in Milan, 1930s–60s*, London: Bloomsbury, 2024.

Beegan, Gerry and Paul Atkinson. 'Professionalism, Amateurism and the Boundaries of Design'. *Journal of Design History* 21, no. 4 (2008): 305–11.

Braga, Marcos. *ABDI e APDINS-RJ*, Second Edition, São Paolo: Editora Edgar Blücher, 2016.

Buitrago, Juan. ALADI. 'Da libertação de nossos povos às leis do mercado'. Doctoral Thesis. Universidade de São Paulo, São Paulo, 2017.

Buitrago-Trujillo, Juan-Camilo. 'The Siege of the Outsiders ALADI: The first Latin American Design Association and its Discourse of Resistance'. *Journal of Design History* 34, no. 1 (2021): 54–68.

Calvera, Anna. 'Local, Regional, National, Global and Feedback: Several Issues to Be Faced with Constructing Regional Narratives'. *Journal of Design History* 18, no. 4 (2005): 371–83.

Čapková, Helena, 'Transnational Networkers – Iwao and Michiko Yamawaki and the Formation of Japanese Modernist Design'. *Journal of Design History* 7, no. 4 (2014): 370–85.

Chakrabarty, Dipesh. *Provincializing Europe: Postcolonial Thought and Historical Difference*, Princeton: Princeton University Press, 2000.
Clarke, Alison J. 'Design for Development, ICSID and UNIDO: The Anthropological Turn in 1970s Design'. *Journal of Design History* 29, no. 1 (2015): 43–57.
Clavin, Patricia. 'Defining Transnationalism'. *Contemporary European History* 14, no. 4 (2005): 421–39.
Devalle, Verónica. *La travesía de la forma. Emergencia y consolidación del diseño gráfico (1948–1984)*, Buenos Aires: Paidós, 2009.
dipti bhagat, 'Designs on/in Africa'. In *Designing Worlds: National Design Histories in an Age of Globalization*, edited by Kjetil Fallan and Grace Lees-Maffei, 23–41. New York: Berghahn Books.
Geyer, Martin H. and Johannes Paulmann, Eds. *The Mechanics of Internationalism: Culture, Society, and Politics from the 1840s to the First World War*, Oxford: Oxford University Press, 2001.
Huppatz, Daniel. 'Globalizing Design History and Global Design History'. *Journal of Design History* 28, no. 2 (2015): 182–202.
Iriye, Akira. *Global Community: The Role of International Organisations in the Making of the Contemporary World*, Oakland: University of California Press, 2002.
Kikuchi, Yuko and Yunah Lee. 'Transnational Modern Design Histories in East Asia: An Introduction'. *Journal of Design History* 27, no. 4 (2014): 323–34.
Kott, Sandrine. 'Towards a Social History of International Organisations: The ILO and the Internationalisation of Western Social Expertise (1919–1949)'. In *Internationalism, Imperialism and the Formation of the Contemporary World*, edited by Miguel Bandeira Jerónimo and José Pedro Monteiro, 33–57. Cham: Palgrave Macmillan.
Laqua, Daniel, Ed. *Internationalism Reconfigured: Transnational Ideas and Movements between the World Wars*, London: I.B. Tauris, 2011.
Lees-Maffei, Grace. 'The Production-Consumption-Mediation Paradigm'. *Journal of Design History* 22, no. 4 (2009): 351–76.
Lees-Maffei, Grace and Kjetil Fallan, Eds. *Designing Worlds: National Design Histories in an Age of Globalization*, Oxford: Berghahn Books, 2016.
Messell, Tania. '*Constructing a "United Nations of Industrial Design": ICSID and the Professionalisation of Design on the World Stage, 1950–1980'*. Doctoral Thesis. University of Brighton, Brighton, 2018.
Messell, Tania. 'Globalization and Design Institutionalization: ICSID's XIth Congress and the Formation of ALADI, 1979'. *Journal of Design History* 32, no. 1 (2019): 88–104.
Mogami, Toshiki. 'On the Concept of International Organization: Centralization, Hegemonism, and Constitutionalism'. In *Networking the International System Global Histories of International Organizations*, edited by Madeleine Herren, 43–52. New York: Springer.
Niezen, Ronald and Maria Sapignoli, Eds. *Palaces of Hope: The Anthropology of Global Organizations*, Cambridge: Cambridge University Press, 2017.
Ozorio de Almeida Meroz, Joana and Katarina Serulus. 'A Theoretical Straddle: Locating Design Cultures Between National Structures and Transnational Networks'. In *Design Culture: Objects and Approaches*, edited by Guy Julier et al., 203–13. London: Bloomsbury.
Saunier, Pierre-Yves. *Transnational History*, Basingstoke: Palgrave, 2013.
Serulus, Katarina. '"Well-Designed Relations": Cold War Design Exchanges between Brussels and Moscow in the Early 1970s'. *Design and Culture* 9, no. 2 (2017): 147–65.
Serulus, Katarina. *Design and Politics: The Public Promotion of Industrial Design in Postwar Belgium (1950–1986)*, Leuven: Leuven University Press, 2018.

Sluga, Glenda. *Internationalism in the Age of Nationalism*, Philadelphia: University of Pennsylvania Press, 2013.
Souza Dias, Dora. 'Icograda: The International Council of Graphic Design Associations, 1963–2013: Transnational Interactions and Professional Networks in Graphic Design'. Doctoral Thesis. University of Brighton, Brighton, 2019.
Souza Dias, Dora. 'International Design Organizations and the Study of Transnational Interactions: The Case of Icogradalatinoamérica80'. *Journal of Design History* 32, no. 2 (2019): 188–206.
Souza Dias, Dora. 'Icograda: The International Council of Graphic Design Associations 1963–2013'. *Design Issues* 40, no. 2 (2024): 28–41.
Toshino, Iguchi. 'Reconsideration of the World Design Conference 1960 in Tokyo and the World Industrial Design Conference 1973 in Kyoto: Transformation of Design Theory', The Proceedings of IASDR2013, 2013.
Twemlow, Alice. 'I Can't Talk to You if You Say That: An Ideological Collision at the International Design Conference at Aspen, 1970'. *Design and Culture* 1, no. 1 (2009): 23–49.
Wang, Yun. *Contemporary Chinese Graphic Design Practice*, London: Bloomsbury, 2025.
Woodham, Jonathan M. 'Local, National and Global: Redrawing the Design Historical Map', Special Issue: 'The Global Future of Design History'. *Journal of Design History* 18, no. 3 (2005): 257–67.
Woodham, Jonathan M. 'Design, Histories, Empires and Peripheries'. In *Design Frontiers – Territories, Concepts, Technologies*, edited by Farias Priscila et al., 8th Conference of the International Committee of Design History and Design Studies, 454–7, São Paulo: Blucher, 2012.

INDEX

Boldface locators indicates figures and tables; locators followed by 'n.' indicates endnotes

Aalto, Alvar 55
Abbott, Andrew 20
abcdesign (Brazil) 298
Abdulla, Danah 9
Abramovitz, José 145
Abstraction-Creation group 45
Academy of Arts & Design, Tsinghua University 300, 310
Acero, Jairo 144 n.15
Acosta, Wladimiro 57, 59 n.55
advertising/advertising agencies 157, 167, 170, 172–3, 211–12, 214, 216–17, 233
   American approach 208–10
   artists 24, 173, 208–9, 212–13, 216–17, 220
   Cuba 26
   and design/graphic design 23, 206–7, 209–12, 210, 213, 218, 220–1
   Italian 209–10, 209 n.16, 219
   Japanese 159, 162
   technicians 208–9
   Tokyo 161
Advertising Artists Gathering (Tokyo) 160–1
Advertising Arts periodical 23–4
aesthetics 25, 57, 101–2, 113, 140, 184, 210, 233, 235, 250, 252, 254, 257, 262, 273, 279
   East Asian 302
   formalist 252, 260–1
   industrial 69–70, 233
   technological 27, 226
Africa 4, 29, 72, 86–7, 92, 98–9, 263, 302–3
   graphic design 35 n.71

   indigenous art and design practices 30
   regional meetings (Icograda) 35
Agrupació de Directors d'Art, Dissenyadors Gràfics i Il lustradors 28
Agrupacíon de Diseño Industrial-Fomento de las Artes Decorativas (ADI-FAD) 90
Ahmedabad Declaration (1979) 10, 10 n.45, 15, 84, 247, 252, 254–60, **256**
Ahn Sang-Soo 302
Aicher, Otl 46, 57 n.51
Aicher-Scholl, Inge 55
Albers, Joseph 51
Alexander, Jane 276 n.22
Alexandrova, Nadeshda 241
Alliance Graphique Internationale (AGI) 15, 31, 214–16, 220, 295, 299
Allianz group (Switzerland) 45
All-Soviet Art Fund 242
All-Union Scientific Research Institute for Technical Aesthetic. *See Vserossiyskiy Nauchno-Issledovatel'skiy Institut Tekhnicheskoy Estetiki* (VNIITE)
alternative design movement 15, 21, 247, 252
Amaral, Tarsila do 41
amateur 267, 273–5, 287, 290
American Institute of Graphic Arts (AIGA) 23, 34, 106, 290
American Society of Industrial Designers (ASID) 64, 69–70, 74–6, 78–81, 85
   and Muller-Munk 67–8, 71
Amir, Sulfikar 84
Andreu, Paul 294
Anglo-American model 65

Anglo-Saxon design 82, 138
anthropology 7, 15, 247, 250–4, 265–6.
    See also quasi-anthropological paradigms
Antropofagia journal 40
Argan, Giulio 57
Argentina 39, 42, 60, 134, 192. *See also* Austral network
    architecture, urbanism, and design 44, 46
    design network in 49–53
    first design organizations in 58–9
    industrial design 58–9, 59 n.55
    industrialization policy 39, 46
    modern discipline 13
    re-foundation of modern architecture 43
    university design programme 54, 54 n.45
Armstrong, Leah 8 n.37, 90 n.17, 90 n.19, 206 n.3
Arp, Hans 41
Art and Design media channel 298
Art Concret magazine 45
Art Directors Club (The United States) 23, 34
Art Directors Club Milano (ADCM) 218–21
Arte Concreto (Concrete Art) group 45, 47
Arte Concreto Invencion (Concrete Invention Art) 45 n.30
Artes de México journal 30
'Art et Publicité dans le Monde' (Worldwide Art and Advertising) exhibition 214
artistic engineering 27, 226
Art Products Factory ARS 242
artron.com 298
Asia 3, 72, 87, 98–9, 101–2, 118, 125, 302
    Asian Regional Group 94
    Asian Typography Professionals Meeting (Tokyo) 172
    regional meetings (Icograda) 35
Asociación Arte Constructivo (Constructive Art Association, Uruguay) 40
Aspen Design Summit 290
Aspen Institute for Humanistic Studies **109–10**, 112–16, 122
The Aspen Times newspaper 271, 281
Associação Brasileira de Desenho Industrial (Brazil) 29

Association Belge des Industrial Designers 184 n.14
Association for Industrial Design (Associazione per il Design Industriale, ADI) 14, 187, 205
    ADCM 218–21
    AGI and Icograda 214–16
    and Aiap 207–9, 213, 215–18, 220
    graphic design/designers (*see* graphic design/designers (in ADI))
    graphic practitioners 208–10, 213, 217
    SIA-D and D&AD 217–18, 221
Association of Commercial Artists (Israel) 23, 32
Association of Industrial Designers (*Asociación de Diseñadores Industriales,* ADIA) 39, 41, 58–9
Associazione Italiana Artisti e Grafici Pubblicitari (Italian Association of Advertising Artists and Graphics) 216
Atkinson, Paul 8
Aubock, Carl 190
Australian Commercial and Industrial Artists Association 32
Austral network 41–5, **43**, 43 n.20, 59
autonomy 134, 134 n.3, 136–9, 141, 149, 151, 200, 223
avant-garde 39–41, 45, 49, 59, 158, 252, 254, 285
Azrikan, Dmitry 225–6, 241, 243

Balaram, Singanapalli 84, 84 n.4, 258 nn.43–4, 261
Baltic applied arts exhibition 227
Bandeira Jerónimo, Miguel 10
Banham, Reyner 57, 268 n.7, 271, 273, 280, 285
Barbieri, Chiara 14
Barcelona Design Centre 97
Barthes, Roland 52
Basic Needs Approach (BNA) 249, 249 n.8, 265
Bass, Saul 159, 165, 273
Baudrillard, Jean 92
Bauhaus 46–7, 52, 55–7, 66, 170, 251
Bayer, Herbert 47, 111–12, 116, 159, 165, 267 n.1
    designed logo for Aspen Institute 109, **110**, 112–15, 123
Bayes, Andrea 278

Bayley, Edgar 45
Beauté France award 101, 184
Beegan, Gerry 8
Beijing CCII (Capital Corporation Image Institution) 300
Beijing Design Week 306, 309
Beijing Gehua Culture Development Group 307
Beijing-Hyundai Auto 291
Beijing Industrial Design Promotion Centre 102
Beijing Youth Weekly magazine 298
Beinart, Julian 273, 280, 287
Belgium
  'Belgian' Artifort furniture 196
  Belgian design policies 185–8
  Belgian Foreign Trade Office 192, 195
  Brussels 100, 179, 181–2, 184, 186, 193
  federalization 200
  Ministry of Public Works 200
  national economy 182
  public promotion in post-war Belgium 182 n.12
Belgo-Luxembourg Economic Union (BLEU) 185, 187
Bell, Daniel 276
Bendito, Fernando 91
Benelux 68, 179, 184–6
Berman, David 298 n.18, 306
Bernadotte, Sigvard **77**, 185
Billism movement 47
Bill, Max 45–7, 55, 57, 57 n.51, 116, 118–19, 121
  form, concept of 49
  HfG in Ulm 56
  Ubertypographie 47
Blackett, Lord 87–8, 105
Black, Misha 58, 64, 68–70, 78, 80, 86–7, 86 n.6, 101, **189**, 190
Blanco, Ricardo 58–9, 59 n.55, 144 n.15
Blank, Luiz 143 n.14, 146, 149 n.20
Boccara, Colette 49
Boletín del Centro de Estudiantes de Arquitectura (Architecture Students' Centre Bulletin) 48, **48**
Bolívar, Simón 138, 141, 148 n.18
Bonet, Antoni 43, 55
Bonini, Ezio 213, 220
Bonsiepe, Gui 58, 84, **143**, 144, 191 n.44, 253
  accusation on Papanek 254

'Development Through Design,' UNIDO 84 n.2
Boorstin, Daniel 275–6
  'Amateurs, Professionals, and the Quest for Lost Innocence' 274 n.15
  'The Prepared Professional' 273, **274**
Booth-Clibborn, Edward **219**
Bourdieu, Pierre 20
Bourgeois, Victor 43
Brazil 40–1, 47, 59, 92, 118, 131–2, 134–5, 138, 180, 190, 255
Breyer, Gaston 51 n.42, 52, 59 n.55
Brown, Wendy, *Undoing the Demos* 285, 285 n.59
Brussels Design Centre 192–6, 198, 200
Brussels World's Fair 1958 (Expo 58) 182, 186
Buchli, Victor 226
Buenos Aires 42 n.14, 44, 44 n.26, 99, 145
  first design organizations 58
  public policy on design 13
  W chair 49, **50**
Buitrago, Juan 13
Bund Deutscher Gebrauchsgraphiker (Germany) 23–4
Bund Österreichischer Gebrauchsgraphiker (Austria) 23
Bureau of European Design Associations (BEDA) 105–6
Burtin, Will 116, 121, 125–6
business-design relationship 64, 70, 78–9, 116, 268, 270, 278, 281, 283–6, 290, 292, 299, 308

Calcaprina, Cino 46
Campo Grafico magazine 24
Camus, Albert 41
capitalism 11, 115, 170, 250
Caplan, Ralph 273, 278
Carboni, Erberto 213–14, 220
Casabella magazine 271
cassette player design 263–4
Castillo, Greg 251, 256
Catholicism 140–1
Cendrars, Blaise 41
Central Academy of Fine Arts (CAFA) Design School 291–2, 295, 298–9, 303–10
Central Committee of the Communist Party of Estonia 223

Centro de Investigación en Diseño Industrial (CIDI). *See* Industrial Design Research Center
Chakrabarty, Dipesh, *Provincializing Europe: Postcolonial Thought and Historical Difference* 21
Chatterjee, Ashoke 255, 257
Chermayeff, Ivan 273
Chicago Institute of Design 55
China 102, 259, 291–2, 300
    Beijing Municipal Government 292, 307–9
    Chinese graphic design 15, 292, 297, 299–300, 308–9
    Communist Party of China 310
    design schools in 298 n.18
    development-oriented society 293
    graphic arts practice 26
    Reform and Opening-up policy 15
China CYTS Tours Holding Co., Ltd 291
China Federation of Literacy and Art Circles 26
China Industrial Design Association 102
China Millennium Monument 306
China National Centre for the Performing Arts **293**, 294, 297–8, 306
China Red Star Design Award 102
ChinaVisual media channel 298
Chinese Communist Party 26
Chinese Communist Revolution 258
Ciba Foundation 251
Ciclo magazine 41, 54
Ciuti, Enrico 220
Clarke, Alison J. 15, 65
Clavin, Patricia 4, 8
Club of Rome, *The Limits to Growth* 197, 255
Clusellas, Gerardo 50, 58
Cobold, Allen 260, 260 n.53, **262**
Cocteau, Jean 41
Cold War 25, 34, 36–7, 74, 77–8, 81, 84 n.3, 111, 128, 183, 194, 226, 241, 251, 254, 256–9
    American 66, 68, 74, 76
    containment strategies 6
    cultural diplomatic politics of 256, 259, 261, 265
    design associations in 25–31
    geopolitics 128, 237
    industrial design's role 15
    political circumstances 11
    and professional imperatives 13
    professionalization 12
    superpowers 29
commercial art/artists 24, 34, 90, 158, 173, 208, 214–15
Commercial Art magazine 24, 157
commercialism 167, 251
Committee of Young Specialists 241
Commonwealth Institute 260 n.53
Communication Arts (The United States) 28, 298
communication technology 5, 302
Communism 149, 259, 310
Compasso D'Oro award (Italy) 101, 184
Concrete art 45 n.28, 47, 49, 55
    Concrete artists 45–7, 57, 59
Concretism 45, 47
Conditions of Contract and Engagement for Graphic Designers 33
Confalonieri, Giulio 214
Congrès International d'Esthétique Industrielle (International Congress of Industrial Aesthetics) 68
Congrès internationaux d'architecture moderne (CIAM). *See* International Congresses of Modern Architecture
consumer capitalism 11
consumerism 115, 157, 173
Container Corporation of America 115, 117, 267 n.1, 270
Cook, Peter 92
corporate design 117, 128
Council of Industrial Design (COID), UK's 68, 89–90, 193
    Design Centre Awards 101
craft/crafting 10, 22, 72, 76, 99, 241, 252, 255–7
Creationism movement 40
Creative Review 288, 298
Crichton, Michael 280, 286–7, 287 n.66
Croce, Benedetto 57
cross-border professional networks 4, 6–7, 13, 63–5
    power and knowledge production 7–11
Cuba 131, 134–5, 138, 303
    Cuba Icograda Congress (2007) 304
    Cuban Revolution 141, 149
    graphic design 26
Cubbin, Tom 223
cultural brokers/brokering 64, 78–82
cultural diplomacy 128, 256, 259, 261, 265

cultural exchange 11, 15, 121, 148, 219, 238, 257
cultural hybridization 44, 65
cultural internationalism 5, 64–5
cultural modernization 39
Cumulus Kyoto Design Declaration 106
Czechoslovakia 27, 27 n.36, 33, 225, 237
Czech Svaz Ceskoslovenskych Vytvarnych Umelcu 27, 34

Deambrosis, Federico 42
Dean, Penelope 15
De Iulio, Simona 209
Delos Symposium (1963–1975) 272
de Majo, Willy 33, 116, 126, 128, 215
De Paepe, Robert 200, 200 n.86
Department of Industrial Art at Estonian State Institute of Art 228
Department of Industrial Design 30
De Poerck, André **189**
des Cressonnières, Geraldine 182 n.8
des Cressonnières, Josine 14, 81, 92, 101, 179–80, 180 n.2, **183**, 184 n.14. *See also* Signe d'Or award
  Belgian design policies 185–8
  Brussels Design Centre 192–6, 198
  Design Commission 199–202, 200 n.86
  early life and education 181–2
  at 8th ICSID Congress, Kyoto **180**
  'Equipment for the Community' conference 196
  '5 Minutes to Convince' lecture 198
  and ICSID 187–92, 192 n.50, 195–8, 198 n.82, 202
  international design community 188–92, 202
  introducing 'design' 199
  male domination 188
  and Prince Albert **194**
  promoting design 181–5
  and Reilly 191 n.47
  at second ICSID Seminar **189**
  social change 196–9
  transnational network of 194, 202
  and Viénot (Henri) 188–9, 191
design/designers 10, 19, 25, 28–9, 35, 49. *See also specific designers*
  design culture 3, 5–6, 10, 13–14, 181, 181 n.4, 202, 227–30, 237, 239, 243, 248, 253, 255, 257, 259, 279, 288–90

design education 60, 64, 104, 255, 295, 306–7, 309
design establishment 9, 15, 91, 101, 271, 276, 278
design institutions 2, 30, 183, 186, 292
design practices 1, 3, 7, 10, 12, 20–3, 27, 29–30, 32–7, 67, 70, 73, 76–7, 79, 81, 120, 161, 206, 208, 212–13, 215, 222, 253, 265, 278, 302, 305
good design 72, 101, 170 n.34, 184, 218, 284–5
history 2, 19, 128, 250, 258
as human-led process 20
organizations (*see specific design organizations*)
policies (*see* policies, design)
as productivity 309
professional 19, 23, 90, 109, 158, 191, 230–2, 237, 278, 296
Design and Development (ICSID/UNIDO congress) 15, 247, 265
  'Industrial Designing is About Caring For People' 258
Design and Industries Association (Britain) 23
'Design as Productive Force' exhibition **305**, 308
Designers and Art Directors Association (D&AD) 217–18, 221
Designersblock (DB) 100
'Design for Development' 252, 254–9, 260 n.51, 261, 265, 265 n.62
  hybridized 10, 260, 260 n.51, 265
'Design for the State' exhibition **201**
'Design from the Netherlands' exhibition 196
DESIGN>In Formation (South Africa) 298
Design Innovationen award (Germany) 101
Design magazine (British) 28, 89, 89 n.13, 93
Design magazine (India) 29
Design Museum in Holon (Israel) 102
Design 360° media channel 298
Design Quarterly magazine 28, 28 n.43
Design Week Mexico 100
Design Zentrum Nordrhein Westfalen 102, 220
Deutscher Werkbund (Germany) 22

Devalle, Veronica 13
developed world 11, 89 n.14, 134 n.3
developing countries 10, 10 n.45, 68, 75, 84, 87–8, 254–5, 264, 303. *See also* underdeveloped countries
developing world 11, 89 n.14, 93
development design 15, 247
Development Working Party 255
d'Harnoncourt, René 118
digital revolution 15, 267, 280
disciplines, design 7, 13, 27, 42, 42 n.16, 52, 59, 74, 104, 181–5, 241, 280–1
Domus magazine 91, 235, 271
Doner, H. Creston 123–5
Dorfles, Gillo 47, 208
Dorfsman, Louis 166, 273
Dova, Gianni 47
Drucker, Peter F. 287 n.66
Drustvo Likovnih Umetnikov Uporabne Umetnosti Slovenije (Slovenia) 28
Dutch Design Center 205
Dutch Design Week 100
Dutch Raad voor Industriële Vormgeving 187
Dwiggins, William Addison 24
d[x]i Magazine (Spain) 298

Eames (Charles and Ray) 252–3, 257–9, 260 n.51
'Making Connections,' IDCA 278
East-West Design Conference 125
Ebin, Alexander 114–15
Economic Commission for Latin America (ECLAC) 139, 139 n.10, 149
Education for Graphic Design, Graphic Design for Education (*Edugraphic*) 34
Ekuan, Kenji 92, 181, 201
at 'Design for the State' exhibition **201**
elite 8, 29, 113, 141, 149, 169, 197, 220, 259, 267, 273, 276
émigré designers 13, 63, 65–6, 116, 121, 268 n.5
ergonomics 227, 242
Escobar, Arturo 11, 248, 250, 265
Encountering Development: The Making and Unmaking of the Third World 249
esotericism 134, 134 n.4
Estonian National Archives 225
Estonian State Council of Scientific-Technological Organisations (*Eesti Vabariiklik Teaduslik-tehniliste ühingute nõukogu* in Estonia, ETTÜN) 230, 232–3, 237, 240–1
Eurocentrism 2, 8, 12, 20, 37, 301
Europe 3–4, 14, 32–3, 64, 66, 73, 76, 78, 87, 98–9, 101–2, 105, 117–18, 121, 125–6, 159, 185–6, 249, 251
avant-gardes 41
commercial artists 24
Common Market 72
design practice 21–3
division of labour 19
European design 23, 74, 79, 187
European design award 186–7
European Economic Community 186
European unification 185–6
Icograda event 34–5
industrial revolution 20
institutionalization of industrial design 14, 182–3, 186
migration 63
professionalization in 8
publications (graphic arts/design) 28
Experimental and Educational Studio of the Soviet Union of Artists 223–4

Facetti, Germano 215, 217
Fallan, Kjetil 19
Farson, Richard 280, 287
Feria de América (Americas Fair, 1953–1954) 50, **51**
Ferrari Hardoy, Jorge 42, 55
Ferrater, Carlos 91
Festival of Britain 68
First Things First manifesto, Garland's 217, 217 n.41
First World 11, 29, 253. *See also* Second World; Third World
First World War 41, 79. *See also* Second World War
Ford Foundation Scholarship 259, 261
foreign design organizations 185, 235
Form magazine 28
Foucault, Michel 271, 285 n.59
Frascara, Jorge, *Graphic Design, World Views: A Celebration of Icograda's 25th Anniversary* 36
Freeman Lau 298
Friend of ICOGRADA system 176
Fukuoka Regional Exhibition 162
Fuller, R. Buckminster

INDEX **319**

true international stature 121, 128
view on internationalism 121
'Furniture from Belgium: From Henry van de Velde until Now' exhibition 196

Gámez, Jesús 142, **142**
Gandhi, Indira 259
Gandhi, Mahatma 258
García, Joaquín Torres, '*América invertida*' painting 141
Garland, Ken, *First Things First* manifesto 217, 217 n.41
GD (Good Design) Mark, KIDP 101
Gebrauchsgraphik magazine 24, 157, 159
Gehua Group 291
Gehua New Century 291
genealogy 21, 60, 134, 134 n.3, 139
Gens, Leo 237
  'Artist and machine' 236
Gentil, Philippe 299
Germany 22, 33–4, 59, 69, 93, 102, 115, 186, 190, 283
  German Democratic Republic 225
  German Design Innovationen award 102
  German Rat für Formgebung institution 187
Gimeno-Martínez, Javier 186 n.19
Glaser, Milton 273, 284–5
glass art/artists, Estonian 228, 230, 237
globalization 3, 11, 36–7, 175, 194, 225, 279, 302
Global Tools 252–3
G-Mark Awards 101
G Mark system (Good Design Products Selection System) 164
Goethe Bicentennial Convocation 113, 115
Gomringer, Eugen 56
Good Design Awards 101
'Good Design' Exhibitions 101
Gordon-Fogelson, Robert 13
Gouldner, Alvin 278
  The Future of Intellectuals and the Rise of the New Class 278 n.29
'Grafica e Pubblicità nel Mondo' (Worldwide Graphics and Advertising) exhibition 214
'Grafici e Industrial Design' (Graphic practitioners and Industrial Design) 210
Graham, Sarah Ellen 258–9

Grand Duchy of Luxembourg 179, 184 n.14, 185
graphic design/designers (in ADI) 14, 24, 27, 32, 34–6, 205–6, 210, 212–16, 221–2, 284. *See also* industrial design/designers
  and advertising (*see* advertising/advertising agencies)
  AGI and Icograda 214–16
  and Aiap 207–9, 213, 215–18, 220
  Chinese 15, 292, 297, 299–300, 308–9
  corporate image 211–13
  design coordination 211–12
  graphic artists 24, 31, 117, 158
  international exchange 310
  Italian 206, 209–12, 214, 217, 220
  Japanese (*see* Japanese graphic design/designers)
  membership 208, 213, 216
  official recognition 212
  organizational strategies of 206–7, 220–1
  professional/professionalization of 14, 24, 157, 207, 221, 302
  SIA-D and D&AD 217–18
'Graphic Design for the Community: Print Around the Clock' exhibition 214
Graphic Design in Japan 175
Graphic Design magazine 31, 164, 166
graphic design organizations 23–5, 30, 33, 309
Graphis magazine 28, 162, 166
  posters sent from JAAC to **164**
Grignani, Franco 213–14, 220
Grisetti, Jorge 57
Gris, Juan 41
Gropius, Walter 55
Grosmann, David 104
Grunfeld, Jean François 201
Guayasamín, Osvaldo, '*Reunión en el Pentágono*' painting 141
Guidotti, Gastone **219**
Guth, Christine 31

Hagerman, Oscar 143 n.14, 146
Hall, Stuart 141 n.13
Hamada, Masuji 158
Hara, Hiromu 159, 161
Hariu, Ichiro 172
Hashiguchi, Goyo 157

Haus Industrieform. *See* Design Zentrum Nordrhein Westfalen
Hayter, Teresa, *Aid as Imperialism* 251
He Jun 294–9, 305
Helsinki Design Week 100
Henrion, F. H. K. 63 n.3, 91 n.21
Hlito, Alfredo 45, 55
Hochschule für Gestaltung (HfG) 55–7, 57 n.51, 193, 260
Huber, Max 47, 207, 211
Huidobro, Vicente 41
human environment 42, 197, 224
humanism 69, 113, 121
Huppatz, Daniel 3
Hutchings, Raymond 225–6

Ibiza, Spain
  Instant City 91–2
  international tourism 91
  Seventh ICSID Conference in 90–2, 197
Icograda Beijing Congress 291–2, 295, 297–8, 306–7, 309–10
  banner of **293**
  CAFA team (*see* Central Academy of Fine Arts (CAFA) Design School)
  poster of **294**
  Xin 293–9
    brainstorm for meaning of **296**
    definition of 295
    as influence 305–9
    as strategy 299–305
ICSID News Bulletin 205, 208, 216
IDEA magazine 164
Iguchi, Toshino 164
Iliprandi, Giancarlo 216, 220–1
Imagined Community 14
imperialism 136, 142
  cultural 134, 251
  professional 264
  US imperialism 138, 141
Import Substitution Industrialization policy 135
India 145 n.16, 252, 254–5, 257–60
  Ahmedabad Chamber of Commerce 257
  Ahmedabad Declaration (*see* Ahmedabad Declaration (1979))
  Congress Party 259
  heritage site 258
  India Design Mark (I-Mark) 102
  India Design Policy 103
  Indian Emergency 259
  'India's Design Dilemma' 260–5, **262**
  modernization programme by Nehru 251, 257
Indian Institute of Art in Industry and the Japan Industrial Designers' Association 77
India Report magazine 257–8, 257 n.40
industrial aesthetics (*esthétique industrielle*) 69–70, 233. *See also* aesthetics
Industrial Art Committee in Estonia 15, 224, 243
Industrial Art Committee (*Tööstuskunsti komitee*, TKK) 223, 225–6, 231, **234**, 238, 241–2
  'Design of industrial spaces' lecture 240
  final years of 240–2
  first meeting of 233
  foundation of 232–9
industrial design/designers 14–15, 27, 32, 52, 55, 59, 64, 67–8, 72, 74, 79, 85–7, 104, 179, 182, 185, 196, 198, 202, 207–8, 212–13, 225, 227–32, 234, 240, 242, 247, 252–5, 257–9, 273, 275–6, 278, 280, 283, 304. *See also* graphic design/designers
  in Argentina 42, 46, 48, 58–9, 59 n.55
  Belgian 182, 182 n.12
  industrial artists 227, 229–30, 232, 234, 237
  international/foreign 68, 76, 81
  in Italy 205
  mainstream 89
  male-dominated environment 188, 202
  Muller-Munk's promotion of 73
  professional 72, 98, 249–50
  Rey on 182
  social change 196
  in the United States 70, 80, 120
Industrial Designers Institute (IDI) 70, 74, 78–80
Industrial Designers Society of America (IDSA) Records 66, 82
Industrial Design magazine 235
Industrial Design policy 87, 199
Industrial Design Research Center 13, 39–41, 58–9
industrialization 19–20, 29, 39, 46, 135, 139–40

innovation 4, 98, 105, 199, 241, 250, 283–4, 286, 290
Institute for Industrial Design for Belgium 179, 182–3, 184 n.14, 185
Institute of Architecture and Urbanism (*Instituto de Arquitectura y Urbanismo*) 46
Institute of Environmental Studies 197
Institute of Industrial Aesthetics (Institut d'Esthétique Industrielle, IEI) 69–70, 85, 187
Institute of Industrial Design and Graphic Art 205
Institute of Technology, Bombay 254
Instituto Cubano del Arte y la Industria Cinematográfica (ICAIC) 26
'Integrated Design' exhibition 117
Intermediate Technology Development Group 251
International Advertising Art/Idea 24, 31
international alliances 13, 63
International Apparel Federation (IAF) 12 n.50
The International Code of Ethics and Conduct for Graphic Designers 33
International Concrete Movement 45
International Congresses of Modern Architecture 42, 42 n.16, 46, 272–3
international cooperation 64, 79–80, 120, 128
International Cooperation Administration (ICA) 75, 77
   design assistance programme 75–6
International Council for Industrial Design (ICID) 76
International Council of Design (Ico-D) 13, 83, **95**, 96, 98, 100, 104–6
International Council of Graphic Design Associations (Icograda) 1, 9, 12 n.50, 13–15, 32 n.63, 33–7, 33 n.65, 58, 63 n.3, 83, 85, 93, 97–8, 105, 157–8, 167, 169
   and AGI 214–16
   aim of 32
   Corresponding Member 34
   Edugraphic conference (1975) 34
   Executive Board 33, 35 n.71, 37, 90, 304
      geography and gender (Icograda/ico-D) **95**, 96
   1st International Student Seminar on Graphic Design 167
   globalization 36–7
   Icograda Beijing Congress (*see* Icograda Beijing Congress)
   Icograda Copenhagen Congress 303
   Icograda Design Education Manifesto 106
   'Icograda General Assembly 21: Minutes, Copenhagen, Denmark, 29–30 September 2005' 304 n.53
   Icograda Seoul Congress 300
   Icograda World Design Congress 97, 176, 294
   inaugural meeting, associations 32, **33**
   and JAGDA 175–6
   membership conditions 34
   Millennium Congress 106
   name change 98
   News Bulletin 167, 175, 216–17
   regional meetings 35–6
   25th Anniversary 36, 98
   'Visualogue' 176, **177**
   'World Communication Design Day' 98
   World Design Day 98
   'World Graphics Day' 98
International Council of Societies of Industrial Design (ICSID) 1, 6, 9, 10 n.45, 12 n.50, 13, 31–2, 58–60, 64, 78, 83, 85, 93, 97–8, 101, 105–6, 145, 187–8, 190–1, 202, 225, 238, 247, 252, 254–5
   American legacy on 82
   American professional standards 69–74
   Archive files 86 n.7, 94
   cross-border exchanges 64, 78, 80
   and des Cressonnières 187–92, 192 n.50, 195–8, 198 n.82, 202
   'Design for Need: the Social Contribution of Design' Conference 94
   'Design for the World' 97
   'Design in a Changing Society' 197
   'Design in Developing Countries Working Parties' 256
   design policies 103–6
   development initiatives 10 n.45, 238
   Dublin ICSID 255
   early years 85–7

Education Commission 88
'The Education of Industrial Designers' seminar 180, 193
Eighth Congress of 179
establishing 66–9
European City of Culture programme/European Capital of Culture 99–100
Executive Board 72, 86–7, 88 n.10, 90
geography and gender (ICSID/WDO) **95**, 96, 103
General Assemblies and Congresses 72–4, 79, 81–2, 85–8, 91, 98, 105
General Meeting 172
ICSID congress in Mexico 131
ICSID-UNIDO Special Commission 97
Kyoto Congress (1973) 92–4
'Soul and Material Things' 92
in late 1960s and 1970s 87
membership (Full Members/Associate Members) 73–4, 77–8, 81–2, 87–8, 88 n.10, 94, 255
and Muller-Munk 64–6, 64 n.4, 69–74, 77–81
name change 73, 86
from 1970s and 1980s 94–6
origination in France 32, 68, 85
proposal for ALADI at 11th Congress of **143**
Seventh ICSID Congress (1971), Ibiza 90–2, 197
'Design in a Changing Society' 90
Sixth ICSID London Congress (1969) 87–8
'Design, Society and the Future' 87, 89
student voices and General Assembly (1969) 88–90, 88 n.10
survey 72
twenty-first-century design activities 100–3
World Cities of Design 97–8
World Design Impact Prize 98
'World Industrial Design Day' 98
International Design Alliance (IDA) 86, 97–8, 97 n.35
International Design Conference in Aspen (IDCA) 1, 9, 13, 15, 63 n.3, 109, 111, 115–21, 128, 267–8, 270–1, 278–81

'Ambient: Interface' conference (2004) 15, 275
ANY Conferences (1991–2001) 272–3
Articles of Incorporation 270 n.8
Board of Directors 268 n.5, 270 n.8, 273, 276, 279–80, 286–7, 287 n.67, 288
Certificate of Incorporation for **269**
critical discourse 271, 273
Design Seminar 113
drop of attendance numbers 288 n.70
'Environment by Design' 89
hijacked by students in 1970 197
IDCA Records 270 n.8
incorporating 122–8
'Insight and Outlook: Views of British Design' conference (1986) 284
integrated design 113, 115–17
International Advisory Committee 125
internationalism 112, 116, 121, 123, 125–9
and Japan Committee on International Design 124–5
letterhead 123–4, **124**, **127**
Middleton's temporary letterhead for 122, **122**
logo (designed by Bayer) 109, **110**, 112–15, 123, 126
'The More Things Change' conference (2001) **288**
naming suggestions 122–3
'New Business of Design' conference (1995) 15, 280, **282**, 282–3
organizational restructuring diagram **289**
and Pizarro 124
professionals/professionalization 273–8
redesign 268 n.7, 287
'Shop Talk' (publicity poster) **272**, 275, 278
sociocultural values 268, 277–8, 281, 289
28th conference ('Making Connections') **277**, 279
international design organizations 1–3, 5–7, 9–12, 14–15, 26, 31–2, 37, 68, 76, 85, 97, 105, 112, 128, 164, 206–7, 214, 221, 224
membership of 214
post-war histories 9, 13

soft power 6
strategic internationalization 6, 63
to transnational networks 4–7, 192
international exchanges 59, 72, 86, 112, 116, 129, 193, 219, 309–10
International Federation of Interior Architects/Designers (IFI) 12 n.50, 83, 86, 97–8, 100, 105, 176
international governmental organizations 5–6, 8
International Industrial Design Exhibition (1960) 187
internationalism 3–4, 9–10, 15, 66, 112, 116, 121, 123, 125–9
  cultural 5, 64–5
internationalization 13, 63, 125–6, 177, 195
  of Japanese graphic design 158–61
International Labour Organization 249
International Liaison Committee of Esthétique Industrielle 69
international non-governmental organizations 5, 8, 12, 22, 31, 64, 302
International Style 40, 42 n.16, 43, 46, 211–12, 225
international trade 63, 74–5, 193
International Trade System 139, 149
inter-social analysis 40
Iran, Knut 34
Iriye, Akira 5
Israel Product Design Office (IPDO) 76
Italian Association of Advertising Artists (Associazione Italiana Artisti Pubblicitari, Aiap) 28, 207–9, 213, 215–18, 220–1
Italian Group of Visual Designers 205
Italy 115, 117, 124
  advertising 209–10, 209 n.16, 219
  graphic design/designers in 206, 209–12, 214, 217, 220
'Italy at Work: Her Renaissance in Design Today' exhibition 117

Jacobson, Egbert 111, 113, 115, 267 n.1
Jakaitė, Karolina 224, 237
Jannello, César 42, 49–53, 51 n.42, 59 n.55
Japan 29, 78, 115, 119–20, 125–6, 308
  Americanization of popular culture 31
  graphic design in 14, 157
Japan Advertising Artists' Club, JAAC (Nippon Senden Bijutsu Kyokai) 14, 31, 157, 161–2
  All-Campus Struggle League for Crushing JAAC 170–1, **171**
  central committee 169 n.25
  end of 167–72
  exhibition applicants number 166, **166**
  exhibition poster of **163**
  General Meeting 171
  International Graphic Exhibition 162
  judging scenes at **168**
  poster exhibitions 162
  posters sent to *Graphis* **164**
  post-JAAC 174
  10th exhibition 168–9
Japan Advertising Club (Nippon Kokoku-kai) 161–2
Japan Advertising Review Organization 173
Japan Committee on International Design 120, 124–5
Japan Design Council (Nippon Dezain Kaunshiru) 162
Japan Designers Association 161
Japan Display Design Association 173
Japanese graphic design/designers 157, 166–7, 169, 172–3, 175
  'Ancient Regime' of 170, 177
  internationalization 158–61
  from JAAC to WoDeCo 161–7
  Nippon Kobo (Japan Workshop) 158–61
  reorganization of 173
Japanese Industrial Designers' Association 92
Japanese-US cultural exchange project 257
Japan Graphic Design Association (JAGDA) 14, 157, 175
  awards 175, 178
  design 177–8
  formation of 172–6
  'Harmonized Checkered Emblem' design 178
  and ICOGRADA 175–6
  membership 175
Japan Institute of Design Promotion (JDP) 102
Japan Lettering Designer Association 173
Japan Package Design Association 173
Japan Productivity Center 120
Japan Sign Design Association 173
Japan Typography Association 173
Japan World Exposition, Osaka 172
Jerlei, Triin 12, 14

Kamekura, Yusaku 159, 161–2, 164, 169, 171, 175
Kandinsky, Wassily 55
Kao, John 279, 282–3
Katsumi, Masaru 164, 167, 172, 175
Kaufmann, Edgard McKnight 43, 101, 159
Kenmochi, Isamu 116, 118–20, 124
    color pictures 120
    koinobori (carp-shaped kite) 120
Kepes, György 118
Kida, Takuya 256–7
Kiyoshi, Awazu 169
Kneebone, Peter 215
Koioke, Shinji **189**
Kojitani 176
Kokoku-kai (Advertising World) 159
Kokusai Shogyo Bijutsu Kokan Kai (Exhibition of International Exchange in Commercial Art) 159
Kono, Takashi 161–2
Korea Institute of Design Promotion (KIDP) 101
Koshy, Darlie 84 n.4
Kott, Sandrine 5
Kreis, Tiiu 236, 240
Kristeva, Julia 52
Kuhlmann, Ellen, context-sensitive approaches 7
Kurchan, Juan 42–3

Laanemäe, Ludmila 241
Lange, Jacques 304 n.53
Latin America/Latin American 3–4, 72, 78, 98, 131, 133–40, 134 n.3, 148–51, 238
    avant-garde architecture 39–41
    Costa Rica 131, 134
    counterculture in 141
    design/designers 134, 135 n.6, 141, 143, 145, 149, 151
    graphic artists 24
    higher education design courses 29–30
    industrialization 29, 135, 139
    Latin Americanism/Latin Americanist 134, 139, 139 n.9, 141, 148 n.18, 149
    migration 41
    modernity 141 n.13
    professionalization of design 14, 39
    regional meetings (Icograda) 35
    Southern Cone of 40
Latin American Design Association (Associação Latino de Diseño Industrial, ALADI) 14, 94, 131, 131 n.1, 139–40
    congresses and assemblies 132, 135 n.5
    'Document of intent' 149, **150**
    Executive Committee 132, **132-3**
    exoticism and identity 145–9
    first ALADI 133–8
    founding members of **137**
    from/for Latin America 150–1
    Interdesign workshop (1978) 134, 143, 143 n.14, 145
    schedule at Valle de Bravo 147
    logo (designed by Gámez) **142**
    proposal at 11th Congress of ISCID **143**
    signatories for **144**
    proposal for formation in India 145, **147**
    'Valle de Bravo Manifesto' 145, **146**
La utopía es posible MACBA exhibition 91
Le Centre de Création Industrielle (CCI), Paris 198
Le Corbusier 41–4, 42 n.14, 42 n.16, 44 n.26
    Athens Charter 272
    Master Plan 42, 42 n.14, 44
    Modulor man 114
Lees-Maffei, Grace 19
Leimei Julia Chiu 300, 302–3
Leonard-Barton, Dorothy 283
Leuppi, Leo 45
liaison committee 34, 68–9, 187–8
Liaison Committee for Industrial Design in the Common Market 187
Liberation Theology 140, 149
Liernur, Francisco 44
Lionni, Leo 116–18, 121–3
    'First International Design Conference' 118
    letterhead for 'International Design Conference' 116
    on Olivetti's design programme 117
Lloyd Wright, Frank 55
local design culture 227–30, 237, 239, 243
local design organizations 224–5
Loewy, Raymond 180, 202
Long Yongtu 306

Louchheim, Aline 119
Lu Jingren 298, 302
   Zhu Xi Bangshu Thousand-Character essay **301**
Luther Plywood Factory 233
Lvov, Igor 27

Making Connections (IDCA conference, 1978) 15, 277–9
Makoto, Nakamura 173
Maldonado, Tomás 50–1, 53, 55–9, 57 n.51, 181, **189**, 193, 197
   defining design 49
   Design, Nature and Revolution: Toward a Critical Ecology 197 n.74
   in design organizations 60
   Nature and Revolution: Toward a Critical Ecology 197
   pre-Ulm period (1942–1954) 45–9
   on visual communication 211
'MAN transFORMS' exhibition 252
Mariño, Mario **143**
Marxist 115, 139, 238, 241
material culture 39, 235, 253, 257, 260–1, 266
Mathur, Saloni 260–1, 260 n.51
MAVO, Russian Constructivists 158
Max Bill **56**, 56 n.48
Medvetz, Thomas 270
   Think Tanks in America 270 n.9, 271 n.10
Méndez Mosquera, Carlos 45, 47, 51, 55
   'Vision' course 52
Messell, Tania 13, 89 n.13, 145 n.17, 188, 192, 196, 238
Metabolism group 169
Metropolis magazine 288
Mexican College of Industrial and Graphic Designers (*Colegio de Diseñadores Industriales y Gráficos de México*, CODIGRAM) 145
Mexico 92, 99, 124–6, 131, 134–5, 143, 145–9
Meyer, Hannes 47
Middleton, Robert Hunter 122–3
   temporary letterhead for IDCA 122, **122**
migrants/migration 13, 41, 63, 65, 140
Mills, C. Wright 276
modernism/modernity 19, 21, 30, 44, 44 n.26, 73, 112, 141, 141 n.13, 225, 237, 250, 261

modern architecture 42–6, 49, 54–7, 140–1
modernization 9, 19, 25, 29, 39, 140, 254
'Modern Japanese Posters' exhibition 158
Modern Publicity magazine 157, 162
Moholy-Nagy, Laszlo 47, 49, 52, 55, 57
   The New Vision 55
   Vision in Motion 55
Mondrian, Piet 41, 55
Monteiro, José Pedro 10
Montréal Design Declaration (MDD) 105–6
Morning Post media channel 298
morphology programme 52
Mosca, Franco **219**
Moscow Design Museum 227
Movimiento Arte Concreto (Concrete Art Movement) 45
Muller-Munk, Peter 13
   as cultural broker 78–82
   dual identity 79
   early life and education 66
   and ICA 75–6
   and ICSID 64–6, 64 n.4, 69–74, 77–81
   American legacy on 82
   and Ilona **71**
   industrial design commissions 67–8
   monographic museum exhibition of 82 n.102
   positions 68
   and SID 67–8, 71
   at Special Exhibition of Industrial Design **77**
   tea service designed by **67**
   in trade fair exhibitions 75
Munari, Bruno 47, 165, 207–8, 211, 214
Museu de Disseny de Barcelona 102
Museum of Contemporary Art of Barcelona (MACBA) 91
Museum of Modern Art (MOMA) 101, 117, 256

Nagai, Kazumasa 166, 173, 178
Napoli, Roberto **143**, 144, 144 n.15
National Alliance of Art and Industry (The United States) 23
national design cultures 181, 181 n.4
national design organizations 2, 26, 66
National Design Policy Work Group (NDP WG) 104

326 INDEX

National Institute of Design (NID), Ahmedabad 84, 254, 257–8, 260, 260 n.53, 263, 265–6
National Institute of Industrial Design (India) 29
National Institute of Industrial Technology (*Instituto Nacional de Tecnología Industrial,* INTI) 58
The National Museum of China **305**, 306, 308–9
nation-states 5–6, 30–1, 180, 258
Nehru, Jawaharlal 251, 255, 258–9, 260 n.51, 261
Nelson, George 111, 252, 273
neocolonialism 253–4, 259, 261, 264
neoliberalism 134, 139 n.9, 285, 285 n.59
Nervi, Pier Luigi 55
The Netherlands 32, 186, 190, 193, 201, 205, 283, 308
Neue Graphik (*New Graphic Design,* Swiss) 28
Neutra, Richard 43
New Economy 268, 282–3, 286
Newman, Ron 295, 304–5
The New York Times 119, 271, 281
Nielsen, Jens 201
Nigerian Association of Graphic Designers 30, 35
Nippon Advertising Artists Council (NAAC) 173
  1st NAAC Exhibition **174**
NIPPON pictorial magazine 159
Niwatari, Ado 161–2
Nizzoli, Marcello 207–8
Nkula-Wenz, Laura 10
non-aligned movement (NAM) 4, 28
non-governmental organizations 5, 8, 64, 302
Noorda, Bob 214
North America 4, 66, 87, 99, 105, 125, 138, 249, 267–8, 273, 282 n.44. *See also* South America
  design's labour force 276, 276 n.22
Noyes, Eliot 91 n.21, 181, 191
Nuestra Arquitectura magazine 43 n.20
Nuevas Realidades (New Realities) exhibition 46
nueva visión magazine 30, 41, 49–51, **53–4**, 54–8
Nueva Visión publishing house 49, 57

Oberti, Guido 46
Ocampo, Victoria 41–2
OCT Design Museum, China 102
Oeri, Georgine 162
Office of International Trade Fairs (OITF) 75
Ohchi, Hiroshi 162
Ohl, Herbert 58
Olivetti Corporation of America 116–17
'Olivetti: Design in Industry' exhibition 117–18
Olympic souvenirs, evaluation of (1977) **232**, 239
Ortega y Gasset 41
Österreichischer Werkbund (Austria) 23

Paepcke, Walter 111, 113–15, 117, 119, 267 n.1
Pakistan Council of Industrial Design 205
Pamio, Oscar 14, 138, 144
Pan-American policy 138
Pan-Pacific Design Congress, Tokyo 175, **176**
Papanek, Victor 250–1, 253–4
  accused by Bonsiepe 254
  Design for the Real World: Human Ecology and Social Change 197, 248–9, 261, 302
  'Project Batta-Koya' 263–4
  'tin can radio' design (decorated) 261, **263–4**
paper and printing systems 19
Peressutti, Enrico 118, 208
peripheral design organizations 15, 223–4
peripheral economies 248, 255, 258
'Persona' Exhibition 166–7
Peter Muller-Munk Associates (PMMA) 67–8, 72, 75–6, 81
Peters, Robert L. 300–1, 304
  'The First Poster Exhibition of China Red Cross Society' 303
  'No Sleeping Dragon – the Dawn of Graphic Design in China' 303
  'A Trip to Shanghai: International Visual Art Master Seminar' 303
Pevsner, Nikolaus 118–19, 121
Picasso, Pablo 41
Piccinato, Luigi 46
Pintori, Giovanni 207, 220
Pizarro, Manuel 124
The Plywood and Furniture Factory 233

INDEX **327**

Poland 225, 237
policies, design 14, 98, 167, 180–1, 198–200, 198 n.82, 202, 247–8, 253, 260. *See also specific policies*
   Belgian design policies 101, 182, 185–8, 192
   global to national 103–5
   India Design Policy 103
   industrial 87, 198, 252
   policymakers/policymaking 90, 250–1, 254, 263, 266
political economy 248, 268 n.7, 269–70, 273, 288, 290
Polo, Rómulo **143**, 143 n.14, 144–6, 144 n.15
Prada Poole, José Miguel de 91
Prati, Lidy 45, 55
Primera Exposición Internacional de Diseño Industrial (First International Exhibition of Industrial Design) 58–9
Print magazine 24
Produto e Linguagem magazine 30
professional design organizations 3–4, 13, 20–3, 29, 63, 73, 84, 93, 97, 227
profession/professionalism/professionalization 2, 12–14, 20, 29, 65, 72, 85, 93, 112, 206, 267, 275
   after Second World War 63
   cross-border 4, 6–11, 13, 63–5
   of design (Latin America) 14, 39
   of graphic design 207
   and IDCA 273–8
   issues of 20–2
   limitations of 37
   promotion 4, 63, 82, 191
Progressive Architecture conference (1995) 284
progressive humanism 69
Provinciali, Michele 207, 213
Pschepiurca, Pablo 44
Pulos, Arthur 76, 78, 81–2, **189**, 192, 252
   'Industrial Design as a Factor' 249
   'The Profession of Industrial Design' speech 248

quasi-anthropological paradigms 15, 253, 260–5. *See also* anthropology
quasi-imperialism 251
Quijada, Mónica 138
Quijano, Anibal 21

Racionero, Luis 92
Radic, Zvonimir **189**
Rand, Paul 162
Red Dot Award Museum 102
Red Dot Awards 102
Redig, Joaquim 144 n.15
Red Star Award 102
Regional Working Groups 94
Regulations Governing Conduct of International Competitions 33
Reid, John 91 n.21, 189–90, 258
   The State of Industrial Design in Developing Countries 257
Reid, Susan E. 241
Reilly, Paul 91 n.21, 190–1
   and des Cressonnières 191 n.47
Reinisch, Jessica 8
Rey, Jean 182
Rey, José 145 nn.16–17
Rodgers, Daniel 181
Rodríguez, Claudio 144 n.15
Rogers, Ernesto Nathan, *Ubicación del arte concreto* (The Place of Concrete Art) 46
Rosi, Franca 144 n.15
Rosselli, Alberto 210–12
Roth, Alfred 43
Royal College of Art (RCA), London 89, 94, 258 n.44, 260

Safdie, Moshe 273
San Francisco Peace Treaty 161
San Miguel de Tzinacapan indigenous community 145–6
Sarlo, Beatriz 44
satellite technology 4
Satomi, Munetsugu 158–9, 159 n.9
   article's poster on *Gebrauchsgraphik* 159, **160**
Saunier, Pierre-Yves, modern nation-states 6
Savez Likovnih Umjetnika Primenjenih Umetnosti Jugoslavije (Yugoslavia) 27–8, 34
Savignac, Raymond 162
Scandinavian design 235, 237, 258
Schockaert, Guy A. 37
Scholl, Inge 46
Schöner Wohnen magazine 235
Schrage, Michael 284

Schumacher, Fritz, *Small is Beautiful: A Study of Economics as if People Mattered* 251
Scientific-Technological Association of Food Industry 241
Second World 11, 84 n.3, 106, 259. *See also* First World; Third World
Second World War 4, 24, 41, 63–4, 83, 90, 101, 157, 159–61, 182, 227, 256, 258. *See also* First World War
Seeger, George 263–4
Seeger, Mia 185, 188
Senezh Studio 224
Serulus, Nina 12, 14
Shanghai Graphic Design Association 300
Shapira, Elana 65
Shapira, Nathan **189**
Shenzhen Graphic Design Association 308
'Shichinin-sha (The Seven)' exhibition 158
shogyo bijutsu (commercial art) 158
Shogyo Bijutsu Kyokai (Commercial Art Association) 158
Shogyo Bijutsu periodical 158
Shultz, Fernando 144 n.15
Signe d'Or award 68, 101, 179, 182–5, 186 n.19, 188, 192 n.53
  Benelux design prize 179, 186–7
  founding members of 184
  jury of **184**, 185 n.17
Silberman, James M. 75
Sina media channel 298
Sipradue magazine 219
Sirel, Helen 229
Sirp ja Vasar (*Hammer and Sickle*) newspaper 228, 239
Smith, Eugene 82 n.100
social organization 21
social sciences 247–8, 248 n.2, 250, 253, 278
Society of Industrial Artists and Designers (SIAD) 90, 217
Society of Industrial Artists and Designers of South Africa 29–30
Society of Industrial Artists (SIA), British 32, 69, 85, 90, 215, 217
  name change (*see* Society of Industrial Artists and Designers (SIAD))
Society of Industrial Designers (SID). *See* American Society of Industrial Designers (ASID)
Society of Typographic Arts (The United States) 23, 34

soft power 6, 220, 247, 251, 256
Soloviev, Yuri 181, 190–1
Sol Sender 298, 308
Sottsass, Ettore 253, 273
sound boxes 134, 134 n.2
South America 34, 99, 118, 302–3. *See also* North America
  Colombia 14, 131–5, 136 n.7, 143, 145, 145 n.16, 180
Souza Dias, Dora 9, 12, 135 n.6
Soviet design organizations 194 n.58, 223–4. *See also* Vserossiyskiy Nauchno-Issledovatel'skiy Institut Tekhnicheskoy Estetiki (VNIITE)
Soviet Estonian Art Fund 242
Soviet Estonian State Planning Committee 242
Soviet Union 15, 25–7, 75, 77–8, 183, 186, 192, 223–7, 233, 237–8, 240–2
Spaak, Paul-Henri 186
Spain 28, 91, 141. *See also* Ibiza, Spain
specialization, design 19–20, 23, 65, 209, 276, 278, 281, 290
'Spirit of Design' program (2001) 280
State Creative Scientific Production Association 242
Steiner, Albe 207–8, 220
Steiner, Henry 299
Stile Industria magazine 210, 212
Stoppa, Bruno 200
The Studio art magazine 157–8
styliste industrielle (Industrial Designer) 85
Suga, Yasuko 14
Sugi, Michio 169
Sugiura, Hisui 157–9
Sugiura, Kohei
  The Birth of the Plastic Arts 302
  Japanese Contemporary Illustrations 302
  Nobuyoshi Kikuchi's Collected Works 302
Summa magazine 30, 54
Surrealism 40
Svenska Affischtecknare (Sweden) 23
Svenska Slöjdföreningen (Sweden) 22
Svenska Slöjdföreningen Tidskift (*Form*) 22
Syndicat National des Graphistes Publicitaires (French) 23

Tada, Hokuu 158
Taeuber Arp, Sophie 41

Tagore 41
Taidepiirtäjäin Liitto GRAFIA Tecknarförbund (Finnish) 23
Tallon, Roger 181, **189**
Tanaka, Ikko 173
Tan Ping 292
Tapiovaara, Ilmari 58
Tara, Bill 126
Tarbeklaas glass factory 228, 230, **236**
Teague, Harry 281, 287 n.68
Tecné journal 41, 43–4
Tedeschi, Enrico 46, 50
Telehor magazine 47
Thackara, John 280, 283, 285
Thapar, Romesh 260
  'Identity in Modernisation' 255, 260
  India and Transition 255
Thatcher, Margaret, 'Design for Profit' campaign 284
think tanks 251, 255, 270–1, 270 n.9, 273, 290
Third World 11, 29, 84 n.3, 249, 258. *See also* First World; Second World
Thomson, Michael 103–4
'three worlds' theory 29 n.44
'Today's Italian Publicity and Graphic Design' exhibition 218–21, **219**
Tokyo Art Directors Club 173
Tokyo Commercial Artist Association 173
Tööstuskunsti nõukogu (Council of Industrial Art) 227–30, 235
Torres García, Joaquin 40–1
Tovaglia, Pino 213–14, 220–1
'Towards Global Histories of Design: Postcolonial Perspectives' 266
transnational networks 6, 31, 65, 192, 211
  des Cressonnières' 194, 202
  graphic design 207, 215, 221
  inter-national to 4–7
Treaty of Rome 186
Tschichold, Jan, *Die Neue Typographie* 47
Turkish Handicraft Development Board 76
Turkish Handicraft Development Office (THDO) 76
Twemlow, Alice 9
Typographische Monatsblätter magazine 24

Udruženje Likovnih Umjetnika Primijenjene Umjetnosti Hrvatske (Croatia) 28
Udruzenje Likovnih Umetnika Primenjenih Umetnosti i Dizajnera Srbije (Serbia) 28
Ulm magazine 28
Ulm School of Design (HfG) 52, 58, 193, 197, 260–3
Umezawa, Tadao 92
underdeveloped countries 89, 136, 263. *See also* developing countries
UNESCO's Creative Cities Network (UCCN) 99
Unión de Escritores y Artistas de Cuba 27
United Nations 26, 31, 131
United Nations Development Programme (UNDP) 134
United Nations Economic and Social Council (ECOSOC) 97
United Nations Educational, Scientific and Cultural Organization (UNESCO) 33–4, 87, 97, 180, 261, 263–4
  2030 Agenda for Sustainable Development 99
  Creative City of Design 99–100
United Nations Industrial Development Organization (UNIDO) 10, 84, 87, 145, 247, 252, 254–5, 257
The United States 3, 8, 14, 25, 27–8, 64, 68, 76, 78, 81–2, 102, 111, 117, 119, 121, 135, 142, 167, 183, 186, 237, 241, 251, 254, 258–9, 268 n.5, 308
  American approach of advertising 209–10
  American designers 64, 68–9, 74–5, 78
  American professional standards, ICSID 69–74
  American way of life 75, 256
  design practice 21
  expansionist policy of 138
  graphic design organizations 23
  imperialism 138, 141
  industrial design/designers in 70, 80, 120
  migration 41
  Pan-American policy 138
  US Office of War Information (OWI) 258

Universidad de Buenos Aires (National University of Buenos Aires) 49, 51–2, 58
Universidad de Buenos Aires, Facultad de Arquitectura (National University of Buenos Aires, Arquitectura) 52
Universidad de Córdoba (University of Cordoba) 52
Universidad de la República (University of the Republic, Uruguay) 51
Universidad del Litoral (University of Litoral) 52
Universidad de Mar del Plata (University of Mar del Plata) 52
Universidad Nacional de Cuyo (Cuyo National University) 51
Universidad Nacional de La Plata (National University of La Plata) 51, 54 n.45
university design programme 40, 42, 54, 54 n.45
UN Sustainable Development Goals (SDGs) 99
urbanism 42 n.16, 44, 46, 52, 57
Urbine, Basilio **189**
Uribe, Basílio 58, **143**, 145
US-Japan Security Treaty 167, 170
USSR 27, 228, 252, 259

Vago, Pierre 64, 64 n.4, 69–70, 77
Vaher, Ingi 15, 223–4, 230–2, **231**, 235, 240–1
   at evaluation of Olympic souvenirs **232**
Valéry, Paul 41
Valle, Gino **189**
V&A museum, Dundee 102
van der Sande, Loek 201
van Doesburg, Theo 41, 45
Vantongerloo, Georges 47
van Toorn, Jan 298
Vázquez, Manuel Villazón **189**
Vechaar Utensils Museum 257
Verband Bildender Kuenstler Deutschlands (East Germany) 34
Verband Deutscher Industrie Designer (Association of German Industrial Designers) 205
vertical studio 51, 51 n.42
Veskimägi, Kaljo-Olev 223

Viénot, Henri 180
   and des Cressonnières 188–9, 191
Viénot, Jacques 68–9, 85
   progressive humanism 69
Vignelli, Massimo 214
Vinti, Carlo 209
visual communication 14, 54 n.45, 93, 166–7, 206, 210–12, 214–16, 221
visual culture 49, 55
visual design 167
Vivanco, Jorge, *Instituto de Arquitectura y Urbanismo* 46
Vserossiyskiy Nauchno-Issledovatel'skiy Institut Tekhnicheskoy Estetiki (VNIITE) 27, 194 n.58, 225–7, 230, 235, 238, 240–1, 243

Waisman, Marina 57
Wang Min 291–2, 291 nn.1–2, 295, 299, 303, 307, 307 n.68, 309
Wang Yudong 309
Wang, Yun 15
Wang Ziyuan 303
Western constructs 8
Whitney, Patrick 308
Williams, Amancio 42, 49, 51, 53
Wolf, Henry 273
Wollner, Alexandre **189**
women 9, 12, 15, 90, 179, 188, 191–2, 240. *See also specific women*
   as factory designers 230–1
   in international design networks 15, 202
   male-dominated context 14, 188
   scientific-technological organizations led by 241
Woodham, Jonathan M. 3, 6, 13, 217, 235
Woodrow Wilson International Center for Scholars, Washington 198
Woolf, Virginia 41
Worker's Club of the Tallinn Plywood and Furniture Factory 233
World Capitals of Design (WCD) programme 98–9, 106
World City of Design (WDC) 97–100
World Conference on Design 125
World Design Capital programme (ICSID/WDO) 10
World Design Conference (WoDeCo), Tokyo 14, 120, 157, 164–7, 171–2, 211

Executive Committee of 165
exhibition sites **165**
'Total Image for the 20th Century' 120
World Design Organization (WDO) 6, 9, 13, 83, 86, **95**, 96, 98–100, 104–6
World Design Summit (WDS) 104, 106
World Design Weeks 100
Wurman, Richard Saul 273

Xiao Yong 292, 295, 303
Xu Ping 295

Yamana, Iwao 159, 159 n.6
Yanagi, Sori 120, 124
Yokoo, Tadanori 170, 170 nn.34–5
Yoshio, Hayakawa 162, 166
Yu Bingnan 292, 299–301, 303–4

Zec, Peter 102
Zen Nihon Shogyo Bijutsu Renmei (Japan National Commercial Art League) 160
Zevi, Bruno 55
Zheng Tao 295